ENHANCING LEARNING

IN

TRAINING

AND

ADULT EDUCATION

Ronald R. Morgan, Judith A. Ponticell, and Edward E. Gordon

Westport, Connecticut
London

Library of Congress Cataloging-in-Publication Data

Morgan, Ronald R.
    Enhancing learning in training and adult education / Ronald R.
Morgan, Judith A. Ponticell, Edward E. Gordon.
        p.   cm.
    Includes bibliographical references and index.
    ISBN 0–275–95016–6 (alk. paper).—ISBN 0–275–95911–2 (pbk.)
    1. Learning, Psychology of.   2. Educational psychology.
3. Personality assessment.   4. Occupational training.   5. Adult
education.   6. Employees—Training of.   I. Ponticell, Judith A.
II. Gordon, Edward E.   III. Title.
LB1060.M677   1998
370.15′23—dc20   95–43763

British Library Cataloguing in Publication Data is available.

Library of Congress Catalog Card Number: 95–43763
ISBN: 0–275–95016–6
       0–275–95911–2 (pbk.)

First published in 1998

Praeger Publishers, 88 Post Road West, Westport, CT 06881
An imprint of Greenwood Publishing Group, Inc.

Printed in the United States of America

The paper used in this book complies with the
Permanent Paper Standard issued by the National
Information Standards Organization (Z39.48–1984).

10 9 8 7 6 5 4 3 2 1

CONTENTS

PART III: ASSESSMENT OF LEARNER CHARACTERISTICS

ILLUSTRATIONS

TABLES

FIGURES

TRAINING APPLICATION BOXES

PREFACE

The overall thesis of the book is to build a strong case for the notion that workplace trainers would be well served if they viewed their work as research. The book consists of nine chapters designed to prepare readers to become workplace consultants. In Chapter 1, the overall thesis of the book is introduced, and the author's workplace training program of research is described. A mastery learning model is presented as a conceptual anchor for the book in Chapter 2. The authors make an effort to present what we know about instructional psychology, cognitive science, mastery learning, and performance-based assessments, and to relate these findings to the workplace. Behavioral views of learning are presented in Chapter 3. In Chapter 4, special attention is directed at emphasizing the importance of taking a cognitive science perspective when trainers are called upon to consult in the workplace. A number of questions are addressed. What biological constraints exist among learners? What psychological constraints exist among learners? What are the differences in the learning characteristics between typical and atypical learners? Can thinking, problem solving, and creativity be enhanced? Within the context of addressing each question, focus is given to manipulating those variables over which we have some control in workplace settings. What we know and don't know about intelligence is presented in Chapter 5. The traditional question has been: Who has it? The contemporary questions have shifted to: What is it? and Can it be increased? An effort is made to build a strong case for the notion that intelligence can be enhanced. The assessment of personality differences among learners is described in Chapter 6. The point to be made here is that we are able to assess personality. Why don't we use these assessments to a greater extent within the context of our efforts to consult in the workplace? In Chapter 7, different models of consultation are described. A special focus is given to instructional consultation. In the last two chapters, an effort is made to present a balanced view of both quantitative and qualitative research methodologies. Postmodern issues related to race, gender, and culture are systematically addressed from a methodological perspective. Considerable focus is given to enhancing diversity in workplace settings.

This book was designed to address a topic that we believe to be **highly relevant to trainers, researchers, and consulting psychologists** interested in the development and implementation of workplace training programs. It should be noted that the book was part of a research project sponsored by the North American Institute for Training and Educational Research. It is the third in a series of books. *Closing the Literacy Gap in American Business: A Guide for Trainers and Human Resource Specialists* (1991) and *FutureWork: The Revolution Reshaping American Business* (1994) were the first two books in the series. The authors wish to express their appreciation to the trainers and managers of Imperial Corporate Training and Development who assisted with the empirical validation of many of the behavioral and cognitive science field training components on which the book is anchored.

PART I

INTRODUCTION

CHAPTER 1

COGNITION AND INSTRUCTION: PUTTING THEORY INTO PRACTICE

INTRODUCTION

American management is running scared in the face of relentless global competition, multicultural issues, and the dizzying pace of technical and societal change. Diversity, multicultural sensitivity, equity, total quality management (TQM), rightsizing, business process re-engineering, international society for organizational standards (ISO-9000), and team building are among the current buzzwords and phrases being invoked in guiding corporate strategic planning. Many employers are asking, "How do I improve my employee's multicultural sensitivity, critical thinking, and problem-solving skills?" Many have claimed to have answers to this complex question. However, it is probably fair to say that few, very few, have provided satisfactory recommendations related to addressing the question.

It is our belief that America now has the training and educational tools to reinvent an increasingly competitive, highly diversified, U.S. business environment. Those businesses that get serious and adopt substantive, lifelong education for workers greatly increase their opportunity to survive, grow, and prosper into the next millennium. However, those companies that decide against investing in their human capital and diversity will increase the likelihood of someday appearing as obituaries in the *Wall Street Journal*. The failure of many American businesses to adapt to changed economic circumstances has become a major social concern. Harry Levinson (1994) claimed that the explanations for these corporate failures are fundamentally psychological. He attributed corporate catastrophes to individual and organizational narcissism, unconscious recapitulation of family dynamics in the workplace organization, dependency, psychologically illogical organization structure and compensation schemes, inadequate management of change, and inability to recognize and manage cognitive complexity. To deal more effectively with such problems, Levinson recommended that boards of directors and senior executives increase their psychological sophistication.

This book was designed to address a topic that we believe to be **highly relevant to trainers, researchers, and consulting psychologists** interested in the development and implementation of workplace training programs. Such programs are growing, and efforts to facilitate them can be significantly enhanced by using what we know about learning and instruction to design workplace training environments.

The book includes detailed descriptions of prominent models of learning and instruction. Given that we have chosen to anchor the contents of the book within the context of the discipline of **educational psychology**, most of the work cited relates to learning in school. We recognize that much of the research literature we use to support our views is primarily based in the laboratory and in schoollike settings. For the most part, we assume that there are few differences in the learning dynamics among adults, children, and youths. Of course, it is our burden to convince our readers that these laboratory-based and school-based research findings are relevant to the workplace.

A number of **common themes** appear throughout the book. At center stage are a cognitive science perspective, an outcome-based education approach, a behaviorally anchored mastery learning model embellished with cognitive science components, and a collaborative instructional consultation model of service delivery. In addition, we have made an effort to **emphasize research methodology** and to encourage our readers to view workplace education and training as research.

We recognize that there is a **literate bias** in most educational and workplace settings. An effort is made to build a strong case for the desirability of this literate bias. With the exception of biologically determined maturational stages of development, we **assume that the learning characteristics among adults, children, and youths are similar.** Special attention is given to six **constructs** (intelligence, personality, the mind, memory organization, motivation, and cognitive style expectancies) that are viewed as being of importance to designers of workplace training environments. Emphasis is also given to modifying those **individual differences** among learners over which we have some control.

In sum, what we attempt to do throughout the book is to build a case for the notion that we use educational and workplace settings as natural laboratories in which to articulate educational, psychological, and sociological theories. That is to say that we recommend that our readers take a **test-train-test hypothesis testing and generating approach** to solving work-related and education-related problems.

Is there currently a comprehensive theory of instructional psychology? What would a cognitive theory add? Why is there a need to reformulate the leading paradigms of instructional psychology within a cognitive context? In this book we attempt to address these questions. First of all, we attempt to build a case for the notion that cognitive individual differences can both constrain and facilitate learning. From what we report, individual differences, especially the cognitive bases of differences of the atypical learner and instructional tasks, appear to have a valid place in the psychology of learning as it relates to designing instruction. The overall thesis presented here is that recent developments in cognitive science may provide additional links between learning theories and teaching.

Presently much research in a number of areas of cognitive science (e.g., expert-novice comparisons, cognitive strategy training, critical thinking, and performance-outcome-based assessment) considered to be relevant to teaching is underway. Detailed cognitive task analyses of instructional sequences are being done, and the training of metacognitive skills and problem solving strategies may help learners master the intellectual skills and the content needed to compete in school and in the workplace. The identification of individual differences in information-processing capacities could be used to design instruction that compensates for a particular deficiency by providing for learners what they cannot provide for themselves. In terms of the atypical learner, identification of individual information-processing differences could be used to pinpoint the appropriate links that would help the learner make a positive adjustment to a challenging school and/or workplace environment before he or she learns to become helpless in it.

Finally, it should be emphasized that most cognitive variables are viewed as learnable. Therefore when we are called upon to design learning environments, we should attempt to include instructional procedures having potential for the modification of these cognitive variables.

Many cognitive instructional systems have been carefully tested in highly controlled laboratory, field experimental, and applied settings. What seems to be needed at this time is a greater focus and appreciation for attempts to relate recent findings in cognitive science to instruction in the workplace. It is our view that greater sensitivity to the possibility of relating cognitive variables to our existing models of instruction will enhance our instructional options and help to account for and minimize individual differences among learners.

OVERVIEW OF CONTENTS

In this section, we present a summary of each of the chapters appearing in the book. Remember that the book is **anchored in the educational psychology** literature and that there are **four themes** presented throughout the book (a cognitive science perspective, an outcome-based education approach, a behaviorally anchored mastery learning model embellished with cognitive science components, and a collaborative instructional consultation model of service delivery). It should be noted that certain components of the chapters are designed to overlap. These **overlapping knowledge structures** are listed in Table 1.1. Readers may find it helpful to refer to **Table 1.1** as they progress through the book. It is our hope that such an arrangement will provide for a smooth transition from one chapter to the next and encourage the reader to relate new information to what is already known.

In **Chapter 2** we introduce a cognitive science perspective to the study of adult learning and development. We begin with a discussion of **three models of instruction** (mastery learning, personalized systems of instruction, and tutoring). Emphasis is given to the commonalities across the three training models (e.g., their emphasis on continuous assessment, remediation, encouragement, and support) rather than the differences. A special effort is made to relate contemporary developments reported in the cognitive science literature to John B. Carroll's (1963) original behaviorally based model of **mastery learning**. Particular attention is given to possible instructional correctives and the special problems related to the application of these models to atypical and/or nontraditional learners.

It is noted that the cognitive scientists claim that the major **differences** in the learning characteristics between **novice** and **expert** human learners are found primarily in the cognitive mediation differences of **attention, cognitive style expectancies, and memory organization**. Individual differences among learners are broken down further into **biological differences** (attention, maturation stages, and temperament) and **psychological differences** (knowledge, language, memory organization, mood, attitudes, personality, cognitive style expectancies, and motivation). It is recognized that the biologically determined differences cannot be modified. However, the assumption is that we can modify many of the environmentally determined psychological individual differences. That is to say that most of the individual difference characteristics of interest to a cognitive scientist are believed to be learnable.

In the last section of Chapter 2, our **workplace research program** is described. Our purpose in presenting this brief description early in the book is to set the stage for encouraging our readers to **view workplace education and/or training as research**. We state throughout this book that there is no best method of instruction and/or therapy that can be applied to all persons in all settings. Most content-laden knowledge has a short shelflife of five years or so. In contrast to content-laden knowledge structures, research methodology seems to have considerable staying power. Therefore, we believe that it is appropriate to put **research methodology** at the center of the stage, to use the knowledge yielded from an empirically

Table 1.1
Organizing Knowledge Structures

- A behaviorally anchored mastery learning model embellished with cognitive science components.
- An outcome-based education approach.
- A collaborative instructional consultation model of service delivery.
- Theoretical comparisons among behavioral-associationistic, gestalt, cognitive developmental, and information-processing views of thinking, problem solving, and creativity.
- A cognitive template view of information processing with filtering viewed as an automatic process and pigeonholing as a cognitive classification process.
- Viewing development as development of attention.
- Viewing differences between children and adults, expert and novice learners, typical and atypical learners as differences in attention, cognitive style expectancies, and memory organization.
- Assume that biologically determined individual differences consist of differences in attention, temperament, and maturational stages of development.
- Assume that environmentally determined individual differences consist of knowledge, language, memory organization, mood, attitudes, personality, cognitive style expectancies, and motivation.
- Assume that there is a literate bias in schooling.
- Six cognitive constructs have lasting value (intelligence, personality, the mind, information-processing conceptualizations of learning and instruction-memory organization, motivation, and cognitive style expectancies).
- Knowledge consists of content knowledge, content-procedural knowledge, and procedural knowledge (general problem-solving strategies) – emphasis is given to automatizing content-procedural and procedural knowledge to free up working memory space for content.
- Emphasis is given to the zone of proximal development (ZPD) – Lev Vygotsky's social framework model-cognitive apprenticeship and reciprocal teaching models.
- Emphasis is given to a test-train-test hypothesis testing and generating approach to solving work-related and education-related problems.
- Viewing workplace education and training as research.
- Promising areas of research consist of expert-novice comparisons/ behavioral-cognitive task analyses/computer simulations of thinking and problem solving; early interventions; prose learning/schema activators; tutoring/mastery learning/PSI; intelligence and personality; and behavior management.

based research program to anchor our work and to guide our training efforts. That said, it is our view that all workplace trainers should view their work as research. It is our recommendation that readers view workplace settings as natural laboratories in which to explore and articulate educational, psychological, and sociological theories.

Chapter 3 consists of an overview of what we know and don't know about learning. The focus of the chapter is on **a behavioral view of instruction.** The first section of the chapter consists of a general discussion of **four learning models** (classical conditioning, operant conditioning, social learning, and cognitive). This is followed by a section in which an attempt is made to relate each of the models to learning in general. Additional sections of the chapter include a brief discussion of the special place of motivation within learning theory, reinforcement versus contiguity theories, the limited role of reinforcement, the existence of cognitive expectancies, and a final section related to attacks on behaviorism.

It is argued that an adequate theory of learning should be able to offer some explanation for the basic **components of the learning curve** (baseline, acquisition, maintenance, and extinction). In the chapter each of the learning models is described, and comparisons are made among them. Each of the major theoretical perspectives is examined within the context of the theory's ability to provide a satisfactory explanation of the various components of the learning curve. We recognize that the reinforcement versus contiguity section, the limited role of reinforcement section, and the existence of cognitive expectancies section are somewhat cumbersome and require careful reading. Some readers may find these sections to be a bit too fine-grained for their purposes. These sections were included because they provide a description of the basic knowledge structures that led to the move away from the behavioral views to the cognitive science perspective. Given that we believe that we should have some strongly supported **reasons for advocating a cognitive science perspective**, it seems necessary to provide a rather highly detailed account of what the behaviorists didn't tell us. In short, as more and more learning theorists identified themselves to a greater extent with notions of the existence of cognitive expectancies and species specific behaviors, an appreciation for a cognitive model became paramount. These sections provide a fine-grained rationale for these changing views.

In **Chapter 4**, an attempt is made to examine learning theory from a contemporary **cognitive scientist's perspective**. This chapter and the research methodology chapter (Chapter 8) are the most highly detailed chapters in the book. The views presented here represent an abbreviated and highly synthesized version of what we know and don't know about cognition. First of all, thinking, problem solving, and creativity are examined from behavioral-associationistic, gestalt, cognitive developmental, and information-processing perspectives, after which a section dealing with a comparative examination of problem-solving behavior across differing behavioral and cognitive theoretical perspectives is presented. This is followed by sections dealing with the development of **schema**, the existence of a **literate bias in schooling**, and what we know and don't know about the **relationship between language and cognition**. A fine-grained description of those **individual difference constraints** introduced in Chapter 2, along with the learnable aspects of thinking and problem-solving, are then presented. In this chapter, an overall attempt is made to develop a case for the notion that the means of instruction can be related to knowledge outcomes. The final sections of the chapter consist of a listing of a few unanswered questions and possible cognitive learning trends for the future.

Chapter 5 begins with a discussion of the clash between traditional and contemporary views of **intelligence**. Special attention is given to the views of Howard Gardner, Robert Sternberg, and Reuven Feuerstein. An effort is made to describe Lev Vygotsky's contributions and to relate his concept of the **zone of proximal development (ZPD)** to Feuerstein's social framework model. Emphasis is given to the importance of a **test-teach-test** and mediated learning **approach** to increase intelligence. It is pointed out that questions related to intelligence have shifted from the traditional psychometric notions of who has it to what is it and can it be improved.

What is intelligence? From a contemporary information processing perspective, **Sternberg (1986)** claims that intelligence consists of three components (metacomponents - knowing what you know components; knowledge acquisition components - content components; and performance components -general problem-solving skills). It is Sternberg's view that we can modify these components and increase intelligence. We attempt to make a case for the notion that **we can enhance intelligence** by using a combination of Sternberg's componential training model, Feuerstein's dynamic test-teach-test model, and Annemarie S. Palinscar's and Ann Brown's reciprocal teaching model.

In the relationship between intellectual assessment and treatment section, we **give special attention to behavioral assessment procedures, curriculum-based assessment (CBA) procedures, and performance-based assessment (PBA) procedures**. Perhaps the most important section of the chapter is the section in which we address the question of whether individual differences can be modified. Here we provide a fine-grained examination of **individual difference** (biological and psychological) **constraints** on learning. As noted in Chapter 2, the **biological differences** consist of attention, maturation stages, and temperament. The **psychological differences** consist of knowledge, language, memory organization, mood, attitudes, personality, cognitive style expectancies, and motivation. It is assumed that we can modify most of these psychological differences. This section is followed by a section dealing with unanswered questions. Here we return to focusing on the **differences between typical and atypical learners** (attention, cognitive style expectancies, and memory organization). Once again, we view these differences from a variety of theoretical perspectives (associationistic-behavioral, gestalt, cognitive developmental, and information-processing perspectives) and attempt to build a case for the possibility of modifying these differences. The final sections of the chapter consist of sections dealing with ethics, consideration of human values and the use of automatic cutting scores in decision making, selection and placement decisions, and equity issues related to the assessment of intelligence.

In **Chapter 6**, an attempt is made to present a practitioner-focused overview of the field of **personality assessment**. The history of personality assessment is far from stable and uneventful. During the 1940s and early 1950s, the field of personality assessment flourished. However, structural and theoretical changes within the profession and society at large resulted in a **period of marked decline in clinical testing during the late 1950s, 1960s, and early 1970s**. Much of the decline was due to newly emerging theories (behavioral and humanistic) and perspectives (psychometric). However, since the mid-1970s, things have turned around. **Personality assessment is popular once again!** What has brought about this positive change? Many of the traditional tests [e.g., the Minnesota Multiphasic Personality Inventory (MMPI-2), the use of the Exner scoring system with the Rorschach] have been improved. New tests have been developed [e.g., the Personality Inventory for Children (PIC), the Beck Depression Inventory, the Millon Clinical Multiaxial Inventory, and the NEO Personality Inventory]. The addition of Millon's personality clusters, the ongoing revision of diagnostic criteria (DSM-III-R, DSM-IV), and the greater acceptance of behavioral-cognitive assessment procedures and performance based assessment procedures (PBA) have contributed to increased interests in the area. In addition, the **pressure to offer short-term, reimbursable interventions** has focused attention on the possibility of using personality measures as a way to facilitate getting under way faster with respect to treatment interventions. In Chapter 6, we review these trends. A special section of the chapter is devoted to a brief description of the most frequently used traditional measures [e.g., MMPI-2, Thematic Apperception Test (TAT), Rorschach, and the California Psychological Inventory (CPI)]. **Behavioral-cognitive assessment procedures** are described in a separate section. The final three sections of the chapter include a relationship between personality assessment and treatment section, a methodological issues related to the treatment utility of assessment section, and a current trends section.

Remember that the basic rationale for inclusion of this chapter and Chapter 5 on intelligence is that **personality and intelligence are considered to be our most important constructs with regard to explaining individual differences among learners**. The assumption is that if we are able to describe the individual differences among our clients, we are in a better position to design interventions to bring about behavior changes. Most would probably agree with the assertion that we are able to adequately assess individual differences for most learners. What we have a great deal of **difficulty** with is **relating our assessments to a treatment plan**. Chapter 6 and the previous chapter dealing with intelligence were designed to describe what we are attempting to do to bring about better assessments and to relate these assessments to a treatment plan.

Chapter 7 was crafted as a summary chapter of the substantive contents of the book. The overall focus of the chapter is to examine our options with respect to **instructional consultation**. For many years, it was assumed that if the schools provided adequate resources and equalized inputs, that the outcomes would be positive. However, with the appearance of the **Coleman Report** in 1966 (Coleman et al., 1966), in which it was claimed that schools could not overcome the socioeconomic class differences of students, the presumed link between the equality of inputs and outputs was shattered. James Coleman and the other authors (1966) maintained that the schools could not overcome the negative effects associated with being poor.

Critics claimed that Coleman's findings were flawed. Researchers made an effort to find schools in which poor students did well. These schools were labeled **effective schools**. Using norm-referenced test scores as a measure of academic success, researchers were able to identify effective schools and the instructional components related to student success in them. In many ways the research findings associated with the effective schools movement served as a major step in **linking school process variables to student outcomes** and in moving us toward our contemporary focus on outcomes. The debates related to the development of a national curriculum, a national assessment system, and the pressure to develop new measures related to evaluating educational and workplace outcomes are all part of the emerging **outcome-based education (OBE)** focus of today.

Advocates of this **OBE approach** to assessing educational and workplace outcomes are using portfolios, products, demonstrations, and transcripts of specific skills rather than course grades to document student progress. The curriculum has been designed to allow all learners to demonstrate mastery of the designated outcomes. A **mastery learning model** of instruction sets criterion-based performance standards identically for all students and allows the time needed to reach that standard to vary. Outcome-based education includes the defining features of the mastery learning model.

Following the introductory sections in which a focus is given to OBE and mastery learning, **three approaches to collaborative consultation (instructional, mental health, and organizational development)** are described and compared. Given the overall cognitive science theme of this book, the **collaborative instructional consultation approach is emphasized**. The next three sections of the chapter describe a cognitive science approach to instruction. Special attention is given to **six constructs** considered to be of importance to a cognitive science approach to instruction. It should be noted that these are the same six constructs **(intelligence, personality, the mind, memory organization, motivation, and cognitive style expectancies)** that are given special attention throughout the book.

The final section of Chapter 7 consists of a series of five **training lectures** that were designed to summarize the substantive contents of the text and to present this information in a format that could be disseminated to your clients when you are called upon to consult.

When experienced researchers think of research methodology, two things are frequently reported (Kerlinger, 1986) to come to mind: (1) the importance of randomization to control for individual differences; and (2) the desirability of having comparison groups. In addition to addressing issues related to randomization and the importance of having comparison groups, an attempt is made in **Chapter 8** to relate research design to statistics and hypothesis testing. First of all, five general organizing statements are presented related to describing the field of research methodology with respect to current issues and trends. Emphasis is given to the shift from univariant to multivariant designs and the **desirability** of conducting **field experiments** in natural settings (e.g., schools, clinics, and workplace settings). This introductory section is followed by a brief overview and comparative summary of **four basic research methodologies** (observation, survey, experimental, and expost facto). Each methodology is discussed and evaluated within the context of internal and external validity. This is followed by a discussion of a number of **faulty and experimental designs**. The final three sections of the chapter consist of discussions related to variance control, basic statistical procedures, and notions of causal inference.

As noted in the summary statements related to Chapter 2, we are attempting to encourage our readers to **view workplace education and training as research**. We state throughout this book that there is **no one best method of instruction** and/or therapy that can be applied to all persons in all settings. Keep in mind that most content-laden knowledge has a short shelflife. Research methodologies have lasting value and provide us with a common means of communication across investigators and/or types of investigations. Once again, we encourage our readers to use the knowledge yielded from an empirically based research program to anchor their work and guide their training efforts. The pragmatic overview of the designs, methods, and statistics presented in Chapter 8 should **set the stage for setting up a research program of your own and/or giving you the basic tools necessary to critically evaluate the work of others.**

In our final chapter **(Chapter 9)**, we present an overview of **methodological issues related to the multicultural revolution reshaping American business**. Once again, we focus on research methodologies, not content. Many employers are asking, "How do I improve my employee's multicultural sensitivity, critical thinking, and problem-solving skills?" Many have claimed to have the answers. But few have delivered on the "how to." This chapter ("Methodological Issues Related to the Multicultural Revolution Reshaping American Business") was designed to deconstruct and then reconstruct this complex topic from a research methodological perspective.

The use of **narrative forms of inquiry** (ethnographic, participant observation, case study, phenomenological, constructionist, and interpretive) as an educational research method for describing teaching and learning processes has generated considerable controversy and excitement. The increasing attention given to postmodern and feminist views and the methodologies associated with these views has created chaos, confusion, and instability among many researchers. That is to say that the use of qualitative narrative methodologies has presented a number of **challenges to many of the assumptions inherent to empirical forms of research inquiry.** One of the contentions with which empiricists typically confront narrative researchers is the belief that every trainer has a story. Each told story that is documented by researchers purports to recount a thick and rich description of the experiences that trainers live in context-specific situations. Such descriptions are thought to play a powerful mediational role for trainers who engage in active reflection ranging from illuminating tacit wisdom that guides practice to assisting trainers in the generation of practice-based theory. Story represents an enormous database from which to develop new understanding about the relationships among phenomena in workplace contexts. However, there are several **questions that empiricists raise** about the utility, authenticity, and claims of veracity of story that beg the question of whether the research community will ultimately sanctify storytelling work as a viable methodological approach.

In this chapter, we analyze the utility of narrative as a legitimate workplace training research tool. Tracing the historical development of research paradigmatic models, we provide a comparative description of sociolinguistic (narrative) and empirical research methodologies, discuss the various definitions and conceptions of narrative/story, explore the sociopolitical conceptual and theoretical frameworks that guide both narrative and technical/empirical forms of research, highlight the disadvantages and advantages of using story as a methodological research tool in the workplace, examine future directions for the use of narrative inquiry, and conclude with a conceptual framework designed to grant story a practical and utilitarian role in the communication processes of trainers, researchers, and academicians. In sum, what **we attempt to do is present a case for balance and the complementary use of narrative forms of inquiry within the workplace community.**

CHAPTER 2

ADULT LEARNING AND DEVELOPMENT: A COGNITIVE SCIENCE PERSPECTIVE

WHAT DO WE KNOW ABOUT ADULTS AS LEARNERS?

In an attempt to enhance the ability of American businesses to compete successfully both at home and abroad, there has been a push to improve worker productivity. Many workplace environments require more sophisticated basic literacy skills (particularly in reading and mathematics) than those generally possessed by the majority of the presently available workforce.

For the most part, the prevailing view has been that the nation's schools were designed to produce what might be called a manufacturing grunt-labor force. That is to say that large numbers of public school students were never expected to become more than functionally literate (i.e., able to read and compute at about the fourth-grade level). Since 1900, about 20 percent of the entire American population has remained at this level of literacy. Most would agree with the statement that the present workforce is composed of many inadequately skilled and poorly educated workers.

The **outcome-based paradigm shift** that is currently taking place in education, business, and industry is clearly evident in the numerous reports appearing in the media. These reports have documented American workers' low academic achievement scores, their lack of preparation for the world of work, and their relatively low rank in international comparative studies. This outcome-based approach includes many skills once demanded only of a few (eg., to think, to solve problems, to be creative, and to learn new skills and knowledge throughout life). It is important to note that the outcomes include more than tangible products. They include thinking, problem solving, attitudinal, affective, motivational, and relationship elements that also contribute to overall performances (Spady & Marshall, 1991).

Findings from current and emerging research suggest that the behaviorist tradition that permeates much of current practice in adult learning and development provides an inadequate design for the increasing demands made by more sophisticated workplace environments (Brown, 1978; Bruer, 1993; Case, 1985; Glaser, 1990; Gordon, Ponticell, & Morgan, 1989, 1991; Gordon, Morgan, & Ponticell, 1994; Levin & Pressley, 1983). Where complex tactical and strategic problem-solving tasks require the assimilation of large amounts of knowledge and high workload requirements rather than fixed procedural sequences, new approaches to training and instruction appear to be needed.

THREE VIEWS OF INSTRUCTION

Three models of instruction have prevailed in adult training and instruction (i.e., **mastery learning, personalized systems of instruction, and tutoring**). In what follows, we attempt to relate theory to practice. An effort is made to focus upon the **commonalities** across these three training models (e.g., their emphasis on continuous assessment, remediation, encouragement, and support) rather than the differences. Trends and existing knowledge related to the effectiveness of each of the models are presented.

An effort is made to relate contemporary developments reported in the cognitive science literature to John B. Carroll's (1963) original behaviorally based model of mastery learning. Particular attention is given to possible instructional correctives and the special problems related to the application of mastery learning, personalized system of instruction (PSI), and tutoring procedures to the atypical and/or nontraditional learner. Those cognitive science components requiring particular attention in the design and implementation of mastery learning, PSI, and tutoring instruction are presented.

Specific attention is given to the **learnable aspects of human thinking and problem solving**. The overall thesis is that most of the cognitive science components are learnable. Therefore when we are called upon to design mastery learning, PSI, and tutoring workforce training environments, we should attempt to include instructional procedures having potential for the modification of the cognitive components presented in the embellished mastery learning model.

Mastery Learning

John B. Carroll (1963) proposed that the degree of learning is a function

Figure 2.1
Carroll's Model of Mastery Learning

$$\text{Degree of learning} = \frac{\text{Amount of time spent on a task}}{\text{Amount of time needed to learn the task}}$$

of the ratio of two quantities: (1) the amount of time a learner spends on the learning task; and (2) the amount of time a learner needs to learn the task.

Carroll's model is depicted in Figure 2.1. This model has served as a behaviorally based theoretical anchor for much of Benjamin Bloom's (1968; 1974) work related to mastery learning instruction. Carroll's formulation implied that by allowing sufficient time to learn a task (i.e., permitting the numerator of the ratio to be larger), and by improving instructional conditions (i.e., decreasing the denominator), most students should be able to reach a criterion of mastery. Mastery learning is an educational procedure in which a learning hierarchy is developed and learners are required to master each unit of the hierarchy prior to beginning a subsequent unit. Mastery usually is determined by end-of-unit tests that learners must pass.

Bloom (1971, 1976) and others (Block, 1971, 1974; Block & Burns, 1976) have argued that mastery learning research supports the claim that mastery learning strategies can raise the achievement levels of approximately 80 percent of students to levels achieved by the upper 20 percent under nonmastery conditions. It should be noted that these findings apply to many academic content areas (e.g., reading, writing, and math) in addition to different types of thinking and problem-solving situations. From these reviews, it seems that most investigators recognize that the tutoring and mastery learning research findings confirm the achievement claims.

The time claims, however, require further investigation. Most tutoring and mastery learning theorists acknowledge that during the initial learning sequences, extra time must be provided to less able learners. However, this extra time is viewed as a temporary "crutch" that becomes less and less necessary with practice (Bloom, 1976).

A number of **critics** of mastery learning instruction (Anderson & Burns, 1987; Buss, 1976; Greeno, 1978; Guskey, 1987; Guskey & Gates, 1986; Mueller, 1976; Resnick, 1977; Slavin, 1987a, 1987b) have argued that in regular nonmastery instructional situations in which time is held constant for all learners, individual differences among students are reflected primarily in differences in achievement outcomes. That is to say that if all students are restricted to learning a lesson in a certain amount of time, then a normal distribution of high, average, and low achievement scores will probably be observed. However, if achievement outcomes are held constant in mastery learning instruction, then individual differences among learners will be reflected by differences in the time needed to learn.

Another way of stating this situation is to say that the assumption of stability in individual differences among students is directly related to the assumption of a time-achievement trade-off. To bring less able learners up to the desired mastery level, additional time must be provided for both learners and instructors. Since individual differences between learners are assumed to be relatively stable, critics claim that these time costs remain relatively constant throughout mastery learning instruction. That is, time is traded for increased achievement of less able students, and time inequality is traded for achievement equality. Thus, there may be a **Robin Hood effect** associated with the use of mastery learning approaches to instruction. Mastery learning may help slower-learning students at the expense of faster-learning students. The important educational resources of instructor time and attention may be used to benefit the slower learners at the expense of faster ones.

From the results of numerous investigations, we know that mastery learning programs when compared to traditional approaches to instruction produce positive gains in academic achievement and student attitudes (Block & Burns, 1976; Carroll, 1989). There is considerable evidence indicating that the effectiveness of the mastery approach depends on the length of the training program and the type of outcome measures used. Robert Slavin (1987a) found that training programs lasting four weeks or longer yielded more positive findings than those training programs lasting less than four weeks.

It should be noted, however, that standardized achievement outcome measures yield much weaker results than performance- and/or curriculum-based outcome measures (Slavin, 1987b) and that group-based mastery learning approaches appear to be extremely difficult to carry out with success in large-scale training projects such as inner city schools (Brophy, 1988).

Personalized Systems of Instruction (PSI)

Although mastery learning and PSI approaches were derived from different theoretical perspectives, they are similar in many ways. Bloom's (1971) learning for mastery strategies evolved from Carroll's (1963) theory of school learning and has had its major impact on elementary and secondary school educators. In contrast, the personalized system of instruction strategy (PSI) developed by **Fred Keller** (1968) evolved from Skinnerian behavioral psychology and has had its major impact on the thinking of university and college educators.

The **basic components** of PSI include self-pacing, the use of human tutors and proctors, the mastery requirement, immediate feedback, and frequent testing over relatively small units. Advocates of PSI assume that traditional instructional procedures do not encourage an adequate number of learner responses or provide learners with personalized opportunities for reinforcement to occur. Keller (1968) proposed that subject matter be divided into brief instructional units, enabling students to study at their own rate, progressing to the next unit when mastery (an 80 to 90 percent correct score) was achieved. Those students who do not master an instructional unit the first time are provided with additional time and individualized (i.e., personalized) tutoring until mastery is achieved.

James A. Kulik's, Chen-Lin C. Kulik's, and Peter A. Cohen's (1979) meta-analyses of PSI indicated that when compared to traditional instruction, PSI produces superior student achievement, considerably less achievement variation, and higher student evaluations. In addition, PSI procedures were found to be unrelated to increased study time or course withdrawals.

Considerable disagreement exists over the respective contributions of each of the basic components (self-pacing, the use of human tutors and proctors, the mastery requirement, immediate feedback, and frequent testing over relatively small units) to the overall effectiveness of the PSI approach to instruction. For example, J. F. Calhoun (1973) found that all of the components make important contributions. However, James H. Block and Robert B. Burns (1976) reported that the mastery requirement produced the strongest effects. Finally, it should be noted that the Robin Hood effect cited above as a potential problem with mastery learning instruction, does not manifest itself with PSI since students work independently (Calhoun, 1973). That is to say that since students work independently with PSI, instructor time and attention are not used to benefit slower learners at the expense of their faster peers.

In sum, PSI gets generally favorable marks when compared with traditional instructional methodologies. It appears to be easily adaptable to a wide variety of instructional situations and has few, if any, empirically demonstrated negative side effects.

Tutoring

Edward E. Gordon and Elaine H. Gordon (1990) reported that large-group-based schooling has dominated the twentieth century, but individual and small-group tutoring approaches to instruction still hold an important role. Peer tutors, afterschool remedial programs, home-bound instruction, and the home-schooling movement are modern expressions of tutoring. Centuries of tutors demonstrated that a child's education was a highly personalized process, supported by the family and guided through the assistance of literate teachers. At their best, tutors remained the best equipped to assess individual differences among their students and to engineer stimulating learning environments (Gordon & Gordon, 1990).

In the nineteenth and particularly in the twentieth centuries, tutoring became an actual part of schooling. Some of the most important Western philosophers developed educational theories based upon their practical experience as tutors. Their tutorial philosophy led to the development of many of our modern educational principles such as continuous assessment, remediation, encouragement, and support. It is important to note that these principles are the same as those assumed to be of importance to advocates of mastery learning and PSI instruction.

A review of the literature indicates that tutoring usually produces positive results. L. F. Annis (1983) reported that tutoring procedures appear to produce positive effects on both tutees and tutors. Summaries of research on tutoring (Cohen, Kulik, & Kulik, 1982; Gage & Berliner, 1992) have indicated that these positive effects have been consistently found on measures of achievement and on affective measures of self-esteem and intrinsic interest in the subject matter being taught. In addition, the results from numerous cross-age, peer tutoring studies conducted with learners across the life span have yielded positive findings (Lippitt, 1969; P. Lippitt & R. Lippitt, 1970; R. Lippitt & M. Lippitt, 1968). In sum, tutoring appears to be a very powerful technique for enhancing student learning across a wide sample of different types of students and content areas.

INDIVIDUAL DIFFERENCES AND THE LEARNABLE ASPECTS OF HUMAN THINKING AND PROBLEM SOLVING

Cognitive scientists (Brown, 1978; Bruer, 1993; Case, 1985; Glaser, 1984, 1990) claim that the major differences in the learning characteristics between novice and expert human learners are found primarily in the cognitive mediation differences of attention, cognitive style expectancies, and memory organization. It is argued here that it is these cognitive mediation differences where the study of individual differences and the learnable aspects of human thinking and problem solving appear to be of particular relevance to advocates of mastery learning, PSI, and tutoring instruction.

Behavioral Views

The behaviorists have viewed individual differences in terms of biological differences and learned habits. Thinking has been viewed as a change in habit strength, problem solving as related to trial-and-error application of existing habits, and creativity as an accidental combination of two or more previously acquired stimulus-response (S-R) chains. In terms of instruction, the accumulation of experience, not the remodeling of experience, has been considered to be of primary importance. From this point of view, instruction involves setting up instructional situations to help learners acquire successful learning habits. The greater the number of acquired habits, the greater the adaptive problem-solving behavior and intelligence of the learner.

Gestalt Views

Gestaltists have focused their attention on individual differences in perception, both biological and psychological. The relationships among attention, perception, learning, and memory have been viewed as particularly important. There is considerable evidence (Bower & Hilgard, 1981) to suggest that most of our perceptions of environmental events are learned. In the process of learning, we develop memories and our memories set up expectancies, stereotypes, and biases that affect the way in which we perceive environmental events. These learned perceptual templates (expectancies) have a great deal to do with stimulus input, and they may facilitate or retard learning.

Gestaltists have viewed stimulus-response associations as mere byproducts of perceptual chunks. They have described two kinds of problem solving: productive (creative-insightful) and reproductive (application of SR habits-simple trial and error learning). Thus, from a gestalt point of view, the primary difference between the novice and the expert learner is considered to be in their learned perceptual templates, which create learning expectancies and which in turn differentially effect stimulus input and memory organization.

Piagetian and Neo-Piagetian Views

For Piagetians and neo-Piagetians (Brown, 1978; Case, 1985), individual differences are considered to be cognitive and have to do with differences in schematic representations. These master cognitive templates (schematic representations) serve as logical problem-solving components. Thinking and problem solving are seen in terms of assimilation and accommodation, and all thinking is believed to be creative. In addition, the neo-Piagetians focus on the development and use of executive processes (i.e., self-controlling processes). They consider equilibration the major type of adaptive problem solving and look at perception as a gestaltist would, viewing individual differences as differences in cognitive expectancies and style (field dependence-field independence; internal and external locus of control).

Novice and expert learners differ with respect to the number of bits of information they can attend to without support from the perceptual field. With age and experience the number of things a person can attend to remains the same (7 + 2), but the bits of information become more cognitively differentiated and sophisticated. From a neo-Piagetian perspective, what develops is attention, and one learns when one is able to acquire a rule (usually a verbal rule) relating new learning to existing cognitive structures. To facilitate learning, a neo-Piagetian would attempt to teach the novice the memory and metamemory (knowing what you know) strategies (e.g., rehearsal, and other active engagement strategies) used by expert learners.

Information-Processing Views

Those individuals associated with the information-processing camp (Bruer, 1993; Glaser, 1978, 1982, 1984, 1986, 1990; Levin & Pressley, 1983; Pressley & Levin, 1983) view individual differences in terms of fixed (attention limitations) and flexible (instructional manipulations) control structures. They are concerned essentially with the description and facilitation of the thinking and problem-solving processes and do not specifically address creativity. They provide detailed task analytic descriptions (computer simulation models) of the expert learner's assimilation processes and construct models to facilitate the acquisition of knowledge among novices.

Individual differences are viewed as the fixed biological control structures of attention, maturational stages, and temperament. Manipulatable flexible psychological control structures comprise differences in knowledge, language, memory organization, mood, attitudes, personality, cognitive style expectancies, and motivation. These flexible control structures are what we attempt to modify to enhance the quality and organization of instruction. For the most part, the neo-Piagetian and the information-processing theorists are closely aligned in their mutual focus on strategy-training procedures directed at the novice learner.

A COGNITIVE SCIENCE MODEL OF MASTERY LEARNING, PSI, AND TUTORING

Given the recent advances with respect to the cognitive science perspective, it is our view that it is now time to embellish the behaviorally based mastery learning model originally proposed by Carroll (1963) to include a number of cognitive variables. An embellished cognitive science model of mastery learning, PSI, and tutoring instruction is presented in Figure 2.2.

From a cognitive scientists' perspective, **individual differences in student aptitude** would consist of differences in attention, temperament, maturational stages of development, existing knowledge and language templates, memory organization, mood, cognitive styles, attitudes, personality, cognitive style expectancies, and motivation. **Quality of instruction** would relate to the ability of the instructor to organize instruction, to set up situations that would enhance meaning and contribute to the development of critical thinking and problem-solving skills.

Figure 2.2
An Embellished Cognitive Science Model
of Mastery Learning, PSI, and Tutoring Instruction

Degree of learning =

$$\text{Degree of learning} = \frac{\text{Time spent (willing or allowed)}}{\substack{\text{Time needed (aptitude, i.e., individual differences)} + \\ \text{(quality of instruction x ability to understand} \\ \text{instructions)}}}$$

Where: **Student aptitude** would consist of the biological differences of attention, temperament, and maturational stages of development and the psychological differences of existing knowledge and language templates, memory organization, mood, attitudes, personality, cognitive style expectancies, and motivation.

Quality of instruction would be viewed as the ability of the teacher to organize instruction, to give it meaning, and to set up problem solving situations which enhance critical thinking.

Ability to understand instructions would consist of the same components as quality of instruction.

It is recognized that we are unable to modify biological differences in temperament and maturational stages. But most of the other components listed in the embellished cognitive science model can be modified. We can enhance knowledge and language templates. It is generally accepted that how efficiently we learn depends to a great extent on what we already know.

From a cognitive science perspective, a major constraint on a novice learner is that their knowledge base and ability to use language to code and store information is very limited. There is a literate bias in schooling that is viewed as enhancing our thinking and problem-solving behaviors. The assumption is that this literate bias allows the expert learner to interpret environmental events in a different way than the novice learner.

It is further assumed that the learner with an internally controlled, field-independent cognitive style interprets his or her environment in a way that differs from the externally controlled, field-dependent learner. For example, the internally controlled learner would attribute successes to effort, persistence, and hard work while the externally controlled learner would be more likely to attribute success to luck. Negative attitudes, low expectancies, and bad moods constrain cognitive performance. Again, the point to be made here is that knowledge and language templates, cognitive styles, attitudes, expectancies, and mood can be modified by the instructor.

WHAT MATTERS?

It is recognized that much of what is presented here is derived from the field of cognitive information processing, a field replete with overlapping ideas and concepts expressed in multiple terms. There are those practitioners who would claim that the field is too complex and the instructional procedures derived from it too cumbersome to use. While most of us may agree that trainers should utilize cognitive information-processing principles in the curriculum and instructional designs they create for all learners, we may not think that this complex theory of learning and instruction can be directly applied to pragmatic training situations.

Should trainers be expected to monitor and shape the cognitive information-processing capabilities of learners? Can a novice learner's attention, cognitive style expectancies, and memory be modified? The research evidence from a cognitive science perspective (e.g., Bransford, Sherwood, Vye, & Rieser, 1986; Bruer, 1993; Foster, 1986; Glaser, 1978, 1982, 1984, 1986, 1990; Glaser & Takaniski, 1986; Greeno, 1989; Pressley & Levin, 1983; Shuell, 1986; Weinstein & Marges, 1986), together with the effective teaching and learning productivity perspectives (e.g., Good & Brophy, 1987; Walberg, 1984; Wang, Haertel & Walberg, 1990), indicates that they can. Several common **factors** that emerge within the context of the research literature supporting the use of mastery learning, PSI, tutoring, and cognitive science models of instruction appear to be particularly **important to trainers**.

Time Actively Engaged in a Learning Task

The amount of time that learners are actively engaged in a learning task (i.e., the concept of academic learning time) is important (Fisher et al., 1978; Stallings, 1980). From a cognitive science perspective, the performance of a task becomes more automatic with repeated exposure to small meaningful components of the task consistently presented over a period of time (Myers & Fisk, 1987). Learning is enhanced by instruction that breaks down complex tasks into small meaningful components that are individually taught.

Small Competency Units Should Be Connected to Existing Knowledge

From a cognitive science perspective, knowledge might be viewed as organized in schemas (i.e., hierarchical structures or networks of concepts, components, and interrelationships). Increasing a learner's ability to develop more elaborate schemas, accessing them more easily, and automating learning procedures enhances learning.

Instruction that facilitates students' relating new information to old is useful. New information is more readily learned when it is organized and

presented in a conceptual structure, using associations, advance organizers, topic headings, and mnemonics. It is important to teach the prototype
first (i.e., concepts, rules, principles), then variations, including real-world
examples and applications. It is also important that learners see the align-
ment among goals, content, instruction, task, and evaluation.

Continuous Feedback and Assessment Should Be Provided

Research indicates that learning is enhanced by detailed and specific
feedback, not only on the correctness of a learner's responses but also on
the appropriateness of a learner's learning strategies (Brophy, 1981; Guskey
& Gates, 1986; Walberg, 1984; Wang, Haertel & Walberg, 1990). In addition,
feedback is important not only on total performance but also on specific
task components, so that the learner can discover sources of error. Continuous assessment that is integrated with instruction enhances the learner's
ability to identify useful problem solving strategies.

Metacognitive (Learning How to Learn) Strategies Should Be Taught

Research indicates that effective learners use mental models to conceptualize task demands, methods for accomplishing the task, and relationships to the task domain (e.g., Brainin, 1985). The best problem solvers are
those who develop detailed mental representations of a "problem space"
before attempting a solution (Norman & Rumelhart, 1981).

Marlene Scardamalia and Carl Bereiter (1983) have found that learners
can be explicitly taught to use learning models and thinking skills. It is
important to find out from learners the models they already use in everyday work or life situations. Learning is enhanced when these existing models are elaborated and refined through the instructional process. Effective
task analysis enables the learner to identify the development of individual
learning models. In addition, using learners' existing models, providing
examples and counterexamples, and structuring situations in which models are applied and tested enables learners to identify "good" models.

Attempts Should Be Made to Establish Motivational Links

Studies have found that learners use two kinds of knowledge to learn,
task knowledge and motivational knowledge (Ames & Ames, 1984, 1985,
1989; Winne, 1991). Motivational knowledge influences students' involvement in learning and stimulates feelings learners associate with the learning experience (Winne, 1985). For adult learners, several motivational factors appear to be important: a stress-free learning environment, peers' academic aspirations, a workplace culture that emphasizes academic achievement and work-related performance, program accessibility, cohesiveness
among program participants, the employer's concern with program suc-

cess, and the individual's value for persistence (Gordon, Morgan, & Ponticell, 1994).

DESCRIPTION OF A WORKPLACE RESEARCH PROGRAM

The nature of these cognitive science approaches is emerging as a growing area of research and interest in business and industry. For example, Edward E. Gordon, Judith A. Ponticell, and Ronald R. Morgan (1989, 1991; Gordon, Morgan, & Ponticell, 1994) have carried out a series of studies in which the embellished model of mastery learning, PSI, and tutoring instruction described above has been applied in the workplace. In these studies, trainer/ administrator teams provided sequentially arranged, systematic training with individuals and/or small groups. A number of specially crafted curriculum scripts were designed to teach workers competencies at the introductory, maintenance, and/or expert levels of performance. Over 300 learning descriptors have been systematically developed and are being used to document academic achievement gains, improved social-emotional outcomes, and the acquisition of selected job-related skills.

Data sets are being collected and examined in several areas of training (see Table 2.1). **Performance differences across time blocks** are being examined in samples of workers receiving individual training. In addition, differences in performance are also being examined in relation to differences in **instructional modes** (i.e., individualized tutoring groups, adult peer tutoring groups, computer-assisted groups, and whole classroom instructional groups).

Comparison of pre- and post-tutoring outcomes are being made across treatment conditions (i.e., individualized tutoring groups, adult peer tutoring groups, computer assisted groups, and whole classroom instructional groups); across time blocks (10 to 19 hours, 20 to 29 hours, 30 to 45 hours); and across types of tutoring interventions (e.g., academic, job-related, social-emotional). Presently, both quantitative and qualitative analyses of numerous data sets are underway. Early indications are that consistent performance differences exist across the time blocks. A six-months to one-year gain in skills improvement appears to occur at around the thirtieth hour of instruction.

In addition, qualitative evaluations by tutee, tutor, and employer indicate growth in academic skills, thinking skills, problem-solving skills, and motivation related to the value of learning in general, academic learning in particular, and work performance. Three important motivational factors appear to be: (1) proximity of the instructional program to the workplace; (2) a supportive workplace environment; and (3) individual perseverance. Emerging data from long-term follow-up reports of workers indicate that they retained what they learned. In addition, their attitudes toward learn-

Table 2.1
Overall Analytic Paradigm

		Treatment Conditions			
		Xa1	Xa2	Xa3	Xa4
		Individualized Tutoring Groups	Adult Peer Tutoring Groups	Computer Assisted Groups	Classroom Control Groups
	Xb1 Academic Xc1 Social-emotional Xc2 Job-related Xc3				
10 to 19		Yb Ya	Yb Ya	Yb Ya	Yb Ya
	Xb2 Academic Xc1 Social-emotional Xc2 Job-related Xc3				
20 to 29		Yb Ya	Yb Ya	Yb Ya	Yb Ya
	Xb3 Academic Xc1 Social-emotional Xc2 Job-related Xc3				
30 to 45		Yb Ya	Yb Ya	Yb Ya	Yb Ya

(Hours 10 to 19, 20 to 29, 30 to 45)

Where: **Independent variables:**
- treatment conditions Xa1, Xa2, Xa3, Xa4
- time blocks Xb1, Xb2, Xb3
- type of intervention Xc1, Xc2, Xc3

Dependent variables:
- academic, social-emotional, and job-related pre- and post-test outcome measures
- triangulation of quantitative and qualitative tutee, tutor, employer, and peer evaluations of tutoring outcomes

ing, their personal motivational levels, and individual work performance showed consistent improvement.

SUMMARY

In this chapter, it has been argued that individual difference in cognition (knowledge and stylistic) and perception can both constrain and facilitate learning. Our view is that individual differences, especially the cognitive bases of differences of the novice learner and instructional task, appear to have a valid place in the psychology of learning as it relates to mastery learning, PSI, and tutoring instruction. Presently much research in a number of areas of cognitive science (e.g., expert-novice comparisons, cognitive strategy training, critical thinking, and performance-outcome-based assessment) considered to be relevant to the implementation of mastery learning, PSI, and tutoring instruction is underway (Bransford, Sherwood, Vye, & Rieser, 1986; Bruer, 1993; Foster, 1986; Glaser, 1978, 1982, 1984, 1986, 1990; Glaser & Takanishi, 1986; Greeno, 1989; Pressley & Levin, 1983; Shuell, 1986; Spady & Marshall, 1991; Weinstein & Marges, 1986).

The findings related to research on cognitive strategy training, metacognitive processes, and computer simulation of expert performance may provide us with **teachable cognitive process variables** that could supplement and perhaps replace traditional intelligence tests in the successful matching of student's individual differences and educational treatment approaches. Detailed cognitive task analyses of instructional sequences are being done, and the training of metacognitive skills and problem-solving strategies may help novice learners master the intellectual skills and the content used by the experts. The identification of these individual differences in cognitive information-processing capacities could be utilized to design instruction that compensates for a particular deficiency by providing for learners what they cannot provide for themselves. Such information could be used to capitalize on the learner's strengths and would appear to be particularly valuable for diagnosing reasons for current learning difficulties and in suggesting mastery learning, PSI, and tutoring instructional procedures (prescriptions) for overcoming them.

What we are proposing here is a **general information processing approach to adult learning and instruction**. Adult instruction should be directed at modifying student attention, cognitive expectancies, and memory. Cognitive information processing is enhanced when learners are actively engaged in the learning task, discuss, rehearse, analyze, problem solve, use graphs to represent experience, and share observations, understandings, and knowledge.

The suggestion here is that when we are called upon to design mastery learning, PSI, and tutoring environments, we should attempt to include instructional procedures having potential for the modification of cognitive learning components (e.g., attention, knowledge and language templates, cognitive strategies, attitudes, expectancies, and mood). We know that mastery learning, PSI, and tutoring instructional systems work. The three instructional systems have been carefully tested in highly controlled laboratory, field experimental, and applied settings. What is now needed is a greater focus and appreciation for attempts to relate recent findings reported in the cognitive science literature to these behaviorally anchored models.

TERMS TO KNOW

Carroll's model of mastery learning (1963)
Keller's PSI model of instruction (1968)
biological constraints on learning
psychological constraints on learning
time achievement trade-off assumption
Robin Hood effect
components of mastery learning instruction
components of PSI
tutorial principles
general laws of learning
differences in the learning characteristics of typical and atypical learners
learned perceptual templates (expectancies)
cognitive templates
executive processes
fixed control structures
flexible control structures
a cognitive science model of mastery learning, PSI, and tutoring
the literate bias in schooling
differences among experts and novices
cognitive components of instruction
the learnable aspects of human thinking and problem solving

QUESTIONS TO CONSIDER

1. Present a comparative discussion focusing on the differences and commonalities across mastery learning, PSI, and tutoring models of instruction.

2. From a cognitive scientist's perspective, discuss the similarities and differences in the learning characteristics of typical and atypical learners.

3. Identify and discuss those cognitive components of instruction having potential for minimizing individual differences among learners.

SUGGESTED READINGS

Readers wanting to study more thoroughly the topics covered in this chapter will find the following references helpful.

Block, & Burns (1976). Mastery learning. In L. S. Shulman (Ed.), *Review of research in education* (Vol. 4). Itasca, IL: Peacock Publishers.
Bloom, B. S. (1976). *Human characteristics and school learning*. New York: McGraw-Hill.

Bruer, J. T. (1993). *Schools for thought: A science of learning in the classroom.* Cambridge, MA: MIT Press.

Carroll, J. B. (1963). A model of school learning. *Teachers College Record,* 64, 723-733.

Carroll, J. B. (1989). The Carroll model: A 25-year retrospective and prospective view. *Educational Researcher,* 18 (1), 26-31.

Gordon, E. E., & Gordon, E. H. (1990). *Centuries of tutoring: A history of alternative education in America and Western Europe.* Latham, MD: University Press.

Gordon, E. E., Morgan, R. R., & Ponticell, J. A. (1994). *FutureWork: The revolution reshaping American business.* Westport, CT: Praeger Books.

Gordon, E. E., Ponticell, J. A., & Morgan, R. R. (1989). Back to basics. *Training and Development Journal* (August), 73-76.

Gordon, E. E., Ponticell, J. A., & Morgan, R. R. (1991). *Closing the literacy gap in American business: A guide for trainers and human resource specialists.* Westport, CT: Quorum Books.

Keller, F. S. (1968). Good-bye teacher! *Journal of Applied Behavioral Analysis,* 1, 79-84.

Kulik, J. A., Kulik, L. C., & Cohen, P. A. (1979). A meta-analysis of outcome studies of Keller's personalized system of instruction. *American Psychologist,* 34, 307-318.

PART II

THEORETICAL FOUNDATIONS OF LEARNING AND DEVELOPMENT

CHAPTER 3

BEHAVIORAL VIEWS
OF LEARNING AND INSTRUCTION

This chapter consists of an overview of what we know and don't know about learning. The focus of the chapter is on a behavioral view of learning and instruction. The first section of the chapter consists of a general discussion of the basic models of learning. This is followed by a section in which an attempt is made to relate each of the models to learning in general. Additional sections of the chapter include brief discussions of the special place of motivation within learning theory, reinforcement versus contiguity theories, the limited role of reinforcement, the existence of cognitive expectancies, and a final section related to attacks on behaviorism.

THE LEARNING CURVE

An adequate theory of learning should be able to offer some explanation for the basic **components of the learning curve**. The first learning curve component is referred to as baseline. **Baseline** refers to those individual differences among learners when a learner is first exposed to a learning task. If a test of your knowledge were given on the first day of your educational psychology class, this would constitute a baseline measure of your knowledge of educational psychology. What would account for differences in baseline performance measures across students in your class? Are these differences related to biological differences, environmental psychological differences, or a combination of both? A theory of learning should offer some explanation for baseline performance differences.

The second component of the learning curve is the **acquisition** component. Here we are referring to an explanation of the actual learning process. How can we explain what you are learning while taking a course in educational psychology? After you have completed the course, one hopes what you have learned will be retained (i.e., the **maintenance** component of the learning curve). Finally, an adequate theory of learning should be able to offer an explanation of why you may fail to retain what you have learned in the course (i.e., the **extinction** component of the learning curve). A diagramatic summary of the basic components of the learning curve is presented below:

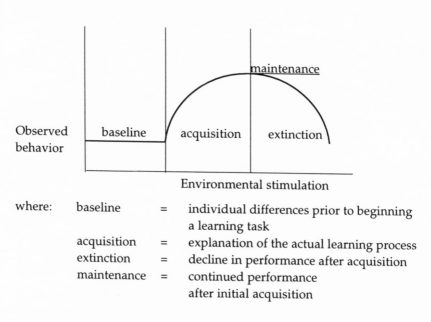

where:	baseline	=	individual differences prior to beginning a learning task
	acquisition	=	explanation of the actual learning process
	extinction	=	decline in performance after acquisition
	maintenance	=	continued performance after initial acquisition

MODELS OF LEARNING

There are **four** basic **learning models** competing for attention (classical conditioning, operant reinforcement, social learning, and the cognitive model). It is a matter of great debate as to how we learn, whether by SS pairings, SR contiguity, use of reinforcing and punishing contingencies, imitation of models, or cognition. Different theorists have different views related to explaining why or how badly or how well we perform in school, on the job, and in life in general. Reading, writing, language, listening, studying, remembering, analyzing, synthesizing, motivation, problem-solving skills, and creativity are but a few of the ingredients required to do well in school and in the workplace. Let us briefly consider some of the major **behavioral theorists** and consider how they would explain learning in general. In the sections that follow, each of the learning models is described and comparisons are made among them. Each of the major theoretical perspectives is examined within the context of the theory's ability to provide a satisfactory explanation of the various components of the learning curve.

Classical Conditioning (SS)

From a classical (SS) conditioning perspective, learning takes place when two stimuli are paired together for a number of trials. One stimulus is referred to as the unconditioned stimulus (UCS) and the other as the conditioned stimulus (CS).

Pavlov. In the original 1927 experimental demonstration of classical conditioning, Ivan Pavlov (1960) paired food powder (a UCS) with a bell (CS) for a number of trials. Before the experiment, Pavlov observed that presentation of food to a dog would elicit salivation. Pavlov attempted to train the animal to salivate in the presence of a bell. To do so, he merely paired the two stimuli (UCS and CS) together for a number of trials. With repeated pairings of the UCS and CS, the animal gradually learned to salivate when the bell was presented.

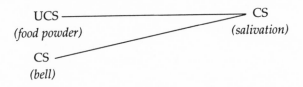

It is recognized that at first glance, this experiment probably doesn't appear to be very important for a person interested in adult learning and development. But as we shall see shortly, Pavlov's contributions continue to have considerable influence.

Watson. Using the same model, John B. Watson and Richard Raynor (1920) designed an experiment in which they demonstrated that early emotions could be acquired using the classical conditioning procedure. Using an infant, Baby Albert, as a subject and pairing a loud sound (UCS) with a rat (CS), they found that the infant would learn to fear the rat.

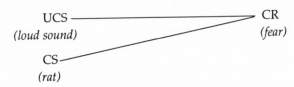

Despite some problems with respect to the failure to replicate the study (Samelson, 1980), the Watson and Raynor study has become one of those anchor studies considered by most psychologists to be of crucial importance. Why? The study is considered important because it represented a demonstration that **early learning** could take place through a process of stimulus pairing and that **emotions** (fear in this instance) were not necessarily innate, but could be learned. It should be noted that if emotions could be learned, they probably could also be extinguished.

Learning Curve Components. When we apply the Pavlovian model to the basic components of the learning curve, individual differences in baseline characteristics of a learner can be described in terms of the learner's previous history of stimulus pairings and the biologically wired UCS difference characteristics of the species. That is to say that baseline performance for Pavlov would consist of previous knowledge acquired by pairing two stimuli together for a number of trials. Individual differences among learners would be represented in terms of differential exposure to stimulus pairs and to the biologically wired UCS differences across species. Acquisition is explained in terms of pairing two stimuli (UCS and CS) together for a number of trials. Extinction takes place when the CS is presented repeatedly without the UCS, and maintenance would take place, if after learning something, a learner would be continuously exposed to UCS-CS pairings. For example, in the case of the Watson and Raynor experiment, fear would be extinguished if the loud sound (UCS) were not frequently presented with the rat (CS), but the fear would be maintained if the UCS and CS were repeatedly paired together in the child's natural environment. From a classical conditioning perspective, the components of the learning curve would be explained as follows:

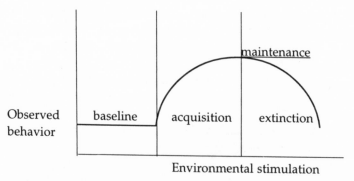

where:

baseline	=	previous stimulus pairs and species appropriate biologically wired UCSs
acquisition	=	pairing two stimuli (UCS and CS) together for a number of trials
extinction	=	discontinue the stimulus pairings
maintenance	=	continue to pair the UCS with the CS

To explain academic learning, heavy reliance would be given to Pavlov's notion of the **second signal system**. All learners (animals and humans) are presumed to learn via using a simple Pavlovian conditioning procedure in which two stimuli (USC and CS) are paired together for a number of trials. Humans, but not animals, also learn by using the second signal system.

After conditioning has taken place, the CS is then paired with a neutral (e.g., verbal) stimulus (NS). This procedure is referred to as the second signal system and allows for the transfer of reinforcement from a UCS to a nonprimary (e.g., verbal) stimulus (NS). Use of the second signal system is frequently used to explain the powerful effects of **language-symbolic learning** within the context of the Pavlovian conditioning model. The second symbol system served as a major variable of interest to A. R. Luria (1966) and is related to the importance of the use of language and symbolization with regard to educational and psychotherapeutic interventions. Extinction would occur if the CS is repeatedly presented without the presence of the UCS. Should the UCS and CS be paired occasionally, maintenance would probably occur.

Finally, mention should be made of **Edwin R. Guthrie** (1886-1959), who was an **SR contiguity theorist**, but not an SS Pavlovian contiguity theorist. His basic law of learning stated that "a combination of stimuli which has accompanied a movement will on its recurrence tend to be followed by that movement." Movements (i.e., muscular movements and glandular secretions) were considered to be the basic data of the theory. Reinforcement served the mechanical function of being useful in learning clean SR associations. Guthrie assumed that learning could take place in one trial. He stated that SR associations reached their full association strength on the first successful pairing of a stimulus and response. It should be noted that for Guthrie, the behavior conditioned is not necessarily the behavior observed. The minute internal movements conditioned are combined to yield complex observed behaviors. Practice, like reinforcement, would facilitate the development of clean associations. Extinction would occur when new learning took the place of what was previously learned. If we wanted to **break a habit**, we would set up a situation where the S and the R would no longer be associated. It should be noted that Guthrie's views related to breaking habits served as the theoretical anchor upon which the desensitization procedures used to extinguish phobias were based (Wolpe, 1981; Woolfolk & Richardson, 1984). See Training Application 3.1

Operant Conditioning (SRS)

Advocates (Thorndike, Skinner, and Hull) of the operant conditioning model use **reinforcement** and **punishment** procedures to shape and control behavior.

Thorndike. Edward L. Thorndike (1874-1949) dominated the field of educational psychology from about 1915 to 1935. He was an SRS theorist who emphasized reinforcement and practice. He believed that skill training was highly specific, and he expected little generalization to occur across learning tasks. His strict behavioral, nonmediational notions of learning have been severely criticized (Bower and Hilgard, 1981). We now know that information (Buchwald, 1967) and awareness (Estes, 1969) facilitate learning. Since Thorndike refused to include these cognitive mediational variables (information and awareness) in his theory and viewed the learning process as being highly mechanical, history has not been kind to his views. Nevertheless, he is given considerable credit for establishing a laboratory approach to educational practice and to advocating that we carefully assess a student's rate of progress. See Training Application 3.2.

Hull. Clark L. Hull's (1943) theory was basically a reinforcement theory, but he did allow some room for goal-directed cognitive mediation (rg-sg habit chains) to occur between the S and the R. One such mediating concept for Hull was the **habit family hierarchy**.

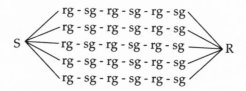

He assumed that knowledge was accumulated through experience. The greater the accumulation, the greater the adaptive ability, intelligence, and problem-solving ability of the learner. The role of the teacher and/or therapist was to increase the number of goal-directed **habit chains** (rg-sg chains). Creativity was explained in terms of an accidental combination of two or more habit chains. For example, if a learner attempted to solve a problem using habit chain 1 but was blocked midway through the chain, he or she could then try habit chain 2, 3, and so on. If by chance, part of habit chain 1 were combined with part of habit chain 4 or 5, a creative solution to a problem could manifest itself. Extinction for Hull was related to failure to receive reinforcement. Hull had many followers (O. Hobart Mowrer, Neal E. Miller, Kenneth W. Spence, Abram Amsel, and Frank A. Logan) and dominated the field of learning from 1935 to 1955.

Skinner. From about 1955 to 1970, B. F. Skinner was center stage. Skinner's model of learning is an operant reinforcement model. He is viewed as a **radical behaviorist** since he advocates a R psychology, not an SR associationistic psychology. He focused his attention on the importance of arranging environmental contingencies to bring behavior under stimulus control. Given his external environmental focus, he considered the mainstream behavioral attempts to determine the nature of reinforcement and to describe the S-R association to be misdirected and without empirical support. Skinner provided evidence supporting the use of four basic ways of handling **contingencies of reinforcement and punishment** to bring about behavior change. For example, in quadrant 1 of the figure presented below, we have a situation in which a learner does something (answers a question, remains quiet) that yields a positive consequence (a smile from the teacher, a pat on the head). This is an example of positive reinforcement, and we would expect this behavior to increase in frequency. In quadrant 1, we have a situation in which a learner engages in behavior that leads to taking away something valued. For example, if a thumbsucker is watching television and you turn off the tube when the child has his thumb in his mouth but turn it on when the thumb is removed, you have set up a punishment by withdrawal of reinforcement situation. By definition, use of a punisher reduces the level of responding while use of a reinforcer increases the level of responding. In this instance, if turning off the television is truly punishing to the child, thumbsucking behavior will decrease in frequency.

	Produce	**Withdraw**
+ Consequence	+ Reinforcement (1)	Punishment by withdrawal (2)
- Consequence	Punishment by hurt (3)	- Reinforcement (4)

In quadrant 3, we have a situation where a child engages in behavior that produces a negative consequence. The child picks a fight with another child, and the teacher hits the child. If the hit is perceived by the child as a negative consequence and not just an attention-getting device, the acting out and fighting behavior will decrease in frequency. Finally, in the fourth quadrant, we have a depiction of a situation where a negative reinforcement contingency is used to control behavior. For most people, the sound of an alarm clock is perceived as a negative stimulus. If one reaches over to turn off the alarm clock, the person has engaged in behavior that has removed a negative stimulus. This behavior is reinforcing, not punishing.

From what is presented above, it would seem that one could build a case in support of using both reinforcing and punishing contingencies to bring behavior under stimulus control. Even though we can control behavior using **punishment**, there is considerable evidence reported in the research literature (Turkington, 1986a) indicating that we not do so. There are reported to be many **undesirable side effects** such as escape, avoidance, and increased aggression associated with the use of punishment. For example, if a teacher paddles a child, the teacher and what the teacher represents (the school, education, etc.) are associated with the punishing event. After receiving punishment, the child may try to avoid, escape, and perhaps aggress toward the teacher and what the teacher represents when given the opportunity to do so. Given these possible undesirable side effects, the recommendation is that we don't use punishment. If we decide that we must use punishment as a last resort, the behavior being punished (e.g., self-destructive head-banging behavior) should be viewed as being more punishing to the learner than the actual punishment (i.e., administration of mild shock to extinguish the self-destructive behavior).

In addition to Skinner's pragmatic focus on reinforcement, he is credited with his work related to manipulating various **schedules of reinforcement and punishment** to bring behavior under stimulus control. If you use a **continuous reinforcement schedule** (i.e., reinforce every desired response), you change behavior very quickly. However, once you discontinue your reinforcement procedure, the behavior extinguishes very quickly. On the other hand, if you use an **intermittent schedule of reinforcement** (i.e., reinforce the first desired R, the third, the seventh, etc.), you find that it takes longer to change the behavior, but once the desired behavior is changed, it is very resistant to extinction. Overall, the best arrangement is to use a combination of continuous reinforcement applied early in the learning sequence followed by intermittent reinforcement.

During the past twenty years, while Skinner's work is certainly considered by many to remain important (Mahoney, 1989; Zuriff, 1980), it is probably fair to say that most educators and psychologists would claim that he has been upstaged by the work of the cognitive theorists.

Finally, brief mention should be made of **Edward C. Tolman** (1886-1959). Tolman serves as a bridge between behavioral and cognitive theories of learning and instruction. Tolman claimed that we learn **cognitive maps**, not a mere set of motor skills. Reinforcement is important with respect to confirming what we expect to learn. Practice would provide an opportunity for building up our cognitive maps. We are motivated to solve problems by cognitive conflict. It is interesting to note that the contemporary focus on expectancies and cognitive styles (Rotter, 1954, 1966) bears some relationship to Tolman's work.

These operant conditioning models appear to be highly useful with respect to explaining learning when we make overt responses that can be selectively reinforced and/or punished. Consider the example of a situation in which we want to increase school attendance. Ronald R. Morgan (1975) conducted a study in which he was able to increase school-attending behavior using a combination of material and social rewards. From an operant perspective, if children are not attending school, the basic problem is that they do not perceive school as a social reinforcer. The job of the teacher is to set up reinforcing situations in the school that would enhance school-attending behavior. Morgan designed a triad reinforcement procedure in which one problem absentee child was paired with two of his or her nonabsentee friends. These friends were carefully chosen by the teacher and were believed to serve as social reinforcers for the absentee child. The contingency set up was that when the absentee child came to school, all members of the triad received a reward. When the absentee child did not come to school, no reward was given to any child in the triad. As in most operant conditioning studies, a continuous reinforcement schedule was used initially to get behavior going, after which an intermittent schedule of reinforcement was used to maintain the behavior. The results of the study supported the use of the triad reinforcement procedure.

Admittedly, use of the operant conditioning model in this instance did not get at the heart of the school-attending problem, which in this case was probably due to the child's negative home situation and lack of academic peer supporters within the child's environment. The traditional approach to the problem would be to talk with the child's family and encourage them to send the child to school. This traditional procedure was tried in this situation but was found to be ineffective. Since the school had exhausted its resources with respect to dealing with the problem, it tried the operant conditioning model as a last resort. The model worked.

Let's consider another example, a person suffering from a snake phobia. From an operant perspective, why would a person be afraid of snakes (or elevators, high places, certain kinds of people, the workplace, etc.)? The operant theorists claim that such fears are learned. If a person is afraid of snakes, it is assumed that the person acquired the fear as a result of their reinforcement and punishment history. Perhaps a relative warned a child to stay away from snakes, to avoid places where snakes might reside (i.e., attended to the child and positively reinforced the child for staying away from snakes). Maybe the child was verbally reprimanded for engaging in behavior that could put the child at risk of being bitten by a snake (i.e., use of punishment by withdrawal of a positive approval contingency). Maybe the child was actually bitten by the snake (i.e., a punishment by hurt contingency).

The point here is that a fear (a phobia, in this instance) is learned, and since it is learned, we should be able to extinguish it. If we learn something through a process of reinforcement and punishment, we should be able to extinguish what was learned merely by reversing the contingencies. That is, we would set up a contingency procedure in which instead of warning and reprimanding a person for approaching snakes, we would encourage the person to learn more about snakes, to visit the zoo and observe snakes, to talk about snakes, and so on. This reversal of reinforcement and punishing contingencies is what is called **desensitization therapy** (Wolpe, 1981).

Learning Curve Components. With respect to describing the components of the learning curve from an operant perspective, individual difference baseline characteristics would consist of a learner's previous reinforcement and punishment history. Acquisition would consist of using one of the four contingencies of reinforcement and punishment. Extinction would take place if we reversed the reinforcing and punishing contingencies, while maintenance would occur if the learner continued to receive rewards and punishers in the natural environment necessary to support the learned behavior.

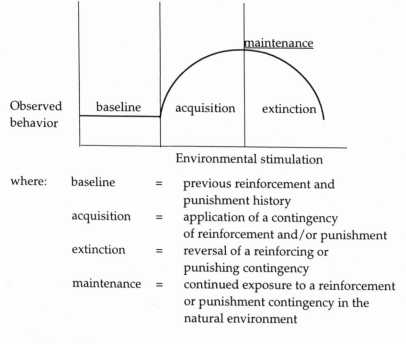

where:	baseline	=	previous reinforcement and punishment history
	acquisition	=	application of a contingency of reinforcement and/or punishment
	extinction	=	reversal of a reinforcing or punishing contingency
	maintenance	=	continued exposure to a reinforcement or punishment contingency in the natural environment

It should be noted that we could also explain the snake phobia example using the classical conditioning model. Let's say that an infant was crawling along a boardwalk when suddenly the board broke, making a loud sound which startled the infant. When the board broke, a snake was exposed under the boardwalk. In this situation, the loud sound is a UCS, the snake a CS, and fear the CR. Using this example, we have merely replaced the rat in the Watson and Raynor (1920) study with the snake. The primary thing to keep in mind with respect to distinguishing between the two models is that when we pair together objects in time (contiguity), we are referring to the classical conditioning model. In contrast, when we use rewards and/or punishers, we are referring to the operant conditioning model.

As noted earlier, the operant conditioning model has been found to be useful with respect to our attempts to explain learning when we make an overt response (e.g., school-attending behavior, acting-out behavior, etc.). It is important to point out that a **chain of S and R associations** is presumed to exist when we attempt to explain **complex behaviors.**

In order for the model to be useful, a learner must make a series of

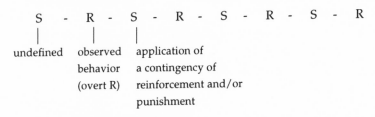

overt responses that can be selectively reinforced and/or punished. One of the major criticisms directed at the model is that many of the most important behaviors of interest to educators (i.e., thinking, problem solving, creativity, learning from attending a lecture, reading, and imitation of a model) do not involve making a fine-grained series of overt responses that can be selectively reinforced and/or punished by the instructor. Therefore, the operant model appears to be of very **limited utility** with regard to its application to many academic and workplace learning situations.

Another problem is that concerns have been expressed that the use of **extrinsic rewards** (i.e., reinforcement) may undermine **intrinsic interests** (Bates, 1979; Deci, 1975; Lepper & Greene, 1978; Morgan, 1984). Yes, using material rewards to encourage a child to attend school may be viewed as a bribe. This procedure, if carried to extremes, might undermine a student's motivation to attend school once the reward contingency is removed. The point is to get the child to come to school using the reward, make sure the child is successful in school once he or she gets there, and to build in natural social contingencies in the school environment so that the child is motivated to get to school on his or her own and to do well once he or she gets there. Admittedly, the balance between the use of extrinsic rewards and intrinsic interests is a delicate one.

One final point should be noted here. When we are using the operant conditioning SRS model, the first S is assumed to exist, but we do not attempt to explain it or deal with it in any systematic way. In the school-attendance example, the first S represents the actual problem (i.e., the family, poverty, etc.), while the R represents whether or not the child attends school. The second S represents application of one of the four contingencies of reinforcement or punishment. Operant conditioners focus their attention only on the overt R and the second S (the contingency of reinforcement and/or punishment). The first S is assumed to be uncontrollable and therefore of little relevance to righting the problem at hand. This procedure is much different from that of a traditional analytic approach in which the focus of treatment would be on the person's understanding of the first S. The analyst would claim that if one ignores the first S and treats only the overt R symptoms, that the problem behavior will manifest itself in another problem behavior (i.e., symptom substitution). The operant conditioners offer some evidence refuting this concern of symptom substitution (Woolfolk and Richardson, 1984).

Although we have presented a discussion of both the SS and SRS learning models as separate systems or approaches, there is considerable evidence to suggest that in most learning situations the two models are combined at least to some extent. When we are reinforced or punished for a certain behavior, everything that is paired in time (i.e., classical conditioning) is also associated with the reinforcing and/or punishing contingency. In addition, the positive demonstration of **biofeedback**, in which an operant conditioning methodology is used to control what we thought to be a classically conditioned involuntary internal response (e.g., pulse rate, blood pressure), raises questions as to the existence of two separate noninteracting models of learning (Miller, 1969).

Social Learning (Soc. L.)

From a **social learning** perspective, a combination of S and R contiguity plus cognitive mediation is necessary for learning to take place. It should be noted that reinforcement and punishment may be helpful but are not considered to be necessary for learning to occur. Use of rewards and punishers is believed to have some influence on performance because if a model is rewarded, the learner is more likely to model the behavior than if the model is punished. The point is that from a social learning perspective, we learn by observing and modeling. We do not need to make an overt response that is selectively reinforced and/or punished. Even though we do not need to make an overt response in order to learn something, we are more likely to emulate a rewarded model's behavior than a punished model's behavior. For example, we can attend a violent film and learn how to be violent, but if the violence depicted in the film is punished rather than rewarded, most of us will not engage in the violent behavior. However, should the violence be rewarded in the film or in real life by our peers, viewing the film could increase our antisocial behavior. Given this situation, it is very important for us to be careful with respect to exposing ourselves and others to antisocial and/or undesirable models. See Training Application 3.3.

The social learning model is very important to educational psychologists and instructors since much of what is learned in school and in the workplace is learned in a **social context** where few overt responses are made. We do learn by attending a lecture where we observe and listen to what is presented by the lecturer. We imitate the behaviors of those around us (teachers, parents, peers, celebrities). Much academic and workplace learning takes place by reading. The lecturers, our parents and peers, books, and workplace training materials serve as our models. While learning to model the models, we are making no overt responses which are selectively reinforced and punished. From a social learning point of view, what is taking place is that we are pairing a S with a R and combining the pairing with thinking (i.e., cognition).

Bandura. Albert Bandura's (1978, 1989) expanded view of the social learning model includes three interrelated components: the learner's behavior (B); individual difference person variables (P) such as intelligence and personality; and the learner's environment (E). This **BPE model** includes components from the other models of learning. Contiguity is viewed as being important, along with cognitive mediation. The environmental contingencies of reinforcement and punishment are not necessary for learning to take place but are considered helpful nonetheless. Finally, individual differences are accounted for with respect to person variables such as IQ and personality differences. The BPE model is a complex, inclusive model and is considered to operate as a dynamic interactive **reciprocal deterministic model** of learning. The model is particularly useful with respect to explaining much of what is learned in school and in the workplace when we attend a lecture, read, and/or imitate models.

Learning Curve Components. From a social learning perspective, the components of the learning curve would be explained as follows:

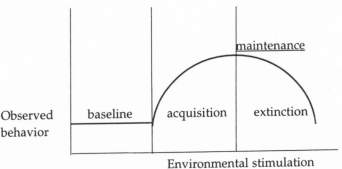

where: baseline   =   previous history of S-R pairings
                              and cognitions related to the pairings
          acquisition   =   S-R contiguity plus cognitive mediation
          extinction   =   eliminate the S-R contiguity
                              and don't think about the model
          maintenance   =   continued S-R contiguity + cognitive
                              mediation occurring within the learner's
                              natural environment

Cognitive Models (SOR)

Today, there are many cognitive learning models (gestalt, cognitive developmental, and information-processing models) competing for attention. The **gestalt model** appears to be of considerable historical importance, and the **cognitive developmental models** receive considerable attention in the research literature. In the discipline of educational psychology, most of the attention today is directed at the **information-processing models**. These cognitive models are designed to explain the complex processes of thinking, problem solving, and creativity. For the most part, these cognitive models are less precise than the behavioral (SS and SRS) and social learning models, but they do provide us with a theoretical anchor that we can use to explain complex behaviors. In the next chapter, an in-depth discussion of these cognitive models is presented. Our purpose in this section is to present a few general organizing cognitive principles of behavior. From a behavioral point of view, learning consists of learning a number of habits. The greater the number of accumulated habits, the greater the thinking and problem-solving ability of the learner. In contrast, from a cognitive perspective, it is not the mere **accumulation of experience**, but rather the **remodeling of experience** that is considered to be of primary importance in the learning process. Likewise, one of the best indicators of what a person will learn in a learning situation is highly dependent on what the learner already knows before entering the learning situation. That is to say that we build upon our past experiences, our past schematic representations of experience. The term **schema** refers to the organized knowledge we possess (i.e., the contents of the mind). These existing schematic representations have a great deal to do with how we organize and interpret our environments. As we interact with our environments, we take in the new information (i.e., the process of **assimilation**), and we change our schematic representations in such a way as to harmonize with the incoming information (i.e., the process of **accommodation**).

Learning Curve Components. From a general cognitive perspective, the components of the learning curve would be explained as follows:

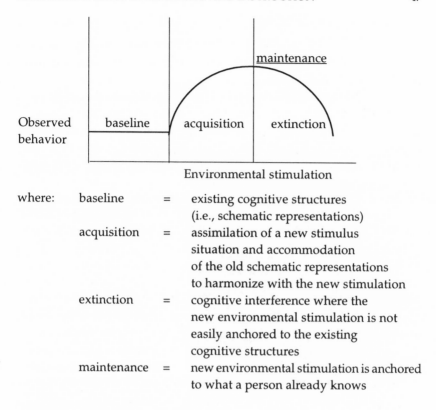

where:

baseline	=	existing cognitive structures (i.e., schematic representations)
acquisition	=	assimilation of a new stimulus situation and accommodation of the old schematic representations to harmonize with the new stimulation
extinction	=	cognitive interference where the new environmental stimulation is not easily anchored to the existing cognitive structures
maintenance	=	new environmental stimulation is anchored to what a person already knows

THE INTERRELATIONSHIPS AMONG THE MODELS OF LEARNING

As noted in the previous section, each of the four models of learning is related to a particular type of learning. These relationships can be summarized as follows:

1. **Classical conditioning (SS)** can be used to explain early learning and emotional development.

2. **Operant reinforcement (SRS)** can be used to explain learning overt responses.

3. **Cognitive theories (SOR)** can be used to explain thinking, problem solving, and creativity.

4. **Social (observational) learning theories (Soc. L.)** can be used to explain learning without making an overt response (e.g., attending a lecture, reading, and imitating models).

Another way to relate the four models of learning to learning in general is to use Robert Gagne's (1985) **eight conditions of learning** as an organizer. **Gagne** developed a taxonomy of learning consisting of the following components:

1. **Signal learning** (essentially the same as classical conditioning; a child learns to fear a rat.)

2. **Associationistic learning** (S-R associationistic learning; a student learns to respond to an S; a student's response to a command such as "Please sit!")

3. **Motor chaining** (a learner acquires two or more S-R motor units and develops a complex motor skill; a child is able to trace a figure.)

4. **Verbal chains** (a learner acquires combinations of verbal units and develops complex verbal skills.)

5. **Multiple discriminations** (a learner responds in different ways to given stimuli.)

6. **Concept learning** (a learner learns to make a common response to a class of stimuli.)

7. **Principle learning** (a chaining or combining of two or more concepts.)

8. **Problem solving** (a learner combines known rules and/or principles into new elements to solve problems.)

Gagne's basic thesis is that each condition of learning, with the exception of the first (signal learning-classical conditioning), serves as a prerequisite for the next higher level of learning. For example, if one expects a student to solve a rather complex problem (condition 8), then one must make certain that a student has already mastered conditions 2 through 7. If a teacher wants a student to learn a concept, then the prerequisite skills would include conditions 2 through 5. It should be noted that Gagne's conditions of learning are considered to be environmentally dependent but not biologically determined stage dependent conditions. That is to say that the job of the instructor is to arrange environmental conditions so that the prerequisite skills are sequentially mastered. The focus here is on arranging environmental conditions (i.e., learning) not on the constraints related to developmental, maturational stages.

Let's get back to the question of relating the four models of learning to learning in general, using Gagne's conditions of learning as an organizer. We have already noted that Gagne's condition 1 is equal to classical conditioning. The operant reinforcement model could be used to explain conditions 2 through 5 without much difficulty. In addition, it is possible to explain the learning of simple concepts and principles using the SRS model. It is not until we desire to explain the learning of complex concepts, principles, and problem solving that we have to rely on the cognitive model for an adequate explanation. The social learning paradigm can be applied to conditions 2 through 8.

The point to be made here is that although the operant reinforcement model appears to be limited to explaining only overt responses, that a great deal of learning (conditions 2 through 5 and maybe conditions 6 and 7) can be explained using the SRS model. Most of us probably assume that we spend much of our time in school and in the workplace solving complex problems. However, for most of us, even in college and in cognitively demanding workplace environments, we spend a great deal of time learning basic terminology (condition 4), learning to make discriminations, acquiring rather simple concepts, and principles. Few of us find ourselves in school and workplace situations in which we are spending most of our time solving complex cognitive problems. Therefore, even though the operant conditioning model appears to be very limited with respect to explaining much of academic learning (i.e., thinking, problem solving, creativity, lecture, reading, and imitation), it has an important place in the overall schooling process. Finally, it should be noted that the social learning model appears to have much to recommend its use given that it allows us to explain conditions 2 through 8.

MOTIVATION

In addition to explaining the components of a learning curve, an adequate theory of learning must offer some explanation of motivation. What is motivation? Most of us assume that motivation is whatever energizes behavior, gives behavior direction, and leads us to a goal. How can we best build motivation into an instructional plan?

Each of the learning models we have discussed above includes a motivational component (McCombs, 1984). Motivation for the traditional classical conditioning and some of the operant conditioning theorists consisted of some sort of **physiological drive** mechanism. A more contemporary behavioral view of motivation is Skinner's use of fixed and variable interval and ratio **schedules of reinforcement** as motivators of behavior. The traditional cognitive view of motivation was to consider it to be a **need** (i.e., a cognitive need to achieve, a cognitive need for competence, a cognitive need to know, to find out to be interested). A more contemporary cognitive view of motivation is to view it as **cognitive conflict** (Sivan, 1986). For example, from a Piagetian perspective, the way to motivate a learner is to present him or her with a problem solving situation that generates a great deal of cognitive conflict (disequilibration). Once the person arrives at a solution to the problem, cognitive conflict is reduced and the learner has established a steady state once again. If we desire to develop to our maximum potential, would we be better off associating with people who are equal to us with respect to their abilities, or would we be better off spending time with people who are more cognitively sophisticated? From a cognitive perspective, we would be better off spending our time with those people who challenge us, those who keep us on the edge of the chair, and those who set up problem situations in which considerable cognitive conflict is generated.

The basic point to be made here is that the contemporary views of motivation offered by Skinner (i.e., the manipulation of schedules of reinforcement) and the cognitive theorists (i.e., cognitive conflict) have much to recommend them in naturalistic school and workplace situations (Geen, 1984). The older physiological drive notions and the cognitively based need notions of motivation, while interesting and of relative importance to learning in general, appear very limited with respect to their educational and workplace utility, since most of us are not in a position to manipulate drives nor to satisfy basic needs. But we can manipulate schedules of reinforcement and set up problematic situations generating cognitive conflict which can be used to motivate and maximize a learner's performance. The different views of motivation are summarized in the figure appearing below.

	Behavioral Theorists	Cognitive Theorists
Traditional views	Physiological drives	Needs
Contemporary views	Schedules of reinforcement	Cognitive conflict

In a final attempt to give meaning to the construct of motivation, let's examine it within the context of a **latent learning** example. In the operant literature, *latent learning* refers to learning without reinforcement. For example, in the diagram presented below, if we had two learners, one learner (1) who received a high incentive for learning (i.e., a high reward condition), and the other learner (2) who received a low incentive for learning (i.e., a low reward condition), what we frequently find is that learner 1 performs significantly higher on the task than learner 2.

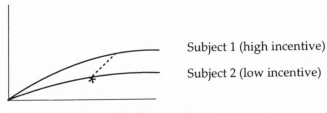

Subject 1 (high incentive)

Subject 2 (low incentive)

✱ Introduction of high incentive

However, if we suddenly introduce the high reward condition to the low incentive learner (2), what we usually find is that learner 2 suddenly performs at the level of the highly rewarded learner 1. In other words, learner 2 was learning even in the low incentive condition but was not performing at a high level because a high incentive system was not applied to the learner's performance. Once incentives were made available, the low performer increased his or her performance level.

Given this example, a **motivator** would be **defined as a stimulus that transforms learning into performance**. In other words, we need a construct such as motivation to transform an internal variable (the unobservable internal learning process) into something external (performance). The inclusion of a motivational construct within our learning theories allows us to connect the internal processes of learning with external performance. We use a schedule of reinforcement as a motivator to transform learning into performance. In addition, we use cognitive conflict as a motivator in a problem solving situation to transform learning into performance.

REINFORCEMENT VERSUS CONTIGUITY

The early behaviorists **Watson** and **Pavlov** did not emphasize the role of reinforcement. Instead, they focused on **temporal contiguity** of stimuli and responses (S-R) and SS associations in learning. With these **contiguity theorists**, the closeness of the stimulus pairs and/or the SR associations was considered to be necessary and sufficient for learning to occur.

Watson claimed that we are all born with a number of SR connections in the form of reflexes. If this inherited behavioral repertoire is preceded by a stimulus for this reflex and paired with another stimulus, the new stimulus will elicit the same response. Thus, **repeated sets of SR pairings** will cause many new stimuli to elicit the old SR bonded response. From this perspective, it is assumed that a series of reflexes is built up until each response in the chain builds a conditioned SR chain for the next response. It should be noted that Watson never systematically discussed the use of rewards and/or reinforcement procedures. However, his **principle of frequency** (i.e., the more frequently we have made a response to a stimulus, the more likely we are to repeat it) and the **principle of recency** (i.e., the more recently we have made a response, the more likely we are to make it again) do seem to be mechanisms for explaining the operation of reinforcement. It is recognized that this was not Watson's original intention and would certainly be denied by him, but these principles (frequency and recency) do tend to encourage repetition of the desired response. Watson would say that a certain act was repeated because many other associated responses dropped out. The response that changes the situation gains in frequency and recency until it is repeated as soon as the stimulus is presented. If you define reinforcement as a condition which follows a desired response and which results in an increase in the strength of that response, then Watson indirectly addresses the reinforcement issue.

Pavlov's physiological explanation of an UCS being repeatedly paired with a CS leading to a CR does allow us to explain why some behaviors are repeated. Pavlov hypothesized that the CS and UCS caused excitation of the cerebral cortex. This excitation spreads from a strongly excited UCS to a weaker CS until the two excitations are in touch with one another. The effect of repeated conditioning is that the CS travels to the same place as the site of excitation from the UCS, even though no biologically wired UCS is present. This conditioning procedure produces the same CR, only in a weaker form. Repeated trials are assumed to strengthen the UCS-CS connection.

Inhibition (either external or internal) counters excitation and lessens the level of performance. Even though Pavlov was a SS contiguity theorist, his mechanisms of **irradiation of excitement** from stronger to weaker areas could be viewed as reinforcing the bonds between the CS and CR.

A major shift in psychological theorizing occurred with **Guthrie** (1959) and his followers. A reinforcer was defined as an event following a response that increased the tendency to repeat the response. That is to say that the focus shifted from the UCS and CS pairing to the end of the response set (rewards). Guthrie's general statement was that if you do something in a situation, you will tend to do it again. If a response accompanies a stimulus once, it (i.e., behavior) will probably occur again. This approach takes no notice of a UCS or the role of reinforcement in promoting re-occurrence of the activity. Guthrie does not use the term reinforcement. However, he does state that whether or not learning occurs depends upon a change creating a new situation. If it **changes the situation**, it becomes the last thing we did in the old situation. We learn not by reinforcement, but by successfully **doing** something. If a response removes the status quo of stimuli, then it is associated with solving a problem and becomes the last step in the problem-solving chain. To Guthrie and his followers, practice and reinforcement helped the learner to make clean associations.

Neo-Guthrians (V. W. Voeks, F. D. Sheffield, and W. K. Estes) attempted to clarify Guthrie's thoughts. **Voeks** (1950) developed a number of **postulates** and added two main ideas: (1) that a stimulus which is paired with or preceded by two incompatible responses will elicit the last response (recency); and (2) that SR contiguity is associated with the operation of external cues and internal movements. **Sheffield** (1965) claimed that **sensory responses may be mentalistic** (i.e., without associated movements). He recognized the roles of **imagery**, perceptual blueprinting, integration of response chains, and cognitive connections. He placed a strong emphasis on the importance of learning **perceptual patterns** and natural units. To Sheffield, our responses are reinforcers, not the reward given afterward. **Estes** (1969) transformed Guthrie's notions further. He is best known for his **mathematically based stimulus sampling theory**. While still favoring association by SR contiguity, he developed models of all-or-none learning and a model in which stimulus elements are constantly changing and constantly sampled by the subject until on successive trials the specific desired stimulus is attached to a certain response. To Estes, outcomes and reinforcers were often, but not always, identical.

The next group of theorists (Thorndike, Hull, and Skinner) spoke directly with respect to the **relative roles of contiguity and reinforcement**. **Thorndike** (1949) focused on animal behavior and the role of pleasure and pain as consequences of our acts. This focus led to his discussion of "satisfiers and annoyers" as reinforcers and punishers. While Thorndike did not discard the importance of the role of SR bonds being formed through contiguity (law of exercise), he did focus primarily on the law of effect (i.e., the creation and strengthening of SR bonds depended not only on a temporal association but also on the effect that followed the response). Loosely speaking, satifiers were considered to be rewards, or the removal of noxious stimuli, and annoyers were considered to be punishers. If a stimulus is followed by a response and then a satisfier, the SR bond is strengthened. If however, the stimulus is followed by an annoyer, the SR bond is weakened.

For **Skinner** (1938), learning was not the conditioning of reflexes, but rather the judicious use of reinforcement to increase the probability of a desired behavior. From Skinner's perspective, complex learning occurs through shaping and the building up of operant SRS chains. Skinner acknowledged positive and negative reinforcement just as Thorndike did. A reward, or removal of noxious stimuli, acts as a reinforcer in that it increases the probability of the desired response. Negative reinforcers work, but not as effectively as positive reinforcers, and have some undesirable negative consequences. Skinner spent much time developing reinforcement schedules (fixed or variable time intervals or fixed or variable ratio schedules). He also examined the role of secondary (i.e., learned), generalized reinforcers in everyday life. A stimulus that is not originally a reinforcer can become reinforcing through repeated associations. To Skinner and Thorndike, reinforcers were primarily associated with external events.

Hull and his followers (Spence, Amsel, Logan, and Miller) empha-sized that: (1) there are possible **internal mechanisms** operating with re-spect to explaining the process of reinforcement; **and** (2) that the **interac-tions** between stimuli and responses are dynamic and not always a prod-uct of a simple, unidirectional process. Hull (1943) postulated a theory in which all reinforcement involved a reduction in the strength of a drive stimu-lus. Drive is considered to be the activating state of the organism and a reduction in this state serves as a reward. Drive is viewed as a temporary state of the learner produced by deprivation of something the learner needs or by painful stimulation. Each drive condition (e.g., hunger) produces a drive stimulus. A rapid reduction in the drive stimulus is considered to be reinforcing.

Hull viewed learning and the operation of reinforcement as the involve-ment of **internal and external rewards (incentive motivation-K).** He also hypothesized that a delay between a response and reinforcement would weaken the tendency to repeat the response. Hull postulated an SOR psy-chology in which the learner does something internal that leads to the re-sponse. These **internal mechanisms** motivate the learner to **anticipate the goal respons**e and to drive behavior toward its ultimate goal. This arrange-ment yields a **S-rg-sg-R configuration**. These SR chains can be long and complex and are considered to have reinforcement properties. Reinforce-ment-based learning in the Hullian tradition is not broken down into a simple two-factor theory (i.e., SS and SRS models of learning). That is to say that **classical and operant learning** are considered to be the result of **one complex interacting system**.

Spence's (1960) concern for the boundary conditions of Hull's theory led him to suggest slight alterations in Hull's theory. To **Spence, incentive motivation (K)** is the total strength of the rg-sg chain. Habit strength did not depend upon reinforcement, but rather upon practice. Drive reduction is not considered to cause reinforcement; rather reinforcement enters through the rg mechanism. This rg is the **anticipation of reward**. Rg is an example of a movement produced stimuli (this notion is similar to Guthrie's) and contributes to the direction and achievement of the goal. This type of rein-forcement does not operate at the end of the SOR chain, but during a chain of responses ending up in a final response.

Amsel (1962) theorized that when a learner expects a reward in a place, situation, or set, the learner makes an rg to the previously learned response. If a reward or goal is not apparent, frustration sets in. Frustration is based on a drive produced by unfulfilled **expectancies**.

The important transition that occurred with Hull and his followers is that: (1) it began to diminish the view of two separate learning approaches (SS and SRS); (2) it paved the way for notions of cognitive structures to be included in theoretical accounts of learning; (3) it led to a relaxation of the condition that only observable and measurable behaviors were worthy of a focus of study; and (4) it was a step in tearing down the mind-body dualism of the past that was a cause of discontinuity in psychological theorizing and research.

Tolman (1932) attempted to bridge the gap between traditional behaviorism and cognitive aspects of behavior by focusing on the subject's beliefs, individual differences, and cognitions. It should be noted that Tolman's theory emphasized objective behavior, not unconscious experience. He focused on the importance of external stimuli but also gave some attention to the importance of **cognitive expectancy factors** that promote, impel, and guide behavior. He and his followers emphasized the importance of **intervening cognitive variables** between a stimulus and a response. Some of their main contributions are as follows:

1. Cognitions from different learning experiences can be put together in novel ways in new situations.

2. Once an individual has learned a cognitive process, they can use these cognitive processes to obtain other goals.

3. Learning can occur without observable evidence (e.g., latent learning).

4. Learners develop **cognitive maps** of SR relationships which can be used to reach a goal even though the original sets of movements are blocked or the perspective of the subject has changed. That is to say that sign-gestalt expectations are acquired, not merely a set of motor habits.

Tolman and his followers are the furthest away from traditional behavioral principles of behavior. Their use of **intervening variables** provides a bridge between the behavioral and the cognitive viewpoints.

Through the development of modern learning psychology, **several tensions** existed and continue to leave a mark on a dualistic two-factor approach (i.e., a combination of SS, SR contiguity, and SRS reinforcement models of learning) to explaining the learning process and behavior. Briefly they are:

1. The active or passive role of the learner.

2. The relative role of contiguity versus reinforcement.

3. The proper focus of study (mentalistic expectancy notions versus the quantifiability of observed, objective behaviors).

4. The need for a theory to accurately explain reality (i.e., the correspondence of the theory to what we know about motivation and the components of the learning curve: baseline; acquisition; extinction; and maintenance).

5. The need to develop different postulates, mechanisms, and so on to explain individual differences (species-specific behaviors) across species or, the possible application of a parsimonious unified theory to all species.

6. Focus on learning simple responses or on learning more complex behaviors (e.g., the use of biofeedback, the learning of language, and the development of thinking and problem-solving skills).

7. The change from an early focus on the situation to that of the variability inherent within the learner.

8. Focus was given to explanations of involuntary behaviors (reflexes) in early research; focus was given to the acquisition of voluntary behaviors in later research.

9. The assumption that it was necessary that behavior be performed in order for learning to take place in early approaches, contrasted with the recognition of latent learning and learning that occurs without making overt responses in the later approaches.

THE ROLE OF REINFORCEMENT

Two theorists, Pavlov and Guthrie, viewed contiguity as the single most important factor in learning. As noted above, **Pavlov** viewed learning as the pairing of two stimuli (a conditioned stimulus and an unconditioned stimulus) together for a number of trials. The learner learns to respond to a previously neutral stimulus. Although Pavlov referred, at times, to the possible reward value of the biologically based UCS, he did not utilize the concept of reinforcement per se. Therefore, there was no real role for reinforcement in Pavlov's paradigm of learning. **Guthrie** was another theorist for whom contiguity, not reinforcement, was the essential law of learning. Guthrie stated that "a combination of stimuli accompanying a movement will, when repeated, tend to result in the same movement." Guthrie's law of learning implies recency; that is, whatever was last engaged in a situation is that which is learned. Guthrie advocated one trial learning, inasmuch as the SR association is believed to be formed in one experience. The role of reinforcement in Guthrie's system is a mechanical one in which reinforcement serves to develop **clean associations** and **prevent unlearning**. Therefore, from Guthrie's perspective, it is not the reinforcing stimuli that results in learning; rather, it is the contiguity of the S and R that produces learning.

The first real reinforcement theorist was **Thorndike**. He could perhaps best be described as an S-R connectionist who emphasized the role of reinforcement in learning. Although Thorndike acknowledged the importance of stimulus-response contiguity, his primary law of learning was the **law of effect**. This law stated that learning was dependent not only upon S-R contiguity, but upon the (reinforcing and punishing) effects that followed a response as well. Thorndike coined the terms "annoyer" and "satisfier" to describe these effects. However, he later deemphasized the importance of **annoyers (punishers)** in terms of weakening of behavior, and focused instead on the role of **rewards (satisfiers)** in terms of strengthening the S-R connection.

Skinner resembles Thorndike in the sense that he emphasized reinforcement as the primary law of learning. Skinner, however, recognized two different kinds of learning, **respondent** and **operant**. In respondent behavior, Skinner recognizes S-S contiguity as being of paramount importance. However, in terms of operant behavior, Skinner is a response psychologist who is primarily concerned with behavior change as a result of reinforcement.

Clark L. Hull, like Thorndike and Skinner, emphasized the importance of S-R contiguity and reinforcement. Initially, Hull viewed habit strength as a permanent bond that accrues slowly as a result of reinforced practice. Studies of **latent learning** (i.e., learning without reinforcement) posed a particularly difficult problem for Hull since habit strength could not account for the rapid changes in performance associated with changes in the magnitude of reinforcement. To correct this difficulty, Hull postulated the variable K (**incentive motivation**) as being related to the amount of reinforcement. This was an important change in emphasis with respect to the role of reinforcement (i.e., from the amount of reinforcement to the number of reinforced trials). Since the major strengthening (learning) mechanism was now associated with the number of reinforcement trials (i.e., upon SR contiguity) and amount of reinforcement was associated with incentive motivation, this change in emphasis signified a lessened role for reinforcement in the acquisition of behavior and a greater reliance upon K (i.e., amount of reinforcement) as the primary determinant of performance but not learning.

Kenneth **Spence** (1960) explored the notion of the operation of K even further. Eventually, he theorized that $K = rg$, where rg is a fractional anticipatory goal response (i.e., an expectancy). Thus, K, as opposed to being related to the SR connection, becomes related purely to the stimulus (because rg is related only to the stimulus). The result of this is that the **incentive component** in Hull's equation refers not to making a response but, rather, to getting to certain anticipated stimuli. Thus, in Spence's reconceptualization of Hullian theory, the role of reinforcement enters only indirectly through rg, and rg can be regarded as the **anticipation or expectation of reward**. In this reconceptualization, Spence effectively eliminated reinforcement as a fundamental concept from Hull's theory. That is to say that reinforcement appears to be of primary importance with regard to explaining performance but not learning. This change represents a large stride toward a more cognitive interpretation of the learning process which prevails today (Burghardt, 1985; Domjan, 1987; Rescorla, 1987).

Finally, another neo-Hullian, **Logan** (1968) further analyzed K and the manner in which reinforcement is related to K. Essentially, Logan's work culminated in an interpretation of S-R contiguity into a S-S (sensory-sensory) **cognitive expectancy view of reward**. Thus, memory traces as well as information become of paramount importance in the operation of reward. It is here that the neo-Hullians are today.

Another theorist who sought an alternative explanation to a strict reinforcement view of behavior was **Tolman** (1932). His law of learning emphasized **cognitive contiguity**. The learner acquires sign gestalts, or **cognitive maps** which are viewed as a learned relationship between environmental cues and the learner's expectations. Thus, the learner acquires a cognitive map as opposed to S-R motor skills. **Reinforcement** operates through the **confirmation of cognitive expectancies**. Tolman's experiments on place and latent learning, as well as reward expectancy, all contributed to the idea that reinforcement is a performance, not a learning, variable. Two neo-Tolmanians, Robert C. Bolles (1972) and Dalbir Bindra (1974), have furthered a cognitive interpretation of learning by formalizing much of Tolman's work. In essence, they were able to move habits beyond a narrow motor habits conceptualization and conceived of both habits and expectancies as intervening variables. The work of Tolman and his followers raised serious questions regarding the adequacy of traditional behavioral views of learning and forced the behaviorists to attempt to formulate explanations for much of the cognitive phenomenon the Tolmanians discussed.

Further tensions between traditional behaviorists and neobehaviorists developed around explanations of the partial reinforcement effect and the relativity versus transitutional notion of reinforcement. In terms of the **partial reinforcement effect (PRE)** (i.e., greater resistance to extinction following partial rewards), traditional behaviorists viewed it as a product of lack of discriminable stimuli. A neobehaviorist, **Amsel** (1962), disputed this interpretation of the PRE, and developed a **frustration theory** to account for PRE. Amsel developed the idea that rg's influence learning through frustration. When the learner expects a reward in a certain place (i.e., makes an rg) and does not find a reward, frustration results. Thus, nonreward of a previously rewarded response becomes an aversive event. In terms of the PRE, rf (frustration) is said to accrue when the learner approaches a goal that has been previously associated with frustration. A learner trained under PRE conditions has had experience training in the presence of rf, whereas a learner trained under continuous reinforcement conditions has not. Thus, when extinction begins, learners under the continuous reinforcement-trained condition begin for the first time, to make rf. This serves to give rise to competing responses and impedes performance faster than for those learners who have had previous experience with rf. Thus, the partially reinforced learner's behavior is more resistant to extinction than the continuously reinforced learner's behavior.

A second area of tension between behaviorists and neobehaviorists concerns the **relative versus transituational generality of reinforcement**. This refers to the question as to whether any reinforcer can be used to increase the probability of any learnable response. Given a particular state of the learner, stimulus events can be roughly divided into two groups (those which affect the learner as reinforcers and those which don't). **David Premack's** (1965) **relativity view** of reinforcement holds that a given event can be used to reinforce some responses but not others. Therefore, reinforcement can be ordered as a hierarchy in terms of the learner's preferences, and a given event can be used to reinforce activities of a lesser value, but not those of a higher value. Thus, an individual's motivation for behaving comes into account in terms of a hierarchy of preferences for reinforcement. This, of course, contrasts with the standard, behavioral-associationistic law of effect, which implies a transituational generality of the role of reinforcement in learning and which would deny that a regard for individual preferences deserves merit.

In summary, we have moved from the SS and SR contiguity theories of Pavlov and Guthrie to the reinforcement theories of Hull and Skinner and have reached a point where most learning appears to take place without reinforcement. We now appear to need cognitive components to explain the learning process. Reinforcement has now been abandoned as a major learning concept, not because of complete disproof, but from lack of interest due to a more cognitive orientation in the field of learning theory and instruction.

THE EXISTENCE OF COGNITIVE EXPECTANCIES

As noted above, Pavlov, Guthrie, and Tolman each developed contiguity theories. **Pavlov's** theory was an SS contiguity theory, with emphasis given to the pairing of an unconditioned stimulus (UCS) and a conditioned stimulus (CS). The timing of this pairing was considered to be of crucial importance. Forward was found to be the most efficient arrangement. In forward pairing the CS is presented about one-half second before the UCS, and then they overlap. Next in effectiveness is the delay condition, wherein the CS is presented for quite some time before the UCS. Next in efficiency is the trace condition wherein the CS is presented and stopped and then the UCS is presented. Least effective, is the backward condition, wherein the UCS is presented before the CS. It should be noted that since the UCS is biologically wired and because of its reinforcing power, there is a link between contiguity theory and reinforcement theory, even though this was not Pavlov's original intent. Finally, some mention should be made of Pavlov's notion of **sensory preconditioning (SPC)**. An SPC procedure consists of the following arrangement. Two neutral stimuli (NS1 and NS2) are paired and presented to the learner before training begins. Then one neutral stimulus (NS1) is conditioned as a conditioned stimulus. After this, the remaining neutral stimulus (NS2) is presented, alone, and the learner elicits the CR. The explanation given for this was that the learner was expecting the UCS because of previous pairings. The demonstration of SPC has added an **expectancy** component and has given a somewhat cognitive cast to Pavlov's theory. The existence of species-specific unconditioned stimuli and the demonstration of SPC tie this theory to internal components. Sensory preconditioning (SPC) also adds expectancies and gives an overall cognitive cast to Pavlov's theory.

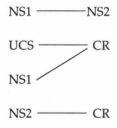

Guthrie formulated an SR, not a Pavlovian SS, contiguity theory. His basic law was that a "combination of stimuli which accompanies a movement will upon its recurrence tend be followed by that movement." That is to say that stimuli followed by internal movements, will tend to be followed by the last internal movement made to them, even if the learner made an incorrect response. The role of reinforcement merely provides an opportunity for a clean SR association to occur. Because of reinforcement, there is less chance that another response will occur and cause unlearning. In Guthrie's theory, the behaviors conditioned are not necessarily the behaviors observed. The unonbservable behaviors conditioned are referred to as **internal movements** that represent learning in one trial and make up the complex acts of observed behaviors. **Maintaining stimuli (rg-sg)** were postulated as motivators to keep behavior going until a goal had been reached. This notion of maintaining stimuli added an internal expectancy component to the theory.

Tolman's theory centered on cognitive expectancy notions. He advocated the importance of contiguity (either SS or SR) and viewed reinforcement as serving to simply confirm whether or not an expectancy had been met. His work with **latent learning** was of particular interest. Rats were allowed to explore a maze before having a goal box introduced. It was found that the rats that explored the maze prior to the introduction of the goal box found the goal box faster than the group not allowed to explore the maze. This finding was considered to be a strong demonstration of **goal learning** (i.e., **cognitive map learning**) taking place without reinforcement. In addition, his work with **place learning** demonstrated that cognitive maps are formed, and these cognitive maps were considered to be more influential than previous motor responses (habits) with respect to directing a learner to a goal. Once again this demonstrated the importance of cognition in learning. This finding taken in combination with the neo-Hullian Amsel's (1962) **partial reinforcement effect (PRE)** findings, changed again the way in which reinforcement was viewed. It was expected that behavior conditioned by continuous reinforcement would be more resistant to extinction than behavior conditioned by intermittent reinforcement, because more reinforcement had been received in the continuous reinforcement condition. However, Amsel found the reverse to be true. Tolman and Amsel attributed the PRE to cognitive expectancies creating persistence, whereas Edward Capaldi (1966) attributed the PRE to a failure to discriminate. Related to Tolman's work, Julian Rotter's (1954, 1966) belief was that the reinforcer, an expectancies of the reinforcer, and the value of the reinforcer were all important.

Thorndike, Skinner, and Hull considered reinforcement to be central to the learning process. Thorndike's original law of effect stated that satisfiers and annoyers strengthened and weakened behavior, but later he eliminated punishment, believing that it was not as effective as reinforcement. He did not believe in cognitive mentalistic notions of learning. Contemporary work by Buchwald (1967) and Estes (1969) showing that learning could take place with **delay of reinforcement**, and research showing that **awareness** facilitated learning, indicated that Thorndike was probably wrong with respect to his emphasis on the importance of reinforcement, since cognitive expectancies seem to have major influences on learning.

Skinner and Thorndike were similar with respect to their views of reinforcement, punishment, and mentalistic components. Skinner included punishment in his theory but viewed it as merely suppressing, not extinguishing, behavior. He had no desire to include mentalistic components, viewing them as excess philosophical baggage (Skinner, 1989). He did allow for drives, but he operationally defined drives as the number of hours of deprivation. He was interested in changing behavior and felt that if one could train a behavior from scratch, that was equivalent to understanding it.

Hull's drive stimulus referred to biological needs and was later changed to drive stimulus reduction, which referred to a **psychological craving**. His theory was a reinforcement theory, with reinforcers serving to reduce drives. As noted earlier, research findings related to **latent learning** caused a problem for Hull since they showed that learning could take place without reinforcement. He changed his theory because of these findings. Originally, the intervening variable habit strength (sHr) was influenced by the dependent variable amount of reinforcement. He changed the amount of reinforcement to the number of reinforced trials directly influencing sHr. A new intervening variable, incentive motivation (K) was created and was directly influenced by the amount of reinforcement. This changed his theory from a reinforcement theory to a contiguity theory. It should be noted that outside of his postulate system he had **three derived mechanisms** that added a cognitive expectancy component to his theory. These were the **fractional anticipatory goal response** (rg-sg) (i.e., a stimulus trace which invigorates the behavior chain, conditioning the response before it and stimulating the response after it to lead the learner to the goal), **goal gradient** (i.e., the response strengthens as the goal becomes nearer), and the **habit family hierarchy** (i.e., a hierarchy of habits that can be used to reach the goal). Neo-Hullian Kenneth Spence (1960) changed the theory by changing K = amount of reinforcement to K = rg, which essentially eliminated reinforcement from the theory and put cognitive expectancies in its place. Once again, Amsel's (1962) work with the PRE confirmed the importance of including the cognitive expectancy variable in the theory. Neo-Hullians Mowrer (1956) and Logan (1968) emphasized the importance of contiguity. Their efforts led up to the contemporary focus on an SS and/or SR contiguity-expectancy theory, not a pure reinforcement theory. These modified views reflect those of **Robert Rescorla** (1987), who is considered by most to be at the cutting edge of contemporary behavioral-cognitive research and theorizing.

On the contemporary scene, contiguity and expectancy, especially notions of cognitive expectancy, are considered to be of major importance. Reinforcement is not seen as the most important variable influencing learning. The discussion presented in this section related to the development and changes in the behavioral theories of learning show how this has come about. As expectancy came to be viewed as important, cognition also became important, and reinforcement declined in importance. This structure has created considerable tension within the behavioral camp of educational-psychological theorizing. Numerous criticisms have been directed at these behavioral theories (Glaser, 1984; Greeno, 1980, 1989; McKeachie, 1976; Wittrock, 1979). It remains to be seen whether Skinner's followers will change their concept of reinforcement from a major learning variable to a performance-motivational variable and accept the role of reinforcement in merely directing attention to what is learned, not learning per se. A number of meaningful reinforcers applicable to adult learners are listed in Training Application 3.4.

WHAT BEHAVIORISM DOESN'T TELL US

In terms of theory, behaviorism has come under attack in four major areas: (1) doubts concerning the operant-respondent distinction; (2) the issue of species specific behavior; (3) the learning-performance distinction; and (4) limitations in explaining complex human behavior (i.e., thinking, problem solving, and creativity).

Operant-Respondent Distinction

Neal Miller (1969) has demonstrated that through the use of **biofeedback** and operant conditioning techniques, visceral responses mediated by the autonomic nervous system can be successfully altered. That is to say that Miller has demonstrated that operant conditioning procedures can be used to bring classically conditioned behavior under stimulus control. This finding sheds considerable doubt upon the appropriateness of the behavioristic use of two-factor theory (operant-respondent) to account for two different kinds of learning. Presently, the main difference between operant and respondent conditioning appears to be that of experimental procedure. The fact that many behaviorists strongly adhere to the operant-respondent distinction is a drawback to the theory in the face of evidence such as Miller's.

Species-Specific Behavior

The issue of species specific behavior (in contrast to the equipotentiality view) concerns the viability of the notion that any response can be attached to any discriminable stimuli. For the most part, behavioristic theory has been viewed as an equipotentiality theory. This notion is in dispute largely because of the identification of a number of species-specific behaviors and the idea of learner preparedness. For example, Keller and Marian Breland (1960) reported many cases of species-specific instinctive behaviors among the animals they trained for the circus that interfered with the shaping of desired operant responses. A related phenomenon is that of autoshaping. **Autoshaping** occurs when an organism is instinctively prepared to make a certain response, and thus does not require any conditioning to make the response. The Brelands' observations, in addition to the demonstration of the phenomenon of autoshaping, disputes the idea of equipotentiality.

Richard J. Herrnstein (1977a, 1977b) addressed this issue by stating that behaviorism is not really an equipotentiality theory because of its recognition of individual differences across species. Thus, from a neobehavioral perspective the organism becomes the final authority on what is learned, and perhaps **self-reinforcement** is what accounts for this. Skinner (1977) responded to this by noting that "phylogeny and ontogeny are friendly rivals, and neither enjoys primacy" (i.e., "the innate susceptibility to a particular type of reinforcement is different than innate behavior", p. 1010).

Learning-Performance Distinction

The issue of the learning-performance distinction has not been adequately accounted for by many of the behaviorists. Behaviorism is basically a performance and reinforcement theory, not a learning theory. As previously stated, studies of **latent learning** indicate that reinforcement influences performance, not learning. Thus, a learning-performance distinction can be made, and some of the behaviorists can be faulted for not doing so. Furthermore, the related issue of motivation, typically defined as a variable that transforms learning into performance, is a rather thorny one for the behaviorists.

The behaviorists have responded to the above issues with the idea that overt behavior must be the unit of analysis and that to go inside the organism in an attempt to ascertain what is really learned is unnecessary in that one need not resort to mentalistic conceptualizations to adequately explain behavior (Mahoney, 1989; Skinner, 1989). Indeed, writers such as Greer (1983) indicate that this is an issue for the field of learning at large, inasmuch as discrepancies exist as to what is being studied and disagreements abound as to the whole issue of the appropriate subject matter of psychology. The learning-performance issue is further complicated by **observational learning**, where the organism must store information for use in later performance. That is to say that there is considerable evidence to indicate that we learn by observation (imitation of models, attending lectures, and reading) without making overt responses. The behavioristic notion of using mediating habit chains to explain observational learning without making an overt response appears not to be completely adequate.

Complex Human Behavior

The final, and perhaps most damaging, general criticism of behavioristic theory is that it is quite limited in terms of explaining complex human behavior (thinking, problem solving, and creativity). The **continuity assumption** that behaviorists abide by is that animal behavior and the process of learning are similar to that of humans. The Kendlers (1962, 1964), however, with their work on reversal and nonreversal shift problems called this continuity assumption into question. What has been found is that there are many types of problems that involve the use of rules, particularly verbal rules, that infrahumans and humans without language are unable to solve. Thus, there appear to be differences (i.e., discontinuities) in the manner in which literate humans and nonhumans learn, think, and solve problems. Thus, the rejection of the continuity assumption, coupled with the fact that the behaviorists assume that an organism must make an **overt response**, severely limits the learning that can be explained by the behaviorists. Such areas as thinking, problem solving, and creativity, which do not entail an overt response, cannot be adequately explained by the behavioristic system. A related issue is the fact that the behaviorists have not provided a place in their system for structures or **constraints** on learning. As a result, the traditional behavioristic system is viewed today as primarily appropriate for explaining some simple human behaviors (Benjamin, 1988; Kipnis, 1987), and the behavior of lower animals (Turkington, 1986b).

In terms of practice, Robert M. W. Travers (1982) supplies a rather **harsh review of behavior modification**. The first problem cited by Travers is that of **triviality**. For example, Travers maintains that one does not need a highly paid psychologist to demonstrate that children will work or modify their behavior in return for a handful of M&Ms and, further, that much of the modified behavior which does occur as a result of behavioral intervention is of a trivial nature. In addition, Travers argues that research purporting to illustrate positive effects of behavior modification has been, for the most part, poorly designed, thus calling many of the behaviorist's conclusions into question. A closely related issue is that of the single organism methodology typically used in the study of behavioral change outcomes. In this regard, Travers writes that a positive outcome is likely to be reported in the research literature while a negative outcome is not. Therefore, the literature is not fully representative of actual results.

Then there are those issues concerning the **transitory** and superficial nature of much of the **behavior change** that does occur as a result of behavior modification. Much research, for example, on token economies does not demonstrate persistent changes after the contingencies of reinforcement are withdrawn. Thus, any so-called learning that does occur appears to be transitory. A behaviorist would counter that this is no different than any other prescriptive discipline. For example, a physician who prescribes lithium as a treatment for manic-depressive illness would not expect the patient to continue to manifest positive change in the absence of the lithium. This brings the issue to the fore with respect to the feasibility or practicality of behavior modification if behavior change is expected to generalize to other situations.

Another difficulty related to the practice of behavior modification concerns the **issue of intrinsic vs. extrinsic motivation**. Researchers such as M. R. Lepper and D. Greene (1978) and E. L. Deci (1975) have indicated that extrinsic motivators (such as use of material rewards) may actually serve to undermine intrinsic motivation and suggests that caution be exercised in the use of extrinsic rewards to enhance learning and/or performance. Counter intuitive notions such as discriminating uses of reward, which are research based, are hallmarks of premature application of principles that lack thorough grounding in basic research (Morgan, 1984). Along similar lines of argument, Samuel M. Deitz (1978) has voiced concern about the shift in the field from applied experimental analysis of behavior to applying behavior analysis. Deitz maintains that a change in emphasis from investigation of independent variables (i.e., treatment variables) to an improvement of dependent variables (i.e., behavioral outcome variables) holds two dangers. The first danger involves that of moving toward a technology prematurely without a sound, well-established body of knowledge. As mentioned earlier with regard to the intrinsic versus extrinsic motivation issue, this danger epitomizes the layperson's notion that a little bit of knowledge is a dangerous thing. It is regrettable that indiscriminate and careless application of behavioral principles to educational and workplace settings has highlighted a lack of thorough, basic knowledge of these principles among many educators and workplace trainers. These prostituted efforts have undermined the credibility of such principles and of psychologists in general. The second danger mentioned by Deitz involves the premature adoption of a technological purpose that ultimately disregards scientific methodology in seeking out new information. The **nongenerative nature of a technology** would ultimately result in a decrease in new uses for behavior modification, since the emphasis would be on the improvement of dependent variables (behaviors), as opposed to exploration and research on relevant independent variables (treatments). Such an eventuality would, of course, stagnate the field.

In fairness to Travers's criticism, he does mention some successes of the use of behavior modification in the realm of psychotherapy. Primarily, this has involved systematic desensitization and the use of biofeedback in such areas as stress management and control of visceral responses. Writers such as R. Douglas Greer (1983) and E. P. Reese (1986) have also emphasized some positive gains that behaviorism has to offer. Greer's viewpoint is that many attacks on behaviorism are due to bias and misinformation and that critics such as Jere E. Brophy (1983) have been unfair in their criticisms. Greer writes of a lack of knowledge in both the social science and behavioristic camps concerning what each camp has to offer the other. This lack of hybridization of ideas and knowledge has resulted in the situation where behavioral social science methodologies tell us how to bring about changes in behavior but provide us with little explanation of the changes brought about. Greer and Reese believe that behaviorism has been given bad press by those who do not completely understand it.

Future trends in the development and application of behavioral theory and practice seem to involve a **move in a more cognitive direction**. Future trends would also include a continued focus on practical applications of behavioral learning principles to the solution of educational, clinical, and workplace problems. A shift toward a cognitive bent is evidenced by the movement of behavioral conditioning theorists toward a more cognitive, stimulus-expectancy brand of associationism and away from strict behavioristic-associationistic, nonmediated S-R theory. W. J. McKeachie (1976) and T. J. Shuell (1986) indicate that this move towards cognition will be accompanied by both intertask and intratask specificity. Greer (1983) and Reese (1986) agree with this assessment, indicating that the field will move in the direction of seeking a set of specific descriptions, rather than a set of general laws. In short, as more and more learning theorists identify themselves to a greater extent with the principles contained in reciprocal determinism, cognition, and specificity of behavior, an **appreciation for the cognitive complexities of behavior** will become paramount.

TERMS TO KNOW

classical conditioning (SS)
operant conditioning (SRS)
social learning (Soc. L)
reciprocal determinism (BPE) model of learning
cognitive (SOR) models of learning
assimilation
accommodation
schema
learning curve components
baseline
acquisition
extinction
maintenance
motivation
cognitive conflict
schedules of reinforcement and punishment
continuous reinforcement schedule
intermittent reinforcement schedule
latent learning

second signal system
habit family hierarchy
contingencies of reinforcement and punishment
radical behaviorist
observational learning
desensitization therapy
biofeedback
principle of frequency
principle of recency
incentive motivation
cognitive map learning
place learning
cognitive expectancy factor
intervening variables
partial reinforcement effect (PRE)
frustration theory
Premack's relativity view
sensory preconditioning (SPC)
behaviorism
cognitivism

QUESTIONS TO CONSIDER

1. Reduced to simplest terms, there are at least four major paradigms competing for attention: classical conditioning; operant reinforcement; cognitive; and social learning or imitation. Describe and discuss each of the four paradigms of learning making certain that you describe the relation of each to learning in general.

2. As an emerging position, specify a number of ways cognitivism differs from behaviorism. Apply each view to an instructional setting.

3. Discuss behavioral and cognitive views of learning in terms of the following variables:
    a. baseline
    b. acquisition
    c. extinction
    d. maintenance
    e. motivation
    f. educational and/or workplace training implications

4. In what ways would each of the following (a-c)view each of these (1-3)?
    a. behaviorists   1. academic learning
    b. cognitive theorists   2. sex-role learning
    c. social learning theorists   3. moral learning

5. Discuss major theoretical accounts of the role of reinforcement and contiguity in learning. Make certain that you explore the tension between traditional behavioral and neobehavioral views of the role of reinforcement and contiquity in learning and that you specifically embed in your discussion the relevant contributions of the neo-Guthrians, neo-Hullians, and neo-Tolmanians.

6. Radical behaviorism and S-R psychology appear to be under constant attack both from within and without. Discuss contemporary criticisms of behavioristic theory and practice. Finally, present some directions for the future related to the development of behavioristic theory and practice.

7. Describe in detail how the six behavioral systematists discussed in this chapter would explain your performance on an academic examination or solution of a workplace problem. (Note: It is assumed that you are a mature, sophisticated learner. Furthermore, it is expected that you respond to the question at hand in such a way so as to craft a few highly detailed examples to enhance the clarity of your response.)

SUGGESTED READINGS

Readers wanting to study more thoroughly the topics covered in this chapter will find the following references helpful.

Bower, G. H., & Hilgard, E. R. (1981). *Theories of learning* (5th ed.). Englewood Cliffs, NJ: Prentice-Hall. (The standard secondary reference related to contemporary theories of learning containing both authoritative descriptions and critical evaluations.)

Hilgard, E. R. (1987). *Psychology in America: A historical survey.* New York: Harcourt, Brace, Jovanovich. (Provides a contemporary overview of the psychology of learning and the relationship of learning to psychology in general.)

Hill, W. F. (1997). *Learning: A survey of psychological interpretations.* New York: Harper and Row. (Focuses on theories that combine the best features of connectionist and cognitive approaches to learning. Selective, easy to read, a well-synthesized overview of the field.)

Koch, S. (Ed.) (1959). *Psychology: A study of a science* (Vol. 2). New York: McGraw-Hill. (A collection of twelve readings on various modern learning theories, most of them written by the theorists themselves. This is the most complete source book available for the classic learning theories.)

Mazur, J. E. (1986). *Learning and behavior.* Englewood Cliffs, NJ: Prentice-Hall. (A presentation of current psychology of learning organized by topics rather than by theories and with a good deal of experimental data on the various issues that concern psychologists of learning.)

Phillips, D. C., & Soltis, J. F. (1984). *Perspectives on learning*. New York: Teachers College Press. (Presents a view of the field from multiple perspectives. Inclusive and easy to read.)

Psychology and learning. (1985). Washington, DC: American Psychological Association. (A short collection of readings related to developments in learning.)

Travers, R. M. (1982). *Essentials of learning: The new cognitive learning for students of education*. New York: Macmillan. (A secondary reference related to contemporary theories of learning. Readable and comprehensive coverage of learning considered to be of importance to educators.)

Training Application 3.1
Emotional "Blocks" to Learning

We sometimes perceive anxiety in individuals attending a training program. They sometimes express fear that they cannot do well in what they perceive to be new and strange activities because they have a mental or emotional block that will prevent learning. At the beginning of training in a workplace setting, it is helpful to develop activities that can help to desensitize participants' fears or anxieties about approaching new learning tasks. For example, a trainer might provide a minicourse the first day to introduce participants to the overall topics and types of activities they will address and in which they will participate. These initial training experiences can emphasize getting to know other participants, the types of learning tasks and participation that will be expected during the training program, and fun! At the end of this first day, participants should be given opportunities to talk about their expectations for the program and to set some personal goals for participation and performance. It is not unusual in training programs for participants to be anxious about the kinds of risks they are going to be asked to take to learn something new and to work with people who are new to them. This kind of opening desensitization day can help to alleviate anxiety and to elicit comfortable feelings. Pairing fun and comfort-producing activities with training may help reduce the individual's perceptions of blocks to his or her successful learning in the training program.

Training Application 3.2
The Importance of Specificity

Despite criticism levied against Thorndike, he makes an important contribution that is useful to trainers. An important principle for learning identified by Thorndike (1912) is: "have a habit formed in the way in which it is to be used" (p. 174). If we apply this principle to training, we can say that participants in a training program need to learn to apply newly acquired knowledge and skills. Thus, (1) applications for content should be taught in conjunction with the content (Thorndike, 1912); (2) skills must be taught in conjunction with different types of application settings (Thorndike & Woodworth, 1901); and (3) individual goals for later utilization of knowledge and skills should be formed to enhance transfer of training into nontraining settings (Gordon, Morgan, & Ponticell, 1994).

Thorndike, E. L. (1912). *Education: A first book.* New York: Macmillan.

Thorndike, E. L., & Woodworth, R. S. (1901). *The influence of improvement in one mental function upon the efficiency of other functions. Psychological Review,* 8, 247-261, 384-395, 553-546.

Training Application 3.3
Modeling

The trainer-as-model is an important construct for workplace training. Modeled demonstrations, incorporated into training activities, are important for the acquisition of complex processes or procedures. Each component skill needs to be explained and then demonstrated slowly and precisely by the trainer. Participants should practice each component skill following the trainer's model. If participants have difficulty with any particular component, the trainer needs to repeat the demonstration before participants move on to the next step. Once all the component steps have been successfully practiced, the trainer models the complete process, and participants practice the complete process.

Two other aspects of modeling are also important. First, the use of context-specific situations in which to ground models helps participants perceive applicability to situations they face themselves in the workplace. Second, the use of practice teams helps participants to observe peers performing the same tasks. Participants can determine their "similarity" to at least one of their peers and can learn from peers' behaviors as they either successfully or unsuccessfully approach the skill they are being asked to demonstrate.

Training Application 3.4
Meaningful Reinforcers for Adult Learners

1. Providing time for participants to identify their expectations for learning and then linking new learning and skills to participant expectations.

2. Setting personal goals for learning.

3. Linking new knowledge and skills with what the adult learner already knows.

4. Valuing participants' personal experiences by providing time for sharing and dialogue.

5. Linking new learning and skills to work-related changes, demands, or events.

6. Demonstrating utility of new knowledge and skills.

7. Linking new knowledge and skills to both personal an organizational values.

8. Providing time for practice of new skills within the training context.

9. Providing team and peer learning activities.

10. Providing opportunities for choice in training activities.

11. Providing praise and supportive feedback to enhance self-esteem.

12. Encouraging risk taking through trainer modeling and acknowledging risk taking in peer modeling.

13. Setting personal goals for transfer of training to workplace uses.

14. Following up with notes of praise to participants' supervisors and/or administrators.

15. Attending to adult comfort needs; self-directed opportunities for "breaks" and "perks" like complimentary afternoon beverages and snacks.

16. Deviating from scheduled timelines; even adults like an occasional fifteen or twenty minutes of early dismissal.

CHAPTER 4

THINKING,
PROBLEM SOLVING, AND CREATIVITY:
A COGNITIVE SCIENCE PERSPECTIVE

In this chapter, we examine learning theory from a contemporary cognitive scientist's perspective. First of all, thinking, problem solving, and creativity are examined from behavioral-associationistic, gestalt, cognitive developmental, and information-processing perspectives. Then we present a section dealing with a comparative examination of problem-solving behavior across differing behavioral and cognitive theoretical perspectives. This is followed by sections dealing with the development of schema, the existence of a literate bias in schooling, and what we know and don't know about the relationship between language and cognition. A fine-grained description of those individual difference constraints introduced in Chapter 2 along with the learnable aspects of thinking and cognition, is then presented. An overall attempt is made to develop a case for the notion that the means of instruction can be related to knowledge outcomes. The final sections consist of a listing of a few unanswered questions and possible cognitive learning trends for the future.

BEHAVIORAL-ASSOCIATIONISTIC VIEWS

During the early part of the twentieth century, the disciplines of experimental and educational psychology were closely aligned with each other. Learning psychologists were actively engaged in both laboratory research and applied research, some of it considered to be relevant to instruction.

As noted in the previous chapter, the laws of learning and instruction were for the associationists, or behaviorists, those dealing with reinforcement and punishment, SS and SR contiguity, trial-and-error learning, and practice. These are the research topics that have continued to occupy the work of behaviorally oriented learning psychologists (Killeen, 1992). When the behaviorists were called upon to explain thinking and problem-solving behaviors, many of them relied on Hull's (1943) notion of the **habit family hierarchy.** The greater the number of habits, the greater the thinking and problem-solving ability of the learner. The focus was on the accumulation of experience, not the cognitive notion of remodeling of experience. Creativity was considered to be an accidental combination of two or more habit chains.

Twenty years ago, McKeachie (1974) pointed out that many of the basic behavioral principles of learning appeared to be in question. He reported that:

1. Knowledge of results is not necessary for learning.

2. Delayed knowledge of results may be more effective than immediate knowledge of results.

3. Rewards do not always function to improve learning, and their effect depends upon the type of reward.

4. Careful planning of a learning program may be no better than a random sequence.

5. Learning by a sequence of small steps may be less effective than learning by larger jumps.

6. Defining objectives may not help improve student learning.

According to McKeachie (1974, 1976), each of the principles confidently proclaimed by the associationists now turns out to be at least partially incorrect. McKeachie is careful to point out that this does not mean that the associationists' attempts to influence education have been undesirable or that the behavioral principles of learning and instruction are completely without value. However, the attempt to make a really systematic effort of application has revealed that what the associationists took to be general laws of behavior are mainly principles that hold only under very limited conditions.

Travers (1982) pointed out that behavioral systems of instruction and intervention (programmed learning, computer assisted instruction, behavior modification, and token economy systems), although popular for purposes of behavioral control and the acquisition of simple behaviors, have met with but limited success with regard to maintenance of behavior changes, learning of complex behaviors (thinking, problem solving, creativity), and learning without making overt responses (learning via lecture, reading, and imitation). Since most behaviors of interest to those of us working in applied settings (schools, businesses, and clinics) involve learning situations in which one does not make an overt response (reading, modeling, and observational learning) and rather complex cognitive types of learning (thinking, problem solving, and creativity), behavioral instruction and intervention appears to be very limited.

It is of particular interest to note that J. A. Bates (1979) has reported that **extrinsically motivated students** learn best with behaviorally based (i.e., manipulated reinforcement based) instruction, whereas **intrinsically motivated students** appear to learn best with cognitively based instruction. Extrinsic rewards are apparently most effective if the person is either not engaging in the task or in situations where the task performance is at a very low level (low intrinsic motivation), but extrinsic rewards are potentially detrimental if the individual is already engaging in the activity at a high level (high intrinsic motivation). Bates found that persons receiving intrinsic rewards for a task feel personally responsible for their performance. However, when receiving extrinsic rewards, they reportedly may feel that they were manipulated.

That said, although the traditional behavioral learning principles do not appear to be universally valid does not necessarily mean that they are without value for teaching and instructional design. McKeachie (1976) provides a succinct summary related to the **utility of behavioral-associationistic learning principles:**

> Knowledge of results is probably important for learning when the knowledge provides information and the learner knows how to correct his or her behavior, but it doesn't make much difference if the learner already has a pretty good idea of how well he has done or doesn't know what to do differently. Contiguity probably makes a difference in learning if the learner soon forgets what he or she did, but it doesn't help when he or she can easily retrieve it from memory and continue to think about it. Rewards probably do affect motivation for continuing learning, since from them the subject learns what activities lead to rewards, but extrinsic rewards which strengthen immediate motivation should not necessarily be expected to strengthen motivation for choosing activities in the absence of anticipation of the reward. Planning and guidance of learning probably is useful within limits, but there may be too much as well as too little. Moreover, some traditional behavioral principles do stand up fairly well. For example: active participation is better than passive learning and meaningful learning is better than rote learning.

GESTALT VIEWS

In the late 1920s and early 1930s, **Western European** Gestalt theorists (Kurt Koffka, 1935; Wolfgang Kohler, 1925, 1929; Max Wertheimer, 1923) were making numerous contributions to the psychological literature of the period. For the most part, Gestalt psychology was ignored by American psychologists. However, today when we speak of cognitive processes and mental operations, the gestalt formulations take on considerable interest for many of us.

Gestalt theory was fundamentally concerned with the psychology of perception, perceptual structures, and the development of perceptual templates. From the Gestaltists' perspective, SR associations were viewed as mere by-products of perceptual chunks. Many Gestalt psychologists attempted to establish relationships among the variables of attention, perception, memory, and learning. It was assumed that most perceptions were learned, that these learned perceptions created perceptual templates through which a learner filtered and pigeonholed new information. That is to say that learned **perceptual templates** set up constraints that either facilitated or interfered with the learning process.

The Gestaltists viewed memories as nonpermanent and reconstructed. In the famous **Bartlett (1932) reconstructed memory experiment**, subjects listened to a story and were then asked to pass the story along to others. What was found was that the story changed as it was passed along from person to person. It was assumed that the original story was reconstructed because of the highly individualized **pigeonholing and filtering** process across learners. That is to say that existing perceptual-cognitive structures influence the manner in which information is initially coded in short-term memory and retrieved in long-term memory.

The concept of perceptual structures led to a concern with **understanding** and/or **insight**. With respect to problem solving, the central concern of the Gestaltists was with the dynamics of insight or "**productive thinking**." One of the basic concepts in the gestalt approach is that there are two basic kinds of thinking. One based on creating a new solution to a problem, is called productive thinking because a new organization is produced; the other, based on applying past solutions to a problem is called **reproductive thinking** because old habits or behaviors are merely reproduced. The distinction between productive and reproductive thinking has also been referred to as a distinction between **insight** and **trial and error**.

Gestalt psychologists systematically investigated how perceptual problems were reformulated into smaller problems or subgoals. A particularly interesting contribution of the Gestalt psychologists was their finding that prior experience could possibly have negative effects in certain new problem-solving situations. This ineffective reproductive application of past problem-solving habits was called **functional fixedness**, rigidity in problem solving, or negative problem-solving set.

Though the Gestaltists talked little about teaching and instructional design, their theoretical notions implied the necessity of **analyzing tasks into components and subcomponents** (i.e., **chunking** both perceptual and other structural components) such that their nature in relation to the whole problem was clear. From a Gestaltist's perspective it is assumed that only when the true structure of problems is understood can principles derived from them be properly generalized. Furthermore, whenever possible, it should be left to the student to discover both the problem and its solution. That is to say that instruction should proceed in a way consistent with the internal perceptual, logical structure of the problem.

According to the gestalt view of instruction, **meaningful discovery learning** is crucially important to the development of creative, productive thinking. Gestaltists emphasized that simply giving the learner the information resulted in rote learning that generally lacked meaning. They attempted to extinguish functional fixedness (i.e., not seeing novel uses for an object) by presenting interesting, thought-provoking problems to subjects experiencing difficulty in problem-solving situations. Gestalt perceptions are supposedly organized according to the **laws of proximity, similarity, common direction, and simplicity**. These laws must be considered when presenting instructional information to a learner. Generally, an individual will focus on the figure and ignore the background (i.e., the learner will remember a unit or a whole better than the specific parts). However, the understanding of how specific perceptual components and their part-whole relationships are to be best taught was never made clear.

Gestaltists suggested that problem-solving exercises could be introduced which focused the learner's attention on certain aspects of the problem structure, thus increasing the likelihood of achieving insight. They also spoke of certain general operations involved in thinking processes **(grouping, reorganizing, structuring, and representing)** from which one might devise ways of teaching. Again these operations were never fully made clear.

All things considered, the Gestaltists enriched the study of thinking, problem solving, and creativity by introducing several provocative ideas: the distinction between productive and reproductive thinking, the idea that thinking occurs in stages, and the idea of rigidity of problem-solving set. Their main tool for understanding such perceptual processes was the idea that **problem solving involves reorganizing or restructuring the problem situation.** Most critics (Bower & Hilgard, 1981; Travers, 1982) have pointed out that the theory is much too vague to be tested directly in carefully controlled experiments.

More recently, cognitive information processing psychologists (Bruer, 1993; Glaser, 1978a; Glaser, 1982; Glaser, 1986; Glaser, 1993; Rothkopf, 1977) and meaning theorists (Ausubel, 1968) have been partially successful in clarifying some of the ideas originally presented by the Gestaltists. For example, David Ausubel (1968) has focused on the importance of **concretizing** (i.e., making information meaningful), **activity** (discovery learning), and the use of **imagery**. **Mnemonics** have been viewed as helpful in storage and retrieval because they provide organization of information, schematic retrieval, and imagery. According to A. Paivio (1971), information encoded both verbally and pictorially (imagery) will be better retained. Meaning theorists have viewed the use of imagery as further elaboration (i.e., making information meaningful). They stress the need to present information in chunks. For example, according to the **short-term memory (STM) chunking** hypothesis (Miller, 1956), an average learner can attend to no more than seven plus or minus two chunks at any one time. From this perspective, attention is viewed as an information-processing resource limitation that cannot be easily altered by instruction. Presumably, if more than this number of chunks is presented, low-priority items will be removed from short-term memory (STM) before meaningful consolidation has taken place in long-term memory (LTM).

In sum, it is assumed that the information presented to a student must be carefully organized in hierarchial fashion from the **general to the specific**. These contemporary information-processing and meaning theory perspectives stressing the importance of active engagement, chunking (presenting wholes before parts), and the meaningful hierarchial organization of information are related, at least in part, to the early Gestaltists' views of learning and instruction. See Training Application 4.1.

COGNITIVE DEVELOPMENTAL VIEWS

As Ernest Hilgard and Gordon Bower (1975) point out, Jean Piaget's views are considered to be important to contemporary learning theorists because they provide a larger context in which to view the acquisition of knowledge and competencies as a consequence of growth and interaction with the physical and social environment. That is to say that Piaget forces learning theorists to be aware of certain developmental variables (growth and maturation) and to focus some attention on the complex interplay between logic and psychology across ages.

In discussing a Piagetian perspective, Lauren Resnick (1976) found it convenient to consider two rather distinct bodies of literature: (1) Piaget's own work (and that of others in Geneva); and (2) neo-Piagetian attempts made largely by American and British psychologists to isolate the specific concepts and cognitive processes underlying performance on Piagetian tasks. A paraphrased summary of Resnick's comments is presented below.

Piaget's Perspective

According to Piaget, knowledge is developed (i.e., **schematic** representations are developed) through maturation and appropriate experience. When children are initially confronted with a problem (**assimilation**), a state of disequilibrium is created. The child seeks a solution to the problem and in the process alters existing schema (**accommodation**). This results in a return to equilibration, but the learner is now considered to be at a higher level of logical thinking. Piaget emphasizes the importance of discovery learning. However, general criticisms of discovery learning approaches have focused on the need for schooling to transmit cultural skills which cannot be easily acquired via discovery.

Much of Piaget's own work was designed to characterize cognitive development in terms of a succession of logical cognitive structures acquired by individuals over time. The **clinical method** (i.e., **case study**) used by Piaget in his research has yielded protocols of children's responses to various cognitive problems (**conservation, transitivity**). The protocols have been interpreted in terms of the child's "having" or "not having" cognitive structures of different kinds.

Piagetian problem-solving tasks have been carefully chosen to exemplify logical cognitive structures that are assumed to be universal. However, most Piagetian problem-solving tasks are not the tasks that are specifically taught in school. One result has been considerable debate over whether Piagetian tasks should become the basis of the school curriculum, whether they are teachable at all, and whether they set limits on what other content can be assimilated and formally taught in schools. Some learning theorists (Hilgard & Bower, 1975) contend that Piagetian tasks such as conservation are interesting and generally accepted, but they are possibly isolated aspects of cognitive development. That is to say that it is recognized that the Piagetian tasks are interesting and well documented in the research literature, but how important are they to instructional design?

In sum, Piaget's cognitive developmental approach provides a unique theory of human cognition. Since the cognitive developmental approach is heavily influenced by biological concepts, theories of human thought based on it remain quite limited since the biological analogy is not perfect. Perhaps Piaget's most important contribution to instruction was his pointing out that there are important cognitive developmental differences between children and adults in the way they approach certain instructional tasks. However, Piaget's logical analysis leaves many unanswered questions related to the understanding of the psychological processes involved in performance on these cognitive developmental tasks.

A Neo-Piagetian Perspective

Much of the English-language research literature on Piaget has focused on locating specific concepts or component cognitive processes underlying the ability to perform well on particular cognitive developmental tasks. There have been numerous studies designed to accelerate cognitive developmental stages (Gelman, 1983). For the most part, conservation and classification tasks have been most investigated, and there has been relatively little systematic study of task characteristics at the stage of formal operational thinking.

Two basic task analytic and **acceleration strategies** can be distinguished in much of this English-language research. One has been to vary the cognitive problem-solving tasks and to examine (i.e., task analyze) the cognitive processes being utilized by the subject in solving the problem. The second research strategy has been to specifically instruct children to solve a Piagetian problem and then to test to see whether they acquire the ability to solve the problem after instruction.

American and British schools of thought have favored acceleration while the Genevian school has not. Richard Anderson and Rand Spiro (1977) believe that schooling assists in the transition from one cognitive developmental stage to the next. Rochel Gelman (1969) demonstrated that conservation could be taught by teaching the child to attend to salient features. However, the child could not verbalize the appropriate cognitive rationale, and the Genevians felt that this was not a true demonstration of conservation.

Current research evidence (Gelman, 1983) supports the view that **language and schooling are important in formal operational thinking but basically unrelated to pre-operational and concrete operational thinking.** All things considered, acceleration training (providing needed experience) appears helpful only for those children from lower socioeconomic environments and children presently in a transition from one stage to the next. It seems as though the concrete operations problem-solving tasks the Genevians studied are psychological "indicators" of general cognitive status rather than educationally important tasks, since they appear, at least in Western urbanized cultures, to be acquired without formal schooling in the normal course of development (Gelman, 1983; Glaser & Resnick, 1972). It may be, however, that formal operations need to be taught explicitly since it is by no means clear that formal operational thinking is universally acquired (Neimark, 1975).

The cognitive developmental approach, particularly the work of Piaget, has been criticized on several grounds. Many of Piaget's theories are so vague or ambiguous that they cannot be adequately tested. Some of the theories that are testable fail to be confirmed.

In fairness, it is important to note that there are those (Kirby & Biggs, 1980) who claim that the Piagetian structuralist perspective is either wrong, incomplete (Brown, 1978; Case, 1978), or irrelevant to teaching. These critics have provided alternative functionally based neo-Piagetian information-processing perspectives related to cognitive development and instruction. For the most part, the neo-Piagetians have taken the position that it is perhaps more productive to focus on the information processing and modifiable components of development, not stages of development.

In response to the question **What develops?**, a neo-Piagetian would respond by stating that **attention** develops. That is to say that the number of things an average person can attend to is **limited to 7 ± 2 objects** and/or events (Miller, 1956). As a person develops, the number of **chunks** a person can attend to remains constant. However, as the chunks become embellished with symbols (particularly linguistic symbols), the chunks become larger and more cognitively sophisticated. From a neo-Piagetian perspective, the **differences between a child and an adult are considered to be similar to the differences between a novice and an expert**. Children (like novices) and adults (like experts) perceive things differently because they are able to attend to different details of a problem given their different perceptual-cognitive templates.

Child *(novice)*	Adult *(expert)*
o	O
o	O
o	O
o	O
o	O

With respect to addressing the question **When do we learn?**, the neo-Piagetian would say that we learn **when we are able to establish a rule** (perhaps a verbal rule) relating new information to existing cognitive structures. However, as Resnick (1976) points out, the unique approach of the cognitive developmentalists provides an emerging source of information which must be eventually assimilated into the broader area of learning theory and instruction.

INFORMATION-PROCESSING VIEWS

Today, information processing is considered to be a branch of cognitive experimental psychology. Numerous information-processing studies have been designed to account for performance differences on cognitive problem solving tasks. Many information-processing models are expressed as computer programs. In these highly formalized computer programs, theoretical validity is usually judged by the programs ability to actually simulate human thinking and problem-solving performance.

Memory Components

Most information-processing theories and models characterized the human mind in terms of the way information is believed to be stored, assessed, and retrieved. Distinctions are made among different kinds of memory. While the details and the labels vary, most theorists distinguish between a sensory register of some kind through which information from the environment enters the system, a **short-term (STM)** and/or **working memory (WM)** in which the actual processing work goes on, and a **long-term (LTM)** (usually a semantic) memory in which knowledge is stored.

sensory register – STM – WM – LTM store

Within this general structure, short-term working memory is center stage. It is only by being processed in working memory that material from the external environment can enter the individual's long-term store of knowledge, and only by entering working memory can information from the long-term store be assessed and used in the course of thinking and problem solving. **Working memory** is considered to have a limited number of "slots" that can be filled, so that it is only by rehearsing, organizing, or by **chunking** material into larger units (so that a body of interrelated information takes up a single slot) that loss of information from working memory can be avoided.

Active Engagement

According to Merlin Wittrock (1978), the cognitive information-processing view of learning sees the learner as active and not passive. It is recommended that the learner be taught strategies for effective encoding and retrieval. Learning to **debug** one's own program (i.e., learning to learn), engaging in **schema-activating activities** (e.g., provision of advance organizers, summary statements, and study guides), and the use of **metacognition strategies** (i.e., training student awareness of cognitive problem solving processes) are viewed as helpful in assisting students to learn.

Wittrock (1978) noted the importance of **cognitive instructional objectives**. He found that behavioral instructional objectives generated learning or recall for information dealing with the specific objectives, not incidental learning. On the other hand, cognitive instructional objectives generated more incidental learning. He concluded that cognitive instructional objectives were generally preferable. Wittrock also noted the importance of **cognitive style variables** in learning (field independent-field dependent; data driven-conceptually driven). **Data driven (bottom-up)** processing means that the learner attempts to retrieve information by matching input with subschema and then activating appropriate schema. **Conceptually driven** students process from the **top-down**. This means that the general schema is entered first and subschema are then activated. Overall, learning is reportedly faster with a combination of top-down and bottom-up processing. Students who use mostly bottom-up processing tend to be easily distracted. Consequently, there have been attempts to teach distractable learners top-down organizational strategies. However, it is important to note that bottom-up processors are not to be viewed as less intelligent. Research (McKeachie, Pintrich, & Lin, 1985) has shown that some bottom-up processors do very well when presented with a problem best solved by analytic processing. Wittrock (1978) discussed how ability and anxiety can influence learning. He reported that high anxiety-high ability students responded well to high structures in information processing, whereas high anxiety-low ability students responded well to low structures.

Organization and Memory

As indicated in the Gestalt psychology section, the famous Bartlett (1932) study of the serial reproduction task, in which the content of a story changed as it was passed along from one person to another, demonstrated that **memories are** essentially **reconstructed**. The assumption here is that the organization or initial encoding of memory is influenced by a number of instructional variables (**schema activators**) such as advance organizers, purpose, prequestions, and instructional objectives. See Training Application 4.2.

Overall, a number of research studies (Rummelhart & Ortony, 1977) supports the view that knowledge is systematically organized in memory. For example, it has been shown that when subjects were given a list of words in random order, they were recalled in categories. When subjects were presented with a list of words already arranged into semantically appropriate categories, retention was greatly improved. This finding supports the view that components of STM assist in the organization of information before it is transferred to LTM for storage. This supports Ausubel's (1968) use of an **ideational framework** or outline that organizes data before presentation and has obvious instructional implications.

The instructional **importance of organized rehearsal** has been demonstrated in numerous investigations (Bower & Hilgard, 1981) concerned with the **serial position effect**. In the typical experiment, items in a list are memorized, and recall has been found to be best for the first and last items. Recall was best for the last items because of the **recency effect** (the items in STM are more easily recalled than those in the long-term memory system). Recall was best for the first items because of the **primacy effect** (they were rehearsed more than the items in the middle of the list and presumably were better consolidated in the long-term memory systems). See Training Application 4.3.

Another phenomenon which illustrates that knowledge may be organized according to general, rather than specific, attributes is the "tip of the tongue" phenomenon. This phenomenon refers to the situation in which subjects cannot recall a word that matches a definition. They can only describe general attributes of the word such as the number of syllables, words rhyming with it, the first and last letter, and so on. However, when shown the word, they immediately recognize it. Presumably, the **depth of processing** (i.e., rote or meaningful rehearsal) influences which stimulus attributes and how many stimulus attributes are encoded.

Teaching cognitive organization strategies may be useful in assisting students, particularly atypical learners, to effectively encode and retrieve information. Atypical learners (e.g., retarded youngsters) demonstrate difficulty in organizing input. It has been demonstrated (Brown, 1978) that atypical learners can be taught rehearsal and organizational strategies, but they have difficulty knowing when to use them. It seems that some sort of master cognitive template is needed to ascertain when a particular strategy should be used. Atypical learners apparently do not use an overall organization strategy when solving problems.

Finally, it should be noted that although an information-processing analysis of instructional tasks is considered by most psychologists to represent a cognitive perspective, the researchers affiliated with this view share the general assumptions as well as a body of empirically derived research methods of the behavioral camp. Information-processing theorists are clearly distinguished from behavioral theorists since they attempt to describe internal, unobservable cognitive-processing components. Their task analyses of instruction differ from the gestalt and Piagetian analyses in that the information-processing theorists engage in empirical attempts (i.e., analyses of computer simulations of expert and novice performance) to describe thinking and problem-solving performance. In addition, they engage in experimental manipulations in which they restructure or translate logical operations into specific temporarily organized and teachable sequences of action.

A COMPARATIVE DESCRIPTION

A comparative summary outline of views of thinking, problem solving, and creativity across associationists, Gestalt, cognition developmental, and information-processing perspectives is presented in Table 4.1.

Table 4.1
A Comparative Summary Outline of Views of Thinking, Problem Solving, and Creativity Across Associationists, Gestalt, Cognitive Developmental, and Information-Processing Theoretical Perspectives

I. **ASSOCIATIONISTS**

    A. **Thinking** — change in habit strength — no overt R.

    B. **Problem solving** — trial-and-error application of existing habit family hierarchies — somewhat easier to explain than thinking since there is an overt R.

    C. **Model** —

        (1) habit family hierarchy:

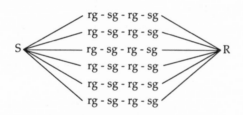

        (2) the greater the number of habits, the greater the level of adaptation, the greater the level of intelligence, the better the problem-solving ability of the learner.

        (3) creativity is viewed as an accidental combination of two or more habit chains.

    D. **External explanation desired.**
        (1) peripheral — external (i.e., muscular movements)
        (2) centralist (i.e., brain activity — EEGs, MRIs)

    E. **Focus on the accumulation of experience, not the remodeling of experience — learner is viewed as passive.**

II. **RULE LEARNING –**
     CONTINUITY/DISCONTINUITY – HYPOTHESIS TESTING

    A. **Thesis** — differences exist between animal and human learners (i.e., discontinuity).

    B. **Example** — Howard Kendler and Tracy Kendler (1962) found that reversal shift problems were more easily solved by adult humans and children with language and that nonreversal shift problems could be solved by animals and children without language. Thus, there appear to be differences between animal and nonverbal human learners (i.e., SR learners) and verbal human learners.

C. **Additional Support** — Jerome Bruner (1966) emphasized the importance of wholes before parts and the desirability of focused gambling strategies as opposed to simultaneous scanning strategies.

III. GESTALT

A. Subject matter of **perception**/popular in the 1920s and 1930s/a Western European position.

B. Focus was on establishing a relationship among attention, perception, memory, and learning (assumed that most perceptions are learned — learners acquire **perceptual expectations** which serve as a **perceptual template** through which incoming stimulation is **filtered** and **pigeon-holed**).

C. **Two types of thinking**
   (1) reproductive (trial and error — SR).
   (2) productive (insight and creativity).

D. Emphasized the importance of using **subgoals** (i.e., chunking) in problem solving.

E. Attempted to reduce rigidity in problem solving by using novel problem training exercises.

F. Example — F. C. Bartlett (1932) reconstructed memory task — as a story was passed from one person to another, the story was recast to reflect the individual differences across persons — (i.e., **memories** were viewed as **reconstructions** of environmental events — memories change to permit better gestalts).

G. Gestalt position presented many interesting problems—put the behaviorists on the defensive—but the explanation of the thinking, problem solving, and creativity process was considered vague and inadequate.

IV. MEANING THEORY

A. More external than the gestalt perspective.

B. Ausubel's (1968) notion of the importance of the **advance organizer** and **ideational framework**.

C. Examples related to prose learning and **mathemagenic (schema activating) activities** (i.e., those behaviors such as outlining, underlining, summarizing, mnemonics, graphic and figural representations that give birth to learning).

D. Importance of active engagement, meaning, and behavior change.

V. COGNITIVE DEVELOPMENTAL

A. **Genevians/Piagetians**
(1) Stage-dependent and stage-independent theory (the development of schema, the assimilation accommodation process, use of cognitive conflict as a motivator).
(2) All thinking is viewed as creative (not necessary to distinguish among thinking, problem solving, and creativity).
(3) Considered imagery to serve as a transition between perception and thought.

B. **American-British experimentalists**
(1) Attempted to accelerate development using strategy training procedures (Bruner, Gelman, Greenfield) — concluded that acceleration was not possible unless the child was near a stage transition point and/or from a deprived environment.
(2) Language did not appear to be necessary for the first three stages but perhaps of importance in formal operational thinking.

C. **Neo-Piagetians**
(1) Brown and Case developed a developmental theory of instruction in contrast to a Piagetian developmental theory of intelligence.
(2) In response to the question What develops?, a neo-Piagetian would say that attention develops. When do we learn? We learn when new learning is related to old learning. The focus is on the importance of the primacy of proactive interference, rule learning, particularly verbal rule learning.

VI. INFORMATION PROCESSING

A. Focus given to establishing relationships among attention, perception, learning, and memory (similar to Gestalt position emphasizing that most perceptions are learned—we acquire perceptual expectancies that serve as **perceptual templates** through which we **filter** and **pigeonhole** incoming information).

B. Developed models of attention (capacity resource limited models and structural data-limited models).

C. Examined the relationship between arousal and performance (an inverted U relationship).

D. Discovered that a learner could **learn to control attention** (e.g., shadow technique — Cherry 1 and 2 ear experiments).

E. Viewed **mental pathologies** (hyperactivity, mental retardation, learning disabilities, autism, depression, schizophrenia) as **attention problems** subject to manipulation and experimental control.

F.   Postulated the existence of **memory components** (the sensory register, short-term memory, working memory, and long-term memory store) — short-term memories are limited, and most problems of atypical learners are considered to be STM problems — long-term memories are considered unlimited, encyclopedic not definitional, and not permanent — to get knowledge from STM to LTM store, it is perhaps best to actively rehearse meaningful, highly symbolized knowledge.

G.   Considered **differences between typical and atypical learners** to be related to differences in attention, cognitive style expectancies, and memory organization.

H.   Assumed that **individual differences** consisted of **biological constraints** (attention, maturational stages, and temperament) and **psychological constraints** (knowledge, language, memory organization, mood, attitudes, personality, cognitive style expectancies, and motivation.

I.   Documented differences between STM recency effects and LTM primacy effects–plus Penfield's demonstration of STM/LTM differences among brain-damaged patients.

J.   Encouraged the use of **mnemonic techniques** to enhance learning (actually increase the amount of information required to solve a problem) (e.g., loci, rhymes, organization).

K.   Encouraged the use of **schema activating techniques** (advance organizers, outlines, summaries, figural and graphic representations).

L.   Focused on the **representation of experience** (distinctions between natural and artificial memories; episodic and semantic memories; spacial, simultaneous, right-brain thinking and temporal, sequential, linguistic left-brain thinking)

M.   Emphasized the importance of overlearning and multiple modality learning.

N.   Considered the role of the teacher and/or therapist to be that of teaching the student and/or client to learn to learn.

O.   Considered individual **cognitive style differences among learners** (internal and external locus of control; field-independent and field- dependent learners; data-driven, distractable, bottom-up learners and conceptually driven, hypothesis testing, top-down learners).

P.   Considered **depth of processing** to be important (i.e., the view that the more symbolic and literate the processing, the deeper the processing and the greater the chances of transfer from STM to LTM store).

Q.   **Content = process** (i.e., not necessary to make distinctions among thinking, problem solving, and creativity since the content for the expert is used to process the incoming stimulation from the environment).

R.   Considered **knowledge** to consist of content knowledge, content- procedural knowledge, and procedural knowledge (general problem- solving skills). Emphasis was given to the notion of automatizing procedural knowledge to free up working memory space so that content could be used to process information.

S. Considerable focus on the **importance of language** learning, rule learning, meaning theory, active engagement, and remodeling of experience, not the mere accumulation of experience.

The behavior of an experienced problem solver as represented by the **associationists** would be influenced by the learner's family of habits, expectancies, and adaptability to environmental cues.

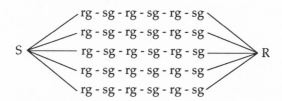

The greater the number of habit chains, the greater the accumulated experiences to choose from in solving a problem. The learner expects (rg - sg) to solve the problem and engages in goal-seeking behavior. The level of inhibition (i.e., fatigue) is believed to influence problem solution. For example, if a student studies for an exam the night before the exam, as opposed to spacing the practice trials out over time, the depth of learning may not be as great had the practice trials been spaced out over time. The greater the reward, the greater the drive reduction after an exam is completed. It is assumed that the greater the number of habits, the greater the understanding of a problem situation. A creative solution to a problem on the examination would be due to an accidental combination of two or more habit chains. Forgetting would occur if the learner were not exposed to situations where the already acquired knowledge and skills could not be used to solve problems.

From a **Gestalt** perspective, the focus of attention would be on how a learner internally represented external events. For example, students respond to questions on an examination based upon their individualized internal representations of material covered in class. Practice for each student involves the active engagement of learning. The more opportunities a student has to establish new relationships concerning material that was presented in class, the better one becomes at restructuring the material. Rewriting notes, participation in study groups, and reading all involve active engagement of the learner.

Motivation is viewed as placing the learner into a problem situation where cognitive conflict is generated because of the challenge or novelty of the situation. Rewards and punishers (good or bad grades) confirm or disconfirm the solution of a problem. Understanding is enhanced, when the learner is able to recognize the relationship of the parts to the whole (i.e., to pigeonhole and filter the information presented in class). Breaking information down into chunks, active engagement, using outlines, figures, and charts should enhance learning. Transfer occurs when common patterns and/or relationships are found. Understanding takes place when the learner can transfer knowledge structures to other problem-solving situations and correctly apply old learning to new situations. Forgetting is assumed to be due to new learning taking the place of what was previously learned (i.e., retroactive interference).

Cognitive developmental theorists would explain student performance by discussing the organized knowledge a student has available for use in solving a problem. Differences in existing schematic representations (acquired knowledge) would account for individual differences. Practice would involve the ability to adapt to the environment by means of assimilation and accommodation. Assimilation transforms new ideas into something that fits into existing cognitive structures. Accommodation involves adjusting one's ideas in order to make sense of reality. That is to say that the old knowledge one has about learning serves as an anchor upon which to accommodate new learning.

Motivation is described in terms of cognitive conflict. The use of rewards and/or punishers would act to confirm or disconfirm a solution to a problem. For example, let's consider the case of a student who put forth a great deal of effort and doesn't receive the highest grade possible. The student's disappointment can be reduced by thinking of the credits received for the course, by being satisfied that as much was learned as possible, or taking into consideration the intrinsic value of learning. Understanding is closely related to the connection between language symbolization and schooling (i.e., the literate bias in schooling). The more schooling a person has, the better that individual's abstract thinking skills. New skills can be acquired more easily if previous skills can be related to them through the use of imagery that is dependent on perception and thought. Transfer occurs through the manipulation of internal representations. These representations are based upon immediate experiences or information stored in memory. Forgetting occurs because new information doesn't fit into existing schematic representations (i.e., retroactive interference). That is to say that new learning replaces old learning.

Information processing theorists would describe individual differences as resource limitations such as attention, memory organization, and cognitive style expectancies. The greater the number of things one can attend to is related to the amount of resources one can effectively use in solving a problem. Practice is important since it provides an opportunity for the learner to remodel experience. The more ways a learner can represent a problem situation, the more useful the practice. Emphasis is given to the importance of active engagement in problem solution. With experience, the content becomes the process. Outlining, using graphic depictions of the problem, and the use of other schema activating strategies such as mnemonics enhances the chances of the content becoming part of the processes used to solve the problem.

Once again, motivation is viewed as cognitive conflict. The problem solver is initiated into activities that move the person toward a goal. Using advance organizers, mnemonics, and practicing are ways in which a learner moves toward the goal of solving a problem. Understanding is achieved when one is aware of how one learns and knows what one must do in order to succeed at a task. For example, a student learns that he or she must read the textbook and perhaps personalize a lecture after each class in order to do well in the class. Transfer occurs because of the primacy of proactive interference. Previous cognitive structures serve as an anchor upon which a learner attaches new ideas. Previous coursework helps an individual because it serves as a base onto which new material is meaningfully attached. Finally, forgetting occurs because of retroactive interference.

SCHEMA

Knowledge is reportedly (Rumelhart & Ortony, 1977) organized in terms of schemata (i.e., schematic representations of the organized knowledge we possess). Schemata are viewed as data structures for representing the generic concepts stored in memory. They are considered to be generalized concepts formed by networks of interrelations among represented objects, events, and situations. According to David Rumelhart and Andrew Ortony (1977), **four characteristics** combine to make schemata powerful for representing knowledge in memory: (1) schemata are used to organize experiences; (2) they can be embedded one within the other; (3) they represent generic concepts that vary with respect to their levels of abstraction; and (4) they are encyclopedic, not definitional. Schemata are considered to be prelinguistic; they can serve as a positive or negative constraint on learning through the operation of the principle of **proactive interference** (i.e., the influence of existing knowledge structures on the acquisition of new knowledge). The more fully developed the schemata, the less likely that they will change. Finally, it should be noted that schemata may serve as **default structures** (Nelson, 1977) when new representations cannot be made on the basis of current input or from memory.

According to Piaget, children are born with a primitive repertoire of action schemata that become more differentiated and coordinated through the process of equilibration and with the aid of maturation and learning. As they develop and mature, children organize schema into operational structures. The **neo-Piagetians** (Brown, 1978; Case, 1978) give a functional interpretation of this view. They believe that all human knowledge is stored in a system of schemata, or operational structures, which are characterized as sets of **executive (i.e., metacognitive) strategies**. The development of operational structures is characterized as a process by which these strategies are reorganized, either in response to increasing awareness of the complexity of a given problem domain or in response to perceived failures to reach a specific goal (cognitive conflict). The **rate of development** depends on four distinct factors: (1) the size of the individual's memory power, or **M-Power**, which is the learner's capacity for attending to several things at once without assistance from the perceptual field; (2) cognitive style expectancies (field dependence/field independence-attributions and/or other sources of resistance to the influence of perceptual sets); (3) the complexity and perceptual organization of the experience the learner encounters; and (4) the learner's affective disposition (mood). According to the neo-Piagetians, M-power is what develops and the metacognitive processes (executive processes, knowing what you know) increase up to the age of eight and perhaps beyond.

Katherine Nelson (1977) adds that concepts arise from the actions of the child with familiar objects, and they are represented internally as event structures, scripts, and ultimately as categories. With increasing age and sophistication, schemata become embedded within themselves and become organized hierarchically. This **embedding process** plus the **hierarchical arrangement** work to facilitate and economize remembering.

Knowledge is reportedly (Rumelhart & Ortony, 1977) retrieved by a process which allows for the convergence of information so that information derived directly from input can be combined with expectations to lead to plausible new schematic representations of experience. The convergence is achieved by a combination of **bottom-up** (data-driven) and **top-down** (conceptually driven) processing. Schemata that are activated by their own constituents are activated from the bottom up; top-down processing arises from schemata activating their constituent subschemata. That is to say that existing knowledge is used in processing new information and in dealing with novel situations. Being viewed as the key units of the comprehension process, schemata serve as a **cognitive template** against which new inputs may be matched and in terms of which they can be comprehended.

The knowledge that a person already possesses (schemata) is considered by many investigators (Vosniadow & Brewer, 1987) to be the principal determiner of what that individual can learn from an educational experience. Overall, the view is that if we change the curriculum, we may get the learning of different knowledge, but not necessarily better learning. If we change the methods of presenting information (i.e., practice and drill versus questions and discussions), no great changes are reported to occur in the short-term outcomes of schooling (McKeachie, 1986).

A child brings a highly individualized knowledge base or schemata to school. In general, the schooling process must deal with the formation and use of schemata (i.e., knowledge that will be learned and modified by schooling). Although there appears to be **no one best fit** between the means of instruction and the knowledge that is acquired, different means of instruction may yield different representations (schemata) that are equivalent for some purposes and different for others. David Olson (1977) believes that because different means of instruction are not alternate routes to the same goal, but single routes to different goals, the choice of a particular means of instruction, like the choice of specific content, must be based upon a consideration of its personal and social consequences. What Olson is referring to is the **literate bias in schooling** (i.e., the transmission of knowledge exclusively by means of written text). The use of written language in schooling appears to have great utility and survival value in our technological culture; however, the exclusive reliance upon text may lead to an underevaluation of practical knowledge and the mother tongue.

Since knowledge acquisition in our culture is conceived of by most writers as a matter of learning by using language, the educational process must teach the child how to comprehend and use language. The child's preliterate, oral schemata must be gradually integrated (through rule learning) with a literate view of reality, a "learning with" view, based upon written language.

Robert Gagne and Leslie Briggs (1979) conceive of knowledge acquisition in terms of learning the intellectual skills of how to comprehend and use language. A student cannot acquire academic knowledge until he or she can manipulate language. Gagne proposes a task-analytic or skills-training approach to enhance the learning of language skills. The skills-training model coupled with criterion-referenced testing appears to be useful because it recognizes that learning problems and prescriptions for remediation are the legitimate territory of the teaching process.

The information processing strategy training approaches reported by Glaser (1978, 1982, 1986) and Michael Pressley and Joel Levin (1983) provide us with a more detailed model of how intellectual operations are acquired and utilized and how environmental and maturational factors can affect this process. The beginning of the identification of the new aptitudes, interpreted in terms of cognitive information-processing variables and constructs, offers hope that we will be able to tailor the treatment to the student instead of forcing the student to fit the curriculum, and thereby help different students attain similar educational outcomes.

THE LITERATE BIAS IN SCHOOLING

Studies (Olson, 1977) of **schooled versus unschooled populations** have revealed consistent differences in their ability to deal with mnemonic skills for deliberate memorizing. Several years of formal schooling seem to be necessary before the emergence of spontaneous attempts to organize, rehearse, or categorize taxonomically for the purpose of memorizing.

Unschooled populations also reportedly (Olson, 1977; Brown, 1978) differ in terms of their ability to transfer problem solutions across tasks, treating each learning and memory task as though it were a new problem. Schooled populations, on the other hand, tend to treat such problems as instances of a general class. Overall, findings from cross-cultural studies (Huttenlocher, 1976) have indicated that unschooled populations develop different metacognitive strategies from the schooled individual.

Ann Brown (1978) has reported that certain forms of logical thinking in response to traditional academic problem-solving situations are dependent upon the intervention of formal schooling. The unschooled as opposed to the schooled populations present a conspicuous absence of **learning to learn abilities**. Furthermore, the effects of an impoverished knowledge base upon LTM can account for many reported learning-developmental difficulties among atypical learners. Intervention in this case could take the form of environmental enrichment. However, training programs themselves are limited by restrictions imposed by the current state of the learner's knowledge base. Piaget supports this position by suggesting that under some cultural conditions, formal operations may not emerge at all because they depend heavily upon Western-type schooling.

Olson (1977) and Brown (1978) have suggested that the move from an oral to a literate culture imposes fundamental changes upon peoples' ways of knowing. The **literate tradition** that is fostered by Western-type schooling emphasizes an abstract decontextualization and formalization of the language. It emphasizes the logical rather than the rhetorical function of language, and it emphasizes the general context-free rule rather than the particular experience. In contrast, the oral tradition, characteristic of the young, the primitive, and the unschooled serves a social, authoritative, and context-bound function of language. It depends upon a form of thinking which is biased by the limitations of auditory memory.

Olson (1977) has stated that our schools have settled on teaching/ learning out of the context of action and through media that are primarily verbal, symbolic, and decontexturalized. Children are expected to make the transition from the context-bound, experientially based, oral culture of preschool life to a context-free, impersonal, learning-for-learning sake atmosphere of the schools. Economic success in our society is defined to some extent in terms of success in school-related occupations.

Those who have difficulties with the **transition from oral to literate cultures** can be termed atypical, deprived, disadvantaged, or different in terms of their preparation for school and the workplace. These atypical learners are hampered by a restricted language code which favors the context-bound, social, rhetorical functions of language rather than the context-free, explicit communicative modes demanded in school and in the workplace. A typical nonliterate children and adults do not make the learning and social adjustment transitions to schooling and working with the ease that literate middle-class children and adults do; some never make the transitions and are marked for failure. These atypical learners lack the prerequisite schemata that allow them to remodel their experiences, they are field dependent, they have difficulty decontextualizing language, they have difficulty dealing with problem situations out of context, and they have difficulty generating aids, mnemonics, and search strategies to enhance deliberate learning. Early failure experiences in school and at work compound the problem by eroding their self-esteem and generating negative expectancies regarding school and workplace performance. As a result, the atypical learner learns to become helpless in the school and workplace environment instead of gaining mastery over it.

The **intellectual deficiencies** typically found **among the disadvantaged** are particularly characteristic of the slow learner. Because of the literate bias in formal schooling, many slow learners appear weak in areas such as the executive processes of monitoring, planning, checking, and reality testing. Their strengths lie in the concrete context-bound areas associated with the oral tradition. Consequently, they have difficulty making the transition from oral to written modes of communication. That is to say that slow learners have difficulty relating their existing knowledge to instructional material by way of rule learning. Their existing oral-based schematic representations appear to function as constraints rather than facilitators in terms of their learning from text. These slow-learning persons appear to have considerable difficulty acquiring the learning-to-learn contexts normally acquired through formal education which would allow them to decontexturalize knowledge, transfer problem-solving strategies to novel situations, and facilitate adaptation without intervention. They do not become mature learners because the literate tradition never quite fits their existing oral cognitive structures.

Early experience in a particular cultural environment provides a learner with a set of values and a set of techniques and skills for learning to learn and for processing incoming information. The middle-class person acquires these metacognitive processes in the home. These processes are the same processes required in school and/or the workplace. They learn because there is an appropriate relationship between their existing knowledge and the instructional material presented to them. In low SES homes, the "problem of the match" is not met (Hunt, 1961). It appears that what the low socioeconomic status (SES) person acquires is discontinuous with what the school and workplace demands. Glaser (1984) stated that in a nonadaptive environment for learning, cultural deprivation is defined in terms of a set of experiences that establishes a discontinuity between preschool experiences, school, and workplace requirements. This discontinuity has a profound negative effect on the atypical learner's behavior in school and in the workplace.

In an attempt to adapt instruction to the atypical learner's individual differences, Glaser (1984) and others (Brown, 1978; Sternberg, 1985, 1986) have proposed that an adaptive educational and workplace environment be provided for these atypical learners which would be designed to modify their values, cognitive styles, and problem-solving skills. That is to say that information-processing variables (attention, cognitive style, and problem-solving skills) would replace traditional psychometric abilities (IQ) in tailoring the instructional treatment to the individual's needs. Instructional prescriptions would also be designed to focus on process education and the training of rule learning, generalization, and transitional metacognitive skills. Enhancing the atypical learner's feelings of personal competence would be considered integrally important.

LANGUAGE AND COGNITION

The question of whether language influences cognition or cognition influences language has received a great deal of attention. Many ideas have been proposed about the relationship between language and cognition. However, we do not yet have a definitive answer to the question.

The early **behaviorists** did not see language as a necessity for thinking. They used the habit family hierarchy, which had no direct connection with linguistic ability, to explain thinking. The rule-learning theorists posited the idea that language is important for thinking since it mediates the process of learning. The advantages associated with hypothesis testing, coming to grips with continuity versus discontinuity issues in learning, and differences between solving reversal-nonreversal shift problems all seemed to require language as a mediator. In sum, language began to play a major role with respect to theoretical accounts of thinking and problem solving.

The **Gestalt theorists** emphasized the importance of imagery and the desirability of forming subgoals when attempting to solve a problem. They stressed the idea that relationships among perceptual chunks are necessary, and many of these relationships were believed to be mediated by language. Meaning theorists (Ausubel, 1968) stressed the importance of language mediating thinking and problem-solving behaviors. The basic idea was that the depth of processing requires linguistic abilities and that the deeper we can process the information, the greater the meaning, learning, and thinking that will occur as a result of deep linguistic processing. Underlining, using summaries and outlines all involve language.

Piaget's view of the relationship between language and cognition was quite different. He said that imagery served as a transition between perception and thought and that we need logic to be able to learn. He claimed that language was not necessary during his first three stages of development, but he did stress that language was probably necessary for a higher level of thought (i.e., stage four formal operations) to occur.

The **neo-Piagetian** ideas were quite similar to the rule learning theorists and the information processing theorists. They assumed that attention was enhanced by the use of language symbolization. Language was viewed as being important to the thinking, problem solving process.

For the **information processing theorists**, the relationship between language and cognition is center stage. They stressed that language is necessary for thinking, creating, and solving problems. They stressed the idea that content = process for the mature learner. A learner uses language to code information that facilitates attention and allows for efficient filtering and pigeon holing of information within the existing cognitive structures. For them, language facilitates elaborate rehearsal, which in turn increases the depth of processing. Thus, for the information-processing theorists, language is considered to be necessary for thinking.

Recent research efforts, as well as research efforts from the past, on the brains of humans have been directed at the **language-cognition question**. "**Split-brain**" operations have been performed to determine whether language is necessary for learning and cognition. The research (Gazzaniga, 1983) has supported the notion that language is localized in the left hemisphere. The **left hemisphere** appears to be specialized with respect to processing time, sequential tasks, and language. On the other hand, the right hemisphere appears to be specialized with respect to processing spatial relationships, simultaneous tasks, and imagery. This lateralization of hemispheric brain functioning sheds some light on the question of whether language is necessary for thinking. For example, in these split brain patients, the cross-over of language from the left to the right side of the brain has been controlled. The **right hemisphere** split-brain patients are able to learn, but they can solve only certain types of problems. The language processes and abilities on the right side of the brain have been found to be not nearly as strong as those localized on the left side.

Other possible relationships between language and cognition are revealed in the work done with **blind and deaf persons**. Visually impaired individuals are limited with respect to the use of imagery and often display developmental delays in object permanence. However, they are capable of thinking and using language. The problem is evidenced a great deal more in the deaf, in whom the development of speech and language is frequently impaired. However, many of these individuals do eventually acquire speech and language, and they are able to think and solve problems at a normal age level if given proper instruction.

A final area of research shedding some light on the language-cognition question is the work with **chimps**. In two groups of studies, one by Premack (1983) and the other by Beatrice T. Gardner and R. Allen Gardner (1969, 1980), there was an attempt made to teach language to chimps. The Gardners used sign language and raised their chimps in a natural (homelike) environment. These chimps did use signs for some words and were able to develop object permanence at a slow pace. Premack's chimps were taught to use a symbolic keyboard and were raised in an experimental laboratory setting. These chimps were found to be able to represent experiences and to use some rule-governed behaviors. However, even though these chimps did learn some language and cognitive abilities, they were not able to develop a sophisticated language evidenced in humans. Also, what language they did learn may have been contaminated by subtle cuing responses made by their caretakers. Thus, it has been determined (Limber, 1977) that there are structural and functional differences between chimpanzee language and the linguistic-cognitive abilities of humans. The chimps do not seem to use language as a social interaction tool in the same way as humans. They were able to use symbols to name objects. However, they did not create their own sentences, use syntax, or evidence generative capabilities. Overall, chimps do not display the cognitive linguistic structures necessary to learn language. Noam Chomsky (1968) referred to humans as having an innate structure that facilitated the acquisition of language. Language is viewed as being constrained by cognitive structures. Humans reportedly have two things necessary to learn language that chimps do not, a hierarchical structure and the ability to generate meaningful ideas. Taken together, the evidence cited above supports the notion that language is a necessary condition for higher level (i.e., human) cognitive activities.

Finally, mention should once again be made of the literate bias in schooling. Academic learning is dependent on linguistic symbolization. Differences between typical and atypical learners typically manifest themselves in differences in attention, memory organization, and cognitive expectancies. Is this because of our language bias or merely reflective of our biased testing procedures? In some cases, it may be the latter, but we assume that in most cases a decreased language ability means a decreased cognitive ability. This is frequently, but not always, the case. We also witness the problems of attention and possible literate bias with respect to evaluating atypical (hyperactive, mentally retarded, and learning disabled) learners. Could many of these problems be lessened by teaching learning strategies that would not only increase attention, but also language and cognition? As can be seen from what is stated above, the precise nature of the relationship between language and cognition remains an unanswered question at this time.

LEARNABLE ASPECTS OF HUMAN THINKING AND PROBLEM SOLVING

In the past, psychologists have aspired to establish general laws of learning comparable to the lawful relations of the traditional natural sciences. For the most part, it has been determined (Bower & Hilgard, 1981; McKeachie, 1976) that the general dynamics of learning (e.g., contiguity, reinforcement, practice, cognition, imitation) apply to all individuals and that the major differences in the learning characteristics between typical and atypical human learners are found primarily in the cognitive mediation differences of attention, cognitive style expectancies, and memory organization. As noted in Chapter 2, it is our view that it is these cognitive mediation differences where the study of individual differences and the learnable aspects of human thinking appear to be of particular relevance to teachers and workplace trainers.

Remember that the **neo-associationists** viewed individual differences in terms of biological differences and learned habits. Thinking was viewed as a change in habit strength, problem solving as related to trial-and-error application of existing habits, and creativity as an accidental combination of two or more previously acquired stimulus-response chains (Herrnstein, 1977a, 1977b; Skinner, 1977). In terms of teaching, the accumulation of experience, not the remodeling of experience, has been considered to be of primary importance. From the neo-associationistic point of view, teaching involves setting up instructional situations to help learners acquire successful learning habits. The greater the number of acquired habits, the greater the adaptive problem-solving behavior and intelligence of the learner.

Gestaltists have focused their attention on individual differences in perception, both biological and psychological. The relationships among attention, perception, learning, and memory were viewed as particularly important. There is considerable evidence (Bower & Hilgard, 1981) to suggest that most of our perceptions of environmental events are learned. In the process of learning, we develop memories and our memories set up expectancies that affect the way in which we perceive environmental events. These learned perceptual templates (expectancies) have a great deal to do with stimulus input and they may facilitate or retard learning. Gestaltists viewed stimulus-response associations as mere by-products of perceptual chunks and described two kinds of problem solving: productive (creative-insight) and reproductive (associationist-trial and error). Thus, from a gestalt point of view, the primary difference between the typical and atypical learner is considered to be in their learned perceptual templates, which create learning expectancies, and which in turn differentially effect stimulus input and memory organization.

For **Piagetians and neo-Piagetians,** individual differences are considered to be cognitive and have to do with differences in schematic representations. These master cognitive templates (schematic representations) serve as logical problem-solving components. Thinking and problem solving are seen in terms of assimilation and accommodation, and all thinking is believed to be creative. In addition, the neo-Piagetians focus on the development and use of executive processes (i.e., self-controlling processes). They consider equilibration the major type of adaptive problem solving and look at perception as a Gestaltist would, viewing individual differences as differences in cognitive expectancies and style (field dependence-field independence; internal and external locus of control).

Typical and atypical learners differ with respect to the number of bits of information they can attend to without support from the perceptual field. With age and experience the amount remains the same, but the bits of information become more cognitively differentiated and sophisticated. From a neo-Piagetian perspective, what develops is attention, and one learns when one is able to acquire a rule (usually a verbal rule) relating new learning to existing cognitive structures. To facilitate learning of an atypical student, a neo-Piagetian would attempt to teach the memory and metamemory (knowing what you know) strategies (rehearsal, representing, and remodeling experience) used by typical learners to atypical learners.

Those individuals associated with the **information-processing** camp view individual differences in terms of fixed (attention limitations) and flexible (instructional manipulations) control structures. They are essentially concerned with the description and facilitation of the thinking and problem-solving processes and do not specifically address creativity. They provide detailed task analytic descriptions (computer simulation models) of the assimilation process and construct models to facilitate the acquisition of knowledge. Individual differences are viewed as the fixed biological control structures of attention, maturational stages, and temperament. Manipulable, flexible psychological control structures comprise differences in knowledge, language, memory organization, mood, attitudes, personality, cognitive style expectancies, and motivation. These flexible control structures are what we attempt to modify to enhance the quality and organization of instruction. For the most part, the neo-Piagetian and the information-processing theorists are closely aligned in their mutual focus on strategy-training procedures directed at the atypical learner.

A COGNITIVE SCIENCE MODEL OF INSTRUCTION

It is our view that it is now time to embellish the behaviorally based learning models of instruction to include a number of cognitive variables. From a cognitive scientists' perspective, **individual differences** in student aptitude consist of differences in attention, temperament, maturational stages of development, existing knowledge and language templates, memory organization, mood, attitudes, personality, cognitive style expectancies, and motivation. **Quality of instruction** would relate to the ability of the teacher to organize instruction, to set up situations that would enhance meaning and contribute to the development of critical thinking and problem-solving skills.

It is recognized that we are unable to modify biological differences in temperament and maturational stages. But **most of the components in the cognitive science model of instruction can be learned**. We can enhance knowledge and language templates. It is generally accepted that how efficiently we learn depends to a great extent on what we already know. From a cognitive science perspective, a major constraint on an atypical or low-achieving learner is that their knowledge base and ability to use language to code and store information is very limited. There is a literate bias in schooling which is viewed as enhancing our thinking and problem-solving behaviors. The assumption is that this literate bias allows the **expert learner** (artist, writer, reader) to interpret environmental events (a painting or story) in a different way than the **novice learner**. It is further assumed that students with an internally controlled, field-independent cognitive style interpret their environment in a way that differs from externally controlled, field-dependent learners. For example, the internally controlled student would attribute successes to effort, persistence, and hard work while the externally controlled student would be more likely to attribute successes to luck or accident. Negative attitudes, low expectancies, and bad moods constrain cognitive performance. The point to be made here is that knowledge and language templates, cognitive styles, attitudes, expectancies, and mood can be modified by the instructor.

Much of what is presented here is derived from the field of cognitive information processing, a field replete with overlapping ideas and concepts expressed in multiple terms. There are those practitioners who would claim that the field is too difficult and the instructional procedures derived from it too cumbersome to use. While most of us may agree that educators should utilize cognitive information-processing principles in the curriculum and instructional designs they create for all learners, we may not think that this complex theory of learning and instruction is suited to instructional situations in which teachers are expected to monitor and shape the cognitive information-processing capabilities of learners. Some may also claim that the information-processing procedures are not suited to instructional situations with students working in isolation or with teachers on individual learning tasks.

At first glance the possible utility of the cognitive science model of instruction may not appear to be clear. We may have a conceptual understanding of each variable, but not the possible interrelationships. For example, how does one attend to and modify the individual differences among learners and the cognitive components of instruction in a practical setting? What does the model mean to a busy educator concerned about how to improve instruction?

What we are proposing here is a general information-processing approach to instruction. Cognitive information processing is enhanced when learners are actively engaged in the learning task, discuss, rehearse, analyze, problem solve, use graphs to represent experience, and share observations, understandings, and knowledge.

The overall thesis being stated here is that when we are called upon to design instructional environments, we should attempt to include instructional procedures having potential for the modification of the cognitive components (attention, knowledge and language templates, cognitive strategies, etc.) presented in the cognitive model. The potential ramifications are many for daily instructional improvements in classroom and workplace settings. We know that cognitive instructional systems work. The cognitive instructional systems have been carefully tested in highly controlled laboratory, field experimental, and some applied educational and workplace settings. What is now needed is a greater focus and appreciation for attempts to relate recent findings in cognitive science to educational practice. It is our view that greater sensitivity to the possibility of relating cognitive variables to our existing behavioral models of teaching will enhance teacher instructional options and better account for and minimize individual differences in learning.

The Cognitive Means of Instruction

What are the overall assumptions related to the educational process? What cognitive science assumptions about the educational process is the instructor making, and how have they been translated into what he or she is doing in the classroom or workplace setting? It is recognized that these assumptions have changed over time and across theories.

Thorndike recommended that we emphasize drill and practice. He looked at everything as if it were reducible to an S-R connection. During the 1930s and 1940s, we emphasized the importance of understanding and meaning. Then Skinner became popular in the 1960s, and we focused our attention on behavior modification techniques and token economies. Lately, we have been looking at the work of people like Feuerstein (Savell, Twokig, & Rachford, 1986). He uses puzzle exercises and abstractions (removed from the content areas) as a way to realize potential. The situation continues to change. Today, the mainstream position is that knowledge develops optimally within a **domain-rich environment**. We seem to be emphasizing the interaction between the knowledge that develops and the cognitive processes. Much of this work has stemmed from the work that compares the problem-solving performance of an expert to that of a novice. For example, M. T. H. Chi (1985) reported that when comparing the memory performance and encoding skills of high-knowledge subjects to low-knowledge subjects, it was found that the difference in performance between the two groups was due to the impact of knowledge. Those learners who had a good knowledge base ended up being much better problem solvers than those with a poorly developed knowledge base. Anderson (1982) postulated that in the first stage of acquiring a cognitive skill, the learner is receiving information and facts (**content knowledge**) about the skill. With practice, this information becomes changed into automatized **proceduralized knowledge**. At this point in the learning process, the learner does not have to exert the same amount of energy to solve a problem. The learner can now use the content to process (solve) other problems in the area. It is a model that allows us to explain how a learner goes from "knowing what" (content) to "knowing how" (i.e., learning problem-solving procedures).

These ideas seem to fit with other notions of how information is organized, stored, and retrieved. It is theorized that as competence is attained, as one moves from being a **novice** to an **expert**, that bits and pieces of information become more interconnected and automatized. The information becomes grouped into meaningful **chunks**, which are easier to access (Rummelhart & Ortony, 1977). The novice's information is considered to be spotty, consisting of terms and constructs in isolation. In contrast, the expert's knowledge becomes more integrated and connected. Cognitive theorists claim that as we acquire knowledge, we acquire schematic organizational representations. These representations evolve and are modified. In the process, more advanced forms of problem solving become possible because we have moved away from merely knowing what to knowing how, and knowing that. The expert is thought to actually see a different problem representation than the novice. That is to say that when an expert and a novice view the same problem situation, the expert is operating on a different level, not discernible to the novice. Novices are saying to themselves, "okay, first —, then —." Whereas experts have sized up the overall problem situation, worked on a possible solution, and are thinking about the next problem. Brown (1978) reported that there are certain **metacognitive**

abilities (executive and self-regulatory processes) which set the two groups (experts and novices) apart. An expert judges performance, engages in time-matching activities, evaluates outcomes, and so on. Brown and others (Garner & Alexander, 1989) have hypothesized that these **metacognitive abilities** can be taught. Finally, it should be noted that the overall goal of instruction from a cognitive perspective is to foster **independent learning** (i.e., learn to learn). See Training Application 4.4.

Glaser (1990) evaluated several programs designed to teach cognitive skills. He noted that there is a strong trend within the research literature supporting a reemergence of learning theory within instructional design. What instructional techniques promise to facilitate the acquisition of new knowledge? **Reciprocal teaching** is one technique that is being used by many cognitive psychologists. The technique has received very favorable reviews in the literature (Brown & Campione, 1986). Two goals are associated with reciprocal teaching efforts: (1) to improve comprehension; and (2) to teach learners a strategy (i.e., an approach to learning situations that can be used across content domains). Briefly, the reciprocal teaching procedure consists of three components. The first component consists of the instruction and practice of self-regulatory and/or executive strategies. Participants are taught to predict, analyze, summarize, and so on. The second component consists of a series of small groups in which learners take turns being the leader and directing the group through the learning process. Initially the instructor, who models and demonstrates the skills to be learned, serves as an expert. The reciprocal teaching methodology focuses on the importance of the social aspect of teaching and learning. The assumption is that learning takes place in a **cooperative environment** and is a social, group experience. For the most part, the reciprocal teaching approach represents a Vygotskian perspective. Lev Vygotsky (1978, 1987; Kosulin, 1986) claimed that we need to create a **zone of proximal development (ZPD)** or the amount of learning possible by a student given proper instructional conditions. During the third component of the reciprocal teaching procedure, we systematically assess the learner's level of functioning; then, with the assistance of an expert, we support the learner's development through the zone. It is assumed that a learner is engaged in a constant process of setting up new ZPDs. We look at the ZPD as being malleable, not fixed, and we look at the reciprocal teaching process as one in which we assist the learner in realizing his or her potential. Vygotsky emphasized that learning first takes place on the external plane. That the learner moves from being an external, highly supported learner to an internalized learner. Internalization is considered to be the key mechanism of change. Once again, it should be noted that Vygotsky emphasized that learning is primarily a social experience.

Wittrock (1978) and many others (Bransford, Sherwood, Vye, & Rieser, 1986; Kimble, 1989; Viney, 1989) have claimed that there is much to be said in support of the cognitive perspective and its potential influence on instruction. Cognitive methods are cheap. (No expensive teaching machines needed here!) Schooling has been blamed for a number of things; one is that it teaches knowledge that is inert, that the knowledge is accessible only under the specific circumstances in which it was taught and learned. The reciprocal teaching method seems to be providing a useful model of instruction that is generative, cheap, and easily reproducible across teaching situations. With reciprocal teaching the learner is actively engaged, learning is a social experience, the learner is submersed within a knowledge domain, there are positive models to emulate, and the potential to be realized is that the learners are walking away with useful cognitive learning strategies that they can apply within many school and workplace contexts.

Individual Differences and Unanswered Questions

Many educators have assumed that the difference between the special education child (atypical learner) and the regular education student (typical) is some sort of deficit in a processing ability. What are the **differences between typical and atypical learners**? What individual difference variables between typical and atypical learners have been identified by each of the theoretical camps? What are the promising interventions?

As we noted earlier, psychologists have attempted to establish general laws of learning, like the ones found in the natural sciences, but have had a great deal of trouble doing so. In general, we have found that the learning principles of contiguity and reinforcement are applicable to all individuals, but the differences between typical and atypical learners seem to lie in the cognitive mediational style differences of **attention, memory organization, and cognitive style expectancies**.

Theorists from different theoretical camps have attempted to deal with individual differences. According to the **neo-associationists**, individual differences are due to **differences in learned habits**. It is the accumulation of experience, not the remodeling of experience that is considered to be important for the teacher. From this perspective, the teacher needs to set up educational situations so that the learner can acquire many habit chains (rg -sg chains). The **Gestaltists** viewed individual differences in terms of **perceptual differences**. Most perceptions are considered to be learned. In the process of learning, we develop memories, our memories set up expectancies, and those expectancies affect the way we perceive. It is here, using these learned perceptual templates that we filter and pigeonhole new information relating it to existing information. It should be noted that these templates can either retard or facilitate learning. **Piagetians and neo-**

Piagetians discussed individual differences among learners with respect to **cognitive differences** (i.e., differences in schematic representations). Thinking and problem solving are viewed in terms of accommodation and assimilation, and all thinking is viewed as creative. Finally, the **information-processing theorists** view some individual differences as being rather **fixed** (e.g., differences in attention, maturational stages, and temperament) and other differences as being **flexible** and modifiable (e.g., knowledge, language, memory organization, mood, attitudes, personality, cognitive style expectancies, and motivation).

What do we know about the differences in attention, memory organization, and cognitive style expectancies among us? We know (Miller, 1956) that **normal learners can attend to 7 ± 2 things**. Typical and atypical learners are thought to differ with respect to the bits of information they can attend to without assistance. We know that with increasing age and experience, the bits become more differentiated and cognitively sophisticated. The neo-Piagetians claim that we learn when we develop a verbal rule. From birth to maturity to old age, what develops? Neo-Piagetians claim that attention develops. While attention is viewed as a rather fixed biologically determined constraint on learning, we are finding that we can control and modify attention somewhat. Cherry's (1953) demonstration of the shadow technique supported this notion. Successful efforts within educational contexts have been made to enhance attention [e.g., Rothkopf's (1977) work with mathemagenic activities; Brown's (1978) work with training metacognitive skills]. In sum, there is evidence supporting the notion that we can increase, direct, and control attention.

Recent research has given us some insight into **memory organization**. We believe that memory has three components (STM-WM-LTM). Working memory is considered to be of particular importance since only the material that gets into WM in the first place will be encoded into LTM. Working memory is thought to have a limited number of slots. F. I. M. Craik's and R. S. Lockhart's (1972) and E. Tulving's (1972; 1985) work on **depth of processing** has indicated that the more ways and deeper we process material the better and easier the recall.

Cognitive style expectancies are considered to be of particular importance with respect to the stable ways in which a learner perceives a problem, encodes, and stores information. H. A. Witkin, C. A. Moore, D. R. Goodenough, and P. W. Cox (1977) found cognitive style differences among learners and dichotomized them into two categories (**field-dependent and field-independent learners**). Field-dependent learners are aware of cues, seek out reinforcement, and are sensitive to the feelings of others. Field-independent learners are more individualistic, intrinsically motivated, and less likely to seek out reinforcement. Bernard Weiner (1974, 1986) developed what is termed attribution theory. **Attributions** are considered to be critical variables related to school achievement and workplace outcomes. Weiner found that there are stable ways in which learners either attribute successes and/or failures. He divided attributions along the **three dimensions of locus of control, stability, and controllability**. Most people hold to an egotistical attribution system (Bar-Tal & Darom, 1979). That is to say that we attribute our successes to internal factors (ability, effort) and our failures to external factors (luck, task difficulty). Jerome Kagan (1966) focused his attention on two types of learners (the analytical-reflective learner who ignores irrelevant stimuli and the global-impulsive learner who is quick to make decisions). For example, an analytical person would look at a set of mismatched chairs and group them together because they all have four legs, whereas, a global learner would group the same objects together based on a purpose (used for dining). Remember, we are talking about cognitive style expectancies here. Both students and teachers have expectancies. We need to be careful about how teachers attribute success and failure to themselves and to others. As Bar-Tal (1979) noted, teachers tend to take credit for their students' successes but blame student failures on external (nonteacher) causes. This tends to be an ego-maintaining mechanism in all of us.

Lee J. Cronbach (1975) examined the split in psychology between the experimental and correlational camps of thought. He reported that the **experimental psychologist** is primarily interested in the variations he or she creates; that individual differences are considered to be annoyances that are relegated to error variance. In contrast, **correlational psychologists** focus their attention on individual differences and predicting variance across treatment conditions. Experimental psychologists search for the one best method of intervention; correlational psychologists describe individual differences among learners prior to and after interventions. Cronbach called for a greater unity between the two disciplines. He called for the development of a unified applied psychology, one that simultaneously deals with individual difference person variables and treatment conditions. His overall plan was to match individual differences in aptitudes (A) to different treatment (T) conditions. He reported that some people learn more easily with one method of instruction than another. He advocated looking at individual differences (A) and varying the treatment (T) at the same time. In this manner, we develop an **aptitude-treatment interaction methodology (ATI)** which provides a procedure to match individual differences (i.e., aptitudes) and different teaching methods (i.e., treatments). Cronbach claimed that there is no way to separate the two and that you can't dismiss one or the other as simple uncontrolled error variance.

More recently, Lauren Resnick (1981) examined the differences between developmental, experimental, and differential psychologists and their respective impacts on education. Resnick noted that the dominant source in educational theory has been developmental and differential psychology. However, neither of these dominant views is compatible with the possible power of education to bring about behavior change. Developmental psychologists have shown us more ways of not interfering with development rather than actively promoting it. For the most part, differential psychologists have classified and described individual difference characteristics among learners. They have encouraged us to adapt our instructional procedures to these individual differences among learners and not to try to change them.

Resnick advocates a shift in our thinking. Because educators and workplace trainers are now dealing with previously invisible segments of the population (special education students), we are no longer in a position to be content with high student drop-out rates, failures in the workplace, and/or illiteracy in general. She notes a shift in social goals and assumptions. We are working toward improving environments for learning. Education and educators are beginning to believe in the **power of education to change things**. The view is that educators are not just the "guardians" of childhood. Educators are the "shapers" of adults and societies.

Resnick sees a great deal of educational potential within the field of experimental psychology, particularly cognitive experimental psychology. For example, we should teach both academic content and problem-solving memory strategies. We need to set up programs to modify student (and teacher) expectancies. It is important for learners to believe that they are in control, to be actively involved, and responsible for their learning. We should make systematic attempts to match aptitudes to treatment conditions in the form of ATI designs of instruction. Richard DeCharms (1976) demonstrated that teachers can be taught to teach learners to feel as origins rather than pawns of their own behavior. The enhancement of a perception of power and/or self-esteem is the key idea here. H. Heckhausen, H. D. Schmalt, and K. Schneider (1985) and F. Fosterling (1985) showed that the motive to achieve can be altered and that we need to get learners to talk to themselves in more appropriate ways. If we know what a learner's attribution patterns are, we can match them to an appropriate instructional procedure to modify them if found to be maladaptive.

We have many laboratory findings waiting to be applied in natural school and workplace settings with atypical learners. We seem to need to free ourselves from the notions that behavior is limited by individual differences and developmental constraints. Yes, atypical learners may have deficient information-processing skills with respect to attention, memory organization, and cognitive style expectancies. The assumption is that, we can indeed modify these variables to minimize individual differences among learners which may constrain learning and performance. See Training Application 4.5.

TRENDS

The overall trend in learning theory has been toward a **shift away from behavioral psychology** to cognitive psychology. Behaviorism has been a learning theory that focuses on observable behaviors and the stimuli that control them. A strict behaviorist does not accept the part played by internal conscious (mentalistic) forces such as purpose and will.

The psychological study of learning from 1930 to 1950 was dominated by behavioristic ideas. The approach was to take a nonphysiological position, to conduct objective studies favoring a peripheral-external view rather than a cognitively oriented centralist-internal view of the learner. Most argued that we stick to the observable data and avoid the study of the mind, the brain, and the nervous system. However, numerous problems with the law of effect and contiguity, along with a need for higher-level explanatory constructs manifested themselves from the early 1940s and throughout the 1950s and early 1960s. By the mid 1960s, the stage was set for the development of a cognitive theory of learning and instruction.

The Gestaltists (Koffka, 1935; Kohler, 1929; Wertheimer, 1923) emphasized the importance of insight in problem solving, the laws of proximity and closure. Their main contention was that the learner behaved and reacted as a whole, even when stimuli are specific, and that mental processes and behavior could not usefully be analyzed into specific elements. From a cognitive perspective, the learning process cannot be reduced to simple S-R associations.

The information-processing theorists dealt with the processing, storage, and retrieval of information in humans and machines. They compared the mind to a digital computer. In the 1970s, researchers (Greeno, 1980) developed detailed analyses of the organization of knowledge for understanding language and solving problems, using computer programming languages that simulated human performance.

Social learning theorists (Bandura, 1978) modified their S-R associationistic position to include cognitive processes. Albert Bandura's (1989) experiments on modeling and observational learning have been important influences in this rather recent cognitive trend. Bandura and his followers stressed beliefs, expectations, choice, and self-reinforcement as important determiners of behavior. In contrast, the radical behaviorists (Killeen, 1992) continue to assert that reinforcement acts on behavior without regard to conscious and/or cognitive processes.

The behavioral peripheralist point of view stressed events that took place on the outside (i.e., muscular movements and glandular secretions). Emphasis was given to drives, habits, and peripheral motor responses. In contrast, the cognitively oriented centralists placed emphasis on cognition, thinking, and problem solving. The mind (brain) was viewed as a mediator between a S and R. That is to say that the mind (brain) really controlled behavior.

Today, the central information-processing view is receiving considerable support. This central processing view (thinking, judging, and making decisions) has been confirmed with the use of **modern-day technologies** (e.g., electroencephalogram [EEG], biochemical changes in glucose levels, positron emission tomography [PET scans], and magnetic resonance imagery [MRI]) that have been used to document brain activities. The cognitivists view learning as a reorganization of perceptions. It is a theory of learning which postulates intervening variables (e.g., expectancies and verbal rules) of a cognitive nature in order to explain the learning process. In contrast, the S-R theorists emphasized external reinforced responses and avoided the use of internal cognitive constructs as explanatory concepts. For the cognitivists, all thinking is believed to be highly personalized and creative. Imagery is viewed as serving as a transition between perception and thought.

Piaget's description of the development of schemata, assimilation, and accommodation has become a useful context in which to explore and test cognitive theory. Developments within neuropsychology have contributed to a better understanding of the learning process. Some of this work improved our understanding of motivation and the nature of reinforcement. However, the central question remains with respect to identifying the physiological basis of a simple S-R association. Much attention is being directed at improving our understanding of the information storage and retrieval process. What we know about the **biological constraints** on learning is being interwoven into the fabric of the basic phenomena of behavioral-cognitive conditioning. Newly emerging fields such as neuroscience, psychopharmacology, behavioral medicine, and behavior toxicology are making dramatic advances, providing new hope that the neural substates of learning will soon be discovered.

TERMS TO KNOW

behavioral-associationistic view of thinking, problem solving, and creativity
gestalt view of thinking, problem solving, and creativity
cognitive developmental view of thinking, problem solving, and creativity
information-processing view of thinking, problem solving, and creativity
habit family hierarchy
perceptual templates
Bartlett's (1932) reconstructed memory experiment
pigeonholing and filtering process
insight

functional fixedness
meaningful discovery learning
schemata
assimilation
accommodation
acceleration strategies
proactive interference
retroactive interference
cognitive style expectancies
neo-Piagetians
schema activators
productive thinking
reproductive thinking
short-term memory (STM)
working memory (WM)
long-term memory (LTM)
chunking hypothesis
cognitive instructional objectives
field-dependent learner
field-independent learner
data driven (bottom-up) cognitive style
conceptually driven (top-down) cognitive style
reciprocal teaching
zone of proximal development (ZPD)
domain-rich environments
proceduralized knowledge
metacognitive abilities
ideational framework
serial position effect
recency effect
primacy effect
depth of processing
cognitive templates
default structures
M-power
the literate bias in schooling
learning-to-learn abilities
novice-expert differences
expectancies
attributions
aptitude-treatment-interaction methodology (ATI)

QUESTIONS TO CONSIDER

1. Discuss the main trends in contemporary research in human learning.
    Make certain that your discussion focuses on theoretical developments

that have stemmed from correcting earlier theoretical misconstructions. Present some directions for the future related to the development of human learning theory and educational/therapeutic practice.

2. Discuss the relationship between language and cognition (thought, problem solving, and memory organization) from a variety of points of view. Be certain to discuss causal directions as you examine the various theoretical perspectives (i.e., does language influence cognition, or does cognition influence language?).

3. The psychology of learning is presumably a field in which the general principles of behavior are systematically addressed. What place, then, does (should) the study of individual differences (constraints) have in such a field? Be specific in identifying promising avenues of theoretical and practical contributions.

4. Is there currently a comprehensive theory of instructional psychology? What would a cognitive theory add? Why is there now a need to reformulate the leading paradigms of instructional psychology within a cognitive context? Discuss the utility of such a theory of cognitive instructional psychology.

5. In every field of inquiry there are difficult questions that continually attract the attention of scholars. Identify what you consider to be the essential unanswered questions in cognitive psychology and discuss how key thinkers have addressed these questions during different historical periods.

6. For many years a commonly used definition of psychology was that it was the scientific study of behavior of organisms. Today, many claim that the behavioral definition needs to be broadened to include the psychology of the mind and brain. Present a discussion of why this broadened view appears to be gaining acceptance in the mainstream. Take a stand on the definitional issue, citing evidence offered in defense of your stand.

7. Discuss the relationship between the means of instruction and the knowledge acquired. In answering this question, make certain that you address the following: How is knowledge organized? How does knowledge develop? How is knowledge retrieved and used? What instructional techniques promise to facilitate the acquisition of new knowledge?

8. Suppose you have to deliver a series of lectures on the psychology of instruction to a very large audience. The audience is composed of educators and workplace trainers; interaction with individuals is impos-

sible. Discuss the most useful information that instructional psychology can offer you to help you make an effective presentation. In your discussion, you should focus on more than one theoretical point of view. Make certain that you cite relevant empirical research supporting your position.

9. In what ways would each of the following (a-d) view each of these (1-3)?
   a. associationists/behaviorists
   b. gestalt theorists
   c. Piagetian theorists
   d. information-processing theorists
      1. thinking
      2. problem solving
      3. creativity

SUGGESTED READINGS

Readers wanting to study more thoroughly the topics covered in this chapter will find the following references helpful.

Bruer, J. T. (1993). *Schools for thought: A science of learning in the classroom.* Cambridge, MA: MIT Press. (Bruer offers a blueprint for educational reform through application of the findings of cognitive research.)

Ceci, S. J. (1990). *On intelligence ... more or less: A bio-ecological treatise on intellectual development.* Englewood Cliffs, NJ: Prentice Hall. (A well-crafted synthesis of what we know and don't know about intelligence. Interesting and easy to read.)

Glaser, R. (1993). *Advances in instructional psychology* (Vol. 4). Hillsdale, NJ: Erlbaum. (A collection of readings describing the research programs of prominent contributors to the field of cognitive instructional psychology.)

Glaser, R. (1986). *Advances in instructional psychology* (Vol. 3). Hillsdale, NJ: Erlbaum. (A collection of readings describing the research programs of prominent contributors to the field of cognitive instructional psychology.)

Glaser, R. (1982). *Advances in instructional psychology* (Vol. 2). Hillsdale, NJ: Erlbaum. (A collection of readings describing the research programs of prominent contributors to the field of cognitive instructional psychology.)

Glaser, R. (1978). *Advances in instructional psychology* (Vol. 1). Hillsdale, NJ: Erlbaum. (A collection of readings describing the research programs of prominent contributors to the field of cognitive instructional psychology.)

Levin, J., & Pressley, N. (1983). *Cognitive strategy research: Educational applications.* New York: Springer-Verlag. (A detailed description of cognitive strategy research efforts applied to educational problems.)

Pressley, N., & Levin, J. (1983). *Cognitive strategy research: Psychological foundations.* New York: Springer-Verlag. (An overview of the psychology behind contemporary cognitive strategy training programs.)

TRAINING APPLICATION 4.1
Organizing or Chunking Information

Presentation of information in training is critical to participants' understanding of that information. Organizing, or chunking of information provides a management strategy that helps learners acquire, process, and recall information. Several chunking strategies can be useful to trainers:

Spatial   Mapping of items describing a physical space.

Time   Chronological sequencing of events.

Procedural   Dividing information into steps or stages of activity.

Cause-Effect   Organizing content around its causes and effects.

Similarities   Organizing content through comparisons and contrasts.
Differences

Form-Function Organizing content by structure (i.e., what is it?) and

                 function (i.e., how does it work?).

Advantages   Presenting information around pros and cons of use.
Disadvantages

TRAINING APPLICATION 4.2
Types of Knowledge

Training can be enhanced when trainers recognize differences in types of knowledge being presented (Paris, Lipson & Wixson, 1983):

Declarative knowledge is knowing what something is or knowing that something is. Declarative knowledge includes facts, beliefs, opinions, generalizations, theories, and hypotheses. Meaningfulness (i.e., linkages to existing knowledge), elaboration (i.e., examples, details, inferences, stories), and organization (i.e., breaking information into components and detailing relationships among the components) enhance the learning of declarative knowledge.

Procedural knowledge is knowing how to perform particular behaviors or activities. Procedural knowledge is enhanced by the learning of concepts (i.e., labeled sets of objects, symbols, or events having similar characteristics), by the acquisition of prerequisite basic skills, and by hands-on practice accompanied by specific corrective or supportive feedback.

Conditional knowledge is knowing why and when to employ either declarative or procedural knowledge. Conditional knowledge is greatly enhanced by the applications of skills, strategies, and resources to a variety of learning tasks. Conditional knowledge is further enhanced by metacognitive skills (i.e., varying self-monitoring activities whereby one checks for one's own level of understanding, predicts outcomes, evaluates the effectiveness of one's decisions and actions, and revises strategies to overcome difficulties).

Paris, S. G., Lipson, M. Y., & Wixson, K. K. (1983). Becoming a strategic reader. *Contemporary Educational Psychology, 8,* 293-316.

TRAINING APPLICATION 4.3
Rehearsal Strategies

, Rehearsal activities that help to keep content active in short-term memory so that it can be processed more deeply for recall (Mayer, 1987) can be important within the training context.

Repetition	Participants repeat a modeled activity or presented content.
Question/Answer	Trainers and/or participants ask questions; participants respond.
Clarifying	Trainers refine misconceptions or errors in participants' responses.
Predicting	Participants predict questions to be asked, meaning of content, or possible applications.
Restating	Participants put concepts, ideas, information, or procedures into their own words.
Summarizing	Trainers and/or participants create an overview of content presented.
Notetaking	Participants write down ideas, definitions, information, procedures, and so forth. Trainers can facilitate note taking by providing a note-taking guide in training materials.
Underlining	Participants are guided to mark important information in their training materials.

Mayer, R. E. (1987). *Educational psychology: A cognitive approach.* Boston: Little, Brown.

TRAINING APPLICATION 4.4
Enhancing Independent Learning

In any learning situation, learners contribute actively to their own learning. There are varying cognitive strategies that can help individual learners become more conscious of their own learning, and thereby increase their learning skills.

Self-monitoring   Participants deliberately attend to the frequency of some aspect of their behavior as they work at a learning task. Self-monitoring assists participants in evaluating the effectiveness of the strategies they use and actions they take during a learning task.

Verbalization   Participants talk through rules, procedures, and strategies to themselves, the trainer, or to peers.

Goal setting   Participants often have doubts about (1) their ability to complete a particular learning task successfully or (2) their using what they learn in training back on the job. Trainers can help participants gain confidence in their abilities and prepare for transfer of training by facilitating personal goal writing as part of the training process.

Self-evaluation   Trainers can provide participants with time for reflection and self-evaluation during the training sessions. At the beginning of a training session, participants can write both learning and performance goals for themselves. At the end of each component of the training sessions, the trainer can cue participants to rate their progress against these goals and either retain, refine, or set new goals for themselves for the next training component. When participants judge their successes against their learning goals, such self-evaluation can be an important motivator.

TRAINING APPLICATION 4.5
Perspectives from Multiple Intelligence Research

The theory of multiple intelligences (MI) focuses on a wide spectrum of abilities as opposed to deficiencies; thus, learners with special needs are perceived more wholistically from a strengths rather than a deficits perspective (Armstrong, 1994).

From a MI perspective, individuals are not viewed as being characterized by a particular label (e.g., LD, ADD), but rather as persons who happen to learn differently. Instead of focusing on standardized tests as the primary indicators of ability, alternative and authentic assessments are used within naturalistic learning contexts to assess learner strengths. Teaching focuses less on remediation and more on variety of activities within real-life problems and events. Instructional materials, strategies, and activities are those that would be good for all learners. Progress toward goals is viewed as more important than performance on a standardized test, and peer cooperation and collaboration are stressed.

A key component of MI theory is that many intelligence weaknesses can be bypassed by utilizing alternative teaching strategies, assessment strategies, and technologies. For example, an individual with weaknesses in the area of linguistic intelligence can be taught to use a tape recorder, a computer scanner, a peer reader/writer, spell or grammar check word-processing programs, and so on.

Armstrong, T. (1994). *Multiple intelligences in the classroom*. Alexandria, VA: Association for Supervision and Curriculum Development.

PART III

ASSESSMENT OF
LEARNER CHARACTERISTICS

CHAPTER 5

INTELLIGENCE: AN INFORMATION-PROCESSING VIEW

THE CLASH BETWEEN TRADITIONAL AND CONTEMPORARY VIEWS OF THE CONSTRUCT

Intelligence has been defined as what an intelligence test measures (Boring, 1923). This psychometric definition of the construct of intelligence and the use of intelligence tests have generated a great deal of controversy because many people question the nature and utility of the construct. This definition of intelligence becomes particularly problematic when people who are not considered to be academically strong display enormous talent.

Because of the apparent discrepancies in human abilities, psychologists and educators continue to question the nature of intelligence. What is intelligence? Can intelligence be improved? The traditional psychometric definition of intelligence appears to be very limited with respect to addressing these two questions. The **questions** have now **shifted from who has it to what is it? Can it be improved?** For many, the construct of intelligence as defined in the first line of this chapter is considered to be a useless myth.

In an attempt to enhance the meaning of the construct of intelligence, **Howard Gardner** (1983) claimed that we need to expand our notion of intelligence. Gardner broke away from the psychometric tradition and focused on the assumption that intelligence can best be studied by examining literature, neurological evidence, descriptions of the mentally deficient and gifted, and/or anthropological reports of diverse people. He postulated that intelligence is divided along **seven** only slightly interdependent **dimensions**. A listing and brief description of each of Gardner's seven types

TABLE 5.1
Gardner's Seven Types of Intelligence

Type	Definition
Linguistic	Found in the nuances of writers and poets (verbal intelligence)
Musical	Refers to intelligence found in the work of famous composers
Logico-mathematical	Present in the higher-order reasoning capacity of scientists
Spatial	Found in the work of engineers and architects who are able to see hidden figures in diagrams
Bodily kinesthetic	Present in athletes and dancers who have an extraordinary sense of awareness of their bodies
Interpersonal	Found in social people who use certain cues and prompts that make them popular and sociable
Intrapersonal	Present in religious people who have a special awareness of their inner feelings and emotions

of intelligence is presented in Table 5.1.

Linguistic intelligence is the kind found in the nuances of writers and poets. This is the kind of intelligence known as verbal intelligence. **Musical intelligence** refers to intelligence found in the work of famous composers. **Logical mathematical intelligence** is present in the higher-order reasoning capacities of scientists. **Spatial intelligence** is the kind of intelligence found in the work of engineers and architects who are able to see hidden figures in diagrams. Athletes and dancers who have an extraordinary sense of awareness of their bodies would be viewed as having bodily **kinesthetic intelligence**. Religious people who have a special awareness of their inner feelings and emotions display **intrapersonal intelligence**. Finally, social people who use certain cues and prompts that make them popular and sociable are considered to have a special kind of intelligence called **interpersonal intelligence**.

His theory focuses on the fact that intelligence is not limited to just linguistic and/or mathematical abilities. The implication is that IQ tests do not measure all seven aspects of intelligence. According to Gardner, each type of intelligence has a system of symbolic codes for processing information. For example, the code reported to be used by the musically intelligent is rhythmic, and the code used by the spatially intelligent is the visual symbol. Each of the seven types of intelligence is considered to be independent but tied together in an overall modular interdependent context. There is some evidence offered in support of Gardner's theory (Gardner & Hatch, 1989). For example, there are cases reported in the clinical literature where people who have lost their speech but not their musical talent. There are individuals who can solve complex digit multiplication problems but are found to be mentally retarded. Thus, we see that if this kind of theory is found to be acceptable, we may be able to develop multidimensional instructional situations through which we can possibly train learners to develop their talents and realize their full potential. Atypical learners should greatly benefit from this type of **multidimensional individualized instruction**. Gardner's "**Project Spectrum**" was designed in an attempt to identify intelligent behaviors within contextual situations. His approach is reflective of another major trend in intelligence research which consist of assessing individual differences from a theoretical perspective and moving away from traditional, atheoretical, psychometric notions of the construct. However, it is important to note that Gardner has been criticized (Brody, 1992) for ignoring the rich research literature related to the hierarchical nature of skills.

Robert Sternberg (1985) postulated a **triarchic theory of intelligence**. He made a distinction among three components of intelligence (the componential, contextual, and experiential components). The **componential element** is considered to be a critical aspect of academic intelligence. A learner who is strong in this aspect of intelligence will probably do well in school because he or she will know how to analyze questions and know exactly what the teacher expects. Such a learner will also be able to see loopholes in arguments. This aspect of intelligence is what most traditional IQ tests are designed to measure. **Contextual intelligence** is considered to be the practical intelligence component. A learner who is strong with respect to this component will know what to do in a problem-solving situation. This aspect of intelligence deals with real-life issues. Unfortunately, few, if any, commonly used IQ tests measure this element of intelligence. The **experiential component** of intelligence stems from experience. This is the insightful component of intelligence. People strong in this aspect of intelligence reportedly use prior knowledge and/or experience with respect to dealing with novel situations. This type of intelligence is close to the Gestalt psychologists' interpretation of problem-solving behavior. The Gestalt psychologists emphasized insight in problem solving, though they also acknowledged that prior knowledge and/or experience does not always prove to be effective in solving problems in novel situations. Once again, the commonly used IQ tests were not designed to measure this aspect of intelligence.

From what was discussed above, it can be seen that traditional IQ tests were designed to measure only one aspect of intelligence (the componential-academic aspect). This means that the utility of the traditional IQ tests appears to be limited to academic matters. These traditional IQ tests have very good predictive validity with respect to predicting who will do well in a middle-class academic situation. They do predict who will do well in school and college. In addition, they do predict who will do well in some cognitively competitive professions (e.g., medicine, law, accounting, and teaching). However, they do not necessarily predict who will be successful in life because other aspects of intelligence that deal with real-life social and problem solving situations are not measured by the commonly used IQ tests. Given this situation, it should not be surprising that the results of a number of longitudinal studies (Schaie, 1980) have shown that some people with high scores on IQ tests as children never became the successful adults we expected them to become. In sum, it is probably fair to say that there appears to be a very questionable relationship between obtaining a high IQ score and success in life. It should also be noted that there is a **difference** between **intelligence** as measured by IQ tests and **creativity** (Halpern, 1989). A student with a very high IQ score is not necessarily creative. In fact, creativity has been found among some students with relatively low IQ scores. A positive relationship has been found between IQ and creativity within the 0-115 range of intelligence. However, beyond the threshold of 115-120, there appears to be little relationship between the two constructs. Given these findings, the emphasis now is to design instructional situations to encourage academic intelligence, social intelligence, and creativity. Researchers are now focusing much of their attention on determining what intelligence is and whether or not it can be enhanced. Attempts are being made in an effort to understand the biochemical changes taking place in the brains of people when they engage in intelligent problem-solving behavior. Such an understanding will, one hopes, assist us with respect to understanding the construct and facilitating our efforts related to the teaching of intelligence in the years to come.

CONTEMPORARY VIEWS

As noted in the previous section, **Sternberg** has objected to the traditional methods used to assess intelligence (Sternberg, 1985). He claims that the present way of assessing intelligence has little to do with understanding individual differences and is of little utility with respect to treatment. As described in the introductory section of this chapter, he proposed a **triarchic theory** of intelligence based on information-processing notions of intellectual development. A diagram of Sternberg's componential theory is depicted in Figure 5.1. His theory appears to have considerable pragmatic utility with respect to education and workplace training. Sternberg's nce the cognitive path of the child.

(1985) views intelligence as evolving from proxi-
he distal factors are considered to be due to genet-
recognized that there is little we can do to change
mal factors include incidental learning and medi-
es. Feuerstein believes that intelligence can be
of mediated learning experiences. He proposed a
to improve intelligence. The initial test serves as a
analysis procedure is used to determine where the
has occurred. During the teaching phase, an at-
nsate for learning that did not occur in the past.
d again to make sure that the **mediated learning**
dressed the problem. Feuerstein's dynamic, task-
pproach appears to have direct applicability to the
The assumption is that in the analysis of the task,
g skills are identified and modified that have wide-
areas of learning as well.

ed above, intelligence can no longer be viewed as
construct. In the next section, we will discuss the
ers an optimistic view of what can be done with
ypical learners, minimizing individual differences,

E BE TAUGHT?

nly, and twenty years ago most probably, it would
erous to talk about teaching intelligence. Intelli-
d as an abstract construct, was thought to be best
nent of it (i.e., through the use of IQ tests). Intelli-
argely stable, static trait. One of the most vocal
he IQ score was that it didn't change (much) over
w did not create an atmosphere conducive to enhance intelligence. However, psychologists have
gnificant amount of the variability in intelligence
unted for by exposure to different environments.
ckdrop of a liberal political atmosphere, new pre-
eadstart) were established throughout the United
anipulate environmental variables that were con-
to the development of intelligence. The assump-
ronmental manipulations would increase intelli-
erformance. In a review of preschool enrichment
(1992) reported that these programs did not pro-

FIGURE 5.1
Sternberg's Componential Theory

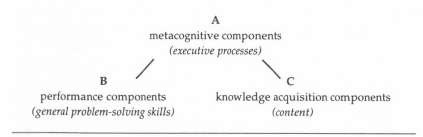

(A) **Metacognitive components** direct learning. The metacognitive componentsare
involved in evaluating, planning, and monitoring learning activities.

(B) **Performance components** include general problem-solving (schema-activating) skills. Examples include use of advance organizers, outlining, summarizing, graphic and figural representations.

(C) **Knowledge acquisition components** consist of content. Content consists of
declarative and procedural knowledge structures.

theory of intelligence is subdivided into **three subtheories** dealing with
the individual's internal world (componential subtheory), the interaction
of the internal and external world (experiential subtheory), and the external world (contextual subtheory).

The first subtheory, the **componential**, is considered to be the "how" of
intelligence. **The componential subtheory is further subdivided into three
components** (the executive processes, the performance variables, and the
knowledge acquisition component). The first component, the
metacomponent, deals with the **executive processes** that regulate everything we do both physically and mentally. The executive processes are involved in evaluating, planning, and monitoring. These are the metacognitive
activities that direct learning. The second component deals with the **performance variables** of encoding, inferring relationships, and comparing
strategic solutions. These general problem-solving skills are believed to be
under the regulation of the executive processes. In many respects these are
the same schema-activating skills (use of advance organizers, outlining, summarizing, graphic and figural representations) discussed in Chapter 4. Increasing these performance (schema activating) skills is assumed to have a
direct impact on intelligence. The third component is referred to as the
knowledge acquisition component. Here the focus is on the learner's ability
to deal with new situations by distinguishing relevant from irrelevant information and the learner's ability to relate new information to old infor-

mation. The knowledge acquisition component represents the internal processes that increase the knowledge base (content) of the individual.

Sternberg's second subtheory is referred to as the **experiential**. Here the internal and external world are believed to be integrated. Sternberg refers to this as the "when" of intelligence. The experiential subtheory was crafted to address the learner's ability to deal with novel situations through selection of information from the external world. The person uses selective encoding to filter relevant from irrelevant information. The learner then selects isolated factors and combines them into constellations of meaningful information. Comparisons are made between new and old information. It should be noted that many aspects of Sternberg's theory are closely related to neo-Piagetian views of learning and development. For example, one important variable assumed to be related to increasing intelligence deals with the development of attention. Attention is considered to be a limited resource. To increase attention, the learner must learn to select relevant information to avoid overloading the memory system with irrelevant information. This allows the memory system to meaningfully reconstruct and encode new information into long-term memory. This process is believed to help the learner distinguish between the encoding of essential and nonessential information. It is assumed that the learner begins to search the existing memory system for relevant information. When the new information is then presented, the learner has already begun the selection of existing templates of knowledge in order to facilitate the acquisition of new knowledge.

Sternberg's **contextual subtheory** deals with a learner's external world. It is the "what and where" of intelligence. This represents the learner's ability to use purposeful selection and shaping of environmental factors to adapt to his or her personal world. Sternberg believes that existing curricula do not relate to the real world. From his perspective, it is essential that we teach the learner to identify and problem solve in the real world. When we measure intelligence, he believes that our measures have little to do with practical intelligence. For example, most problem-solving situations in school come in neat little packages with specific solutions. In the real world, few problems have neat solutions. Sternberg believes that the ability to deal with these novel situations is an important aspect of intelligence that needs to be systematically assessed and nurtured. He has designed a program of instruction entitled Intelligence Applied (IA) to address these issues. Through direct teaching of situations transferrable to real life, Sternberg claims that we can "teach" intelligence.

Lev Vygotsky's (1978) model of intelligence is highly dependent on a **social framework** in which the child's intellect unfolds through maturation and interaction with the environment. Like **Jerome Bruner** (1966), Vygotsky emphasizes the learner's involvement in his or her environment.

FIGURE 5.1
Sternberg's Componential Theory

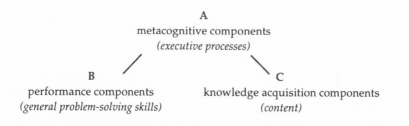

A
metacognitive components
(executive processes)

B
performance components
(general problem-solving skills)

C
knowledge acquisition components
(content)

(A) **Metacognitive components** direct learning. The metacognitive componentsare involved in evaluating, planning, and monitoring learning activities.

(B) **Performance components** include general problem-solving (schema-activating) skills. Examples include use of advance organizers, outlining, summarizing, graphic and figural representations.

(C) **Knowledge acquisition components** consist of content. Content consists of declarative and procedural knowledge structures.

theory of intelligence is subdivided into **three subtheories** dealing with the individual's internal world (componential subtheory), the interaction of the internal and external world (experiential subtheory), and the external world (contextual subtheory).

The first subtheory, the **componential**, is considered to be the "how" of intelligence. **The componential subtheory is further subdivided into three components** (the executive processes, the performance variables, and the knowledge acquisition component). The first component, the metacomponent, deals with the **executive processes** that regulate everything we do both physically and mentally. The executive processes are involved in evaluating, planning, and monitoring. These are the metacognitive activities that direct learning. The second component deals with the **performance variables** of encoding, inferring relationships, and comparing strategic solutions. These general problem-solving skills are believed to be under the regulation of the executive processes. In many respects these are the same schema-activating skills (use of advance organizers, outlining, summarizing, graphic and figural representations) discussed in Chapter 4. Increasing these performance (schema activating) skills is assumed to have a direct impact on intelligence. The third component is referred to as the **knowledge acquisition component**. Here the focus is on the learner's ability to deal with new situations by distinguishing relevant from irrelevant information and the learner's ability to relate new information to old information. The knowledge acquisition component represents the internal processes that increase the knowledge base (content) of the individual.

Sternberg's second subtheory is referred to as the **experiential**. Here the internal and external world are believed to be integrated. Sternberg refers to this as the "when" of intelligence. The experiential subtheory was crafted to address the learner's ability to deal with novel situations through selection of information from the external world. The person uses selective encoding to filter relevant from irrelevant information. The learner then selects isolated factors and combines them into constellations of meaningful information. Comparisons are made between new and old information. It should be noted that many aspects of Sternberg's theory are closely related to neo-Piagetian views of learning and development. For example, one important variable assumed to be related to increasing intelligence deals with the development of attention. Attention is considered to be a limited resource. To increase attention, the learner must learn to select relevant information to avoid overloading the memory system with irrelevant information. This allows the memory system to meaningfully reconstruct and encode new information into long-term memory. This process is believed to help the learner distinguish between the encoding of essential and nonessential information. It is assumed that the learner begins to search the existing memory system for relevant information. When the new information is then presented, the learner has already begun the selection of existing templates of knowledge in order to facilitate the acquisition of new knowledge.

Sternberg's **contextual subtheory** deals with a learner's external world. It is the "what and where" of intelligence. This represents the learner's ability to use purposeful selection and shaping of environmental factors to adapt to his or her personal world. Sternberg believes that existing curricula do not relate to the real world. From his perspective, it is essential that we teach the learner to identify and problem solve in the real world. When we measure intelligence, he believes that our measures have little to do with practical intelligence. For example, most problem-solving situations in school come in neat little packages with specific solutions. In the real world, few problems have neat solutions. Sternberg believes that the ability to deal with these novel situations is an important aspect of intelligence that needs to be systematically assessed and nurtured. He has designed a program of instruction entitled Intelligence Applied (IA) to address these issues. Through direct teaching of situations transferrable to real life, Sternberg claims that we can "teach" intelligence.

Lev Vygotsky's (1978) model of intelligence is highly dependent on a **social framework** in which the child's intellect unfolds through maturation and interaction with the environment. Like **Jerome Bruner** (1966), Vygotsky emphasizes the learner's involvement in his or her environment.

The learner is seen as a creator of his or her own existence through active participation in the environment. However, Vygotsky sees the adult's role as being particularly important with respect to the intellectual development of the child. The adult is viewed as being the natural teacher who imparts the language and culture to the child. Initially, the child is considered to be other directed; that is, the adult "teacher" guides the child's learning. As the child develops, he or she becomes self-directed as he or she internalizes the information gained from the historical cultural milieu through the adult. A particularly applicable component of Vygotsky's theory to education and training is the concept of the **zone of proximal development (ZPD)**. The adult assesses where the child can function independently and the child's optimal level of performance (i.e., the child's performance with the aid of an adult "expert"). The difference between these two levels of functioning is referred to as the ZPD. It is within this area that Vygotsky believes that cognitive development (intelligence) can best be facilitated. To increase intelligence, then, it is necessary to know what the learner knows. In this way, the adult expert can bridge the distance between independent learning and potential levels of learning. From this perspective, it is believed that instruction outside the zone of proximal development will slow cognitive development. Eventually, the child learns his or her own zone of proximal development and is able to use the thinking and problem-solving (i.e., **scaffolding**) techniques that the adult modeled as he or she becomes more self-directed. This viewpoint lends credence to the movement away from traditional psychometric assessment instruments toward a **test-teach-test, criterion-referenced, performance-based form of assessment**. Vygotsky views language development, interaction with culture, and the child's use of imagination, make-believe, and play as important functions to facilitate cognition. Therefore, to increase intelligence it is believed to be important to provide opportunities for the child to engage in imaginative play. It is important that the child interacts in a cultural milieu. Finally, it is assumed that language enrichment will positively affect the development of intelligence.

    J. B. McLane (1987) has discussed the development of intelligence within the context of the **nature versus nurture** debate. According to McLane, intelligence is believed to be highly canalized across species from the ages of 0-2. In cases of intellectual deprivation, McLane believes that returning the child to a species-appropriate environment will correct a deprivation taking place during the first two years of life. In regard to this early stage, it is assumed that little can be done to "teach intelligence." However, beyond the age of two, intelligence is believed to become less canalized and is subject to environmental influence. At this point, differences among learners occur. Intervention can then greatly change intellectual functioning. At this point, the assumption is that the intervention of a Vygotsky-like expert model can greatly influence the cognitive path of the child.

Reuven Feuerstein (1985) views intelligence as evolving from proximal and distal factors. The distal factors are considered to be due to genetics and SES status. It is recognized that there is little we can do to change these factors. The proximal factors include incidental learning and mediated learning experiences. Feuerstein believes that intelligence can be changed through the use of mediated learning experiences. He proposed a **test-teach-test** approach to improve intelligence. The initial test serves as a medium in which a task analysis procedure is used to determine where the break down in learning has occurred. During the teaching phase, an attempt is made to compensate for learning that did not occur in the past. The learner is then tested again to make sure that the **mediated learning teaching experience** addressed the problem. Feuerstein's dynamic, task-analytic, test-teach-test approach appears to have direct applicability to the teaching of intelligence. The assumption is that in the analysis of the task, particular problem-solving skills are identified and modified that have wide-ranging effects on other areas of learning as well.

Given what is reported above, intelligence can no longer be viewed as a static, biologically fixed construct. In the next section, we will discuss the current research that offers an optimistic view of what can be done with respect to working with atypical learners, minimizing individual differences, and teaching intelligence.

CAN INTELLIGENCE BE TAUGHT?

Fifty years ago certainly, and twenty years ago most probably, it would have been fairly preposterous to talk about teaching intelligence. Intelligence, though recognized as an abstract construct, was thought to be best revealed through assessment of it (i.e., through the use of IQ tests). Intelligence was viewed as a largely stable, static trait. One of the most vocal arguments in support of the IQ score was that it didn't change (much) over time. Such a point of view did not create an atmosphere conducive to encouraging attempts to enhance intelligence. However, psychologists have long maintained that a significant amount of the variability in intelligence test scores could be accounted for by exposure to different environments. In the 1960s, against a backdrop of a liberal political atmosphere, new preschool programs (e.g., Headstart) were established throughout the United States in an attempt to manipulate environmental variables that were considered to be detrimental to the development of intelligence. The assumption was that these environmental manipulations would increase intelligence and later school performance. In a review of preschool enrichment programs, Nathan Brody (1992) reported that these programs did not produce significant lasting increases in IQ test performance. That is to say, that some of these programs raised IQ scores, but these increases were not maintained. It should be pointed out that Brody was careful with respect to noting that the programs may have produced positive changes in the children's expectancies and aspirations. In sum, it is probably fair to say that the final verdict with respect to the utility of preschool enrichment programs using the Headstart model is not yet in.

Current theoretical work and the empirical research findings related to supporting these theories are demonstrating that intelligence can be taught. Sternberg's information-processing model and Vygotsky's social/cognitive model are stimulating the development of instructional methodologies designed to teach intelligence. By taking full advantage of the aspect of **Sternberg's model** in which emphasis is given to the executive components' regulation of the learner's physical and mental activities and the need to link the executive components with the nonexecutive components, researchers are attempting to enhance intelligence. Important links are being made in this area with respect to teaching learners to regulate their planning, monitoring, and encoding of information activities. Tasks involving metacognition are considered to be of extreme value. Sternberg proposed the idea that the learner's internal world is a process of mediating information through the use of metacomponents (planning, evaluating, monitoring) and performance components (comparing solutions strategies and being able to distinguish the essential from the nonessential details). It should be noted that direct teaching of metacognitive strategies has had mixed results (Weinstein & Marges, 1986). The strategies have been found to be useful for slow learners and low-average-ability students. However, the results related to their use with high-ability students have been found to be less promising. The assumption is that high-ability students develop their own metacognitive strategies. Therefore, teaching strategies to these students may conflict with their own well-developed problem-solving strategies. However, for lower-ability students this is an area in which the teaching of intelligence has had some success.

The traditional psychometric models that viewed intelligence as being relatively static are beginning to give way to the notion of viewing intelligence as being a dynamic structure (Sternberg and Feuerstein). These dynamic models imply that intelligence can be improved and that intelligence can be taught. By utilizing a test-teach-test model, researchers are able to underscore problem areas. By teaching the learner how to perform various cognitive tasks, by emphasizing such important information processing components as monitoring, planning, and evaluating, the learner often shows improvement not only with respect to performance of a specific skill, but has also been taught how to be more intelligent.

The **Dynamic test-teach-test** approach to assessment is receiving a great deal of attention in the research literature. Researchers such as Sternberg (1985), Feuerstein (1985), and Anne Marie S. Palinscar and Ann Brown (1984) are utilizing it as a means for teaching intelligence. According to Sternberg (1985), we are at a point in our understanding of intelligence such that a strong commitment should be made in the areas of understanding specific processes as opposed to the inadequate general processes that the psychodiagnosticians glean from their factor-analytic models of intelligence and psychometric measurements. Sternberg is making a call for specific process analysis. This has direct application to the teaching of intelligence since improving these processes provides a real means for learners to teach themselves how to improve their intellectual capacities. The future of this area of research looks promising.

Many efforts to increase intelligence have been made within the past two decades. These research programs have been embedded within the context created by theorists who view intelligence from a dynamic test-teach-test (versus static) perspective.

Ann Brown and Joseph Campione (1986) conceptualize intelligence as including an architectural and an executive system. The architectural component is the biological or hardware part of the system. For the most part, this component of the system cannot be modified. But much can be done by working with the executive process part of the system. Particular attention has been directed at training control processes (e.g., learning strategies) and metacognitive processes (i.e., awareness of one's thoughts). For example, in the **reciprocal training** instructional program designed to teach reading, Brown and Campione (1986) emphasize the teaching of metacognitive strategies (e.g., self-monitoring and rehearsal) within a co-operative learning model. Brown and Campione believe that these strategies need to be explicitly taught.

Brown (1978) and **Palinscar and Brown** (1984) have been involved in work that was designed to demonstrate that intelligence could be taught. They attempted to develop a link between Sternberg's executive and nonexecutive components. Using a **reciprocal teaching model** of instruction, they attempted to encourage a gradual transition from the expert teacher teaching the novice learner to the learner himself or herself doing the actual teaching. These efforts included such things as teaching the novice learner how to ask him- or herself clarifying questions and teaching the learner how to summarize and clarify the central point of a reading passage. The Palinscar and Brown reciprocal teaching procedure fosters the acquisition of metacomponential skills (monitoring, planning, and evaluating). These skills are viewed as being intellectually generative. That is to say that they improve intelligence since they give the learner insight into ways in which they can learn how to learn. With respect to Sternberg's model of intelligence, this procedure helps the learner improve at the third subunit of his componential subtheory (the knowledge-acquisition component). Therefore, not only are Palinscar and Brown generating intellectual growth at the metacomponent level, they are also facilitating intellectual growth at the knowledge-acquisition componential level as well (i.e., the declarative content knowledge level).

As noted earlier, **Vygotsky** (1978) posited the notion of the zone of proximal development (ZPD) as being of vital importance to the intellectual growth of the child. The zone of proximal development is defined as the zone between what the child (novice) is able to do on his or her own and what the child (novice) is capable of doing with adult (expert) assistance. It is within this zone of proximal development that the greatest potential for intellectual growth can be made. Therefore, if researchers and teachers can identify a learner's zone of proximal development, then instruction designed to improve the learner's intelligence within this zone will fare best.

Feuerstein (1985), working out of a model of intelligence very similar to Vygotsky's, has developed an instrument called the **Learning Potential Assessment Device (LPAD)**. This tool was designed to identify where the learner is with respect to his/her ZPD. Use of this tool may facilitate our efforts to improve intelligence since locating the area for the greatest intellectual growth potential can be identified, and instruction can then be designed to enhance intelligence.

Feuerstein believes that many cognitively deficient learners were culturally deprived. He maintains that there are two kinds of learning experiences (direct exposure learning experiences and mediated learning experiences in which an expert instructor teaches a novice learner). Thinking and problem-solving skills are believed to be transmitted through these experiences and culturally deprived learners are considered to be deprived of the opportunity to develop many of these thinking skills.

Feuerstein's **instrumental enrichment program** was designed in an attempt to teach these thinking skills that he sees as necessary with respect to equipping a learner to benefit from instructional experiences and to learn on his or her own. Feuerstein believes that intelligence is not static and must be seen as a process rather than a product.

It is probably fair to say that Feuerstein and the metacognitive theorists (Sternberg, Brown, Campione, and Palinscar) recommend that in designing instruction, we should pay attention to where a learner is developmentally, their knowledge base, and what they are able to learn (i.e., assess the zone of proximal development - ZPD). As a person learns, the ZPD is believed to be in a state of constant flux. From this point of view, intelligence represents the ability of a person to change as a result of instruction. For Sternberg (1985), this dynamic process is represented by the dimensions of procedural actions (applying old rules and strategies) and flexibility (developing new ones). That is to say that intelligence encompasses a dynamic compromise between these dimensions as the learner faces new challenges.

At some point, we may have to come back to the question of whether or not what we are increasing as a result of these instructional efforts is in fact intelligence. Or whether the researchers/theorists are simply training subjects to do better on the tests (performance-based outcome measures) they are using. This possibility, of course, brings us back to the old question of just what is intelligence? At present, the cognitive programs of research designed to improve thinking and problem-solving performance look very promising.

THE RELATIONSHIP BETWEEN INTELLECTUAL ASSESSMENT AND TREATMENT

Traditional psychometric assessment procedures have not been found to be very useful with respect to assisting us with our interventions and/or treatment plans. At best, our assessment efforts have yielded diagnostic labels that have resulted in placements in specialized treatment programs. For example, a child identified as being learning disabled (LD) may be placed in a treatment program developed for that particular diagnostic group where the focus is on the use of more concrete materials, manipulation of materials, and self-help activities. Another child identified as being behavior disordered (BD) may be placed in a treatment program in which emphasis is given to learning self-control techniques and management of aggressive behavior. And yet another child identified as being educably mentally handicapped (EMH) may be placed in a setting where the focus is given to reinforcing small increments of academic improvement and strategy training. That is to say that the treatment program is designed for the diagnostic category (LD, BD, EMH) rather than for the individual learner. The psychological processes identified in the assessment process are not directly related to the treatment plan.

Traditional intelligence tests were developed to measure the underlying constructs of intelligence. Tests like the frequently used Weschler tests are dichotomized into verbal and performance components. Alan Kaufman (1979) developed another dichotomy that he referred to as simultaneous and sequential components of intellectual ability. Jerome Sattler (1982) argues that our intervention and/or treatment programs are not clearly aligned with these commonly assessed constructs. That is to say that these frequently used traditional constructs seem to have little pragmatic value with respect to relating them to our treatment programs. Recent studies have also shown that the labels that we assign to exceptional learners (LD, BD, EMH) have little treatment utility (Hayes, Nelson, & Jarrett, 1987; Matarazzo, 1990). Not only do the tests not adequately delineate the differences among these groups of exceptional learners, it has been found that these groups are not really treated very differently in terms of our intervention efforts.

Behavioral assessment procedures have become a popular alternative to traditional intellectual assessment procedures. Behavioral assessment procedures include direct behavioral observations, self-reports, behavioral interviews with significant people in the client's life (teachers, parents, employers, peers) and possibly physiological measures. Proponents of the behavioral assessment method claim that this type of evaluation of the learner within the context of a natural learning environment (classroom and/or workplace) is more valuable than a traditional assessment method with respect to determining a treatment plan. With this method, a baseline of the targeted problematic behavior is determined, manipulations of the environment are employed, and follow-up assessments to determine the effectiveness of the treatment are made within the context of an ongoing test-teach-test program of intervention.

There is also a growing interest in **information-processing assessment procedures**. As noted in the previous sections, Feuerstein (1985), Sternberg (1985), Gardner (1983), and others have examined traditional assessment procedures and have found them to be lacking. The intellectual constructs identified to date do not adequately address the underlying mental processes related to treatment. Gardner feels that we evaluate intelligence too narrowly. Sternberg suggests that test items be used for task analysis to determine what mental processes need to be modified. He also objects to the lack of generalizability of the traditional test performance measures to real life situations.

As noted earlier, **Feuerstein** (1985) developed an assessment measure that is designed to assess latent learning potential. Through use of the **LPAD (Learning Potential Assessment Device)**, the learner's cognitive deficits are identified. Through participation in a series of mediated learning experiences, the learner is taught those specific processes and problem-solving strategies that are found to be lacking. That is to say that the treatment program that Feuerstein has created [Instrumental Enrichment (IE)] is directly related to the LPAD assessment instrument.

Sternberg (1985) addresses the assessment issue through the use of his Multidimensional Abilities Test. This test covers a wide range of content, including practical content. His test-teach-test program referred to as Intelligence Applied is being used in an attempt to relate formalized instruction to real-world problem-solving situations. This information processing approach to assessment is gaining in popularity because of its direct link to treatment.

Another area that is gaining in popularity is directly related to the studies of **Vygotsky** (1978). Using his concept of the zone of proximal development (ZPD), the novice learner is assessed with respect to what he or she can do with the assistance of an expert and what he or she can do independently. The assessor interacts directly with the learner during the testing to determine latent learning potential. Through this dynamic social interaction process, the assessment signifies what the learner is able to do independently, what is lacking, and what the learner's potential to move forward is.

Another recent trend in assessment has to do with the development of curriculum-based and/or performance-based assessment procedures. As noted above, traditional testing has been found to have very little relationship to instruction. **With curriculum-based assessment (CBA) and/or performance-based assessment (PBA),** there is a direct link with instruction. Failures that occur in traditional testing may reflect a lack of exposure to the material to be learned. In contrast, failures that occur within the context of CBA or PBA are viewed as true learning failures. Here the material is not unfamiliar to the testee. In addition, CBA and PBA procedures do not have practice effects associated with their use, and they can therefore be used for ongoing monitoring of performance. With CBA and PBA, instructors can develop a treatment plan directly from the assessment. That is to say that instructors are able to change instruction based on the information from the testing. J. Ysseldyke, M. Thurlow, J. Graden, C. Wesson, S. Deno, and B. Algozzine (1982) found that CBA was particularly useful when working with atypical (i.e., exceptional) learners. Finally, it should be noted that I. E. Gallagan (1985) found that CBA is less culturally and racially biased than traditional assessment instruments.

From what is reported above, it seems as though assessment is undergoing many changes. Many traditional constructs have not held up well to empirical scrutiny, and the assessment-treatment match has been found to be very weak. A static view of assessment is giving way to a more dynamic test-teach-test approach including behavioral assessments, information processing, curriculum-based, and performance-based measures. These changes are slow, however, as many psychologists and educators hang on tenaciously to the traditional IQ measures. It is recognized that norm-referenced traditional assessment procedures do have some value with respect to anchoring a learner's performance to a large representative sample. The overall trend, however, is to include less formal and more varied performance based measures in our assessment batteries. See Training Application 5.1.

CAN INDIVIDUAL DIFFERENCES BE MODIFIED?

Traditional behavioral theorists deemphasized individual differences. They focused their efforts on establishing general principles of behavior and documenting similarities across different species. However, with increased evidence of species-specific behavior (Breland & Breland, 1960) and an increased focus on investigating characteristics and problems of human learning from a cognitive perspective, the importance of **individual differences (i.e., biological and psychological constraints on learning)** moved to the center of the stage. Human mental structures have been found to be more complex, and human mental capabilities have been found to be greater than that of other species. This complexity seemingly is accompanied by greater intraspecies individual differences. The study of individual differences appears to be particularly important from an applied perspective. With respect to investigating learning from instruction, a detailed examination of individual differences may facilitate our understanding of the interaction taking place between these differences and our instructional methods. Through such an examination, information may be obtained, in fact, has been obtained, that will be useful to us with respect to guiding our instructional efforts. In assessing a person's intelligence, thinking and problem-solving skills, cognitive style, attributions, and setting up treatments within a dynamic test-teach-test context, it is assumed that information about a person's individual differences can greatly facilitate the intervention process. In this section, **biological (maturation, temperament, attention) and psychological (knowledge, memory organization, emotion, mood, language, personality, cognitive style, and motivation) constraints** on learning will be described, and theoretical and practical contributions related to their use and possible modification will be identified.

Biological Constraints

Maturation and Temperament. Maturation and temperament are considered to be biological constraints that are not very amenable to change. Piaget viewed cognitive growth as the result of qualitative changes in thinking that correspond to biologically determined maturational stages of development. This view has been widely supported in the research literature. The information-processing theorists view cognitive growth as a combination of qualitative and quantitative changes in knowledge. These changes are presumed to be a function of both physical maturation and experience. Information-processing theorists have attempted to explain observed differences between the way children and adult learners use cognitive strategies to solve problems. Adult learners not only learn and solve problems more rapidly, but also approach learning tasks in different ways than younger learners. For example, children under the age of five rarely rely on language as a mediator in their thinking processes while older children and adults consistently use language to facilitate problem solving. In addition, children do not consistently use rehearsal and other memory strategies to facilitate learning until about age nine or ten.

Attention. Attention is another biological constraint that may be only partially amenable to change. The span of attention or memory span refers to the amount of information that can be obtained from a single brief exposure to the environment and immediately recalled from short-term memory (STM). With regard to the normal individual, the amount of information that can be attended to is believed to be limited in quantity to 7 ± 2 distinct units (Miller, 1956). A person's attentional capacity reportedly is fully developed by age two (Case, 1978, 1985). However, with experience a person is able to hold larger amounts of information in STM by chunking or organizing lower-order units into seven or so higher-order units. Learning, then, is viewed as a matter of segregating, classifying, and grouping elementary elements into a smaller number of richer, more densely packed chunks. From an information-processing perspective, attention is viewed as being the primary problem with respect to such mental pathologies as retardation, autism, depression, schizophrenia, hyperactivity, and so on.

Psychological Constraints

Knowledge. From the information-processing perspective, knowledge is believed to be arranged in hierarchies that gradually develop throughout our lives. A person first acquires lower-order skills onto which higher-order skills are anchored. It is assumed that learning occurs when a person can relate new knowledge to existing knowledge through the use of rules (particularly verbal rules). It is assumed that deficits in lower-order skills and/or knowledge bases will impede the learning of higher-order skills that will in turn impair our thinking and problem-solving abilities.

Memory organization. Memory organization appears to be crucial with respect to the transfer of information from the STM to the LTM system. In fact, one of the major differences between atypical and typical learners appears to lie in the former's inability to organize information for transfer to the LTM system and to use strategies (e.g., rehearsal, mnemonics, and production of images) that typical learners ordinarily use in order to keep meaningless information in STM before transferring the information to the LTM store.

Emotion (state-dependent memory). Emotions may have a substantial impact on how information is processed during problem solving (Lazarus, 1991; Zajonc, 1984). For example, research has indicated that emotional reactions reduce flexibility in problem solving and that frustration reduces fluency. Thus, some people experiencing strong emotional reactions may be less likely to access some of their knowledge and bring that knowledge into working memory. Emotions appear to be differentially attached to certain components of declarative (content) knowledge and procedural knowledge and are selectively triggered in the retrieval activation process. Thus, identification of a concept with a strong emotion attached to it brings the emotional response into the working memory along with the concept. Emotional reactions can be so ambiguous and painful that it is difficult for a person to cognitively process relevant information pertaining to the emotional reactions, or they can be so painful that strong avoidant patterns of responding are developed and repressed.

Mood. Mood as a constraint can also be subsumed under the concept of state-dependent learning. These mood states may manifest their effects on learning in two ways: (1) they may affect the nature of the materials selected for encoding; and (2) they may provide access routes to coded memories. The experimental work conducted by Gordon Bower (1981) and his associates indicates that learning is mood dependent.

Language. Language appears to be an important tool through which learning is accomplished. Achievement of higher levels of thought are believed to be closely tied to verbal development. Verbal memory appears to be a very important component of the memory system, in that new knowledge may be meaningfully integrated into this system. Although there are other forms of memory (imagery and episodic), these are likely to remain at a relatively primitive level, until the knowledge they contain can be further encoded in a detailed verbal symbolic form. Thus, language is believed to be the key to success with respect to academic intelligence, doing well in school, and achieving in the workplace.

Personality. Personality variables may either constrain or facilitate the learning process. For example, introversion-extraversion (I-E) is a commonly identified personality dimension. The I-E dimension has been conceptualized as directing one's attention habitually inward more than outward (I), or vice versa (E). With respect to problem solving, introverts may have difficulty detecting problems in the environment, and extroverts may have difficulty getting problems properly encoded. In short, personality differences will most likely be evident when information is encoded and are believed to be related to problem detection, formation, and solution (Lazarus, 1991).

Cognitive style. The manner in which people process data or information (i.e., their cognitive style) is another major source of variation in performance and, consequently, in thinking and problem solving. Several dimensions have been used to describe individual differences in cognitive style (e.g., top-down vs. bottom-up processing, reflective vs. impulsive, and field-independent vs. field-dependent styles). With regard to the first cognitive style dimension, persons who hypothesize aspects of the entire pattern in the sensory array in order to identify specific parts use a top-down style. Those who use specific lists and pieces of sensory input to generate problem solutions use a bottom-up style. For the most part, the top-down hypothesis testing processing style is more efficient and is more advantageous in academic work. The bottom-up processor's attention seems to be more distracted.

With regard to the reflective-impulsive cognitive style dimension, reflectives are usually considered to be more efficient problem solvers, whereas the impulsives plunge in, make mistakes, and then have to back up to arrive at a correct solution (Kagan, 1966; Neimark, 1975). It should be noted that these findings are tempered by the type of problem to be solved. With regard to the field independence-field dependence cognitive style dimension, field-independent learners seem to learn more under intrinsic motivation conditions, have more definite internalized values and standards to regulate their behavior, persevere more, and are more systematic in their learning activities. Field-dependent learners, in contrast, are better at perceiving relational networks, are better at incidental learning of social stimuli, and adapt better to new requirements (Heppner & Krauskoff, 1987).

Motivation. Those who study motivation are primarily concerned with how actions are activated and selected. Motives regulate the extent to which learning is energized and the direction of behaviors (i.e., what is learned). From a cognitive science perspective, a person's cognitive system mediates most external or internal instigators to action. This cognitive mediating system gives rise to individual differences among learners. The assumption is that human reactions to such common motivators as strong environmental stimulation and/or biological drives can be cognitively controlled. That is to say that rather than being moved by external forces, human beings are most often motivated by cognitive representations of future outcomes. It is believed that we can learn to control these cognitive motivators (expectations). A second source of cognitive motivation lies in goal-setting and self-reinforcement (i.e., in self-regulatory processes) (Bandura, 1978). Self-motivation results from setting and making commitments to goals and defining standards by which one evaluates his or her goal-attaining behavior. Self-regulation seems to be at the heart of such phenomena as achievement motivation, power motivation, competence motivation, curiosity, and our thirst for "knowledge of results." See Training Application 5.2.

UNANSWERED QUESTIONS

Many educators and trainers have assumed that the difference between the atypical learner and the typical learner is due to some sort of deficit in a processing ability. Is this deficit view supported in the literature? In this section, we address the following questions: What are the documented differences between typical and atypical learners? How are individual difference variables explained by theoreticians from different camps of thought? What holds promise for future interventions?

As noted earlier, psychologists have attempted to establish general laws of learning, like the ones found in the natural sciences, but have had a great deal of trouble in doing so. In general, they have found that the learning principles of contiguity and reinforcement are applicable to all individuals but the **differences between typical and atypical learners** seem to lie in the cognitive mediational style differences of **attention, memory organization, and cognitive style expectancies**. As was noted in Chapter 4, theorists from different theoretical camps have dealt with individual differences in thinking, problem solving, and creativity from different points of view.

According to the **neo-associationists,** individual differences may have biological origins and/or have to do with differences in learned habits. It is the accumulation of experience, not the cognitive remodeling of experience, that is considered to be important to the neo-associationists. From this point of view, we need to set up learning situations so that learners can acquire more habits.

The **Gestaltists** viewed individual differences in terms of perceptual differences. Most perceptions are considered to be learned. In the process of learning, we develop memories, our memories set up expectancies and those expectancies affect the way we perceive environmental events. It is here, using these learned perceptual templates that we filter and pigeon-hole information. It should be noted that these templates can either retard or facilitate learning.

Piagetians and neo-Piagetians look at individual differences with respect to cognitive differences. These cognitive differences have to do with schematic representations. Thinking and problem solving are viewed in terms of a process of accommodation and assimilation, and all thinking is viewed as being creative.

The **information-processing theorists** view individual differences as being either fixed (differences in attention, maturation, and temperament) or flexible (knowledge, language, memory organization, mood, attitudes, personality, cognitive style, expectancies, and motivation).

What do we know about the differences in **attention, memory, organization, and cognitive style expectancies** among us? We know (Miller, 1956) that **normal learners can attend to 7 + 2 things**. Typical and atypical learners are thought to differ with respect to the bits of information they can attend to without assistance. We know that with increasing age and experience, the bits become more cognitively differentiated and sophisticated. The neo-Piagetians claim that we learn when we develop a verbal rule. From birth to maturity to old age, what develops? Neo-Piagetians claim that attention develops. While attention is viewed as a fixed biologically determined constraint on learning, we are finding that we can learn to control and modify attention. Cherry's (1953) demonstration of the shadow technique supported this notion. Successful efforts within educational contexts have been made to enhance attention (e.g., Rothkopf's (1977) work with schema-activating mathemagenic activities and Brown's (1978) work with training metacognitive skills). In sum, there is evidence supporting the notion that we can increase, direct, and control attention.

Recent research has given us some insight into **memory organization**. We believe that memory has three components (STM-WM-LTM). Short-term memory (STM) and working memory (WM) are considered to be of particular importance since only the material that gets into STM and WM in the first place will be encoded into LTM. Short-term memory is thought to have a limited number of slots (7 + 2). Craik's and Lockhart's (1972) and Tulving's (1972, 1985) work on depth of processing has indicated that the more ways and deeper we process material, the better and easier the recall.

Cognitive style expectancies are considered to be of particular importance with respect to the stable ways in which a learner perceives, encodes, and stores information. H. A. Witkin, C. A. Moore, D. R. Goodenough, and P. W. Cox (1977) found cognitive style differences in expectancies among people and dichotomized learners into two categories (field-dependent and field- independent learners). Field-dependent learners are aware of cues, seek out reinforcement, and are sensitive to the feelings of others. Field-independent learners are more individualistic, intrinsically motivated, and less likely to seek out reinforcement. Bernard Weiner (1986) developed what is termed **attribution theory**. Attributions are considered to be critical variables related to school achievement outcomes. Weiner found that there are stable ways in which learners either attribute successes and/or failures. He divided attributions along the three dimensions of locus of control (internal and external), stability (stable and unstable), and controllability. Most people hold to an egotistic attribution system (Bar-Tel & Darom, 1979). That is to say that we attribute our successes to internal factors (ability, effort) and our failures to external factors (luck, task difficulty). Jerome Kagan (1966) focused his attention on two types of learners (the analytical-reflective learner, who ignores irrelevant stimuli, and the global-impulsive learner, who is quick to make decisions). Remember, we are talking about cognitive style expectancies here. Both students and teachers have expectancies. We need to be careful about how teachers attribute success and failure to themselves and to others. As Delbir Bar-Tal (1979) noted, teachers tend to take credit for their student's successes but blame student failures on external (nonteacher) causes. This tends to be an ego-maintaining mechanism in all of us.

Cronbach (1975) examined the split in psychology between the **experimental and correlational camps of thought**. He reported that the experimental psychologist has been primarily interested in the variations he or she creates (i.e., that individual differences are annoyances that are relegated to error variance). In contrast, correlational psychologists have focused their attention on individual differences and predicting variance across treatment conditions. Experimental psychologists search for the one best method of intervention; correlational psychologists describe differences among learners prior to and after interventions. Cronbach called for a greater unity between the two disciplines. He called for the development of a unified applied psychology, one that simultaneously deals with individual difference person variables and treatment conditions. His overall plan was to match individual differences in aptitudes (A) to different treatment (T) conditions. He reported that some people learn more easily with one method than another. He advocated looking at individual differences (A) and varying the treatment (T) at the same time. In this manner, we are able to develop **an aptitude-treatment interaction methodology (ATI)** that provides us with a procedure to match individual differences (i.e., aptitudes) and different teaching methods (treatments). Cronbach claimed that there is no way to separate the two (i.e., the aptitudes and the treatment) and that you can't dismiss one or the other as simple error variance.

More recently, Resnick (1981) examined the differences among developmental, experimental, and differential (correlational) psychologists and their respective impacts on education. Resnick noted that the dominant sources in educational theory have been developmental and differential psychology. However, neither of these dominant views is compatible with the power of education to bring about behavior change. Developmental psychologists have shown us more ways of not interfering with development rather than actively promoting it. For the most part, differential psychologists have classified and described individual difference characteristics among learners. They have encouraged us to adapt our instructional procedures to these individual differences among learners and not to try to change them. Resnick advocates a shift in our thinking. Because educators and workplace trainers are now dealing with many previously invisible segments of the population (special education students), we are no longer in a position to be content with high student drop-out rates, failures in the workplace, and/or illiteracy in general. Resnick noted a shift in social goals and assumptions. We are working toward improving environments for learning. Education and educators are beginning to believe in the power of education to change things. The view is that educators are not just the guardians of childhood. Educators are the shapers of adults and societies. Resnick sees a great deal of educational potential within the field of experimental psychology, particularly cognitive experimental psychology. For example, we should teach both content and procedural memory strategies. We need to set up programs to modify student (and teacher) expectancies. It is important for learners to believe that they are in control, to be actively involved, and responsible for their learning. We should make systematic attempts to match aptitudes to treatment conditions in the form of ATI designs of instruction. DeCharms (1976) demonstrated that teachers can be taught to teach learners to feel as origins rather than pawns of their own behavior. Heckhausen, Schmalt, and Schneider (1985) and Fosterling (1985) showed that the motive to achieve can be altered and that we need to get learners to talk to themselves in more appropriate ways. If we know what a learner's attribution patterns are, we can match them to an appropriate instructional procedure or modify them if found to be maladaptive. We have many laboratory findings waiting to be applied in natural school and workplace settings with atypical learners. We seem to need to free ourselves from the notions that behavior is limited by individual differences and developmental constraints. Yes, atypical learners may have deficient information-processing skills with respect to attention, memory organization, and cognitive style expectancies. The assumption is that, we can indeed modify these variables to minimize individual differences among learners that may constrain their learning activities and problem-solving performance.

ETHICS

Perhaps the most basic law that has had a profound impact upon psychology and educational psychology dates back to the 1954 **Brown vs. Board of Education** decision, in which it was decided that separate is different rather than equal and that the placement of black and white students in separate facilities violated the equal protection clause of the 14th Amendment. This decision has clearly had an impact with respect to the regular education initiative (REI), where it is again being argued that the provision of separate educational training programs for disabled, atypical learners is not equitable. That is to say that children with disabilities should not be segregated in special classes because of their uniqueness.

The **Americans with Disabilities Act of 1990 (ADA)** is a recent statutory law that is a revision of Section 504 of the Rehabilitation Act of 1973. This law is an attempt to begin to remedy the discrimination against individuals with disabilities in the areas of education, employment, transportation, recreation, communication, voting, access to public areas, and so forth. It emphasizes the notion that separate is not equal and that **inclusion** in society is necessary to protect the rights of disabled persons.

The **Individuals with Disabilities Education Act (IDEA-1990)** is another recently established law that is a reauthorization of the landmark Education for Handicapped Children's Act (commonly known and referred to as **PL 94-142**) that mandated a free, appropriate education in the least restrictive environment for all children with disabilities. This act, unlike the ADA, is funded and created a permanent federal grant program to the states. It is required that all children be placed in the least restrictive environment and that procedures be implemented to insure that all children have the opportunity to learn with a diverse sampling of their peers.

The **Larry P. vs. Riles Case** (1979) emphasized that placement outside the regular classroom was justified only if the child was receiving additional benefit from the special classroom. It was decided in this case that the use of an IQ test for the placement of African-American educable mentally handicapped (EMH) children in a special classroom was considered to be discriminatory. In California, the recommended practice was to replace the IQ test and to use measures of adaptive behavior, interviews, and past performance to determine whether or not a minority child was to be placed in an EMH setting. However, in another case, the **PASE vs. Hannon case** (1980), it was determined that the use of IQ tests for the placement of African-American students in EMH classroom was not discriminatory. Only a few items on the WISC were found to be culturally biased. Therefore, the PASE decision said that it was indeed all right to use IQ tests for the placement of students (of any ethnicity) into EMH programs. Taken together, these two cases have raised our awareness to the notion of possible bias related to our measures of intelligence and have encouraged us to continue to revise our tests and assessment procedures to insure that they are as culturally fair as they can be.

The **Buckley Amendment** (1972) is another federal statute relating to access, confidentiality, and accuracy of educational and/or psychological records. Adults have the right to review their records. In addition, parents have the right to view their child's record in its entirety and to see whether there are any inaccuracies reported in the file. The raw data collected from assessment are considered to be the child's property. If requested by the parents, school officials are required to surrender the assessment information. It must be added, however, that school officials also have the ethical responsibility to do all that they can to protect the confidentiality and validity of the test protocols. The only information that is considered to be "our own" is our personal information (i.e., private notes taken about a client and not reported to others).

It is important to note that when we (educators and/or workplace trainers) assess behavior, we are obligated to keep all information confidential with two exceptions. In the case of persons who plan to harm themselves and/or others (**Tarasoff vs. Board of Regents**, 1976) or if there is suspected abuse taking place, we are required to warn the threatened person(s) and to report the situation to legal authorities. That is to say that if we suspect abuse, we are considered to be mandated reporters by laws and we must report all abuse to the proper authorities. If a third party has been identified, we have to take reasonable and professionally appropriate steps to inform them of the possible danger.

Finally, it should be noted that professional standards include protecting the welfare of the consumer (getting informed and voluntary consent, letting them know about the effectiveness of the treatment provided), using culturally fair measures, using our services responsibility, supporting moral and legal standards (federal and legal statues apply to us), establishing and maintaining professional relationships (we have to work as a member of a professional team), maintaining confidentiality, and maintaining professional competencies to perform assessments and/or interventions.

CONSIDERATION OF HUMAN VALUES AND THE USE OF AUTOMATIC CUTTING SCORES IN DECISION MAKING

In order to make informed decisions with regard to the **placement** of persons in school and workplace settings, test results are frequently used to improve decision making. The public perception of this process is that a somewhat arbitrary **cutting score** is used to decide which learners are to be assigned to a particular program of study. Because the cutting score is perceived by many to be rather arbitrary, and because the score is based on test results that are viewed as not being totally valid or reliable nor reflecting a person's ability in all aspects of schooling or working, many believe that serious errors are made when we attempt to relate assessment results to educational and/or workplace placements. The trick is to attempt to minimize the errors in the direction of special concern for certain types of human values. Generally, **two types of errors** are considered (false positives and misses).

Graphically, the miss-false positive situation looks like this:

	II	I
SUCCESSFUL	miss	correct decision
FAILURE	III correct decision	IV false positive

CUTTING SCORE

REJECT   ACCEPT

where: Scores appearing in quadrants I and III represent correct decisions.
Scores appearing in quadrant II are misses (i.e., false negatives).
Scores appearing in quadrant III are false positives.

The assessor starts out with a hypothesis. There is no difference between the assessed person and the person in the normal population. A **false positive** would occur if, based on a person's test results (the person's score was above the cutting score), he or she were considered to be "normal" but subsequently failed in school and/or at work because of learning, intellectual, personality, and/or behavior problems that had not been detected. A **miss** (i.e., a false negative) would occur if, based on a person's test results (the person's score was below the cutting score), he or she were called "atypical" but would have succeeded in a regular class and/or normal workplace setting if given the opportunity. A true-to-life example related to minimizing misses exists in the legislation (PL 94-142) that changed the definition of the educable mentally handicapped (EMH) to include only those children having IQs two standard deviations or more below the mean (55-70) in addition to having limited social intelligence. Prior to the enactment of PL 94-142 in 1975, EMH children had been defined as those having IQs of only one or more standard deviations (70-85) below the mean. Many of these mildly retarded children were found to be able to do as well in regular classes as in special EMH classes. That is to say that they represented misses. Given the lack of empirical evidence supporting special class placement for these children, it was decided that it is better to give them an opportunity to succeed in a regular (mainstreamed) class, free of the stigma associated with the assignment of a diagnostic label. That is to say that it was decided that we were willing to give a person with a relatively low IQ score a chance to perform at an acceptable level in a regular class. We moved the cutting score to the left (from 70-85 to 55-70) to minimize the number of possible misses.

Sometimes, more accurate decisions are made when base rates are taken into account than when decisions are made merely on the basis of predictive validity. The important thing is to use the method of prediction that minimizes errors (misses and false positives), while maximizing concern for human values and the ultimate ramifications (societal and personal) of the decision.

You must consider the **type of decision** to be made and its overall importance. Generally, in **academic and workplace situations**, you want to guard against the misses. But in **life or death situations** (e.g., when a person threatens to harm others or appears to be suicidal, when a surgeon decides whether or not to operate on a tumor, or when you wish to train pilots to fly airplanes), one would move the cutting score to the right to ensure that false positive choices are not made.

When assigning cutting scores, one must attempt to take into consideration potential assessment biases, particularly those due to **cultural differences**. Disproportionate numbers of persons in lower SES, racial and/or ethnic minority groups tend to fall into the "miss" category, probably not as much from true IQ or personality differences as from the fact that the tests tend to be normed on middle-class, white, English-speaking persons. To the extent that there are cultural differences in levels of success or failure, bias is introduced. Assessors have made moves to attempt to alleviate some of this potential bias by mandating that tests be given in a person's native language or primary mode of communication and also by allowing no single procedure to be the sole criterion for recommending a person's placement in a special program, class, or workplace setting.

In general, the average IQ scores earned by groups of minorities tend to be lower (15 to 20 points lower) than those earned by groups of nonminorities (Brody, 1992). Findings such as these add considerable fuel to the nature-nurture debate. While we as assessors of intelligence and personality do not wish to eliminate all differences that truly and inherently exist among people, it is important that we attempt to **minimize bias** due to the specification of the criterion, the type of standardization group used for test result interpretation, and the language in which the test is administered. The fact that there is indeed a **literate bias in schooling**, which is reflected by the relatively high predictive validity of the verbal components of IQ tests to school and/or workplace performances, is a source of bias to be recognized and reckoned with when considering human values regarding the facilitation of equal and appropriate opportunities for all.

We must also be aware of the extent to which situational variables and an individual's prior experience enter into test results and how these factors influence the determination of the cutting scores in the overall decision-making process. In addition, an awareness of naturally occurring learner characteristics (e.g., SES) may act to predispose an evaluator's and/or instructor's expectations about a learner's performance and thus may enter into the decision-making process. Performance expectations are based on these characteristics, so human values may also play a major part here.

SELECTION AND PLACEMENT DECISIONS

Predictive validity and incremental validity are the keys to the process of making accurate selection and/or placement decisions. **Incremental validity** is a primary concern because it represents the "amount" of value a given instrument or piece of information provides to the overall decision-making process without being redundant and reaching a point of diminishing returns. Essentially, the more incremental validity information one has, the better the prediction. **Predictive validity** refers to the correlations between a set of predictors and the criterion of interest.

Another side of the selection and placement decision issue is whether or not one is using an appropriate criterion and/or predictor(s). These are issues related to bias. **Bias** may be involved in determining the criterion. For example, in decision making, tests should be used to discriminate on relevant factors, not irrelevant ones. Although IQ scores discriminate rather well between those who are successful in school and/or the workplace and those who are not, they also seem to discriminate between those of different SES and/or racial groups. Are the tests "fair"? Yes and no. Yes, they are fair in that they predict school and job success equally well across SES and racial groups (Brody, 1992). But many low SES and nonwhite groups do not do well on these IQ tests, apparently for related (the literate bias in schooling) but perhaps unjust reasons (not being a part of mainstream middle-class culture). The issue of possible bias also applies to the use of personality tests such as the MMPI in that "appropriate" behavior in one group (enacting nonaggressive middle-class values) may be considered "deviant" in another (reflecting the need to aggress to survive in the inner city). That is to say that the majority standards apply in norming the tests. The question becomes: Are the test validating criteria fair? Other areas of possible bias involve using tests for purposes for which they were not designed (e.g., using the MMPI or Rorschach for a job/employment decision in a nonclinical population). Should test use be viewed as a purely scientific (i.e., psychometric) process, or should consideration be given to qualitative judicial/social components of the decision-making process? With respect to coming to terms with the issue of bias, the jury is still out.

The **relationship** between **assessment** and **testing** is another relevant issue. The difference between assessment and testing is in some ways related to bias; psychologists sometimes say that testing can be done by a monkey, but it takes a person to do an assessment. The assessment process is viewed as going beyond mere testing in that it involves integrating various sources of quantitative and qualitative information such as knowledge of learning, human development, theories of intelligence, and personality theory. That is to say that when we assess behavior, we approach the task from a **holistic perspective**. Testing consists of compiling the data set without the interpretive dimension of integrating the information and applying our clinical expertise to systematically building and testing hypotheses.

Sometimes factors such as inexperience and overconfidence, which usually go together, come into play in selection and placement decisions. These factors may adversely affect our professional judgments.

In addition to the social justice issues mentioned earlier, some attention should be given to **privacy** and **inviolacy** issues. Clients are not always aware of the kinds of information we are gathering with our various assessment tools. Our assumption is that if they do know, the test results could possibly be skewed by a client's **response set** (i.e., deliberately attempting to project a certain image of themselves) or a client's distorting **response style** (i.e., a stable pattern of response). The client also has a right to some privacy with respect to taboo subjects such as sexual practices and religious views that are not directly related to a job or school selection decision. Ethically, the assessor's responsibility is to protect the best interests and rights of the client. There is not always a clear-cut situation, and conflicts may arise with respect to determining who the client is. That is to say, is the client the child, the parents, or the school? Is the client the employee or the employer?

Finally, there are a few issues related to the **special problems of assessing children**. Judgments that one might make on the basis of using intelligence and personality tests should not be the same for children as for adults. When dealing with children, it is very important to look at where the child is developmentally. Given that the psychometric adequacy of many of the tests is rather questionable when the tests are used with adults, the psychometric adequacy of the tests is even more questionable when the tests are used with children. Behavioral-cognitive approaches are perhaps best, although serious psychometric problems also exist with these approaches. Checklists and rating scales designed to assess a child's intellectual functioning and personality are often completed by parents and teachers who may inadvertently impose their own distorted perceptions on the child they are rating.

EQUITY ISSUES RELATED TO THE ASSESSMENT OF INTELLIGENCE

The overall theme of this chapter was to keep intelligence tests in perspective. That is to say that intelligence is only one measure of worth. First of all, it was noted that there are many eminent psychologists and educators who question whether intelligence tests have any real meaning. However, it was also noted that most scholars in the field believe that intelligence tests do indeed measure important thinking and problem solving skills that may be reasonably thought of as intelligence.

African-American/White Differences

It is recognized that IQ tests are good predictors of academic and job success when the criterion is performance in a middle-class academically competitive situation (Brody, 1992; Herrnstein & Murray, 1994). It is also recognized that intelligence test scores are not fixed. The tests have been found to be equally predictive across ethnic groups. Yes, there are differences between African-Americans and whites, and these differences have remained constant for several decades. The differences appear to develop early, sometime after the first year of life. That is to say that the differences are present prior to school entry. The magnitude of the difference (one standard deviation) has not been found to change over the elementary school years.

What are the reasons for these differences? There is considerable evidence supporting a biological explanation for whites. Much less data exist for African-Americans. We need more data related to African-American adoption studies and transrace adoption studies. Since the two groups are exposed to different environments, it is always possible to attribute group differences to the environment. African-Americans and whites are reared in quasi-segregated environments in which they have different cultural exposures to art, music, and language. It is probably fair to say that Jensen (1980) and Herrnstein and Murray (1994) are correct in asserting that measures of environmental influence do not account for African-American/white differences. However, it should be noted that the genetic hypothesis is not confirmed by the disconfirmation of environmental influences. These are indirect, incomplete arguments. In sum, the genetic hypothesis is not clearly testable at this time.

Japanese and Chinese Groups

It is interesting to note that in the early 1920s, Japanese and Chinese groups were reported to exhibit cognitive deficits. Today, these groups exhibit a consistent pattern of stronger performance, particularly on nonverbal tests. Japanese and Chinese children and adults also tend to be more lateralized with respect to processing information. These positive differences have been found to increase with age. It has been hypothesized that a differential emphasis on formal and abstract elements in the Japanese and Chinese curricula might increase fluid intelligence. Much remains to be done to explain these differences (Flynn, 1991).

Gender Differences

Many researchers have documented female superiority with respect to verbal ability (Halpern, 1991). However, these positive differences have declined and now represent only one-tenth of one standard deviation difference. This small difference appears to have little, if any, practical or theoretical significance. Males have greater spatial abilities. In addition, males are able to break sets more easily and are able to solve certain types of problems more quickly. Males are also like the Japanese and Chinese groups in that they appear to be more lateralized. To date, there is little convincing data supporting a socialization explanation for these gender differences.

Future of Intelligence Tests

It is probably fair to say that on balance, the tests are more nearly right than wrong. The tests increase accuracy with respect to special education placements. At the same time, the tests are at least partially responsible for the warehousing (labeling) of children and adults. One could argue that special education and tracking programs may have only marginal influences over what a child learns in school. The elimination of IQ tests for placement would probably have only a marginal influence with respect to special education placements.

The tests inform us that race in America is weakly linked to differences in academic aptitude. Attacking the tests will do little to mask the underlying reality revealed by the tests. We may have come as far as we can with the assessment of intelligence by psychometric procedures. We do not have a clear explanation for the documented differences across groups. The genetic hypothesis is not clearly testable at this time. Our attempts to modify intelligence have made some progress. It is recommended that continued attention be given to alternative assessment procedures (e.g., Sternberg's strategy training procedures, Feuerstein's dynamic assessment procedures, curriculum-based assessment procedures, performance-based assessment procedures). The basic question remains. Can we accommodate and/or eliminate the individual differences in cognitive functioning within and across groups in the years to come?

TERMS TO KNOW

intelligence
Robert Sternberg
triarchic theory of intelligence
componential intelligence
metacomponents (executive processes)
performance variables
knowledge acquisition components
experiential component
contextual intelligence
Howard Gardner's seven types of intelligence
Lev Vygotsky
zone of proximal development (ZPD)
scaffolding
Reuven Feuerstein
dynamic assessment
mediated learning teaching experience
test-teach-test approach

reciprocal teaching model
Learning Potential Assessment Device (LPAD)
instrumental enrichment program
behavioral assessment
information-processing assessment procedures
curriculum-based assessment (CBA)
performance-based assessment (PBA)
biological constraints
psychological constraints
aptitude-treatment-interaction methodology
a miss (false negative)
a false positive
predictive validity
incremental validity
holistic perspective
response style
response set
inclusion
Brown vs. Board of Education (1954)
The Americans with Disabilities Act (1990)
The Individuals with Disabilities Act (IDEA 1990; PL 94-142, 1975)
Larry P. vs. Riles (1979)
Pase vs. Hannon (1980)
Buckley Amendment (1972)
Tarasoff vs. Board of Regents (1976)

QUESTIONS TO CONSIDER

1. Present an evaluative discussion of the ways in which researchers are now attempting to assess and teach intelligence.

2. The view of intelligence has changed from a rather static model that examined it in terms of factor analysis to an approach that utilizes information-processing and developmental constructs. This latter approach allows for pragmatic methods of changing "intelligence." Discuss those developments that are changing the way we are viewing intelligence and what can be done to assess and/or modify intelligence.

3. In every field of inquiry there are difficult questions that continually attract the attention of scholars. Identify what you consider to be the essential unanswered questions in the field of intelligence and discuss how key thinkers have addressed these questions during different historical periods.

4. Does there continue to be a reason to measure intelligence? If yes, what

is (are) the reason(s), and how do we measure it in a valid way? If no, why not? How (and with what) will we replace the importance focused on the measurement of intelligence in our society?

5. Critically evaluate the extent to which assessment information has been successfully used to plan treatment interventions. In your discussion make certain that you present a detailed description and critique of assessment interventions.

6. Write a short essay concerning the use of automatic cutting scores in making decisions and the possibility of their ignoring human values.

7. Discuss the legal regulations of psychology with respect to psychological assessments and interventions. Make certain that your answer integrates the ethical standards of the profession, statutory law, and case law.

8. Publication of *The Bell Curve: Intelligence and Class Structure in American Life* (Herrnstein & Murray, 1994) has stimulated considerable discussion about an old argument. Discuss the basic premises of the authors, the nature of the data they use to support their position, the reasons that their views are controversial, and the book's likely implications for future study in the area.

SUGGESTED READINGS

Readers wanting to study more thoroughly the topics covered in this chapter will find the following references helpful.

Brody, N. (1992). *Intelligence*. New York: Academic Press.

Ceci, S. J. (1990). *On intelligence ... more or less. A bio-ecological treatise on intellectual development*. Englewood Cliffs, NJ: Prentice-Hall.

Gardner, H. (1983). *Frames of mind*. New York: Basic Books.

Herrnstein, R. J., & Murray, C. (1994). *The bell curve: Intelligence and class structure in American life*. New York: Free Press.

Sternberg, R. J. (1986). *The triarchic mind: A new theory of human intelligence*. New York Cambridge University Press.

TRAINING APPLICATION 5.1
Assessment Models

The outcomes-based paradigm shift is also shaping how we view assessment. For decades we assumed that assessment was an end in itself. Now we look to assessment as a vehicle for learning improvement. It is important to ask what is gained by various assessment models.

Norm-referenced standardized tests	Provide a global picture of what a population in general knows in a timed-testing situation.
Criterion-referenced tests	Provide information about an individual's proficiency in or mastery of a specific skill or set of skills.
Curriculum-based measurements	Provide measurement of an individual's performance on a single type of task repeated over time as a measure of progress toward a specific long-term learning goal. For example, to determine reading accuracy an individual completes a weekly one-minute reading passage. Each week the number of words correctly read in the passage is calculated and graphed. The passages are about 250 words in length and randomly selected from materials used in the literacy training program or in the workplace. An optimal performance, or goal line, is set each week as a target for improvement.
Alternative assessments	Provide a collection of products that demonstrate coherence of knowledge across content domains, problem solving, access and utilization of information, automaticity of basic skills, and metacognitive skills. Performance portfolios are judged against specific performance standards known as rubrics.
Authentic tasks	Provide a measurement of essential performances that are measured in "authentic" problems and situations. Authentic tasks are product oriented; they call upon individuals to use multidimensional problem-solving skills to collect and assemble information, to define alternatives, to select a problem solution, and to evaluate the possible outcomes of that solution. Authentic tasks are untimed, and performance is measured against a set of scoring criteria that are made explicit to the individual prior to their engagement in the assessment. Authentic tasks also utilize learner self-assessment, providing standards by which learners can review and analyze their own performances.

TRAINING APPLICATION 5.2
Enhancing Motivation

Trainers can use varying instructional practices to convey information to participants about how well they are learning. Students can use these motivational cues to assess "learnability" of content being presented (Schunk, 1991, pp. 256-257).

Purpose of instruction	Referring to the uses participants will make of content to be learned.
Content difficulty	Referring to the level of knowledge or skills needed to be successful in a learning task.
Cognitive processing	Varying the kinds of strategies participants use to process information (e.g., video presentation requires less mental effort from participants than lecture).
Strategy training	Overt training of learning strategies concurrently with content presentation.
Instructional presentation	Presenting information in organized small chunks, utilizing various instructional design strategies to enhance recall.
Performance feedback	Providing opportunities for participants to check their progress against personal goals, training outcomes, or improvement targets. The trainer also provides participants with specific corrective or supportive feedback during learning tasks.
Models	Providing opportunities for participants to observe the trainer and/or peers successfully demonstrating a learning task.
Goal setting	Providing opportunities for participants to set personal learning and performance goals prior to training, and to review their progress toward these goals during training.
"Perks"	Small, unexpected rewards tied to participants' progress (e.g., extended break, early dismissal, afternoon snacks, performance certificates).
Attributional feedback	Linking participants' successes or failures to specific causes within their own performances.

CHAPTER 6

PERSONALITY ASSESSMENT

HISTORY OF PERSONALITY ASSESSMENT

The **history of personality assessment** has been described by some as far from stable and uneventful. When personality assessment techniques were first introduced in the 1940s and 1950s, personality assessment flourished, and many clinical psychologists prided themselves on assessment as their main clinical function. However, after World War II ended, many structural and theoretical changes took place within the profession and society at large that ultimately led to a period of marked decline in clinical testing during the late 1950s, 1960s, and early 1970s.

In the immediate postwar era, the field of psychodiagnosis (a combination of psychodynamic and psychometric theories) was prominent. At that time, personality assessment was viewed in a positive light. A clinician's main purpose/goal was to assess and describe an individual in as full, multifaceted, and multileveled way as possible. A number of objective and projective procedures were used to tap both conscious and unconscious processes. Use of clinical judgment and inference were highly valued, as well as the process of integrating assessment findings into a coherent whole. However, this positive situation did not last. Many factors began to emerge that ultimately led to a serious **decline** in personality assessment. It is ironic to note that although a decline in testing took place during the late 1950s, 1960s, and early 1970s, today many of us are gradually returning to our once highly valued assessment roots.

The factors and occurrances that contributed to the decline in personality testing (during the postwar era) were reviewed by Sheldon J. Korchin and David Schuldberg (1981) and Theodore Millon (1984). The two major events that reportedly led to this **decline** included the following: (1) new roles opened up for clinical psychologists that included more prominent therapeutic, administrative, and research-oriented roles; and (2) the newly emerging theories (humanistic and behavioral) and perspectives (psychometric) were to some extent found to be incompatible with the clinical assessment process. **Humanists** viewed testing as an intrusion on the client and a process that deprived the client of individuality, dignity, and the ability to be his or her own assessor. In addition, the claim was made that assessors also labeled their clients instead of viewing them as unique individuals. **Behaviorists** rejected intrapsychic processes and were only interested in observable behavior. For the most part, the behaviorists rejected traits and focused their attention on situational factors. That is to say that they rejected most personality assessment tools based on personality constructs (traits). **Psychometricians** criticized clinicians and devalued the subjective/intrapsychic judgments made by them. They emphasized the importance of reliability, validity, and other measurement issues (objectivity). They devalued the artistry involved in traditional assessment procedures. Other factors such as abuses of tests by using them to deny opportunities to disadvantaged persons in personnel assessment and the fact that testing was expensive and was intended to be used within the context of long-term treatment (which was no longer the norm) also helped contribute to a decline in testing.

In addition to the two major events cited above, there was a concurrent **decline in personality theory**. The behaviorists were not interested in the assessment of individual differences and/or establishing coherent gestalts. Their focus was on describing and manipulating observable behaviors. Very little attention was given to personality variables. Millon (1984) also noted the negative influence of a very damaging book written by Walter Mischel and published in 1968. Mischel (1968) challenged the utility of personality constructs, intrapsychic coherence, and the notion of behavioral consistency. In addition, Millon reported that there had been a decline in the 1960s of the intuitive, analytic, abstract-minded, ambiguity-tolerant student pursuing graduate degrees in psychology. At the time, **graduate training programs** were **deemphasizing testing** and if it was taught, it was not done so by experienced role models.

In spite of all the negative influences mentioned above, many **new and encouraging trends** are developing within the field of personality assessment. Both Millon (1984) and Korchin and Schuldberg (1981) recognize the trend reverting back to former **holistic approaches**. They cite the MMPI as a good example. The **MMPI** is considered to be an empirically sound instrument. Clinicians are now using the MMPI scales in a cohesive, holistic, and integrated manner. In addition, some projective tests such as the Rorschach that were severely criticized for their low empirical value are now being improved (e.g., the development of the **Exner scoring system** for the Rorschach). The use of the clinical interview as an informal means of assessment has also emerged. In addition, some clinicians now use one or two TAT cards or Rorschach cards to get a quick fix on a client's reality testing during **crisis intervention interviews**. Millon also reported a re-

cent resurgance of interest in psychoanalytic theory particularly with respect to object relations theory.

Perhaps two of the most profound trends in personality assessment
include **Millon's personality clusters** and the consequent development of
the Millon personality scales (Millon, 1981, 1984). The inclusion of a separate DSM III-R and IV axis (**Axis II**) for personality disorders that are thought
to be long-standing and stable personality styles provides additional support and continuity to the field. It should be noted that Millon (1984) cau-
tions us to remember that these positive developments are just a start and
that the DSM III-R and IV diagnostic criteria and personality clusters currently in use remain only crude first approximations that lack diagnostic
comparability, a strong empirical foundation, and syndrome comprehen-
siveness.

There has also been a recent focus on and emergence of **behavioral-
cognitive assessment** procedures. Attempts have been made to merge
behaviorial and cognitive approaches to assessment. Researchers in the
area have been particularly interested in conducting research studies designed to examine which therapies work best with which types of clients
(Beck, 1991). The cognitive theorists have been very interested in studying
cognitive style. Cognitive style is thought to be one of our most stable traits
and includes field dependence versus field independence, internal versus
external locus of control, reflective versus impulsive thinking, a person's
ability to attend to and chunk information, expectancies, and attributions.
Those cognitive-behavioral researchers who want to determine what type
of treatment works best with a particular type of client focus their efforts
within the context of a typical **ATI design** as indicated below:

| | therapeutic treatments | | |
	X1a	X2a	X3a
	X1b		
stable			
aptitudes	X2b		
(cognitive			
style	X3b		
categories)			

where: X1a - X3a = treatments
        X1b - X3b = stable aptitudes (e.g., IQ, cognitive style,
        attention, attitudes, attributions, expectancies)

An attempt would be made to measure changes on the more unstable aspects of behavior (e.g., how the person does on a series of outcome measures) across different treatments and different cognitive styles. However,

some resistance (Bowers, 1973; Buss, 1989) to the notion of the existence of stable traits continues with those closely associated with the work of Mischel. As mentioned before, Mischel (1968) had a great impact on the decline of personality assessment. He questioned the very nature of the stability of the commonly accepted personality traits, maintaining that one cannot be certain a trait is stable just because it doesn't change over time. Mischel, a social learning psychologist, believed that environments don't change much either, so how do we know that a "stable trait" is simply not just a function of continuing to be exposed to a "stable" environment?

Another promising area of research reflecting newer trends in personality assessment includes studies designed to detect individual differences in **reaction time** that are believed to be indicative of a cognitive style difference among respondents (Eysenck, 1982). For example, a researcher would record response times on problem-solving tasks related to assessing a reflective versus an impulsive style of thinking. It should be noted that reaction time is thought to be one of the few stable traits we can realistically assess in children since even IQ (our most stable trait) and cognitive style (our second most stable trait) are thought to be variable in children under the age of eight.

Finally, as stated above, there has been a recent trend toward using the traditional assessment techniques (TAT cards, Rorschach cards) more informally in an effort to quickly assess a client's reality bases in crisis intervention situations, to determine psychological mindedness and resistance to change, and to break the ice with guarded clients. These test results could also be used within the context of a test-treat-test procedure as an ongoing part of individual or group psychotherapy. In sum, from what is reported above, personality assessment has an interesting history and there are many emerging trends that promise to yield a positive future for the field.

APPROACHES TO ASSESSMENT

Richard I. Lanyon and Leonard D. Goodstein (1992) discussed three approaches to personality assessment (the rational-theoretical, empirical, and internal consistency approaches). They related this trichotomy to **two historical trends** in the development of personality assessment. The rational-theoretical approach was aligned with **clinical** interests and yielded projective assessment techniques. The empirical and internal consistency approaches sprung from **academic** roots, where the focus was on the measurement of individual differences using empirically derived tests. This academic orientation permitted the assessment of personality via paper-and-pencil tests that were easily administered to groups. These tests could be objectively scored, and the results were amendable to statistical manipulations and descriptions.

The clinical emphasis of the **rational-theoretical approach** grew out of the influence of Freud and the Gestalt psychologists. For the most part, these theorists were concerned with global assessments. They assumed that a client could project his or her personality onto an ambiguous field. In contrast, those aligned with the **empirical** and **internal consistency approaches** attended to the overt, specific aspects of personality as evidenced by answers to structured questions on paper-and-pencil tests. Given that some responses are susceptible to social desirability and faking, lie and validity keys were developed to control for response sets and response styles.

There are differences, of course, between the empirical and internal consistency approaches to personality assessment as well as differences between these two approaches and the rational-theoretical approach. They all differ in the source of the stimuli presented to the subject. For the rational theoretically derived instruments, test stimuli are selected that seem to tap behaviors of special interest to the author of the instrument. If the test author is strongly aligned with a specific theory, he or she chooses items designed to assess those constructs within the context of the theory of interest. Examples of rational-theoretically based instruments include sentence completions, the Edwards Personal Preference Schedule (EPPS), the Rorschach, TAT, and projective drawings. On the other hand, empiricists select test stimulus items because of their empirically demonstrated power to discriminate among the groups of interest. Tests based on this approach include the MMPI, Personality Inventory for Children (PIC), and the California Personality Inventory (CPI). Items for the internal consistency approach are a product of using factor analytic procedures on an item pool. Items are chosen that load on factors. These items are assumed to tap the same psychological variable. Originally, the items were developed out of some theoretical framework where the meanings of the factors were elucidated by rational objectives. The internal consistency approach has yielded tests such as R. B. Cattell's 16 PF, Louis and Thelma Thurstone's Temperament Schedule, and J. P. Guilford's scales.

What is the comparative utility of these three approaches to personality assessment? The instruments based on a **rational-theoretical approach** have been found to be useful as ipsative measures, allowing for comparisons within an individual, but appear to be limited with respect to interindividual comparisons. Advocates of the rational-theoretical approach assume that the client can accurately judge himself or herself and truthfully respond. Items that are content relevant are viewed as better than subtle items. However, it should be noted that the psychodynamic theorists believe that many clients receiving psychological evaluations are not able to accurately judge themselves and truthfully respond to the items put to them. In general, there are many limitations associated with the use of the rationally derived instruments. For example: (1) few approaches to personality assessment can really be considered theoretical; (2) fine-grained molecular theories are presently in vogue, while most of the rationally derived instruments are based on a molar framework; (3) most psychologists today are more psychometrically than clinically oriented; (4) there are empirical problems with respect to distinguishing whether a subject's responses are representative of real life or based only on fantasy.

Empirically derived tests fare considerably better than the rationally derived instruments in terms of prediction of behavior (Polyson, Peterson, & Marshall, 1986). However, problems remain with respect to providing a theoretical explanation or determining the underlying etiology of a problem behavior. If the test author fails to cross-validate the items, the test may be replete with errors, and the assessor of personality should be aware of this possibility. Also, if one is interested in assessing an individual suspected of falling within the normal range of behavior, in most instances normative groups were selected for their extreme responses, so it is difficult if not relatively meaningless to assess normal individuals with most of these empirically derived instruments. Finally, there are other factors that could diminish the utility of these empirically derived instruments: (1) little, if any, theoretical information is yielded; (2) the item pool may not be sensitive to group differences and thus not yield discriminating items; and (3) other differences between and among groups may go undetected and distort the test results (i.e., scale factors are probably not "pure").

The predictive usefulness of tests based on the **internal consistency approach** must be demonstrated empirically (i.e., utility is not intrinsic to factorially derived scales). While Raymond B. Cattell (1965) believes that factors reflect personality traits, Walter Mischel (1973, 1977, 1979, 1981, 1984) said that factors may be nothing more than response distortions. That is to say that factors merely reflect the behavioral consistencies constructed by observers and test authors, not the actual consistencies in an individual's behavior.

Lanyon and Goodstein (1992) stated that the emphasis placed on the differences among these three approaches to assessing personality has been to the detriment of the field of personality assessment as a whole. Some psychologists such as Richard Levy (1985) believe that the projective, paper-and-pencil distinction is a spurious one. Paper-and-pencil inventory devices can be and most often are responded to projectively. Psychologists often use a paper-and-pencil profile for global assessment, and projective techniques can be, and often are, scored objectively and interpreted according to carefully constructed norms and empirical evidence. As in many other areas of contemporary psychology, it appears as though personality assessment is now moving toward a more unified, eclectic position.

TRADITIONAL ASSESSMENT

Personality tests typically administered to adult and adolescent subjects include the Thematic Apperception Test (TAT), Rorschach, Bender Visual Motor Gestalt Test, Minnesota Multiphasic Personality Inventory (MMPI-2 or MMPI-A), the Millon Clinical Multiaxial Inventory-III (MCMI-III), sentence completion inventories, the Edwards Personal Preference Schedule (EPPS), California Psychological Inventory (CPI), selected human figure and object drawings, self-reports, and sibling-spouse-employer-friend personality ratings. Children are typically administered the Childrens' Apperception Test (CAT), Rorschach, the Personality Inventory for Children (PIC), Bender Visual Motor Gestalt Test, House-Tree-Person Test, Draw a Person Test, a sentence completion test, verbally administered self-reports, and sibling-friend-parent-teacher personality ratings. A clinical interview is conducted with all clients. A brief description of some of the instruments listed above is presented in this section.

Edwards Personal Preference Schedule (EPPS)

The **Edwards Personal Preference Schedule** (Edwards, 1954, 1992) was developed by A. L. Edwards and was first published in 1953. Its theoretical foundation rests on H. A. Murray's (1938) need-press theory of personality. The EPPS is a nonprojective, forced-choice, objective personality inventory that **measures fifteen normal need variables** (achievement, deference, order, exhibition, autonomy, affiliation, intraception, succorance, dominance, abasement, nurturance, change, endurance, heterosexuality, and aggression).

The instrument is untimed. An average college student completes it in about **forty minutes**. The EPPS was initially designed for college students, although norms exist today for subjects from high school to adult age. Items are written at a seventh-grade reading level.

The eight-page test booklet contains 225 items. There are nine items for each of the fifteen need variables; each item is paired twice with one from every other need, yielding a total of 210 items. Respondents must decide which of each forced pair is more characteristic of them. In addition, fifteen items are repeated to obtain a reliability estimate of the respondent's consistency. The EPPS produces a score for each of the fifteen needs listed and described in Table 6.1 and a consistency score (c).

Table 6.1
Summary Description of the Edwards Personal Preference Schedule Scales

1. **ach-Achievement**: To do one's best, to be successful, to accomplish tasks requiring skill and effort, to be a recognized authority, to accomplish something of great significance, to do a difficult job well, to solve difficult problems and puzzles, to be able to do things better than others, to write a great novel or play.

2. **def-Deference**: To get suggestions from others, to find out what others think, to follow instructions and do what is expected, to praise others, to tell others that they have done a good job, to accept the leadership of others, to read about great persons, to conform to custom and avoid the unconventional, to let others make decisions.

3. **ord-Order**: To have written work neat and organized, to make plans before starting on a difficult task, to have things organized, to keep things neat and orderly, to make advance plans when taking a trip, to organize details of work, to keep letters and files according to some system, to have meals organized and a definite time for eating, to have things arranged so that they run smoothly without change.

4. **exh-Exhibition**: To say witty and clever things, to tell amusing jokes and stories, to talk about personal adventures and experiences, to have others notice and comment upon one's appearance, to say things just to see achievements, to be the center of attention, to use words that others do not know the meaning of, to ask questions others cannot answer.

5. **Aut-Autonomy**: To be able to come and go as desired, to say what one thinks about things, to be independent of others in making decisions, to feel free to do what one wants, to do things that are unconventional, to avoid situations where one is expected to conform, to do things in positions of authority, to avoid responsibilities and obligations.

6. **aff-Affiliation**: To be loyal to friends, to participate in friendly groups, to do things for friends, to form new friendships, to make as many friends as possible, to share things with friends, to do things with friends rather than alone, to form strong attachments, to write letters to friends.

7. **int-Intraception**: To analyze one's motives and feelings, to observe others, to understand how others feel about problems, to put oneself in another's place, to judge people by why they do things rather than by what they do, to analyze the motives of others, to predict how others will act.

8. **suc-Succorance**: To have others provide help when in trouble, to seek encouragement from others, to have others be kindly, to have others be sympathetic and understanding about personal problems, to receive a great deal of affection from others, to have others do favors cheerfully, to be helped by others when depressed, to have others feel sorry when one is sick, to have a fuss made over one when hurt.

9. **dom-Dominance**: To argue for one's point of view, to be a leader in groups to which one belongs, to be regarded by others as a leader, to be elected or appointed chairman of committees, to make group decisions, to settle arguments and disputes between others, to persuade and influence others to do

what one wants, to supervise and direct the actions of others, to tell others how to do their job.

10. **aba-Abasement**: To feel guilty when one does something wrong, to accept blame when things do not go right, to feel that personal pain and misery suffered does more good than harm, to feel the need for punishment for wrong doing, to feel better when giving in and avoiding a fight than when having one's own way, to feel the need for confession of errors, to feel depressed by inability to handle situations, to feel timid in the presence of superiors, to feel inferior to others in most respects.

11. **nur-Nurturance**: To help friends when they are in trouble, to assist others less fortunate, to treat others with kindness and sympathy, to forgive others, to do small favors for others, to be generous with others who are hurt or sick, to show a great deal of affection toward others, to have others confide in one about personal problems.

12. **chg-Change**: To do new and different things, to travel, to meet new people, to experience novelty and change in daily routine, to experiment and try new things, to eat in new and different places, to try new and different jobs, to move about the country and live in different places, to participate in new fads and fashions.

13. **end-Endurance**: To keep at a job until it is finished, to complete any job undertaken, to work hard at a task, to keep at a puzzle or problem until it is solved, to work at a single job before taking on others, to stay up late working in order to get a job done, to put in long hours of work without distraction, to stick at a problem even though it may seem as if no progress is being made, to avoid being interrupted while at work.

14. **het-Heterosexuality**: To go out with members of the opposite sex, to engage in social activities with the opposite sex, to be in love with someone of the opposite sex, to kiss those of the opposite sex, to be regarded as physically attractive by those of the opposite sex, to participate in discussions about sex, to read books and plays involving sex, to listen to or to tell jokes involving sex, to be become sexually excited.

15. **agg-Aggression**: To attack contrary points of view, to tell others what one thinks about them, to criticize others publicly, to make fun of others, to tell others off when disagreeing with them, to get revenge for insults, to become angry, to blame others when things go wrong, to read newspaper accounts of violence.

16. **con-Consistency score**: This score is based on a comparison of the number of identical choices made in two sets of the same fifteen items. The probability of 9 or more identical choices occurring by chance is about 0.30. The probability of 10 or more is 0.15. The probability of 11 or more identical choices being made by chance is about 0.06. The manual suggests that if the consistency score is 11 or higher, the subject is not making choices on the basis of chance alone. A **con** score of 9 or 10 is considered to be acceptable.

For the most part, the information contained in the EPPS manual is not convincing with respect to its articulation of the instrument's validity. The validity data reported in the manual appear to be scanty and inadequate. It is probably fair to say that the EPPS has suffered a handicap from its inception since validity was not emphasized in the original scale development.

In terms of norms, the original manual (Edwards, 1954) contained a data set from 749 college women and 760 men. The revised manual (Edwards, 1992) contained an additional data set based on 4,031 male and 4,932 female heads of households. The newly revised norms (1991) are based on a representative national sample of adults.

In terms of reliability, the revised manual reported spilt-half reliability coefficients for the college student norm group ranging from 0.60 to 0.87 with a median of 0.78. Test-retest coefficients are also listed; these are based on a sample of 89 college students and range from 0.55 to 0.87 with a median of 0.73. For the most part, the reliability of most of the EPPS scales is roughly comparable to that of other personality inventories. Edwards (1992) reported internal consistency estimates of his scales ranging from 0.60 to 0.87. The deference scale was the least reliable scale and the heterosexuality scale was the most reliable.

It should be noted that Edwards (1992) recognized that subjects tend to endorse desirable and reject undesirable items on personality inventories. He sought to minimize this through the use of scaled forced-choice items. Critics have noted, however, that judgments of social desirability are influenced by context; statements in pairs do not necessarily retain the same scale value assigned to them individually. Another argument raised by the critics is that social desirability values are not stable entities equally valid in all times and places; the generalizability of such values is considered to be questionable. Anne Anastasi (1982) stated that a forced choice technique has not been found to be as effective as had been anticipated in controlling faking or social desirability response sets. Research on the EPPS has failed to demonstrate many significant links between test scores and external behaviors, or between test scores and underlying constructs. Finally, it should be noted that a practical consideration in clinical use is that some respondents find forced-choice items to be awkward and rather difficult.

Minnesota Multiphasic Personality Inventory (MMPI-2)

The **MMPI-2** (Butcher, Dahlstrom, Graham, & Tellegen, 1990) consists of 566 self-referenced statements to which subjects respond as applying to them (true) or not applying to them (false). Responses are scored objectively and yield scores for four validity scales and ten clinical (personality descriptor) scales. A summary description of the four MMPI validity scales and the ten clinical scales is presented in Table 6.2 Separate norms are available for males and females. T scores are used to construct a profile that serves as a means to generate inferences about the examinee's personality. The MMPI-1 was published in 1943. It was developed to provide a more efficient way of arriving at appropriate psychodiagnostic evaluations. The MMPI-2, like its predecessor, utilizes an empirical keying approach in the construction of its scales. The items have been empirically derived in an effort to differentiate among groups of subjects who are members of a certain psychodiagnostic category (e.g., the clinically depressed, the violent and dangerous, the manipulative, the narcissistic, etc.).

Table 6.2
Summary Description of the MMPI-2 Validity and Clinical Scales

Validity Scales: ? (Cannot Say) Number of items left unanswered.

L (Lie) Fifteen items of overly good self-reports, such as "I smile at everyone I meet." (Answered True). Dissimulation.

F (Frequency or Infrequency) Sixty-four items answered in the scored direction by 10 percent or less of normals, such as "There is an international plot against me." (Answered True) Highly independent to failing bad to notorious.

K (Correction) Thirty items reflecting defensiveness in admitting to problems, such as "I feel bad when others criticize me." (False) Concern for a good image. Tries to please people and/or conform.

Clinical Scales:

1 or Hs (Hypochondriasis): Thirty-three items derived from patients showing abnormal concern with bodily functions, such as "I have chest pains several times a week." (Answered True)

2 or D (Depression) Sixty items derived from patients showing extreme pessimism, feelings of hopelessness, and slowing of thought and action, such as "I usually feel that life is interesting and worthwhile." (Answered False)

3 or Hy (Conversion Hysteria) Sixty items from neurotic patients using physical or mental symptoms as a way of unconsciously avoiding difficult conflicts and responsibilities, such as "My heart frequently pounds so hard I can feel it." (Answered True)

4 or Pd (Psychopathic Deviates) Fifty items from patients who show a repeated and flagrant disregard for social customs, an emotional shallowness and an inability to learn from punishing experiences, such as "My activities and interests are often criticized by others." (Answered True)

5 or Mf (Masculinity-Femininity) Sixty items from patients showing homo-eroticism and items differentiating between men and women, such as "I like to arrange flowers." (True scored for femininity)

6 or Pa (Paranoia) Forty items from patients showing abnormal suspiciousness and delusions of grandeur or persecution, such as "There are evil people trying to influence my mind." (Answered True)

7 or Pt (Psychasthenia) Forty-eight items based on neurotic patients showing obsessions, compulsions, abnormal fears, and guilt and indecisiveness, such as "I save nearly everything I buy, even after I have no use for it." (Answered True)

8 or Sc (Schizophrenia) Seventy-eight items from patients showing bizarre or unusual thoughts or behavior, who are often withdrawn and experiencing

delusions and hallucinations, such as "Things around me do not seem real!" (Answered True) and "It makes me uncomfortable to have people close to me." (Answered True) (Imaginative to delusional)

9 or Ma (Hypomania) Forty-six items from patients characterized by emotional excitement, overactivity, and flight of ideas, such as "At times I feel very 'high' or very 'low' for no apparent reason." (Answered True) (Hypo to Hyper activity)

0 or Si (Social Introversion) Seventy items from persons showing shyness, little interest in people, and insecurity such as "I have the time of my life at parties." (Answered False) (Shy to exhibitionist)

The eight original MMPI-1 **clinical scales** were initially developed utilizing two criterion groups. The normal subjects group consisted of relatives and visitors of hospital patients, recent high school graduates, and medical patients. The clinical group consisted of patients representing all major psychiatric diagnostic categories (as clinically diagnosed at the time of the test construction). At a later time, the Masculinity-Femininity (Mf) scale and the Social Introversion (Si) scale were added to the test profile.

MMPI Scale Number Designations	MMPI Scale Personality Descriptors
1	Hypochondriasis
2	Depression
3	Hysteria
4	Psychopathic deviate
5	Masculinity-femininity
6	Paranoia
7	Psychasthenia
8	Schizophrenia
9	Hypomania
0	Social introversion

The **four validity scales** (?, L, F, K) were developed in an effort to detect deviant test-taking attitudes. The "Cannot say" scale is the total number of omitted items or those answered both true and false. Sometimes items are omitted because of carelessness, confusion, indecision, or lack of information or experience necessary to answer. Omitted item content frequently indicates an attempt on the part of the respondent to avoid admitting undesirable things. A very large number of omitted items lowers the scores on the other scales.

The **L scale** (Lie Scale) was designed to detect a deliberate, unsophisticated, and naive attempt to present oneself in a favorable light. These items were rationally derived and assess the strength of a person's unwillingness to admit even minor character weaknesses. A high L scale score indicates that a person is trying to create a favorable impression. A low L score indicates that a person is responding frankly to the items.

The **F scale** (Infrequency Scale) was designed to detect those approaching the test-taking task in a way different from that intended. It was developed by comparing endorsement frequency of items in the normal criterion group. Deviant responses involve responding to items endorsed by fewer than 10 percent of the normals. The F scale serves multiple functions. It is an index of test-taking attitude and is useful in detecting deviant response sets. If profile invalidity can be ruled out, it is considered to be a good indicator of degree of psychopathology and/or psychological distress.

The **K scale** (Correction Scale) was designed to identify ego strength and clinical defensiveness. A very high K score calls into question the validity of responses to all items. In addition, the K scale is used as a correction factor for some of the clinical scales. Its application to the clinical scales allows for greater differentiation among them.

Administration and Scoring. The manual indicates that individuals 18 years of age or older with at least eight years of successful schooling should be able to complete the MMPI-2. It can be administered individually or in groups. Several forms of the MMPI-2 exist, (e.g., for individual or group administration, for the visually impaired, or for those with limited facility with English).

The MMPI-2 can be either hand scored, using templates for each scale, or computer scored. The interpretation of the MMPI-2 is configural in nature. Although some useful information may be gained by considering a T-score on an isolated scale, the interpretive value greatly increases by considering the pattern of both the four validity scales and the ten clinical scales in relation to each other.

Critique. The MMPI-2 remains the instrument of choice for the routine assessment of the nature and degree of emotional upset in adults (inpatient and outpatient). An exception is with an inpatient population with predominantly psychotic reactions. The original MMPI-1 can be used with an adolescent population as young as 12 or 13 years of age. However, a hazard in such use is that this group frequently shows discrepancies between verbal self-descriptions and real-life behavior, so that test results often either grossly overstate or understate pathology. The newly constructed MMPI-A (Archer, 1992) is the recommended instrument to be used with adolescent subjects. The MMPI-2 is also considered to be the instrument of choice for screening or assessing emotional distress in workplace and research populations.

Strengths of the MMPI-2 include its strong empirical derivation and norming, its documented utility in assessment, and its utility with respect to the efficient utilization of a professional's time (if not the examinee's), when compared to traditional assessment instruments such as the Rorschach and TAT. The huge body of research generated with the MMPI-1 (over

6,000 citations) is considered to be a strong foundation onto which to anchor the ongoing research findings related to the newly revised MMPI-2. The extensive research literature suggests that a naive interpretation of MMPI-2 profiles is probable unless the interpreter is aware of the complexity and nuances of the meaning of configurational generated scores. Considerable clinical sophistication in the use of the MMPI-2 is necessary before its actuarial power can be appropriately utilized.

For the most part, recent research has supported the reliability and validity of the instrument. Most psychologists would probably agree that the MMPI-2 is our best personality assessment instrument. Readers desiring to learn more about the MMPI-2 may find the 1991 edition of the Roger L. Greene book to be very helpful.

Personality Inventory For Children (PIC)

The **Personality Inventory for Children** was developed over a 20-year period (Wirt & Lachar, 1981). There have been two revisions (Lachar, 1982; Wirt, Lachar, Klinedinst, & Seat, 1984). It was developed at the University of Minnesota as a downward extension of the MMPI in an attempt to create an objective personality scale for children. It has both an atheoretical-empirical and a rational foundation. Items were chosen by a combination of empirical and rational procedures.

The PIC consists of 600 true or false items; it is not a self-report instrument. Rather, it is completed by an informant who knows the child, preferably the child's mother.

The PIC is normed for respondents who are three years through 16 years of age. It yields 33 scores: one general screening score (adjustment); three validity scales; twelve clinical scales (achievement, intellectual screening, development, somatic concern, depression, family relations, delinquency, withdrawal, anxiety, psychosis, hyperactivity, and social skills), and seventeen experimental scales. As with the items, the scales were developed using a combination of a logical, rational, and atheoretical-empirical test construction procedures.

Because of the length of the original form, the PIC has been reformatted (Lachar, 1982) so that if only the first 131 items are completed, an informant Defensiveness scale and four broad factor-derived scales that reflect the major content dimensions of the PIC item pool can be obtained. If the first 280 items are completed, a Development scale and shortened versions of the remaining 14 profile scales can also be scored.

Scoring. Although the length of the complete PIC may prove to be a daunting task for the informants, the administration of the inventory is relatively simple for the examiner. The interpretation of the instrument, however, is complex. The authors provide a six-stage interpretive approach,

profile studies, and a sample series of mean profiles for a variety of diagnostic groups. It is considered to be important that interpretations be based
on information published in both the manual and the accompanying mono-
graph.

Critique. Although the PIC was developed as a downward extension
of the MMPI, important differences exist between the two instruments. The
group on which the 600 items were normed include 2,390 children tested
between 1958 and 1962 in the Minneapolis public school system and from a
single medical clinic. Although large numbers of children were involved
(about 100 boys and 100 girls at yearly intervals between 5 1/2 and 16 1/2
years), its norms do not reflect the more stringent and useful standard of a
nationally stratified random sample of children. The sample also appears
to be somewhat antiquated; how adults perceive children has changed a
great deal since 1962.

Perhaps the major problem of standardization of the PIC is its infor-
mant-respondent format. There is the confounding possibility of broad
variability across types of respondents (mothers, fathers, grandparents,
guardians, teachers, etc.), and yet no separate norms have been developed
for types of respondents. It is extremely unlikely that for any specific child
the respondents would give the same answers. The concern is that the PIC
personality profile may be largely a function of the type of respondent completing the instrument.

Another possible problem with the instrument is that it is not uncom-
mon for respondents to complete the PIC at home. Of course, response
contamination is feasible in this situation since family discussion of response
choices may occur among family members.

Test-retest reliability studies are reported in the manual. Reliability
estimates across scales range from 0.35 to 0.94 with psychiatric patients,
and 0.34 to 0.91 and 0.68 to 0.97 in two studies of normal children. The
reliability of the PIC subscales fluctuates widely across scales and across
samples. Only a few scales consistently demonstrate adequate reliability.
It should be noted that there is a danger of overinterpreting error variance
on the PIC.

A large number of validity studies are described in the PIC manual.
However, the interpretation of these studies is hampered by the lack of an
underlying theoretical structure against which to test construction and validation of the instrument. The studies cited seem to be most promising with
respect to classifying children with psychological disorders and less useful
with respect to general clinical treatment applications.

The interpretation of the PIC is complicated by a lack of uniformity in
the T score elevations across scales. For example, some of the validity and
clinical scales have clinically significant T score levels below 70, while other
scales require higher levels of elevation to be considered clinically signifi-

cant. This variation across scales makes interpretation from the profile sheet rather difficult and cumbersome. Interpretation is further complicated by the use of a multiple scale construction format (empirical versus rationally derived), as well as the array of different criterion and validation groups reported in the manual. Perhaps what is needed most is the development of a more straightforward, integrated, and user-friendly manual.

To the author's credit, the revised manual and shortened form of the PIC (Lachar, 1982; Wirt, Lachar, Klinedinst, & Seat, 1984) retain the performance values of the original 600-item scale. A direct approach to scale reduction led to the inclusion of items based on several criteria, including item-to-item raw scale correlations and the representation of scale content dimensions based on results obtained from scale item factor analyses. Intercorrelations between scales on the original format were compared to intercorrelations on the revised format; little difference in the relative magnitude of correlations appeared. The revised manual (1982) reports that the shortened format scale reliability and validity data supports the conclusion that the shorter scales function in a similar manner to the full-length scales.

Critics seem to be most optimistic in recommending the research applications of the PIC in any of its lengths (131 items, 280 items, or 600 items), but caution against an indiscriminate clinical use or a naive approach to interpretation.

Bender Visual Motor Gestalt Test

The Bender Visual Motor Gestalt Test was first published in 1938 as an adaptation of Max Wertheimer's (1923) verbal technique of assessing visual perception. Wertheimer used a series of figure designs for research in visual gestalt psychology. Bender adapted nine of these figures as a nonverbal measurement of gestalt functioning in the perceptual-motor sphere. Instead of having examinees describe the designs, as Wertheimer did, Bender had them copy the figures.

L. Bender (1946) described the gestalt function as: "that function of the integrated organism whereby it responds to a given constellation of stimuli as a whole . . . any deviation in the total organism will be reflected in the final sensory motor pattern in response to the given stimulus" (p. 54).

The designs of the figures were constructed so as to illustrate different principles of gestalt psychology. The test is applicable for subjects four years of age and older.

Scoring. The task given examinees is straightforward (to copy the design of each figure). Many clinicians interpret the Bender Gestalt intuitively and subjectively. However, several objective scoring systems have been developed for use with adults or children. The most widely used objective method is the Pascal-Suttell scoring system (1951), standardized and quantified on an adult population and based on matched samples of normals and abnormals. E. M. Koppitz (1975) has standardized the Bender Gestalt Test with children. Utility in assessing school readiness and in predicting educational achievement of first graders has been demonstrated. Some attempts have been made to impose a projective function on the Bender Gestalt task by adding to the copying phase an elaboration phase, a free association phase, and a test-the-limits phase.

Critique. There has been a great deal of criticism directed at some of the adaptations of the Bender Gestalt Test, particularly against those who have attempted to make it a projective personality test. Perhaps it would be best to create a new projective technique utilizing Bender Gestalt findings and insights rather than attempting to extract every last drop of projective material from a test not originally designed to assess personality.

While attempts to introduce objectivity and quantification to the scoring of the Bender Gestalt Test seem helpful, perhaps a more fundamental need is for research on construct validity to determine the meaning of what the test measures. Test-retest reliability is low. Reliability can be affected by a number of factors. Results are easily affected by fatigue. Performance can be affected by modifying the directions for administration of the test. Even advance information about the number of designs to be copied, or the position of the stimulus cards relative to the copy sheet, or the shape or size of the copy sheet can affect performance. Examiners need to be aware of the effects of administration procedures on outcomes.

The Bender Gestalt Test is frequently used to diagnose organicity; it is often included in batteries primarily used to detect brain damage. It is recommended for inclusion in diagnostic examinations of adults and children beginning at age four because of its contribution with respect to the evaluation of perceptual-motor functioning, neurological impairment, expressive styles, and maladjustment. Its brevity and innocuousness makes it useful as an icebreaker to introduce the examinee to a test battery.

There are at least seven forms of the Bender Gestalt Test (the Visual Motor Gestalt Test, the Hutt Adaptation of the Bender Gestalt Test, the Bender Visual Motor Gestalt Test for Children, the Watkins-Bender Gestalt Scoring System, and the Canter Background Interference Procedure for the Bender Gestalt Test). Each uses the same nine figures borrowed from Wertheimer, but with variations of administration, scoring, and interpretation procedures.

All things considered, even with significant limitations in validity and reliability, the Bender Gestalt retains an important role as a screening instrument for the detection of brain damage. The use of the test to assess personality characteristics is considered to be very problematic.

Thematic Apperception Test (TAT)

The **TAT** was first published in 1935 by Henry Murray and is based on his need system. In its current form, it consists of 19 achromatic cards involving ambiguous scenes and one blank card. Some cards are used with all subjects; others are gender specific and/or age specific. The TAT may be used with subjects who are age four and above. Specific forms have been created for young children (CAT), the aged (SAT), and others.

The original procedure outlined by Murray in the test manual requires two one-hour sessions, 10 cards being employed during each session. The cards reserved for the second session were deliberately chosen to be more unusual, dramatic, and bizarre, and the accompanying instructions urge respondents to give free play to their imagination. Most clinicians use abridged sets of specially selected cards, seldom giving more than 10 cards to a single respondent.

Current thinking related to the utility of the TAT is that it is a useful projective instrument for tapping fantasy in a manner that leads to diagnostic conceptualizations of individual personality and/or group dynamics. It might more accurately be described as a "constructionist" device, since the respondent constructs the responses through the use of imagination and fantasy.

Administration and Scoring. The TAT is normally administered in an interview situation with one individual. It provides more structured stimuli than the Rorschach and is more obvious in intent. It should be noted that the examiner sits in a side-by-side seating arrangement with the examinee.

The examiner introduces the TAT roughly as follows: "This is a test of imagination, one form of intelligence. I am going to show you some pictures, one at a time; and your task will be to make up as dramatic a story as you can for each. Tell me what led up to the event shown in the picture, describe what is happening at the moment, what the characters are feeling and thinking; and then give the outcome. Speak your thoughts as they come to your mind. Do you understand?" (Bellak, 1993).

The examiner records the respondent's stories verbatim. If the full set of twenty pictures is used, they are usually broken into two sessions, each of which may take an hour. However, as noted above, in practice examiners usually use only ten stimulus figures (cards).

The basic assumption underlying the interpretation of the TAT is that the stories reflect the subject's internal needs and the perceived external (environmental) press. These needs and press are particularly apparent in the way in which the subject talks about the "hero," that is, the main person with whom he or she seems to be identifying in each story. Other persons in the pictures reflect attitudes toward significant people in one's experience. In addition to looking at the hero and other major characters, the assessor notes the theme of each story, whether the plot reflects success or failure, how problems are resolved, and the content of the stories. Presumably, these themes reflect the person's views about his or her own life. The assessor's purposes are to develop and check hypotheses about why the person tells the story, what personality determinants seem to be significant, and how the person copes with different kinds of situations. The assessor notes productivity, reaction times, signs of strong emotion, unusual words or expressions, repetitions, the intellectual quality of the verbal responses, and the examinee's attitudes and interests in taking the test.

Finally, it should be noted that the TAT has no single accepted procedure for scoring and interpretation.

Critique. The quantity and quality of research stimulated by the TAT marks it as a highly successful contribution to the search for knowledge about personality. However, from a psychometric point of view, the TAT cannot be judged successful. Studies of psychometric qualities raise many questions about its use for clinical and/or other applied purposes. Based on TAT research and clinical usage, several critical points have been noted: (1) TAT responses are subject to conscious control by the subject; (2) although the predominant effect seems to be a direct relation between TAT fantasy and behavior, no conclusions will hold for all motives and subject backgrounds; and (3) the high ambiguity of the pictures relates to a weak relationship between story content and a respondent's overt behavior. In sum, the TAT does appear to be a useful indicator of a respondent's general interests, motives, and areas of emotional disturbance, but it is not a psychometrically sound measurement device with respect to differentiating personality traits among individual respondents.

The central problem of validity is in establishing the relationship between fantasy imagery as reflected in the TAT stories and overt behavior in real life. That is to say that it is not possible to make a statement about the relationship between TAT fantasy and behavior that will hold for all motives, ages, and both sexes.

Concurrent validity in terms of similarity of inferences from TAT scoring and assessments with other procedures has not been encouraging. Concurrent validity, in terms of differential results with contrasted groups of subjects, remains satisfactory. This finding indicates that there may be some justification for including the TAT in a diagnostic workup of patients. Variations in scoring have been introduced in order to improve the validity of inferences (e.g., computer scoring of content).

While supporting the projective hypothesis, the sensitivity of the TAT to temporary situational conditions may complicate the detection of more enduring personality traits. Interpretation of the constructs assessed by the TAT must also take into account the finding that measures of the same needs through such instruments as the EPPS, and Adjective Check List have shown little correspondence of results. Such discrepancies limit the generalizability of scores. The question of internal consistency of TAT responses has also received considerable attention in the research literature.

A fair amount of normative information has been published regarding the most frequent response characteristics for each card, including the way each card is perceived, the themes developed, the roles ascribed to the characters, the emotional tones expressed, speed of responses, length of stories, and the like (Bellak, 1993). Although these normative data provide a general framework for interpreting individual responses, most clinicians rely heavily on "subjective norms" built up through their own experience with the test. A number of quantitative scoring schemes and rating scales have been developed that yield good scorer reliability. However, since their application is rather time-consuming, such scoring procedures are seldom used in clinical practice. Although typically given as an individual oral test in a clinical situation, the TAT may also be administered in writing and as a group test.

The TAT has been used extensively in personality research. Although researchers have been unable to establish criterion-related validity of the TAT for specific uses, such studies contribute to the construct validation of TAT interpretations. A basic assumption that the TAT shares with other projective techniques is that the present motivational and emotional condition of the subject affects his or her responses to an unstructured test situation. The technique has provided the vehicle for a great deal of clinical work. One can find numerous applications to a variety of psychological problem areas, such as delinquency, brain damage, asthma in children, bilingualism, mental retardation, obesity, phantom pain, achievement, affiliation, sexual identity, power, and schizophrenia. Overall, there appears to be a tacit acceptance of the notion that the TAT is an acceptable methodology for personality study and not a test per se, so the emphasis on validation research has diminished, and a more flexible and informal use of scoring variables and scoring systems has emerged.

There is concern that all the TAT cards are black and white and ethnically homogeneous. It has been postulated that the black and white cards at least partially account for the predominantly somber emotional tone of the majority of the TAT productions. However, researchers who have introduced color and/or ethnicity variation into the TAT cards have found few significant differences in productivity and emotional tone between the color and noncolor series and the ethnicity homogeneous and ethnicity heterogenous series.

It is recognized that examiner bias can easily be introduced into the test environment and interpretation of the stories. That is to say that the TAT content is viewed as a joint expression of goodness of fit between the examinee and his or her environmental status and between the examiner and examinee expectancies for interaction. Readers desiring to learn more about the TAT may find the 1993 edition of the Bellak book to be very helpful.

Children's Apperception Test (CAT)

Although the original TAT is said to be applicable to children as young as four years of age, the **Children's Apperception Test (CAT)** was specially designed for use between the ages of 3 and 10 years (Bellak, 1993). The CAT cards substitute animals for people on the assumption that young children project more readily to pictures of animals than to pictures of humans. Contrary to the author's assumption, however, several researchers who used children from the first grade up found either no difference or, more often, greater productivity of clinically significant material with human rather than with animal pictures. In response to these research findings, a human figure modification of the test (CAT-H) has been developed for use with children especially those with a mental age beyond 10 years. Unfortunately, there is no data provided by the test developers related to supporting the validity and/or the reliability of the instrument. No norms have been published.

Like the TAT, the Children's Apperception Test (CAT) is a constructionist technique consisting of a series of 10 pictures depicting anthropomorphic animals in a variety of situations that require the 3- to 10-year-old child to make up stories related to the pictures presented. The purpose is to facilitate an understanding of a child's thoughts, needs, drives, and feelings regarding important relationships, situations and conflicts at both a conscious and unconscious level.

As noted above, concerns over the relative merits of the use of animal versus human figures led to a human modification of the CAT (CAT-H) in which human figures were substituted for animals with slight variations in the context of the pictures. No clear advantages of human over animal forms have been reported in the research literature, with the exception being for children between the ages 7 to 10 who have a mental age beyond 10 years. It is speculated that these children find the animal pictures too childish and respond more favorably to the human forms. Finally, it should be noted that a supplement form (CAT-S) has been developed to elicit children's responses to issues of physical activity, physical injury, competition, body image, sexual conduct, or classroom situations.

Critique. The nature of the traits and characteristics purportedly measured are believed to be primarily motivational and emotional in nature. Therefore, issues related to consistency over time (test-retest reliability) and internal consistency (split-half reliability) may not be applicable in this instance. That is to say that emotions and motivations may not be expected to be stable over time. Being based on psychodynamic theory, the CAT continues to be questioned by others from different theoretical orientations. An interview approach involving conversational transactions between examiner and child has been suggested. Advocates of this interview approach view the CAT as a clinical tool that can elicit a wide range of responses. The instrument may be used as an effective ice-breaker to establish therapeutic rapport and is considered to be less susceptible to faking when presented as an informal interview.

Rorschach

The ten inkblots that constitute the **Rorschach Test** evolved from an observation Hermann Rorschach made that patients identified as schizophrenic seemed to respond differently to the Klecksographie inkblot game compared to others. From a series of experiments utilizing 40 inkblots on patients and nonpatients, Rorschach developed a code that classified responses according to the area of the blot used (whole, large detail, etc.), the features used (a shape, color, etc.), and the contents (human, animal, etc.). He suggested that this method might prove diagnostically useful, especially in identifying schizophrenics, and in detecting personality traits, habits, or styles. The year after he first published it as his Form Interpretation Test (Rorschach, 1921), he died. During the next twenty years, five American Rorschach systems were developed (Beck, Klopfer, Hertz, Piotrowski, and Rapaport and Schafer). All of these systems shared the same method but were widely divergent with respect to procedures used to score and interpret responses. These different systems yielded different kinds of records. For the most part, the scores and interpretative postulates were found to lack empirical support. Recently, an attempt to develop a comprehensive Rorschach system (Exner, 1974, 1978, 1993; Exner & Andronikof-Sanglade, 1992; Exner & Weiner, 1982) using standardized administration and scoring procedures combined with the findings related to a systematic ongoing research program has helped offset many of the weaknesses of the earlier, competing systems. John E. Exner's systematic plan of research has led to the development of a test with empirically established psychometric and clinical properties.

Although the Rorschach protocol often includes projections, it is misleading to label it a projective technique. Rather, it is a procedure that provokes many of the perceptual-cognitive problem solving operations of an examinee. It should be noted that imagination was seen by Rorschach to have little to do with the basic problem-solving processes being tapped by the test. According to Exner (1993), the essential task requires subjects to misperceive the stimulus (they are, after all, aware that they are responding to just an inkblot) and thus project something of themselves into the response. A problem-solving situation is created which provokes a complex of psychological operations that culminate in decision making and verbal responses. These operations include encoding of the stimulus field, classification of the stimulus field and its parts, discarding some potential answers through ranking or censorship, and selecting from remaining answers because of style, traits, or a psychological state that is activated by the task demand. There is a tendency toward behavioral redundancy in Rorschach-related operations that creates a greater probability that certain kinds of responses will be selected than others. This redundancy is reported to be one of the possible strengths of the Rorschach since it allows for the establishment of a consistent and reliable protocol of responses.

Scoring. Of each response reported by a subject, four things can be said: the response is directed at perceiving all or some part of the blot; one or more properties of the blot are perceived (form, color, movement, or shading); some class of content is specified (like human, animal, or thing); and it is a percept seen by other people either commonly or rarely. Interpretations are simply descriptions of the patterns of perceptual, cognitive, emotional, and/or social strategies used in coping with the problem-solving task. The Rorschach, then, is perhaps not to be viewed as a test, but rather as a behavior sample.

As noted above, the Rorschach is considered to be a test of perception, not imagination. It consist of five chromatic and five achromatic cards, to which the average adult will give 22 responses. Scoring involves coding each response for its location, determinants, and content. The testing task involves two parts: the initial response given by the examinee and the inquiry made after all responses have been given to all ten stimulus cards. A verbatim record is made of the initial responses. During the inquiry, each response is read back to the examinee. Nondeductive questions are put to the examinee in an attempt to clarify the location, determinants, and content. The goal of the inquiry is to ensure that the examiner sees the percept as the examinee does. The cardinal rule of scoring Rorschach responses is that the code should represent the cognitive operation that occurred at the time the subject gave the initial response. Any additional information generated during the inquiry is not to be confused with that generated in the initial responses. Only the perceptual and cognitive problem-solving processes reflected in the original responses are formally coded and scored.

Each response is carefully coded on a structural summary form. These codes do not yield ordinal scores, as used with intelligence and/or achievement tests, but rather a reduction of verbalizations to a systematic structural summary format. Rorschach scores crucial to interpretation are the frequency scores for each of the codes, the percentages, ratios, and other metrically useful derivations of them. These are collectively referred to as the structural summary.

Critique. It is often assumed that the interpretation of the Rorschach is driven by psychoanalytic theory. While analytic theory has been used in the interpretation of Rorschach tests, it was not Rorschach's intention to tie the test to this single theory. Likewise, the development of the Exner comprehensive system is not tied to analytic theory. Exner (1993) stated that if any theoretical influence pervades the comprehensive system, it is cognitive theory.

Reliability studies in the past often made no distinction among the various Rorschach interpretation systems. Reliability among raters using the various Rorschach interpretation systems was found to be weak. However, when a single interpretation system was used, such as Exner's comprehensive system, interrater reliability coefficients have been found to be consistently high among most expert raters.

Since stimuli are meant to be novel, test-retest reliability appears to be irrelevant in this instance. Split-half reliability is also considered to be irrelevant, since each stimulus is distinct (i.e., we expect homogeneous response patterns not heterogeneous response patterns). Interscorer reliability, when using trained scorers and Exner's comprehensive system, has been reported to be from 0.87 to 0.99 (Reznikoff, Aronow, & Rauchway, 1982). By and large, Rorschach interpretation rests on understanding individual subjects rather than on group-based nomothetic data sets. Rorschach validity has been questioned based on studies of content interpretations. There is, however, strong validating data related to the use of the overall structural summary.

The Rorschach has been used with subjects as young as three years old. Normative data exist for children and adolescents as well as for normal adult and clinical populations. Yet, the basic principles of interpretation remain the same for all age groups. Exner (1993) is unequivocal on this point: "Rorschach behavior means what it means regardless of the age of the subject" (p. 21).

Perhaps the most extreme negative view taken toward the Rorschach is the notion that the rate of scientific progress in clinical psychology might well be measured by the speed and thoroughness with which it gets over the Rorschach. A more optimistic view is that the Rorschach is still of value due to the development of more focused, psychometrically refined, and theoretically relevant scales. Perhaps the Rorschach should be considered to be more like an interview than a test, useful in exploring a broad spectrum of personality dimensions.

The most consistent criticism of the Rorschach method involves examiner-induced bias. Examiner expectancies can be communicated both verbally and nonverbally. Transient stress, verbal reinforcement, gender, and experience of the examiner have been reported to affect responses. Exner (1993) has recommended strategies designed to minimize this bias (never sit across from the examinee, use uniform instructions, etc.).

In summary, it is probably safe to say that after a period of decline, the Rorschach is generating new support, particularly with respect to the use of Exner's comprehensive system.

California Psychological Inventory (CPI)

The **California Psychological Inventory (CPI)** was developed to predict what normal people will do in particular contexts and to identify how they would be described by others. The instrument is based on a number of folk concepts that are believed to be everyday variables used by ordinary people to understand their own and others' behavior. The original edition of the CPI, published in 1956, contained 18 folk concept scales. The revised 1987 edition of the CPI contains two additional folk concept scales, as well as three structural vector scales. Three of the 20 folk concept scales serve as validity scales to detect unreliable or invalid protocols. Of the 20 folk concept scales, 13 were developed by the empirical method. These are the scales for Dominance (Do), Capacity for Status (Cs), Sociability (Sy), Independence (In), Empathy (Em), Responsibility (Re), Socialization (So), Tolerance (To), Achievement via Conformance (Ac), Achievement via Independence (Ai), Intellectual Efficiency (Ie), Psychological-Mindedness (Py), and Femininity/Masculinity (F/M). Four scales [Social Presence (Sp), Self-Acceptance (Sa), Self-Control (Sc), and Flexibility (Fx)] were developed using the rational method of scale development.

The three validity scales were developed through a mixed strategy not classified as either empirical or rational (Gough, 1987). These scales are Good Impression (Gi), which is used to identify people trying to "fake good"; Communality (Cm), which assesses random responding; and Well-Being (Wb), which is used to identify people who may be "faking bad."

Factor analytic studies have supported the notion that there are four higher-order factors among the 20 folk concept scales (Gough, 1987). These factors have been labeled as extroversion, control, flexibility, and consensuality. The three structural vector scales were developed by selecting items that correlated highly with the factorial axes. These scales are: v.1, Internality; v.2, Norm-Favoring; and v.3, Self-Realization. The combination of scores for v.1 and v.2 divided people into four ways of living or types: Alphas (outgoing), Betas (reserved), Gammas (adventurous), and Deltas (disaffected). V.3 provides a level or quality of functioning for the type.

The folk concept scales can be broken down into four classes (Wegner, 1988). Class I (Do, Cs, Sy, Sp, Sa, In, and Em) measures pose, ascendancy, self-assurance, and interpersonal adequacy. Class II (Re, So, Sc, Gi, Cm, Wb, and To) measures socialization, maturity, responsibility, and interpersonal structuring of values. Class III (Ac, Ai, and Ie) measures achievement potential and intellectual efficiency. Class IV (Py, Fx, and F/M) is a mixed group of intellectual and interest modes.

The 462 items in the 1987 version of the CPI (12 were deleted from the original CPI's 480 items) are a series of true/false statements, in which respondents mark true for those items with which they agree and false for those times with which they disagree. The items are printed in a reusable test booklet.

Administration and Scoring. The CPI is largely self-administered and usually takes 45 minutes to one hour to complete. The testing can be divided into two or more sessions for slow readers or in special circumstances. No rigorous controls are needed to establish dependable results; thus, administration can take place under varied conditions ranging from the more standard supervised testing conditions to take-home testing or mail-out and mail-back testing.

Standard scores are used for each scale, with a mean of 50 and a standard deviation of 10. All of the scales, except for F/M, are scored so that higher values are associated with the conventionally favored standing in the variable. This arrangement facilitates interpretation of the profile. For example, higher scores on the sociability scale indicate a person who likes to be with people and is friendly, while a lower score indicates a person who feels uneasy in social situations and is shy. The answer sheet can be scored by hand or returned to the publisher, Consulting Psychologists Press, for processing by computer.

Critique. In terms of the practicality of using the CPI, it has numerous positive aspects. It has a comprehensive, yet easy-to-read manual, as well as an easy-to-read and understand test booklet. Though lengthy, the questions do not appear to alienate the reader. The incorporation of the three validity scales is important for determining whether the response sets of faking good, faking bad, and/or random responding have occurred. Scoring can be done by hand or computer. Different options are available depending on the level of interpretation the user wishes.

Regarding the reliability data, the test-retest correlations are not extremely high but are adequate enough to indicate that the CPI is stable and can be used with confidence. However, the internal consistency correlations are low on many scales. There is certainly sufficient evidence of convergent and predictive validity. The validity studies have clearly provided evidence that the CPI is capable of making predictions about the way normal people will behave and be described by others. Hence, the CPI appears to achieve its ultimate goal.

BEHAVIORAL-COGNITIVE ASSESSMENT

Behavioral-cognitive assessors (Beck, 1991; Miller & Berman, 1983) focus their efforts on observable behaviors and controllable environmental variables. A **target behavior** is carefully selected and defined. It is observed and recorded in a systematic and standardized fashion in terms of some scaling dimension (e.g., frequency or duration of a specified behavior). Time and event sampling procedures are used to ensure reliability as well as a representative sampling of targeted behaviors. It should be noted that cognitive assessments are included in the behavioral cognitive analyses of the targeted behavior problem. The behavior of interest is conceptualized in terms of what the stimulus of the target behavior is, the response made to the stimulus of interest, the relationship of contingencies of reinforcement and punishment to the response of interest, and other environmental antecedents and consequences related to the target behavior. In light of this systematic behavioral analysis of target behaviors, specific treatment outcome goals are articulated and a treatment plan is formulated and implemented. After treatment has been applied, the target behavior is again assessed to determine the adequacy of the treatment.

There are at least four (4) basic **differences between behavioral-cognitive and traditional assessment procedures**. First, behavioral-cognitive and traditional assessors have different views of **personality structure**. Traditional assessors rely on the centralist or dispositional perspective in which there are presumed to be underlying personality traits and structures to what is being observed. Behavioral-cognitive assessors focus only on what is actually observed and avoid postulating underlying personality constructs. A second difference is in terms of the **content assessed**. In traditional assessment, test items are frequently ambiguous (e.g., inkblots, drawings, pictures, incomplete sentences). In contrast, behavioral-cognitive assessors attempt to use specific and observable measures of target behaviors (e.g., number of aggressive responses, time needed to solve an analogue problem). A third difference is in terms of **interpretation**. Those associated with the traditional approach use the assessment data sets as signs or symptoms of underlying conscious or unconscious processes. Behavioral-cognitive assessors focus on the observables and do not attempt to postulate underlying causes (i.e., cognitive and/or personality dispositions). That is to say that behavioral-cognitive assessors analyze the target behavior in terms of the context, contingencies, and stimulus and response units. The fourth and perhaps most important difference is that in traditional assessment, **treatment** is often **separated from assessment**. In behavioral-cognitive assessment, the treatment is viewed as an ongoing integral part of the assessment process (i.e., an ongoing dynamic assess-treat-assess process).

In short, behavioral-cognitive assessment is criterion-referenced.

Traditional assessors rely more on norm-referencing procedures using traits or other mentalistic descriptors of behavior. In the behavioral-cognitive approach, the target behavior is carefully specified, analyzed, and treated followed by a test to evaluate the adequacy of the treatment.

It should be noted that there are combinations of naturalistic, controlled, and some unsystematic methodological components used by behavioral-cognitive assessors. Using naturalistic observation methods, a behavioral-cognitive analysis is done in a natural setting without interfering with the behavior observed or controlling it in any way. The problem, of course, is the possibility of reactive effects since the presence of the observer can change the behavior in some way. In addition, it is possible that the observer may be somewhat biased with rspect to recording targeted behaviors. Such problems must be carefully controlled by using multiple observers and/or unobtrusive observational procedures (e.g., a hidden camera, a confederate observer, etc.).

A number of specific methods are frequently used with respect to **controlled behavioral-cognitive observations**. One is the use of an **analogue situation**. The client is instructed to perform some problem-solving task that is designed to sample how the client would behave in some natural setting. For example, a phobic client might be exposed to a graded series of phobic stimuli to assess the phobia. A person might be encouraged to engage in some problem-solving task designed in such a way so as to ensure failure. The client's attributions to failure would be hypothesized to reflect what would actually occur given a natural problem-solving situation in which the client experienced failure. The major problem with the analogue approach is the creation of an analogue task that truly reflects the natural occurrence of the target behavior.

Another frequently used approach is **role playing**. The client is asked to role play something, such as family or workplace interactions. Focus would be given to assessing the context of some problematic behavior. As in the analogue method, a trained observer would record the series of events.

Self-reports and/or **self-monitoring** procedures can also be used. Self-reports can be written, oral, or in the form of a structured interview. The problem of course, is that the reporting may not be accurate and/or may be distorted in some way. Self-monitoring procedures can be used in which the client records his or her own behavior by counting it or recording it with various devices or scoring sheets. It should be noted that self-monitoring itself could influence the behavior (i.e., a reactive effect could manifest itself).

A final means of behavioral-cognitive assessment could include **physiological measures**. Procedures such as computerized tomography (CT), magnetic resonance imaging (MRI), skin resistance, catecholamine levels, and so on could be used to assess and monitor target behaviors.

It should be pointed out that there are **three levels of analysis** with respect to behavioral-cognitive assessment procedures: (1) assessment of **overt behaviors**; (2) assessment of **cognitive behaviors**; and (3) assessment of **emotional and/or physiological levels** of behavioral functioning. In whatever type (e.g., analogue, role playing, self-reporting, use of physiological measures) of behavioral-cognitive assessment used, the level of analysis is clearly specified and this specification determines the specific method of observation to be used. For example, if one wishes to assess current concerns, a self-report method or an interview might be used. If the problem is believed to be one of attribution, an analogue problem-solving role-playing situation could be used. If the behavior of interest is physiological, the method might include an alpha-wave monitoring biofeedback procedure to treat highly stressed clients. At the overt behavioral level, to treat such things as phobias, tics, aggressive behavior, or social insensitivity, observations in controlled or natural settings are frequently used. Or a multimethod approach may be necessary since behaviors like anxiety may manifest themselves at all three levels of analysis.

Finally, it should be noted that some traditional assessment measures could be used within the context of a behavioral-cognitive assessment procedure. For example, the TAT could be used to indicate a client's attributions and/or locus of control. The Rorschach could be used to assess a client's problem-solving ability and/or reality base (Weiner, 1994; Weiner & Exner, 1991). Depression scales (e.g., the Beck Depression Inventory) could be used to monitor the efficacy of treatment for depression.

In sum, behavioral-cognitive assessment techniques appear to be growing in use. The distinct contribution of the behavioral-cognitive assessment approach is its integration with the treatment plan. Much work related to establishing the psychometric adequacy of the approach remains to be done.

THE RELATIONSHIP BETWEEN PERSONALITY ASSESSMENT AND TREATMENT

The history of assessment in psychology has not typically placed a heavy emphasis on relating the assessment to treatment, and it is because of this lack of a link between the two processes that the ultimate utility of our assessment techniques have been highly questioned. Mischel (1984) said, "We have entered the age of infinite examination and compulsory objectification where evaluation (assessment) has replaced torture" (p. 357). If indeed our assessment techniques are only for comparing individuals to the norm, then the batteries of tests we put clients through could be likened to forms of modern "torture." In the past couple of decades, however, a much stronger emphasis has been placed on relating the assessment information and techniques to treatment and the results have proven to be a very worthwhile endeavor.

Korchin and Schuldberg (1981) and J. C. Perry (1992) have made an effort to explain how the process of assessment can be used to gain an accurate picture of where the individual is currently functioning and then using that information to determine what intervention or treatment techniques would be the most effective. Assessment is explained as a necessary starting point if we are going to find ways of truly helping people; few would argue that it is better to proceed from ignorance than from knowledge. By means of assessment, we are actively trying to gain as much knowledge as we can about the person so that our treatment effect will be positive.

Assessment is the process by which we gain necessary understanding of a person so that we may make an accurate and informed decision with respect to designing a treatment plan for the person. Through gathering information from many sources, we gain a picture or a working model of the person and a sample of their behavior. In order to design, implement, and evaluate a treatment plan, we go through a thorough process of evaluating the person. We then attempt to integrate the disparate multidimensional findings into a coherent whole that accurately describes the person. The bottom line is that it is the assessor, not the tests themselves, who is at the center of the assessment process. The tests are merely the tools that the assessor uses to aid his or her systematic study of a person.

In order to successfully plan interventions and treatments, we use a variety of assessment techniques including interviews, psychological and educational tests, and observations. **Triangulation of results** (i.e., utilizing multiple measures) helps to ensure that you will come up with reliable results that are an accurate description of the person with whom you are working. The various means of assessment that have been found to be helpful with respect to predicting outcomes of treatments include the following: behavioral assessments, clinical interviews, environmental assessments, medical/neuropsychological assessments, objective personality tests, and projective techniques.

Behavioral assessment techniques are helpful not because they tell you why the person does what he or she does. They are helpful because they tell you when, where, and under what circumstances a person does what he or she does. They provide information of immediate relevance to the planning of treatment programs for clients so that you have an idea, based on their history and experiences, of how they will behave. Admittedly, more work needs to be done to improve the psychometric purity of this assessment procedure.

The **clinical interview** continues to remain a critical factor in the overall assessment process. It is considered to be particularly important with respect to determining effective treatments because it is through this interview that the assessor is able to integrate all of the information obtained. By means of a structured or semi-structured interview, the assessor is able to gain an integrated picture of the person's present level of functioning in their environment and their past history of adjustment.

Environmental assessment has become popular in recent years. An attempt is made to decentrate the individual and to look at the broader environmental conditions in which an individual is embedded. This contextual information is believed to be invaluable with respect to trying to plan a successful intervention. For example, you would not return a substance abusing child to his or her home and expect them to have an easy time recovering if you knew that the child's parents were convicted drug dealers who probably had not stopped dealing drugs even after the police had gotten involved.

Objective personality **measures** of assessment have also been shown to be helpful with respect to making treatment recommendations (Polyson, Peterson, & Marshall, 1986). For example, the MMPI profile can yield information as to whether or not a person will do well in therapy. If a person has a high score on scale 3, then they are probably denying a problem and are highly defended. Counseling probably wouldn't work in this instance. Likewise, if a person has a high L and scale 1 score they are most likely not psychologically minded, probably deny psychological problems, and will be resistent to our intervention efforts. Tests such as the MMPI also yield a goodly amount of self-report information that can be used as an integral part of planning an effective treatment. In addition, the results from **projective tests** have been found to be helpful in determining whether or not a person would do well in certain types of treatment (Polyson, Peterson, & Marshall, 1986). For example, if the subject's Rorschach protocol includes only a few movement responses, the chances for a quick change are probably not good. **Medical assessments** and **neuropsychological assessments** have been shown to be very helpful when a damaged portion of the brain has been identified and as a result, the neuropsychologist is able to help the patient plan alternate means of completing tasks and ways to compensate for a learning and/or emotional deficit (Heinrichs, 1993; Lykken, McGue, Tellegen, & Bouchard, 1992; Restak, 1994).

Testing could perhaps best be described as an objective, technical process whereas assessment could be best described as a holistic, insightful process. That is to say that assessment goes beyond testing. The assessor is challenged to look beyond the numbers. From an ecological perspective, the assessor attempts to describe how a person is currently functioning in his or her environment. Then, an effort is made to help this person in his or her adaptive struggles of life. If the assessor is going to be succesful, multiple measures need to be used to describe the person interacting with their environment.

METHODOLOGICAL ISSUES RELATED TO THE TREATMENT UTILITY OF ASSESSMENT

Steven C. Hayes, Rosemary O. Nelson, and Robin B. Jarrett (1987) and J. C. Perry (1992) do an excellent job reviewing current research trends related to the **treatment utility of assessment**. They reported that one reason for the decline of assessment in the 1950s and 1960s was that it had not proven its value with respect to fostering favorable treatment outcomes. Paul E. Meehl (1954, 1959) maintained that there was no published empirical evidence supporting the practical value of assessment. Twenty-two years later Korchin and Schulberg (1981) stated that this still seemed to be the case. Can personality tests offer the type of information needed to be used in the development of a treatment plan? McReynolds (1968, 1982, 1989) stated that not much well-designed research has been done in the area. Can personality tests actually help therapists with their treatment efforts?

In spite of the many negative attitudes and overall pessimism seen in the field, even Meehl (1954, 1959) recognized in his foresight that there is a definite need to ask in what way and to what extent assessment information helps therapist treat their clients. Why has this area of research been so solely neglected in spite of its perceived value? Hayes, Nelson, and Jarrett (1987) reported that there has long been confusion related to the psychometric concepts and methods relevant to and appropriate for this special type of research. In addition, they said that therapists seem to be having a difficult time fusing the two roles of being a therapist and a psychometrically oriented testing clinician. It is recognized that many clinicians view testing as an invasion into the therapeutic alliance. Given our limited knowledge base in the area, it is far too perfectionistic to expect psychometric purity of many of the personality assessment instruments we use in clinical practice. The time is ripe for research to expand in the area.

On the optimistic side, Hayes et al. reported a recent upswing in research studies designed to demonstrate the treatment utility of assessment information. With the advent of the development of many different types of therapies as opposed to one or two theoretical orientations, this type of research has become a necessity. It is now considered to be important to determine what treatment works best with a particular type of client and a particular type of therapist. It is probably fair to say that most practitioners do not assume that one therapy will work for all individuals. Those days are gone! In addition, Hayes et al. observed that today there are more assessment instruments available. This too, lends itself to increased efforts to merge assessment and therapy.

An **outline of the research findings related to various types of treatment** and the usefulness of each is included in the **Hayes** et al. (1987) article. The first type of study listed in the article is a **simple post-hoc study**.

This is a sort of backward study in which a group of subjects is assessed, and then they are all administered a treatment. After the treatment, the assessment information that was used to predict who would respond to the treatment and who wouldn't is systematically analyzed. Some concerns about this type of study include the fact that there is no comparison group. Because of this limitation, it cannot be determined with certainty what specific individual difference characteristics among the participants were actually related to the differential treatment outcomes.

The second type of study listed by Hayes is the **a priori study**. This type of study is considered to be superior to the post hoc type study. Different kinds of apriori studies are described and illustrated. One of these, the **obtained differences approach**, is somewhat comparable to the post-hoc type study. But here, subjects are divided into groups (predicted responders and nonpredicted responders) based on pretreatment assessment differences prior to receiving treatment. It should be noted that both groups receive the same treatments. That is to say that the groups were divided into predicted responders versus nonpredicted responders before treatment as opposed to administering treatment and then dividing them into groups (the procedure used in the post hoc type of study). A varient of this approach is to create a situation in which the collection and/or availability of the assessment data to the therapist is varied while the treatment given to the subjects is the same. Another a priori approach is the **manipulated use approach**. Here the same assessment data set is available to all therapists, but they use this information in varied ways. Here all of the therapists may use the data to refer a client for either one of two types of treatment. These a priori arrangements allow for better control of individual differences across treatment group conditions. If outcomes are found to vary across groups and/or conditions, it would provide evidence to support the use of the test to facilitate treatment.

A third kind of study could be set up as a **multiple dimension design**. Here several combinations of the variables are used to create a factorial design. For example, two or more variables (individual difference measures and different treatments) are set up within the context of an ATI factorial design. One would ask whether two or more different available assessment data sets have varying effects on two or more treatments? This type of study has an advantage over the others because it allows us to test for interaction effects. That is to say that the researcher may not only find out if there is improvement with a specific type of treatment, but also determine what various individual difference factors contribute to this differential effect and in what ways.

A fourth type of study is a **time-series between subjects design**. Here individual cases are studied, but then several of these cases are later collapsed into groups for comparison. There is an advantage to this type of study in that it allows the researcher not only to compare groups, but to examine also the individual data sets to determine what factors contributed to success and/or failure in treatment for each individual subject across time and/or phases of treatment. A **within subjects time series design** is used in situations in which two or more treatments are compared with respect to their utility for use with the same subjects. Here, all subjects are subjected to all treatments. This rather complex design has much to recommend it with respect to the provision of comparison groups and control for individual differences.

Hayes et al. maintained that all of the above designs can be used to test the treatment utility of assessment techniques and to help further theoretical developments in the area. Following these procedures, researchers can determine which specific components of the assessment data sets provided the best predictors related to the treatment outcome measures. In addition, given these data sets, we would be in a position to address the following question. Is it the actual process of assessment rather than the tests themselves that produces outcome differences across treatment groups? For example, does a particular type of assessment set up certain dynamics related to the therapeutic relationship? That is to say that if a client is given frequent evaluations of his or her therapeutic progress, does this assessment information increase the frequency of reinforcing responses made by the therapist and/or is the client more psychologically minded and aware?

Admittedly, we have our work cut out for us. As noted earlier, **Mischel** (1968, 1973, 1977, 1979, 1981, 1984) reported that personality assessment information appeared to have very limited utility with respect to its use in therapy. He preferred empirical/actuarial assessment approaches over rational/theoretical approaches. He claimed that even some laypersons could do just as well at assessment as experienced clinicians. It should be noted that he did give high marks to some of the empirically derived tools such as the MMPI. In fact, he claimed that the **incremental validity** of assessments increased very little with the addition of more measures after the IQ and MMPI findings had been interpreted and used to make predictions related to outcome possibilities. That is to say that examination of a typical MMPI profile can reveal a need for treatment and prognosis. For example, a high 2, 7, and F score taken in combination with a low 3 score indicates that the client is probably a good candidate for treatment. A person achieving a high 2, low 9, and high 0 score is probably suffering from situational depression and is a good candidate for medication. A person with a high 8, low 6, and high 7 score may best be assisted using psychotropic medication. A high 0 score could mean that the person would do better in individual as opposed to group treatment. A high 4 and 9 score indicates that the person would probably be best served by a long-term treatment approach. Finally, a person with a high 1, 3, and K score is probably extremely guarded. Theraputic intervention will probably prove to be difficult at best in this instance.

For the most part, other than advocating the use of the MMPI, Mischel questioned the use of other personality assessment instruments. However, others have reported that there is value with respect to the periodic use of the TAT cards to determine how well the client is doing in therapy (Bellak, 1993). The Rorschach protocol can be used to determine a person's reality ties and a person's coping patterns (Exner, 1993). Examination of the emotional indicators taken from the Bender can be used to determine the degree of psychological distress (Schraa, Jones, & Dirks, 1983). In sum, at least from a methodological point of view, it seems as though the stage is set for advances to be made with respect to relating assessment information to treatment.

TRENDS

All things considered, it is probably fair to say that the field of personality assessment is gradually becoming revitalized after experiencing a major **decline in the 1950s, 1960s, and 1970s** (Zilbergeld, 1984). Prior to World War II, the area of personality assessment flourished. However, during the war and afterward, the emphasis shifted to treatment that was seldom connected directly to the assessment process. The **Rogerian revolution**, with its position that psychological tests were detrimental to the counseling-therapeutic process and the **behavioral position**, with its emphasis on observable behaviors instead of inner dispositions, traits, or personality structures, greatly contributed to the decline in the use of personality tests. Another significant factor was the very poor research results reported in numerous studies (Mischel, 1968) that raised serious questions with respect to the stability of personality constructs and the psychometric adequacy of the most commonly used personality tests. Currently, however, a number of positive trends and research findings have emerged that indicate that the field of personality assessment is increasing its role and place in psychology.

This **revitalization** is seen in a number of surveys that indicate that many more psychologists are using personality tests today than in the 1970s. At conventions of the American Psychological Association, the National Association of School Psychologists, the American Educational Research Association, and other professional associations, the time devoted to personality assessment issues and personality assessment research is growing. Even with the criticisms, personality testing is still required for many jobs and is now being emphasized to a much greater degree in graduate training programs. Surveys of the job placement sections of the **APA Monitor, NASP Communique**, and the **Educational Researcher** indicate that over

90 percent of the jobs advertised in clinical, counseling, school, and industrial psychology require some training in personality assessment and approximately 80 percent require projective testing skills. It is particularly interesting to note that after many years of use and disuse, and considerable controversy, many traditional personality assessment tests continue to be valued as part of the overall assessment process. Korchin and Schuldberg (1981) noted that the top-ranked personality tests are the MMPI, Rorschach, TAT, Incomplete Sentences, Bender, and Draw-a-Person Test. While most of these tests have some predictive validity and reliability problems associated with their use, they are reported to be used in most applied settings (Polyson, Peterson, & Marshall, 1986; Hogan & Nicholson, 1988). Instead of relying on just one or a few tests to provide a diagnostic picture of a person, a battery of tests approach is being using today with the emphasis on viewing the clinician as a **hypothesis generator** and tester. That is to say that the tests are now being used to confirm or negate hypotheses within the context of a broad-based assessment, treatment-oriented approach.

One of the major trends today is an **attempt to relate and integrate assessment information with therapeutic interventions** (Butcher, 1992; Matarazzo, 1990, 1992; Stricker, 1992; Vane & Guarnaccia, 1989). Testing and therapeutic treatment have been separated for many years and tests are now being used as part of the overall therapeutic process itself. Ironically, many of the previous opponents of such a combination are leading the way with respect to this trend. For example, humanistic psychologists are using some tests in an informal collaborative fashion with their clients. That is to say that the test results are used not as a definitive answer or label with the therapist having the final judgment with respect to the design of the treatment plan, but as part of the self-exploration of the client. Tests specific to this process are being developed at this time. Interestingly, many practitioner-oriented therapists, despite their initial uncomfortability with "personality assessment" in the traditional sense (since assessment of personality structures implied underlying unobservable traits and personality structures), have led this movement to integrate assessment and treatment. In fact, with respect to **behavioral-cognitive approaches**, assessment and treatment are viewed as inseparable (Stein & Young, 1992). A person is tested, type of treatment is determined by observations, treatment is then applied, and finally testing is done again to see if the treatment has been effective. **Aptitude-treatment interaction (ATI) research findings** appear to be particularly significant in this regard. The emphasis in ATI research as it relates to the area of personality assessment is on the treatment outcomes and their relationship to certain stable cognitive aptitudes. **Social psychological aptitude variables** such as the cognitive styles of internal and external locus of control, field dependence and independence, type of attributions, and expectancies have been repeatedly studied to ascertain their differential effects on treatment outcome measures.

Thus, the assessment process appears to be becoming more integrated within the psychotherapeutic process. Assessment helps the therapist choose a particular approach to treatment with a client. That is, with the combined behavioral-cognitive assessment intervention focus, the atheoretical-empirical strengths of the DSM III-IV systems of categorization, and the ATI research being done showing that certain therapies are better with certain types of clients and/or problems, pretherapy assessment becomes crucial. Today assessment information is viewed as important during therapy in that it helps the therapist see if there is progress or if he or she is perhaps missing something with respect to the functioning of the client. After therapy, assessment is used to systematically evaluate if and how the client was helped.

An ongoing battle continues with regard to the differential utilities of **clinical versus actuarial approaches** to assessment (Matarazzo, 1986). In the clinical approach, the clinician is viewed as the central part of the process in that clinical judgement governs the predictions and judgements of the overall assessment process. In the actuarial approach, the tests stand on their own based on past empirically established relationships between the test and a selected criterion group. The overall trend today seems to be on the actuarial side. Findings from numerous studies (Lanyon & Goodstein, 1992; Matarazzo, 1986; Mischel, 1968) have indicated that the actuarial approach is equal to or better than the clinical judgment approach. The actuarial approach has been found to be better both in the predictive aspect of the assessment process as well as in the clinical description of the assessed person. Despite the claims of many practitioners that the clinician is central and better, the actuarial approach continues to be reported as being equal to or better than the clinical approach. In fact, a linear rather than configural or weighted combination of test results is producing very good descriptions of personality (Greene, 1991) thus countering the claim that clinical diagnosticians have unique configural processing abilities when engaged in the assessment process.

The use of computers is part of this actuarial trend. Automated administration, scoring, and even **computer-generated narrative descriptions and interpretations** of projective personality tests are now being used a great deal. Examples include the Roche and Caldwell MMPI-2 reports (Greene, 1991) and the Exner Rorschach reports (Exner, 1993). There are, however, some problems associated with this trend in that it is being used and perhaps relied on more than may be warranted. Given the generally positive, but rather limited empirical base, many more reliability and validity studies with varied populations are needed to document and improve the automated approach to assessing personality.

Presently, numerous objective personality tests are being developed and improved that contribute to the continued revitalization of the field. The **MMPI-2** was recently revised, and the specialized content scales are being refined. Work is being done to improve the predictive and descriptive weaknesses of the instrument. For example, research findings reported in the **Advances in Personality Assessment** series (Spielberger & Butcher, 1982-1992) indicate that consideration of some demographic factors are important with respect to interpreting the MMPI. Different norms are needed for sex as well as age (e.g., adolescents need to be scored differently). Ethnicity studies (Westermeyer, 1987) are also being done showing some, but not many, differences between the response patterns of black-white subjects. Education, occupation, and intelligence also appear to relate to scores on the MMPI-2 (e.g., the more intelligent and educated have lower L and higher K scores). In addition, it has been reported that subtle items do not seem to be necessary to arrive at an accurate MMPI-2 code type descriptor. The **Millon Multiaxial Clinical Inventory III (MCMI-III)** appears to be a promising instrument, but more research on its psychometric properties needs to be done. In short, objective personality tests are now being improved and stringently analyzed in an attempt to enhance their psychometric, predictive, and treatment utility properties.

Projective tests have also been greatly improved. Several scoring systems have been developed that have increased the interscorer reliability of the inkblot tests. The **Exner Comprehensive Scoring System** has greatly improved the scoring and interpretive reliability of the **Rorschach**. The **Holtzman Inkblot Test (HIT)** with its greater number of cards and only one response required per card has facilitated the development of an alternate form. The HIT appears to be emerging as a very useful research instrument that is enhancing our understanding and use of projective assessment. Alternate-form reliability indexes are possible to compute with the two forms of the HIT and research using the HIT is helping us understand how personality develops. That is, recent research (Swartz, Reinehr, & Holtzman, 1983) is showing how certain content scale scores stabilize during adolescence and adulthood. Thus, new inroads are being made with respect to understanding how personality changes and what specific components of personality remain stable. Finally, it has been found that some projective tests (the TAT and Rorschach) have high interscorer reliabilities associated with their use. Since heterogeneous responses and the encouragement of novelty are viewed as important aspects of many projective protocols, a case can be made for the notion that traditional internal consistency and test-retest measures of reliability appear to be inappropriate criteria to use with respect to evaluating the psychometric adequacy of projective tests (Reznikoff, Aronow, & Rauchway, 1982).

Another important trend today is that associated with the **interactionist position** (Bowers, 1973; Buss, 1989). Assessment people are realizing more and more the complexity of trait and situational influences on personality. Neither approach is considered to be complete with respect to assessing personality. There is also a trend related to combining medical and psychological assessments. Health psychologists investigate how psychological variables influence health, illness, and recovery. Thus, there is a need for testing in these areas to systematically investigate and document these interrelationships. Psychopharmocologists reportedly need assessment information to help decide which drugs are appropriate for treatment. Neuropsychological assessors are attempting to establish relationships between neurological variables and functional deficiencies.

There is a renewed effort in creating and psychometrically improving tests for certain critical areas of need. For example, in **crisis intervention**, practitioners are becoming more clear about what assessment procedures can be useful in managing crises. Since crisis intervention demands a focused and efficient means of assessing and treating the person in crisis, new assessment tools are being developed that are designed to be brief and specific. Efforts are being made to improve our ability to predict suicide (Eyman & Eyman, 1991). Scales are being tested to screen for **alcohol and drug abuse**. Most of the scales currently being tested fall short of reliability and validity requirements with the possible exception of the MMPI correlates (a 4-2-7 profile for alcoholism; a 4-8-9 for substance abuse) and the promise of the MacAndrew's MAC scale. However, because of the heterogeneity of the drug- and alcohol-abusing population, much work remains to be done in this area (Megargee, 1985). Similar research (Biaggio & Mauro, 1985; Monahan, 1992) is being conducted in an attempt to predict **violence** (e.g., an elevated 4-3 MMPI profile and/or aggressive content scores on projective instruments such as the TAT and Rorschach). There is a great need for good assessment techniques in this area, and thus there are numerous cognitive, behavioral, and physiological measures currently being developed and tested. Much work remains, however, since the constructs of violence, anger, hostility, and aggression are not easily differentiated or predicted.

There is some research being done related to assessing intelligence and personality using measures of **reaction time**. Promising results are being found with the advantage being a direct and **culture-free assessment** of intelligence and/or personality. Eysenck (1982) is associated with this work and has hypothesized that 10 percent of the variance in intelligence may be accounted for by personality dimensions.

The development of the **Perceptanalytic Dream System** (Piotrowski, 1983) is another example of the way in which the field of personality assessment is being expanded. Using the TAT structural summary method, dreams are being analyzed in an attempt to document similarities between TAT structural properties and dreams (i.e., dreams are assumed to be similar to TAT stories in that there is usually a hero, both use imagery, and the type of ending is considered to be of importance).

Finally, the **clinical interview** remains a very important part of the overall assessment process. In fact, Lanyon and Goodstein (1992) report that the clinical interview is very helpful in accurately describing individuals and that not much incremental validity is gained by adding other tests to the interview.

That said, the area of personality assessment appears vibrant, with much research taking place and many new approaches manifesting themselves. After a long period of decline, the usefulness of personality assessment is once again being shown and further refined.

THE BIG-FIVE MODEL

It is clearly documented that measures of cognitive ability and normal personality, structured interviews, simulations, and assessment centers predict workplace success and leadership reasonably well (Bass, 1990; Howard & Bray, 1990; Hughes, Ginnett, & Curpky, 1993; Sorcher, 1985; Yuki, 1989). Nonetheless, Robert Hogan, Gordon J. Curpky, and Joyce Hogan (1994) claimed that many companies seem to be unaware and/or reluctant to take advantage of psychological assessment services. As a result, workers and executives are usually selected on the basis of their technical skills rather than their social and leadership skills. **Why aren't psychologists more involved in the process of worker and executive selection?**

R. M. Stogdill (1948, 1974) reviewed research on personality and emergent leadership in a variety of workplace situations. He concluded that measures of dominance, extroversion, sociability, ambition or achievement, responsibility, integrity, self-confidence, mood and emotional control, diplomacy, and cooperativeness were positively related to success in the workplace and emergent leadership.

Hogan, Curpky, and Hogan (1994) claimed that the personality characteristics described in Stogdill's reviews can be anchored onto the **big-five model** of personality structure endorsed by many modern personality psychologists (Costa & McCrae, 1988, 1992; Costa & Widiger, 1993; Digman, 1990; Goldberg, 1993; R. Hogan & Hogan, 1992; McCrae & Costa, 1986, 1987; Passini & Norman, 1966). The five personality descriptors (surgency, agreeableness, conscientiousness, emotional stability, and intellect) included in the big-five model provide us with an organizer that can be used to integrate personality research findings across studies. Hogan, Curpky, and Hogan (1994) noted that "the conscientiousness dimension is related to conformity, prudence, constraint, will to achieve, and work. Dominance, extraversion, and sociability reflect surgency; responsibility, achievement, and integrity fall into the conscientiousness dimension; self-confidence, mood, and emotional control are part of emotional stability; and diplomacy and cooperativeness resemble agreeableness" (p. 496).

D. A. Kenny and S. J. Zaccaro (1983) reported that between 48 percent and 82 percent of the variance in worker and executive success was due to personality characteristics. There does appear to be a consistent relationship between high scores on the dimensions of the big-five model and being successful in the workplace.

Most would probably agree with the statement that the best way to predict worker and executive success is to use a combination of cognitive ability, personality, simulation, role play, and multirater assessment instruments and techniques. Although personality assessment is part of this, there is considerable disagreement as to whether personality measures on their own can predict worker and executive potential. Hogan, Curpky, and Hogan (1994) claimed that numerous and at times incompatible personality descriptors have obscured the usefulness of personality measures for assessing worker and executive potential in the workplace. Once again, they argue that the big-five model will substantially enhance our ability to integrate research in the area.

Why do leaders fail? V. J. Bentz (1985) and Harry Levinson (1994) reported that a number of leaders and corporations fail for personal rather than structural or economic reasons. Positive characteristics associated with leadership include intelligence, confidence, and ambition. Leadership characteristics associated with failure include playing politics, moodiness, and dishonesty. Bentz concluded that the failed leaders had an overriding personality defect or character flaw that alienated their subordinates and prevented them from building a team. Levinson (1994) reported that the psychological characteristics associated with corporate failure include "individual and organizational narcissism, unconscious recapitulation of family dynamics in the organization, exacerbating dependency, psychologically illogical organization structure and compensation schemes, inadequate management of change, and inability to recognize and manage cognitive complexity" (p. 428). To address these problems, Levinson (1994) and Bentz (1985) recommended that executives and boards of directors become more psychologically sophisticated.

Finally, it should be noted that the big five model reflects the **bright side** of personality. Effectiveness requires both the presence of these positive characteristics and the absence of what we call **dark side** characteristics (i.e., irritating tendencies that alienate subordinates and interfere with a person's ability to form a team). Hogan et al. (1994) claim that it is hard to detect these dark side characteristics using interviews, assessment centers, or inventories of normal personality because they coexist with high levels of self-esteem and good social skills. That said, it is our recommendation that we make a systematic effort to assess our clients bright side and dark side tendencies.

SUMMARY

In general, the overall popularity of using projectives has dropped somewhat, but there does appear to be a positive movement afoot to **resurrect projective assessment**. Admittedly, there continue to be numerous problems with projective tests with respect to the lack of objective scoring procedures and the problems with reliability. With regard to the Rorschach, while interscorer reliability appears satisfactory, other forms of reliability such as split-half and alternate forms may not be applicable since novelty and heterogeneity of responding are encouraged. The high and uneven number of responses given to the blots continues to constrain our attempts to construct a more psychometrically sound test. However, the highly structured and empirically validated Exner scoring system represents a very positive approach to the refinement of the Rorschach as a well-developed, psychometrically sound projective test. On the other hand, some practitioners are advocating using the Rorschach and other projective measures such as the TAT as less of a test (i.e., as a component of a clinical interview technique designed to sample individual and/or group behavior). Given the positive reviews of the actuarial approaches reported in the literature, the trend with respect to objective personality tests such as the MMPI and the Millon tests is toward increased use of **automated assessment**. Here the cookbook actuarial data set is fed into a computer, that then produces a comprehensive descriptive narrative interpretation with a great deal of statistical, predictive power.

Behavioral-cognitive assessment procedures also appear to have a key to the future. Use of formalized behavioral-cognitive assessment procedures has increased with the rise of the cognitive science theoretical perspective within the mainstream of psychological science. Behavioral-cognitive assessors remain close to observations, while steering clear of risky inferences. With a skill deficit conception of the problem, behavioral-cognitive assessors emphasize that specific task requirements, representative of the situations in which the behavior occurs, be carefully assessed. From this perspective, assessment leads directly to an intervention plan. Behavioral-cognitive assessment procedures have been broadened to include an assessment of the cognitive components of cognitive styles, expectancies, attributions, and beliefs. Combined methods including interviews, self-reports, rating scales, analogue assessment, role playing, and direct observation are used to systematically assess the interaction between the person, his or her behavior, and the environment. Thus, multifaceted behavioral-cognitive assessment procedures appear to be moving toward greater inclusiveness of salient determiners of behavior that will hopefully lead to a more complete identification of problem behaviors and selection of an appropriate treatment plan.

The **clinical interview** continues to be a popular procedure. It allows for both general and specific data to be gathered, it allows for great flexibility for adapting to the needs of the client, and facilitates the development of a positive therapeutic relationship. Since it serves as a strong link between assessment and treatment, and is a main tool in behavioral-cognitive assessment, work is now being done to make it a more objective and structured procedure (Matarazzo, 1978).

Environmental assessment has become important with the rise of the interactionist position. Efforts have been made to assess the nature of the environment in general, looking at broader conditions such as how persons conceptualize the environment and themselves. In terms of medical uses, there has been considerable growth in the field of **neuropsychology**. With the development of better instruments and technology, such as the Halsted-Reitan assessment battery, better quantification of biological variables as they relate to psychological variables is now possible (Heinrichs, 1993; Lykken, McGue, Tellegen, & Bouchard, 1992; Restak, 1994).

In sum, the trends reported in this chapter point to a growing view of tests as a set of procedures useful for assessment, not as isolated instruments of testing. A more focused technique with better psychological integrity is developing, one that takes into account environmental factors as well as the person's subjective views. This in turn should lead to better clinical judgments, better treatment plans, and better descriptive information in the years to come.

TERMS TO KNOW

assessment
humanistic views of personality assessment
behavioristic views of personality assessment
Millon's personality clusters
DSM-IV
Axis II
rational-theoretical approaches
empirical approaches
internal consistency approaches
behavioral-cognitive assessment
Edwards Personal Preference Schedule (EPPS)

Minnesota Multiphasic Personality Inventory (MMPI-2)
Personality Inventory for Children (PIC)
Bender Visual Motor Gestalt Test
Thematic Apperception Test (TAT)
Children's Apperception Test (CAT)
Hermann Rorschach Test
Theodore Millon
California Personality Inventory (CPI)
clinical interview
social psychological aptitude variables
automated personality assessment
an interactionist position
actuarial assessment
incremental validity
environmental assessment
triangulation

QUESTIONS TO CONSIDER

1. Present a review of the emerging trends in the use of projective and nonprojective personality tests that may lead to a revitalization of the field of personality assessment. In responding to this question, make certain that you identify a number of promising avenues of research where significant contributions may be possible.

2. Psychology is presumably a field in which the general "principles" of behavior are systematically addressed. What place, then, does (should) the study of the assessment of individual differences (**constraints**) have in such a field? Be specific in identifying promising avenues of theoretical and practical contributions.

3. Critically evaluate the extent to which assessment information has been successfully used to plan treatment interventions. In your discussion make certain that you present a detailed description and critique of assessment efforts that have been used to plan treatment interventions.

4. Define behavioral-cognitive assessment. Distinguish between behavioral-cognitive and traditional assessment procedures. Make certain that your response includes a comparative summary of common methods of behavioral-cognitive assessment and that you indicate how traditional assessment procedures could be used within the context of behavioral-cognitive assessment.

5. What are the relevant issues in the use of personality tests for the selection and placement of individuals? Make certain that you critically discuss the appropriate use of different types of personality tests and that you identify the legal and ethical conditions that apply.

SUGGESTED READINGS

Readers wanting to study more thoroughly the topics covered in this chapter will find the following references helpful.

Archer, R. P. (1992). *MMPI-A: Assessing adolescent psychopathology.* Hillsdale, NJ: Lawrence Erlbaum.

Bellak, L. (1993). *The Thematic Apperception Test, The Children's Apperception Test, and the Senior Apperception Technique in clinical use (5th ed.).* Boston, MA: Allyn and Bacon.

Ciminero, A., Calhoun, K., & Adams, H. (1977). *The handbook of behavioral assessment.* New York: Wiley.

Diagnostic and statistical manual of mental disorders: DSM IV. (1994). *American Psychiatric Association (4th ed.).* Washington, DC: American Psychiatric Association.

Exner, J. E. (1993). *A Rorschach workbook for the comprehensive system.* Bayville: Rorschach Workshops.

Greene, R. L. (1991). *The MMPI-2: An interpretive manual.* New York: Allyn and Bacon.

Harvey, J. H., & Parks, M. (1981). *Psychotherapy research and behavior change. The Master Lecture Series (Vol. 1).* Washington, DC: American Psychological Association.

Lanyon, R. I., & Goodstein, L. D. (1992). *Personality assessment.* New York: University Press of America.

Millon, T. (1981). *Disorders of personality DSM-III: Axis II.* New York: Wiley.

Ogden, D. P. (1985). *Handbook of psychological signs, symptoms, syndromes.* Los Angeles, CA: Western Psychological Services.

Ogden, D. P. (1969). *Psychodiagnostics and personality assessment: A handbook.* Los Angeles, CA: Western Psychological Services.

Spielberger, C. D., & Butcher, J. N. (1982). *Advances in personality assessment (Vol. 1).* Hillsdale, NJ: Lawrence Erlbaum.

Spielberger, C. D., & Butcher, J. N. (1983). *Advances in personality assessment (Vol. 2).* Hillsdale, NJ: Lawrence Erlbaum.

Spielberger, C. D., & Butcher, J. N. (1983). *Advances in personality assessment (Vol. 3).* Hillsdale, NJ: Lawrence Erlbaum.

Spielberger, C. D., & Butcher, J. N. (1984). *Advances in personality assessment (Vol. 4).* Hillsdale, NJ: Lawrence Erlbaum.

Spielberger, C. D., & Butcher, J. N. (1985). *Advances in personality assessment (Vol. 5).* Hillsdale, NJ: Lawrence Erlbaum.

Spielberger, C. D., & Butcher, J. N. (1986). *Advances in personality assessment (Vol. 6).* Hillsdale, NJ: Lawrence Erlbaum.

Spielberger, C. D., & Butcher, J. N. (1988). *Advances in personality assessment (Vol. 7).* Hillsdale, NJ: Lawrence Erlbaum.

Spielberger, C. D., & Butcher, J. N. (1990). *Advances in personality assessment (Vol. 8).* Hillsdale, NJ: Lawrence Erlbaum.

Spielberger, C. D., & Butcher, J. N. (1992). *Advances in personality assessment (Vol. 9).* Hillsdale, NJ: Lawrence Erlbaum.

PART IV

CONSULTATION AND PROFESSIONAL PRACTICE

CHAPTER 7

INSTRUCTIONAL CONSULTATION

OUTCOME-BASED EDUCATION

Many times paradigm shifts are not center stage. The outcome-based paradigm shift that is currently taking place in education has not been linear, but it is clearly evident in the numerous school reform reports appearing in the media. These reports have documented American students' low achievement scores, their lack of preparation for the world of work, and their relatively low rank in international comparative studies. Educational accountability has become a prominent theme among professional educators and the public at large.

For many years, it was assumed that if schools provided adequate resources and equalized inputs, that the outcomes would be positive. However, with the appearance of the **Coleman Report** in 1966 (Coleman, 1966) in which it was claimed that schools could not overcome the socioeconomic class differences of students, the presumed link between the equality of inputs and outputs was shattered. James Coleman et al. (1966) maintained that the schools could not overcome the negative effects associated with being poor.

Critics claimed that Coleman's findings were flawed. Researchers made an effort to find schools in which poor students did well. These schools were labeled **"effective" schools**. Using norm-referenced test scores as a measure of academic success, researchers were able to identify effective schools and the instructional components related to student success in these schools. In many ways, the research findings associated with the effective schools movement served as a major step in linking school process variables to student outcomes and in moving us toward our contemporary focus on outcomes. Additional evidence related to documenting the shifting paradigm to outcomes can be seen in the increasing number of meta-analyses being conducted and in the findings related to Herbert Walberg's (1984) educational productivity research program. The debates related to the development of a national curriculum, a national assessment system, and the pressure to develop new measures related to evaluating educational and workplace outcomes are all part of the emerging **outcome based education (OBE)** focus of today.

MASTERY LEARNING INSTRUCTION AS A GUIDING FORCE

Advocates (Spady & Marshall, 1991) of this **OBE "approach"** to assessing educational and workplace outcomes are using portfolio's, products, demonstrations, and transcripts of specific skills rather than course grades to document student progress. The curriculum has been designed to allow all learners to demonstrate mastery of the derived outcomes. **A mastery learning model** of instruction sets criterion-based performance standards identically for all students and allows the time needed to reach that standard to vary. Outcome-based education includes the defining features of the mastery learning model.

In the traditional school, time is fixed, or constant, for all students, and the outcomes vary among students. In the OBE school, outcomes are held constant, and the time for mastery is allowed to vary among students.

This new OBE literacy that requires fundamental and total restructuring of the educational system includes many capacities once demanded only of a few (e.g., to think, problem solve, be creative, and to learn new skills and knowledge throughout life). It is important to note that the outcomes include more than tangible products. They include attitudinal, affective, motivational, and relational elements that also contribute to overall performances (Spady & Marshall, 1991).

Authentic assessment (OBE) involves assessment activities like those currently used in the world outside the classroom (e.g., work samples, performances, exhibitions, and self-evaluation reports). Several areas of education have a long history of using authentic performances or products as a means of assessing students' learning. For example, physical educators, art teachers, music teachers, and vocational and technical arts teachers have all used, to some extent, students' products or performances to determine whether the learning objectives of a class have been mastered.

A Good Chance for Success

If the basic ideas associated with the use of mastery learning and OBE have been around for some time, and it has only been recently that these ideas seem to have caught on in a major way, what took so long for the educational and business communities to discover and embrace them? W.G. Spady and K. J. Marshall (1991) claim that three factors seem to have been at work. First, until the middle 1980s, the public education system of the

United States was relatively immune from serious threat. That is to say that the public education system did not have to improve in order to survive. Second, the current basis of the attack on the traditional education system is focused on the low-quality products it is producing. Third, there is now documented evidence supporting OBE results.

Skeptics might claim that OBE is just another educational fad. It is recognized that we have tried many of the categories associated with mastery learning and OBE before, such as an emphasis on continuous assessment, remediation, encouragement, and support. Many of these strategies have been viewed as being unsuccessful in the past, why would we expect them to be successful now? Today, the OBE perspective appears to be persuasive both inside and outside of education. For the most part, **it is the quality paradigm shift in business and industry that is driving the paradigm shift in education**. Most previous reform efforts have been driven only by the educational community, not the business community.

APPROACHES TO COLLABORATIVE CONSULTATION

One way to categorize consultation delivery systems is to assume that there are **three basic approaches** to consultation (instructional, mental health, and organizational development). **Instructional consultants** attempt to apply knowledge taken from learning, development, and research methodology to instructional situations. The instructional consultation process takes place within the context of a problem-solving situation. The first step is to carefully **assess the problem situation**. Attention is directed at assessing the individual difference characteristics of the learner(s) along with describing and task analyzing the learner's environment. Questions are asked related to determining what needs to be changed and whether change is possible given the constraints of the situation. What constraints (biological, psychological, political, etc.) exist in the situation? Is change possible given the realities of the situation? Once the initial assessment process is done, then an attempt is made to design a **treatment plan** using what we know about learning, development, and research methodology to guide our efforts. It should be noted that the treatment plan is considered to be tentative in that we apply it, systematically determine if it works, then revise it, evaluate it again, and revise it a second time, and continue this **test-teach-test hypothesis testing process** until the problem is solved.

In order to be an effective instructional consultant, one needs to acquire a strong knowledge base with respect to learning, development, and research methodology. It is recommended that an effort be made to stay abreast of the most current work taking place in these disciplines.

Instructional consultants **view teaching and therapy as research**. The overall assumption is that most knowledge has a limited shelf-life (maybe five years or so). Instructional consultants ask themselves the following questions: What constitutes the core knowledge base of psychology and education? What constructs (intelligence, personality, the mind, information-processing conceptualizations of learning and instruction, motivation, and cognitive style) have lasting value? What knowledge is considered to be most exploitable for application to educational practice? How can a study be best designed to remediate a problematic situation? Instructional consultants recognize that there is **no one best method of intervention**. We know that there are multiple paths of treatment yielding similar outcomes. A rather safe and realistic course of action is to recommend using a test-teach-test (hypothesis testing) format set up within the context of an **aptitude-treatment-interaction (ATI)** design of intervention.

Mental health consultants focus their attention on whether it is best to recommend primary preventions, secondary interventions, or tertiary interventions designed to address problematic behavior(s) and/or situations. Should **primary prevention** be considered to be the best course of action, all individuals in the situation would receive treatment. For example, if it were decided that all individuals in school and/or in the workplace could profit from exposure to problematic situations involving coming to terms with moral dilemmas, a treatment program could be designed and implemented in which persons would be asked to solve problems related to resolving these dilemmas. Such an effort would be undertaken in an attempt to embrace a person's level of moral functioning at school, or in the workplace. The basic idea is that ethical practice would be enhanced as a result of the treatment. Of course, it is recognized that there are many situations where this type of treatment would not be considered to be an appropriate intervention.

With **secondary intervention**, the focus of treatment is directed at only those individuals considered to be at risk. Early intervention efforts related to identifying and providing stimulating environments for all high-risk minority children would be an example of a secondary intervention program.

Most mental health consultants focus their attention on **tertiary intervention** efforts. Here the problem behavior has already manifested itself. The learner is behind his or her peers with respect to academic achievement, work performance, social functioning, and or emotional development. Tertiary intervention represents the sort of treatment prescribed where a child is referred for a psychological evaluation because he or she is not doing well in school. A person who seeks out therapy as a means of enhancing their social emotional adjustment would be another example of a tertiary intervention procedure.

Organizational development consultants focus their attention on attempting to correct malfunctioning organizational structures. That is to say that the problem is assumed to exist within the organizational structures (e.g., faulty teacher-student administrator relationships or faulty worker-manager relationships) of the workplace or school, not the individual workers or students. **Gerald Caplan** (1970) has provided us with a useful categorization system with respect to distinguishing large-scale organizational development approaches to consultations from individual and small group types of consultations. He described **four types of consultation** (direct, indirect- individual client, indirect-group intervention, and organizational development.) With **direct consultation**, the focus is on providing one-on-one services to an individual. An example of direct consultation would be conducting psychotherapy with an individual client in an effort to improve their emotional level of functioning. With **indirect consultation**, the consultant may assess the individual difference characteristics of the client or situation and design a program of intervention that is to be carried out by others (the teacher, the administrator, the work supervisor). The point to be made here is that indirect consultation (in both individual and group forms of practice) is a means of systematically assessing a problem, designing a treatment program, and then monitoring the implementation of the treatment program. But indirect consultants usually do not serve as the actual treatment agents. The treatment plan is carried out by someone else (a teacher, administrator, or work supervisor). Finally, an **organizational development** approach to consultation would be used in those situations in which a problem is considered to exist within the organizational structure of a school, institution, or business. An organizational development consultant would focus their attention on assessing the organizational structure of the client's school or workplace. A special attempt would be made to carefully assess the interpersonal dynamics of the workers and supervisors (teachers-students-administrators-employers-employees). Workshops would be provided in which these dynamics could be assessed and discussed. Then a large-scale treatment plan would be crafted and implemented within the context of the organization. Once again the consultant would use knowledge in the areas of learning, development, and research methodology to construct the intervention plan. But unlike the plans devised for Caplan's first three types of intervention (direct, indirect-individual, and indirect-group) in which the treatment plan was designed to focus on the individual client and/or a small group of clients, the organizational development treatment plan would be carried out within the organizational structure of the client's school or workplace not at the individual and/or small group level of direct and indirect consultation.

In closing this section, the basic idea to keep in mind is that regardless of the approach taken to consultation (instructional, mental health, or organizational development), the knowledge base of learning, development, and research methodology should provide a solid guiding force for our efforts to improve performance levels among our clients. This knowledge base taken in combination with an ATI (aptitude-treatment-interaction) approach to designing treatment plans and carrying out the treatment plan(s) within the context of a test-teach-test problem-solving approach to interventions, has considerable potential for solving many of our problems both in school and in the workplace. Once again, remember that we are advocating teaching, therapy, and consultation as research. The information presented in the learning chapters (3 and 4) and the research methods chapters (8 and 9) should be particularly helpful with respect to designing and implementing the treatment component of our consultation efforts. In addition, the information contained in the assessment chapters (5 and 6) should be helpful with respect to assessing the individual differences (the aptitude component of our ATI model of intervention) of our clients.

Finally, it should be noted that what we are advocating here is a **collaborative consultation** approach. That is to say that the assumption is that the consultant(s) and the client(s) are viewed as equally valued participants in the consultation process. Each provides a special expertise (i.e., a knowledge base and a set of problem-solving skills) that is shared equally among the participants. The client's input particularly with respect to the assessment of individual differences is considered to be invaluable within the context of the overall consultation process. By the same token, the consultant's specialized knowledge base in learning, development, and research methodology is considered to be useful with regard to designing, implementing, and monitoring the treatment plan.

The next three sections of this chapter describe a cognitive science approach to instruction, after which a series of five training lectures is presented that is designed to address the following question:

> Suppose that you are called upon to deliver a series of lectures on the psychology of instruction to a large audience. Discuss the most useful information that has potential for relating knowledge in psychology to instructional practice. In your discussion attempt to focus on more than one theoretical point of view. Finally, make certain that you cite relevant empirical research supporting your position.

What we have attempted to do in this lecture series is to summarize the substantive contents of the text and to present this information in a format that could be disseminated to your clients when you are called upon to consult.

A COGNITIVE SCIENCE APPROACH TO INSTRUCTIONAL CONSULTATION

Currently there is no comprehensive theory of instructional psychology. In its early stages, the psychology of learning was behaviorally focused. It was thought that in order for psychology to be considered a science, we must study only observable behaviors. Cognitive processes were ignored. However, in recent years, it was found that these internal cognitive processes could no longer be ignored and thus the cognitive revolution began. Along with this development of cognitive theory in psychology, there was a parallel movement with respect to a cognitive focus in instructional design.

As noted earlier in the text, from a **cognitive scientist's perspective**, learning results from active engagement on the learner's part. Knowledge is considered to be organized as a set of mental structures (schemata), with learning occurring as a result of changes in these structures because of active problem-solving engagement. Indeed, covert processes such as thinking, problem solving, and creativity are now being emphasized, and seen as critical components of the overall learning process. With the pervasive view of the utility of cognitive science, there was a need for learning theorists to reformulate the behavioral paradigms within a cognitive context. Likewise, in instructional design, the overall trend has been a shift away from behavioral approaches to cognitive approaches.

Given our present knowledge base, a cognitive theory of instructional psychology seems to be the best theory that we have to offer at the present time. Using a cognitive theory allows us to explain the learning curve components. In addition, most individual differences are considered to be data and/or resource limitations that can be modified by instruction. Of course, biologically determined differences such as attention, temperament, and maturational stages cannot be modified, but psychological differences such as knowledge, language, memory organizations, mood, attitudes, cognitive style expectancies, and motivation can be modified. From this point of view, instead of fitting learners into specific methods of instruction, we are learning to adapt instructional methods to the learner's individual differences. This is being achieved by focusing on cognitive strategy training, rule learning training, and increasing a learner's feelings of personal competence. In sum, we are finding that we can modify thinking and problem solving skills.

Developmental issues are also considered to be important with respect to understanding instruction. We know that while a learner's **M-power (memory power)** is fixed at a young age, the size of the learner's chunks can be increased through the use of metacognitive strategies, schema-activating activities, the teaching of procedural knowledge to free up working memory space, and the use and refinement of linguistic symbolization. We know the areas in which atypical learners differ from typical learners (attention differences, memory organization differences, and cognitive style expectancy differences), and we have designed instructional strategies to address these differences.

Throughout this book, we have given special attention to six constructs considered to be of importance to a cognitive science approach to instruction that seem to be adding to our knowledge and understanding of the instructional process. These **constructs** appear to have explanatory power (i.e., the ability to explain the behavior of individuals in different situations and the ability to predict future behavior), they are flexible (i.e., broadly defined), and they have some social value (i.e., are considered to be worthwhile to the public at large).

Intelligence is one such construct. It appears to have explanatory power for academic success, it is flexible, and has social value. Assessment of intelligence is now being viewed as a beginning instead of an end point. The focus has moved away from who has it, to what it is and to how to accurately assess it and improve it. Sternberg (1986) sees intelligence as modifiable through the training of thinking and problem-solving skills. He views this as happening when learners develop expertise in attending to relevant stimuli, properly identifying the problem at hand, generating hypotheses, and selecting and implementing proper plans and/or strategies.

The assessment of differences in **personality** characteristics among learners assists us with respect to making predictions about school and workplace performance. Although it is less precise than those predictions based on intelligence, it is probably fair to say that most educators and trainers value the personality construct.

Another construct of special interest to the cognitively oriented instructional design specialists is the **mind**. It is thought that through the understanding of **the relationship between the mind and the brain**, this will help us to explain and control behavior. The ability to control bodily functions by attending to selected environmental cues (e.g., biofeedback), the relationship between stress and the immunization system, and the relationship between anxiety and learning are three areas in which we are learning more about mind-brain-behavior relationships. It is assumed that as we learn more in the area, our understanding of the learning process will increase and provide us with valuable approaches to use in remediating learning problems.

Information-processing constructs related to **memory organization** have received considerable attention in the research literature. We now know that active engagement facilitates memory and schematic development by making information meaningful and therefore easier to retrieve. We also are finding that the use of schema activating (mathemagenic) strategies (e.g., advance organizers, summaries, outlines, figural and graphic representations) improve memory and retrieval.

The construct of **motivation** has also generated much interest and research. Attribution theorists (Weiner, 1986) emphasize the importance of a learner's locus of control. They claim that learning becomes maladaptive when a person attributes success to external forces and failure to internal forces. Lepper and Greene (1978) reported that if a task has high intrinsic interest for a person, use of an external reward system may have a negative motivational effect. Through such research, we are learning that we can match a person's motivational style to instruction and that we can actually modify maladaptive motivation.

A related construct, **cognitive style**, has led to an increase in our understanding of the teaching and learning process. A person's cognitive style is defined as the way a person differs with respect to their perceptions, storage, and retrieval of information. Field-independent persons are generally individualistic, have a low need for external reinforcement, are intrinsically motivated, and are inner directed. Field-dependent persons tend to depend on environmental supports and others, have a high need for external reinforcement, are extrinsically motivated and other directed. The assumption here is that one would use different teaching strategies to teach field-independent and field-dependent learners.

Given the **documented utility of a cognitive science approach** to instruction, there does seem to be greater correspondence with reality than there was with the behavioral models of instruction. Cognitive theorists can explain complex behaviors, and at the same time take individual differences/constraints into account. Such a theory is pragmatic and relatively easy to implement. It should be noted that the approach is also relatively inexpensive since in most cases we don't need to use expensive courseware. What we are trying to say here is that implementation of a cognitive theory of instruction is possible in most instructional situations and actually rather simple. The following **suggestions** are made with respect to implementing such an approach:

1. Consider using the reciprocal teaching methodology.
2. Teach procedural knowledge so that you maximize the chances of the content becoming the process.
3. Teach metacognitive abilities.
4. Teach learners to feel in control and responsible for their learning.
5. Match aptitudes of students to learning conditions.
6. Teach mathemagenic (mnemonic and schema-activating) strategies.
7. Teach thinking and problem-solving strategies that have potential for activating existing knowledge structures so that incoming knowledge can fit with old knowledge (i.e., focus on anchoring new information to existing cognitive situations and always keep in mind the importance of the principle of the

primacy of proactive interference).
8.   Teach techniques geared toward enhancing meaningful learning (e.g., use
     advance organizers). According to Ausubel (1978), use of advance organizers
     helps to bridge the gap between new and old information by giving the new
     knowledge meaning (e.g., use mapping techniques).

The instructional design strategies are summarized in Training Application 7.1.

In summary, although there is currently no one best and/or comprehensive theory of instruction, the cognitive science models of instruction seem to be our best bet at the present time. These models have been found to correspond well with reality, and they are coherent, inclusive, pragmatic, and reasonably parsimonious. We are no longer severely limited by individual differences and developmental constraints. That is to say that we are finding that we can shape learners and make changes that will assist us in our efforts to bridge the gaps between typical and atypical learners.

A BROADENED COGNITIVE VIEW OF BEHAVIOR

Looking back to the 1920s through the early 1960s, one can readily see that behaviorism was in the forefront of psychology. Psychology was still a newly developing field and was very much concerned with being accepted as a scientific field of study. It was then believed that if it was to be recognized as a genuine science, attention should be directed at studying observable behavior. As a result, research was focused on learning contingencies, punishment, and reinforcement. Only that which was observable was believed to be acceptable to the scientific community.

As psychology developed further and perhaps became more sure of itself, it became apparent that by focusing only on the observable that our research efforts were not addressing the way people think and solve problems. We were ignoring the importance of the thought processes taking place inside of our minds. By focusing only on the observable, we were missing a tremendous amount of information of what was going on inside a problem solver's head prior to solving a problem. What needed to be included in our study of behavior was an examination of the human brain and mind. It was decided that this neglect of the human mind and the way people think had to be systematically addressed. No longer could psychology focus only on observable behavior. As a result of these changing views, cognitive science began to take the forefront of psychological research in the late 1960s and early 1970s.

The importance of addressing the mind in addition to behavior seems to be logical and basic to the overall learning process. Through studying individual thought processes, we can better understand how people learn and then effectively aid them when their means of thinking and problem solving are not proving beneficial to them. Current research has shown that this is an area that has tremendous potential with respect to working with atypical learners.

With the shift to including cognition in addition to behavior, we now have a better understanding of how knowledge develops and the learning process. We know that knowledge is an organized set of mental structures (content) and procedures (procedural knowledge) and that learning takes place when there is a change in these mental structures and/or procedures. The **cognitive scientists** have underlined the importance of getting students to be **active learners** if we want them to truly understand and remember what we want them to learn. One way of getting them to be active is to have the students **construct meaning for themselves** when they are introduced to new material. The student needs to have a knowledge base of some related information onto which the learner can anchor the new information and construct meaning. Using a method in which the student actively retrieves old information and then builds on that information will help to insure that learners are actively engaged in the learning task. Passive learners will not learn as much as active learners who are forced to use their existing knowledge structures to process information. By creating a bridge between new information and old information, we are increasing the chances that a learner will genuinely understand the material presented and will then be able to remember the information at a later time when it is needed (Ausubel, 1968).

Given this broadened cognitive view of behavior, we will now focus our attention on how we can relate this cognitive view to instruction. Through understanding such terms as schemata, short-term memory, working memory, and long-term memory and what can be done to improve learning effectiveness at each stage of the learning process, we can better address the needs of atypical and maladaptive learners.

The term **schemata** refers to how our knowledge is organized. It is viewed as a framework in which information of a conceptual unit is organized. Schemata are assumed to be expandable, generative, and efficiently organized. For some, it is helpful to think of different schemata as representing different drawers in a file cabinet. Each drawer has its own schemata (its own category), and in each drawer we have information filed alphabetically according to topic so that the information may be retrieved easily when it is needed. When we first create a new file, it is relatively open and unused, but the more information we gain in a given category and on a given subject, the more the drawer becomes filled. We learn and add information to our schemata through activating previous knowledge, anchoring the new information onto the previously learned knowledge, and then integrating the information together so that it is more efficiently organized. In order to truly learn and understand something and be able to remember it at a later time, we must have some previous knowledge to which we can relate (anchor) this new information.

Information is first encountered through our **sensory register**. In order to perceive the information, we have to first attend to the stimuli. If we decide that we want to hold onto the information for a short time, through active engagement and rehearsal we can hold the information long enough to reach our **short-term memory**. This type of memory is of a limited duration and will fade unless we decide we need to consolidate and further rehearse the information and have it permanently stored in our **long-term memory system**. The knowledge we have gained relating to these specific memory types has been very helpful in understanding how people learn and why some people may have difficulty retrieving needed information. Recent neuropsychological research (Restak, 1984, 1988, 1994) has greatly enhanced our understanding of brain-mind-behavior relationships and has helped us with respect to relating our assessments to treatment when working with individuals who have memory problems. Through identification of specific brain structures related to different memory functions, we can aid persons who have had damage to a given area by teaching them to compensate for their loss.

The use of **schema-activating techniques** (advance organizers, mnemonics, analogies, figural and graphic representations, etc.) that are designed to promote active learning and increase understanding have helped us improve instruction. These techniques facilitate understanding of material and aid in effective recall of information at a later time.

Throughout this book we have emphasized six **cognitive constructs** that have aided us with respect to our scientific study of the human learner. The six constructs selected for special review were intelligence, personality, information-processing constructs of memory organization, mind-brain-behavior relationships, cognitive styles, and motivation. **Intelligence** has aided us in predicting who will succeed in school and in some cognitively demanding workplace situations. Remember that it doesn't always effectively predict who will do well in life. Much research has been done by Gardner (who views intelligence in contextual situations; 1983), Sternberg (who believes that through use of training techniques and strategies that we can teach intelligence; 1986), and Feuerstein (who emphasizes the importance of the adult expert who selects, shapes, and filters information for the learner and the high impact culture has on the learning process; 1985). Each of these theorists believe that we need to expand our current definition of intelligence and that intelligence can be modified and taught at least to some extent. It is commonly believed that a person's **personality** has a great deal to do with whether or not a person is successful in school, in the workplace, in life in general. Although the field of personality assessment is not as well developed as the field of intelligence testing, and we recognize that we are not always able to accurately predict who will do well in school, the workplace, or life in general, most of us consider the personality construct to have some value with respect to our assessments, predictions, and outcome-monitoring activities. The field appears to be growing, and the personality assessment instruments are being refined. Research related to supporting the **information-processing constructs of memory organization** includes all of the previously discussed information related to meaningfulness and the importance of building a bridge between what was previously known to the new information being introduced to a learner. The **mind-brain-behavior** construct receives support from research on biofeedback (Miller, 1969) and the finding that negative self-statements can alter the biochemical balance in a person's brain and thus lead to depressed affect (Beck, 1976). Research related to the **cognitive style** construct includes the work done with learners who are field dependent and those who are field independent. For example, Witkin, Moore, Goodenough, and Cox (1977) did research in this area of learning style and found that the field-independent learners tended to be more confident, less likely to look to others for reinforcement, and they were typically inner directed. Field-dependent learners, on the other hand, looked to others for support, were less confident, and were less likely to be in positions of leadership. Of all of the cognitive constructs mentioned, motivation probably has the most important implications for those of us working in the fields of education and training. Motivation includes such things as needs, values, attitudes, and aspirations. It can be described as a regulatory process that directs and guides learning and behavior. Thus it can readily be seen why it is so important to educators and trainers. If you have a learner who is not motivated to learn, he or she is simply not going to learn. However, there are things you can do to try to change a learner's level of motivation and help him or her become a better learner. Abraham Maslow's (1954) research program relates to the importance of addressing lower-level needs before one can address higher needs. Bernard Weiner (1986) defined attribution as including locus of control, controllability, and stability and found that most of those learners who attributed success to an unstable external locus of control were maladaptive learners. If you could change a learner's locus of control and get the person to realize that he or she can have an impact on personal success, this individual could then become a more adaptive learner. Bates (1979) reported that intrinsically motivated students performed better with cognitively based instruction, and extrinsically motivated students performed better with behaviorally based instruction. DeCharms (1976) found that those learners who were able to view themselves as origins of their behavior rather than pawns were able to free themselves from feelings of helplessness, were able to improve their achievement and were able to set more appropriate goals for themselves.

Through our efforts to include these six cognitive constructs in our instructional design work, we have greatly increased the range of techniques and tools we can use when working with learners who are having difficulty learning. Cognitive scientists have tremendously broadened our repertoire of potential interventions and greatly helped our success rate when dealing with atypical learners. By focusing on these six aspects of cognition that can be effectively manipulated and broadening our focus from simply studying overt behaviors, we are now helping to make students better learners.

INDIVIDUAL DIFFERENCES

By means of studying individual differences, we can better understand where an individual's unique characteristics may be strengthening or weakening his or her current functioning. By assessing an individuals relative strengths and weaknesses, we can describe a learner's behavior and then try to come up with intervention strategies designed to improve the learner's current level of performance.

There are individual differences such as maturation, attention, and temperament that we know that we really cannot manipulate. These individual differences are considered to be **biological constraints**. We are born with them and live our lives with them and have little if any control over them. However, there are also quite a few other individual difference constraints that we can manipulate. These are the constraints to which we look when we are trying to help an individual better adapt to his or her learning environment. These are the **psychological constraints** and include knowledge, language, memory organization, mood, attitudes, personality, cognitive style expectancies, and motivation.

In helping students to learn better in their learning environment, we can look to these psychological constraints and determine which type of intervention would best address a learner's needs. For example, if a learner with a disability were mainstreamed into a class or work situation and then had a difficult time adapting (e.g., not mixing with others, feeling isolated, expecting to fail, and perceiving others as having an advantage), a very helpful method of intervention would be to use **reciprocal teaching, cooperative learning** and/or **peer tutoring procedures**. The focus here would be on manipulating what you knew you could (e.g., the disabled students' knowledge base, language skills, expectancies, attitudes, and mood). The use of reciprocal teaching, cooperative learning, and peer tutoring procedures have been reported to improve students' achievements in the classroom, their relationships with their peers, and their attitudes toward themselves and toward school. These techniques have been shown to be effective with respect to the manipulation of a student's knowledge base, language skills, attitudes, mood, and expectancies (all of which are considered to be psychological constraints on learning). These interventions have been found to be helpful for not only those learners with special needs, but also for typical learners as well. It is believed that their effectiveness can be attributed to the fact that they serve to remediate basic academic skills, reinforce active engagement in learning activities, and promote critical thinking.

Different means of assessment are used to document **individual differences** among learners. For example, if you chose to use a dynamic assessment approach (**Feuerstein**, 1985), you would assess a learner's ability to learn and then try to help the learner develop beyond that point. General principles of learning and development would be recognized and used to support the person's learning environment.

In **authentic assessment**, each learner is evaluated individually. It is believed that the best way to accurately assess and evaluate the learner's performance is by means of creating a **portfolio** of each individual learner's efforts, progress, and achievements. The focus is not only upon collecting data and making diagnostic decisions, emphasis is also placed on the interpretation of the data and the use of it to develop intervention strategies. The information that is obtained from authentic assessment procedures can be used to determine how each learner is functioning as an individual in his or her unique learning environment. The first step is to document the skills (individual differences) of the learner. Next, an attempt is made to examine the interactions taking place in the learning environment in an effort to see what can be manipulated to make the learner better and more effective. This is a very positive approach because poor academic performance is not seen as the result of some deficit in the student. Rather, poor performance is viewed as being a result of inappropriate interactions taking place between the skills of the learner and his or her learning environment. The assumption is that we can change the environment, modify learning skills, and enhance learning.

Assessment of individual differences among learners provides us with an **overall structure** and a **framework** onto which we can begin to study individual differences and assess which differences are helping and which differences are hurting an individual learn. It is from that point that we can begin to look to ways to help learners modify their skills and teach them to compensate for their deficits.

TRAINING SCENARIO LECTURE SERIES

In this final section of this chapter we present a series of **five training lectures** that represent a synthesis of the cognitive science information contained in this book. Given that our clients are most likely composed of individuals with varying levels of competence regarding the psychology of instruction, we would want to be sure that everyone had a good knowledge base related to the general learning models and the cognitive science perspective. It should be noted that the lectures are purposely designed to overlap. Such an arrangement provides for a smooth transition from one lecture to the next and encourages a learner to relate new information to what is already known. We would advise the instructional consultant to split up the information in the following way:

1. Training Lecture 1:   An **overview** of the **learning models**
2. Training Lecture 2:   The **impact** of **cognitive science** on learning theory and instruction
3. Training Lecture 3:   The **means of instruction**
4. Training Lecture 4:   The means of instruction and the **knowledge acquired**
5. Training Lecture 5:   **Developmental issues** of relevance to learning and **current trends** in research related to instruction

Training Lecture 1: An Overview of the Learning Models

We would begin our lecture by carefully framing the contents of the lecture for our audience. By definition, a **frame** is a network of related ideas. By explaining (as an advance organizer) the topics we selected to discuss in our lecture (e.g., learning theory models, relating the cognitive science knowledge base to instruction, etc.), we would be able to direct the attention of our audience to the topics at hand. Our lecture would be designed to focus on basic information since without prior knowledge of the background of our audience, we would make an effort to structure our lecture to allow our audience to anchor the contents to their existing cognitive templates. That is to say that we would attempt to speak within the context of our audience's zone of proximal development (ZPD).

First of all, we would point out that theories of learning can be explained in terms of the **learning curve components**. The **baseline** learning curve component refers to those individual differences among learners when a learner is first exposed to a learning task. The **acquisition** component refers to explanations of the learning process. The **maintenance** component refers to what has been retained and the **extinction** component refers to what has been lost or forgotten with the passage of time and/or interference.

Then, we would describe the four different theoretical **models of learning**. **Classical conditioning theorists** explain learning as taking place when two stimuli (a UCS and a CS) are paired together for a number of trials. From this perspective, learning is viewed as taking place through stimulus pairing. In this model, the baseline is considered to be the learner's previous history of stimulus (UCS-CS) pairings. Individual differences can be explained by differential exposure to stimulus pairs and to possible biological differences existing among the biologically wired unconditioned stimuli (species specific UCS wirings). Acquisition is seen in the USC-CS pairings for a number of trails. Maintenance occurs with continuous UCS-CS pairings and extinction occurs when the pairings are discontinued. This model appears to be well suited to explaining early learning and emotional development.

Operant conditioning theorists introduced the idea of using reinforcement and punishment procedures to shape behaviors. Baseline is explained by the learner's previous reinforcement and punishment history. When we arrange the environment to bring the learner's behavior under stimulus control, we have a positive demonstration of acquisition. Maintenance occurs if the learner continues to receive rewards and/or punishers for a targeted behavior in their natural environment. Extinction occurs if we reverse the reinforcing and punishing contingencies.

Social learning theorists claim that learning takes place when there is a combination of S-R continuity and a cognitive mediator. We learn by observing and modeling. Learning curve components in this model consist of a baseline of previous exposures to models. Acquisition occurs through exposure to models in the learner's environment. Extinction occurs with the elimination of the exposure to the models.

There are many **cognitive models** of learning. The cognitive information processing model has been greatly influenced by Gestalt and cognitive developmental ideas. **Gestalt** psychologists introduced the idea of learned perceptual templates. These templates were viewed as setting up constraints that either facilitated or interfered with learning. They introduced the idea of productive (insight) versus reproductive (trial-and-error) thinking. They also introduced the idea of chunking, or analyzing a task into subcomponents, in an effort to see the parts in relation to the whole. Gestalt psychologists claimed that memories were constantly being reconstructed (e.g., Bartlett's famous reconstructed memory experiment).

Cognitive developmental theorists can be divided into the Piagetian (Genevan) and neo-Piagetian (camps of thought). **Piaget** claimed that there were important developmental differences between a child and an adult. He introduced the concepts of schema, assimilation and accommodation of experience, disequilibration, and the importance of an active learner interacting with a stimulating and supportive environment. **Neo-Piagetians**

discussed the value of engaging in a cognitive task analyses. They varied problem-solving tasks in an effort to examine the cognitive processes used by subjects to problem solve. They stressed the value of relating language and schooling to cognition (e.g., we learn when we establish a rule, particularly a verbal rule).

Cognitive **information processing theorists** (cognitive scientists) used the computer program analog to explain thinking and problem solving. They focused on the way information is stored, assessed, and retrieved in the mind. They claimed that the memory system was divided into four components (i.e., the sensory register, short-term memory, working memory, and the long-term memory store). They examined differences between expert and novice thinkers and problem solvers. These cognitive scientists claimed that it is not the accumulation of experience (a behaviorist's notion), but rather the remodeling of experience that is of primary importance to the learning process. What a person will learn depends on what he or she already knows when first exposed to a learning situation. The assumption is that we build on past schematic representations. (Schemata are defined as the organized knowledge we possess.) The baseline in a cognitive, learning theory model is considered to be the learners existing schemas or cognitive structures. Acquisition is explained by assimilating a new stimulus situation and accommodating old schema to incorporate the new information. Maintenance occurs when new environmental information is anchored to what a person already knows, and extinction is explained in terms of cognitive interference when new information isn't easily anchored to the existing cognitive templates.

After discussing the learning curve components and the four theoretical models of learning, we would note that Robert Gagne (1985) created a **taxonomy of learning** that can be used as an organizer to interrelate the models of learning just discussed. His model consists of eight conditions of learning. These conditions are arranged in a hierarchy each serving as a prerequisite for the next higher condition of learning with the exception of the first condition (signal learning). Condition 1 is explained by the classical conditioning model. Conditions 2 through 5 could be explained using the operant conditioning model. The social learning model could be used to explain conditions 2 through 8, and the cognitive model could be used to explain problem-solving behavior (condition 8). The classical conditioning model can be used to explain early learning and emotional development. The operant conditioning model can be used to explain learning of overt responses. Social learning theorists introduced a model emphasizing the powerful effect of modeling and imitation. The social learning model appears to be well suited to explaining learning when one reads or attends a lecture. Finally, it should be noted that the cognitive models allow us to explain the thinking, problem-solving, and creativity process. Today, behaviorism is viewed by many as basically a performance-motivational theory, not a full-blown learning theory. It seems as though the animal-human analogy can only go so far in explaining learning without consideration being given to the value of language and rules used in thinking and problem solving.

In the final section of lecture one, we would discuss **motivation**. What is motivation? Motivation energizes behavior and gives it direction. It leads to a goal by turning learning into performance. Each learning theory has a motivational component associated with its use. The behaviorists viewed motivation in terms of physiological drives and schedules of reinforcement. Cognitive theorist view motivation in terms of need theory and/or cognitive conflict or disequilibration. As educators and trainers we are not in a position to manipulate physiological drives. However, we can benefit from the behavioral idea of using schedules of reinforcement. It is important to keep in mind that the question of using extrinsic rewards and the possibility of their undermining intrinsic interests, continues to be debated. We can create problematic learning situations in which cognitive conflict is used as a motivator to maximize student performance.

The overall purpose of the first lecture was to give the audience a general knowledge base (anchor) related to an overview of learning theory. By describing the four models of learning, how they relate to the components of the learning curve, how they address the construct of motivation, and how they correspond with reality, the stage is now set for the second lecture (the impact of cognitive science on learning theory and instruction).

Training Lecture 2: The Impact of Cognitive Science on Learning Theory and Instruction

There has been a **shift toward the cognitive science perspective** in recent years. This shift seems to have resulted from the realization that cognitive mediation is very important in the learning process. In fact, too important to ignore any longer. Today, most learning theorists have made a place for the inclusion of a cognitive component in their models. This cognitive component is considered to be necessary with respect to explaining thinking, problem solving, and creativity.

The documented importance of the **relationship of language to cognition** has prompted most learning theorists, even the behaviorally minded theorists, to reformulate their paradigms. For example, the associationistic anchored **rule learner** group considered language to be important with respect to mediating the process of complex learning. The meaning theorists arose from the Gestalt movement. They emphasized the role of language with respect to enhancing meaning and facilitating the depth of processing of information. The neo-Piagetians considered language to be very important because it had considerable potential for enhancing attention. Finally, the cognitive information-processing theorists viewed language and cognition as going hand in hand. They viewed language as being necessary for the coding of information. From their perspective, the use of language allows for the efficient filtering and pigeonholing of information within the context of a learners existing cognitive structures.

The notion of the **literate bias in schooling** is the result of the view that language is considered to be an important determiner of cognition. Indeed, it is considered to be impossible to acquire complex academic knowledge until one is able to manipulate language. The mastery of language in achieving school and workplace success is one of the ways in which the **unschooled mind** differs from the **schooled mind**. Other differences between the schooled and unschooled mind include the unschooled person's inability to transfer thinking and problem-solving skills to novel situations, their difficulty in using aids such as mnemonic devices for enhancing memory, their lack of prerequisite schemata to allow for the remodeling of experience and the development of different metacognitive learning strategies. Unschooled persons have not **learned to learn** and are context bound. That is to say that the content never becomes the process for such individuals, for they lack the prerequisite information needed for anchoring new incoming information to well-developed knowledge structures.

Atypical learners are considered to be similar in some respects to the unschooled in that important metacognitive strategies and a well developed prerequisite knowledge base are lacking. It is assumed that **experts** interpret their environment in a different manner than **novices**. The literate bias in schooling allows them to do so. Expert learners are usually less dependent on environmental supports and are internally controlled processers of information. That is to say that they don't need a great deal of reinforcement from their external environment. Their superior knowledge base allows them to have better memories and recall. Experts are able to move from knowing "that" to knowing "how," by learning procedural knowledge that allows their limited working memory space to be freed up so that their specialized content knowledge can then be applied to solving problems. Since their knowledge becomes organized around meaningful symbolic representations of experience, they have faster and better recognition patterns of perceptions than novices.

When observing **atypical learners, differences in attention, memory organization**, and **cognitive expectancies** become evident. Most atypical learners lack good anchors. Given that new information is built upon older existing knowledge, the **primacy of proactive interference** is a hindrance for many of them. While typical learners **remodel experience** (building the new onto the old), atypical learners appear to merely accumulate experiences without being able to relate new experiences to their poorly developed existing knowledge structures. For typical learners, their existing sche-matic representations can serve as default structures when new representa-tions can't be made on the basis of incoming stimuli. For atypical learners, this does not appear to be the case.

Although the difference between typical and atypical learners, and ex-perts and novices for that matter, are considered to be vast, **some remediation is possible**. Through the teaching of strategies (strategy train-ing), the use of schema activators, and mathemagenic activities, one can attempt to modify the atypical learner's ability to attend to the important features of a problem, their memory organizational abilities, and their cog-nitive expectancies. These differences between the typical and atypical learn-ers are viewed as representing differences in cognitive structures (schema). **Individual differences** are assumed to be either **fixed** (biological differ-ences such as attention, temperament, or maturational stages of develop-ment) or **flexible** (psychological differences such as knowledge, language, memory organization, mood, attitudes, personality, cognitive style expect-ancies, and motivation). These flexible constraints on learning can be modi-fied through a focus on process education and training. This is where the use of schema activators come into the training picture. By actively engag-ing the students in the learning process, attention improves, memory im-proves, and internal cognitive expectancies are developed. Some examples of **memory and/or comprehension directed schema activators** (mathemagenic activities) include the following:

1. Use **advance organizers**.
2. Encourage **underlining** of prose material (only useful if used sparingly; train learn-ers to know what is important and what is not important).
3. Encourage learners to **summarize** information (better if student constructed rather than instructor constructed).
4. Use **mnemonic techniques** (e.g., use of acronyms, first letters, keywords, rhymes - especially useful for learning new, unfamiliar information such as mathematical concepts and/or a foreign language).
5. Train learners to **ask questions** and **take notes**.
6. Break down learning tasks into behavioral and/or cognitive components (i.e., **task analyze** and use behavioral and/or cognitive instructional objectives).
7. Encourage use of **figural** and/or **graphic representations** of information.

Overall, these strategies work best if they are **student generated**. By teach-ing atypical learners and novices to attend to relevant stimuli, their chunks become larger and more sophisticated. In sum, they become better think-ers and problem solvers.

In lecture 2, an attempt was made to focus on the contributions that cognitive scientists have had on the understanding of the overall learning process. The importance of developing good language skills and formal-

ized schooling appears to be clearly demonstrated in the research literature. In addition it does seem to be important to build new knowledge
onto a strong anchor. By examining the differences between typical and
atypical learners, and expert and novice learners, educators and trainers
can modify these differences by using what we know about strategy training, metacognitive awareness, and encouragement of active engagement in
problem-solving tasks.

Training Lecture 3: The Means of Instruction

Given what we know about learning theory and instruction (Bruer,
1993), it seems that there is **no one best method of instruction**. Behaviorists stressed reinforcement, punishment, and the accumulation of habits.
These habits reportedly influenced thinking and learning ability. The focus
was on the accumulation of experience. Behavioral ideas have considerable value when applied to the learning of simple skills, rote learning, and
control of undesirable behavior. The cognitive theorists felt that information needed to be meaningful to be learned and claimed that the use of
language symbolization and imagery were important to the overall learning process.

In **a cognitive model**, it is assumed that environmental information
enters sensory registers and from there it is processed in a (time limited)
short-term, working-memory system, after which it enters a long-term
memory system where it is stored for retrieval. Only by entering the limited short-term memory system can information get coded and entered into
the long-term memory store. The more ways and the deeper we process
information, the easier the recall. In addition, the more the encoding process relies on **meaning**, the more likely the recall. This notion of relating
meaning to recall constitutes what is known as a **depth of processing view**.

Knowledge is believed to be stored in a system of **schematic structures**
that are developed through active involvement with the environment. With
time and experience these structures are remodeled and greatly expanded.
Language is believed to be critical to learning because a learner uses language to code information.

This **coding process** is believed to facilitate attention and allows for the
efficient filtering and pigeonholing of information into the context of a
learner's existing cognitive structures. That is to say that language symbolization is believed to allow for deep elaborative rehearsal that eventually frees up a learner's limited working memory space to allow for more
and deeper meaningful processing of the information at hand. With experience, oral (i.e., preliterate) schema gets integrated within the context of
rule learning and a literate view of reality. This is not necessarily an automatic process. Some learners (unschooled learners) have a very difficult

time moving from using oral to literate schematic representations. This places many of them at an educational disadvantage. Admittedly, our schools and most contemporary workplace settings contain a strong literate bias. The oral learning tradition is constrained (bound) by auditory memory limitations. The literate school and workplace cultures impose a logical, abstract thinking, and problem-solving context upon our interpretations of environmental events. Considerable research has been done on the development of reading and writing skills with this literate bias in mind. With social learning theory as a base, teachers model literacy, teach writing and reading, and reinforce the use of print and language at an early age.

As noted earlier, behaviorists stressed the importance of trial and error learning, reinforcement and punishment, accumulating experience, and drill and practice. Cognitive scientist's focused their studies on documenting the differences between **novice and expert problem solvers**. It seemed that the major difference between the two groups was due to the impact of knowledge. First the learner appears to need to receive facts (content) about a skill and with practice that content is eventually converted to **proceduralized knowledge**. The learner needs less energy at the proceduralized stage of problem solving because the **proceduralized information** has become **automated**. At this point it is assumed that the learner can use his or her cognitive processes and schematic representations like an expert problem solver. That is to say that the learner moves from knowing that (declarative content knowledge) to knowing how (proceduralized knowledge). As competence is acquired (moving from novice to expert levels of performance), many bits and pieces of information become interconnected. Previous learning serves as a contextual anchor on to which we attach new ideas. This notion is consistent with contemporary views related to the importance of the primacy of proactive interference. This interconnected knowledge is assumed to become grouped into meaningful chunks that are easier to access. In sum, the view being advocated here is that we rework our schematic representations and move from knowing what, to knowing how, to knowing that.

Default structures represent what we have inside our heads. We use these default structures to access what we know and to assist us with our problem solving efforts. It is assumed that learners learn better by using strategies to represent experience. With a goal of embellishing our memory chunks or developing large-scale functional units, we can provide the learner with appropriate procedures to facilitate learning. For example, in teaching we begin by assessing required skills needed in a specialized domain of knowledge. We analyze the skills and identify subcomponent skills. Then we attempt to teach the skills to the client. We can activate prior learning by using advance organizers, asking questions, presenting text cues, underlining prose, using mnemonic techniques, and encouraging active engagement of the material to be learned.

The knowledge the learner has about his or her learning and the decisions made about its use is referred to as **metacognition**. It has been demonstrated that metacognitive skills can be taught (Brown, 1978). Learners need to know which strategies work best for them and when to use them. Cognitive scientists attempt to establish relationships among the basic components of learning (e.g., attention, memory, perception, and learning). It is assumed that most perceptions are learned. These learned perceptions create templates through which the learner filters and pigeonholes new information. Sometimes these templates serve as constraints. For example, when we approach a reading task, we impose our cognitive templates on the information at hand. That is to say that we are **context dependent**. With the increasing development of cognitive templates, some learners become more rigid with respect to processing new information. Should this occur, it then becomes more difficult for them to anchor new information onto these existing structures because they have become very context dependent.

Most learning theorists address **individual differences**. Associationists view individual differences in terms of learned habits and/or accumulated experience. Gestalt theorists view individual differences as differences in a learner's cognitive and perceptual templates. Piagetians refer to different schematic representations among learners. Finally, the information processing theorists view individual differences in terms of **biological constraints** (attention, maturation, and temperament) that are considered to be more or less fixed constraints and psychological constraints (knowledge, language, memory organization, mood, attitudes, personality, cognitive style expectancies, and motivation). These **psychological constraints** are considered to be manipulable. Atypical learners are assumed to have defective template filters (e.g., defective attention, language, attitudinal, etc., filters). This view empowers the trainer and learner. By using various thinking and problem-solving strategies, we can manipulate and improve many of the various psychological constraints imposed on the learner.

The assumption that we learn when we develop a verbal rule has been stated above. Vygotsky (1978) claimed that we learn within the **context of a social situation**. That is to say that we learn within a **zone of proximal development (ZPD)**. An innovative learning strategy many trainers are now using is the **reciprocal teaching strategy**. First of all, we assess a student's level of competence. Then with the assistance of an expert model, we support the learner's development within the constraints of the learner's ZPD. Gradually, learners become more of an expert (autonomous) and assume control of their own learning.

Finally, it should be noted that these cognitive learning theories have been criticized by some as being too complex and unmanageable when attempts are made to put them into practice. However, all things considered, it is our view that these cognitive learning theories represent our best models. They allow us not only to explain complex behavior but also offer many manageable strategies designed to facilitate high levels of thinking and problem solving behavior. Glaser (1984, 1990) discussed many ideas related to using our knowledge of psychology to recommend instructional practices. He described the characteristics of competent learners and recommended several procedures (modeling, reciprocal teaching, strategy training, etc.) designed to assist us in our efforts to analyze instructional tasks and design instructional components to reach our goals of training competent learners.

Training Lecture 4: The Means of Instruction and the Knowledge Acquired

Once again, it should be stressed that there seems to be no one best **method of instruction**. Instead, there are multiple routes leading us to similar outcomes. The **behaviorists-associationists** stressed the use of reinforcement, punishment, and the accumulation of experience (habits). This building up of a hierarchy of habits was assumed to facilitate the development of thinking and problem solving skills. The focus was on the **accumulation of experience** not on the cognitive notion of the remodeling of experience. Behavioral means of training and instruction, although popular and useful in controlling problem behaviors and in acquiring simple behaviors, seems limited with respect to explaining complex thinking and problem solving behavior.

The **cognitive information processing theorists** said that information needs to be meaningful in order to be learned and that the use of imagery is important with respect to encoding and remembering. Cognitive theorists attempt to explain complex thinking and problem solving behavior. They claim that it isn't the mere accumulation of experience but rather the **remodeling of experience** that is important to learning. In addition, it is desirable to know what a learner already knows as we build on our past experiences. It is important to relate (anchor) new information to our existing cognitive structures.

Remember that behaviorists explain **individual differences** among learners as differences in the accumulation of learned habits. Gestalt theorists see individual difference as differences in learned perceptual templates through which learners filter and pigeonhole information. Piaget and the neo-Piagetians view individual differences as existing in a learner's schematic representations. The information-processing theorists see individual differences in terms of rather fixed biological templates (attention, maturation, and temperament) and more flexible and modifiable psychological templates (knowledge, language, cognitive styles, personality, attitudes, and mood).

From such descriptions of learner characteristics came the idea of matching these different learner variables to different treatment conditions. Remember that the premise is that there is not any one best method of teaching or learning. That is to say that there are **multiple routes yielding similar outcomes**. From this perspective, it is recommended that we view the teaching-learning process within the context of **aptitude treatment interaction (ATI)** situations. In sum, we view teaching as a test-teach-test research project set up within the context of an ATI design.

How is knowledge organized? We believe that knowledge is organized **schematically**. The organization is dependent on maturation and experience. Schema or knowledge structures represent concepts stored in memory. All human knowledge is thought to be stored within a system of schema structures developed through active involvement with the environment. These schematic representations affect how the learner will view, approach, and interpret information. With age and experience, schema become embedded and organized. They are influenced by our **prior experience** and they represent dynamic, constantly changing structures. Through the motivational process of **cognitive conflict**, learners are faced with problems. In problem-solving situations, the learner alters (accommodates) his or her schema to incorporate new information. This process is assumed to result in a higher level of thinking. Schema can serve as a constraint to the learning process. That is to say that we can become rigid and dependent on our learned context dependent schematic representations. It may become more difficult for us to pigeonhole (categorize) more and more information onto our anchors as we continue to learn more and more.

How do we **encode** information to build on our anchors? We believe that environmental information is encoded first in our sensory registers, next into short-term and working memory, and finally into our long-term memory store. **Short-term** and **working memory** are considered to be **limited to 7 + 2 chunks**. It is assumed that the more ways and the deeper we process information, the easier the recall. The more the process relies on meaning, the greater the chance that the information will be encoded and available for later retrieval. As noted earlier, Glaser (1984, 1990) discussed several tactics and strategies that are considered to be helpful with respect to facilitating the encoding process.

In our culture, knowledge acquisition involves **language**. Oral schema must gradually be integrated with literate schema. It seems that several years of formal schooling are needed for this transition and that **many disadvantaged, unschooled, and/or atypical learners have problems moving from an oral to literate tradition** because they have **restricted language codes**. Language in an information processing model is considered to be paramount to the development of higher level thinking. That is to say that content is equal to process for mature, expert learners. Learners use language to code information. This coding facilitates attention and allows for the efficient filtering and pigeonholing of information.

With the goal of embellishing our knowledge (memory) chunks or building large-scale functional units, we can provide the learner with appropriate knowledge schema for interpreting and integrating new information. The use of schema activators seem to help place new information in memory so that it can be retrieved and activated. Advance organizers help direct attention. How learners develop a schema is facilitated by the use of adjunct questions. In addition, mnemonics aid encoding and make information easier to remember. Such aids facilitate developing our default structures. The overall goal is to free up working memory space to process more information.

From an information-processing perspective, what develops? Attention develops. The number of things a person can attend to is assumed to be limited to 7 + 2 chunks, but the chunks can become embellished with symbols and are particularly enhanced by the development of linguistic symbols. Studies designed to determine the differences between experts and novices have found that they differ in the ways that they attend to different details of a problem-solving situation. We learn when we develop a rule, particularly a verbal rule that relates new information to a learner's existing cognitive structure.

Knowledge acquisition proceeds from declarative (content-propositional) to procedural. Cognitive scientists recommend that we teach content, procedural content, and procedural knowledge (general problem-solving skills-schema activators). It is recommended that at first we would do well to focus our attention on the acquisition of content. At the same time, we should acquire procedural knowledge. Afterwhich we should attempt to automatize our procedural knowledge in an attempt to free up working memory space for content. Again, schema activators (use of figures, and graphs, advance organizers, mnemonics, etc.) should be used to direct encoding and facilitate remembering. These procedures provide a way to facilitate the targeted information into the long-term memory system. Identifying what is important in a lesson facilitates memory. The knowledge the learner has about what strategies are useful to his or her individual style and when to use them is called metacognition. That is to say that metacognition represents personal knowledge about individual learning. Metacognition strategies have a powerful effect on learning. We should assess our students ZPD and recognize the power of modeling. To facilitate the learning process, we can use reciprocal teaching procedures, mathemagenic activities, and monitor skills. Hopefully, we will be able to effect positive change using these recommended procedures.

Training Lecture 5: Developmental Issues of Relevance to Learning and Current Trends in Research Related to Instruction

Our understanding of the psychology of instruction would not be complete without some understanding regarding developmental issues as well as getting some idea as to where the field is headed.

From a **neo-Piagetian perspective,** attention develops as we mature, and we are able to learn when we have acquired rules (i.e., verbal rules) allowing us to relate new information to older existing information. Knowledge is seen as being stored and anchored in a complex system of schematic representations governed by sets of executive processing strategies. The **rate of the development** of schema is considered to be dependent on the size of the learner's M-power (the learner's memory power capacity to attend to a number of schema at once); the learner's cognitive style; the complexity and cognitive-perceptual organizational representations of experiences the learner has encountered; and the learner's affective disposition (mood). While **M-power** (memory power) is thought to be fixed at a very young age, we do have the ability to greatly expand the size of our chunks. This expansion can be achieved through increasing a learner's content, content-procedural, and procedural knowledge base.

Use of the **reciprocal teaching method** (Palinscar & Brown, 1984) is another way through which individuals can be trained to enlarge their chunks and become more sophisticated learners. This method of instruction improves comprehension while at the same time teaches strategies that can be used to improve the learner's self-regulatory executive functions. In this manner, learning takes place in a **social context,** and in a **cooperative learning environment.** The learner is brought through his or her **zone of proximal development (ZPD)** up to the next higher level. A movement from an external to an internal plane accompanies this change. In this manner, learners are actively engaged (discussing, rehearsing, and analyzing information) and they share their knowledge and observations with others. This teaching procedure is thought to enhance overall cognitive processing.

To complete the final lecture, it is our view that the audience should become aware of **trends** in the area (i.e., where the research related to the psychology of instruction is headed). Glaser (1978, 1982, 1986, 1993) listed the following six areas of research that seem to be reflective of current research in the field:

1.   **Comparison of expert and novice problem solvers.** Through behavioral and cognitive task analyses, the way experts go about learning and solving problems is carefully examined and described. The goal is to find the best learning and problem solving techniques, isolate them, and then try to teach them to atypical learners.

2.   **Early interventions**. The focus here is on how to improve early assessments, how to best identify at risk learners, and provide early interventions.
3.   **Prose learning, mathemagenic activities, and schema activators**. The focus here is on strategy training, use of advance organizers, active engagement, underlining, outlining, summarizing, use of figural and graphic problem solving procedures that have been demonstrated to improve memory and comprehension.
4.   **Intelligence and personality**. The focus here is on developing more accurate ways to assess intelligence and personality and to relate these assessments to a treatment plan.
5.   **Tutoring, mastery learning, and PSI**. Attempts are being made to examine the similarities across these approaches and to add cognitive components to these instructional models.
6.   **Behavior modification with a cognitive cast**. Here the focus is on an attempt to integrate the older behavioral models of learning and instruction with the newer cognitive strategies.

In summary, this series of lectures was designed in an attempt to help explain the utility of focusing on a cognitive psychology of instruction. By describing the learning models, the cognitive science perspective, developmental issues, and areas of current research, we hope that your audience would walk away from the lecture series with a solid foundation of knowledge related to what we know and don't know about the psychology of instruction.

TERMS TO KNOW

outcome-based education (OBE)
Coleman Report (1966)
effective schools
mastery learning model
authentic assessment
collaborative consultation
instructional consultation
mental health consultation
organizational development consultation
test-teach-test hypothesis testing approach
viewing teaching and therapy as research
aptitude-treatment-interaction (ATI) designs
M-power (memory power)
schema-activating techniques
biological constraints
psychological constraints
depth of processing
content knowledge
content-procedural knowledge

procedural knowledge (general problem-solving skills)
default structures (large-scale functional units)
zone of proximal development (ZPD)
neo-Piagetian perspective
reciprocal teaching method

QUESTIONS TO CONSIDER

1. Suppose that you are called upon to deliver a series of lectures on the psychology of instruction to a large audience. Discuss the most useful information that has potential for relating knowledge in psychology to instructional practice. In your discussion attempt to focus on more than one theoretical point of view. Finally make certain that you cite relevant empirical research supporting your position.
2. Is there currently a comprehensive theory of instructional psychology? What would a cognitive theory add? Why is there a need to reformulate the leading paradigms of instructional psychology? Discuss the utility of such a reformulated theory.
3. Discuss the relationship between the means (i.e., methods) of instruction and the knowledge that is acquired. In answering this question, make certain that you address the following questions: How is knowledge organized? How does knowledge develop? How is knowledge retrieved and used? What instructional techniques promise to facilitate the acquisition of new knowledge?
4. To what extent have the following areas of investigation led to productive research efforts in the study of instructional psychology?
    a. comparison of expert and novice problem solvers
    b. early interventions
    c. prose learning, mathemagenic activities, and schema activators
    d. intelligence and personality
    e. tutoring, mastery learning, and PSI
    f. behavior modification

    Treating the areas separately or together, state briefly their relevance and utility to school and/or workplace learning.

SUGGESTED READINGS

Readers wanting to study more thoroughly the topics covered in this chapter will find the following references helpful.

Bruer, J. T. (1993). *Schools for thought: A science of learning in the classroom.* Cambridge, MA: MIT Press.

Gagne, R. M. (1985). *The conditions of learning (4th ed.).* New York: Holt, Rinehart and Winston.

Glaser, R. (1978). *Advances in instructional psychology (Vol. 1).* Hillsdale, NJ: Erlbaum.

Glaser, R. (1982). *Advances in instructional psychology (Vol. 2).* Hillsdale, NJ: Erlbaum.

Glaser, R. (1984). *Education and thinking: The role of knowledge.* American Psychologist, 39, 93-104.

Glaser, R. (1986). *Advances in instructional psychology (Vol. 3)*. Hillsdale, NJ: Erlbaum.

Glaser, R. (1990). *The reemergence of learning theory within instructional research*. American Psychologist, 45(1), 29-39.

Glaser, R. (1993). *Advances in instructional psychology (Vol. 4)*. Hillsdale, NJ: Erlbaum.

Spady, W. G., & Marshall, K. J. (1991). *Beyond traditional outcome-based education*. Educational Leadership, 49, 67-72.

Walberg, H. J. (1984). *Improving the productivity of America's schools*. Educational Leadership, 41, 19-30.

Training Application 7.1
Instructional Design Strategies

Instructional design has been greatly enhanced by strategies learned from cognitive science (West, Farmer, & Wolff, 1991). Several strategies can enhance the presentation and processing of information in training.

Chunking strategies	Strategies used to organize information for recall (e.g., spatial, narrative, procedural, cause-effect, similarity-difference, form-function, advantage-disadvantage).
Frames	Grid, matrix, or framework used to visually display large amounts of information. The frame easily lends itself to displaying facts, details, examples, and principles organized in cause-effect, similarity-difference, form-function, advantage-disadvantage chunking strategies.
Concept mapping	Graphic display of concepts and relationships between or among concepts usually in a "spider," "hierarchy," or "chain" format. Concept maps are appropriate for concepts, propositions, and relationships, but not for factual detail.
Advance organizers	A brief prose passage, usually about a paragraph in length, that introduces the main body of the presentation. It links what is already known to new material by outlining, arranging, or logically sequencing the main points or procedures to follow.
Metaphor	A verbally cued, rich image that connotes general knowledge and similarity.
Rehearsal strategies	General repetition and study strategies that keep information active in working memory (e.g., repetition, questions and answers, summaries, underlining, notetaking).
Imagery	Pictures in the mind that are representations of something physical. they are like rich videos or movies that allow for recall of substantial detail.

| **Mnemonics** | Artificial memory aids helping to organize information for memorization (e.g., HOMES - the names of the Great Lakes, Huron, Ontario, Michigan, Erie, and Superior). |

West, C. K., Farmer, J. A., & Wolff, P. M. (1991). *Instructional design: Implications from cognitive science.* Englewood Cliffs, NJ: Prentice-Hall.

PART V

TRAINING AND ADULT EDUCATION

CHAPTER 8

THE INTERFACE OF SCIENCE AND PRACTICE: THE ROLE OF THE TRAINING PRACTITIONER IN APPLYING SCIENCE

Fred Kerlinger (1986) reported that when experienced researchers think of research methodology, two things frequently come to mind: (1) the importance of randomization to control for individual differences; and (2) the desirability of having comparison groups. In addition to addressing issues related to randomization and the importance of having comparison groups, we attempt in this chapter to relate research design to statistics and hypothesis testing. First of all, five general organizing statements are presented related to describing the field of research methodology with respect to current issues and trends. This introductory section is followed by a brief overview and comparative summary of four basic methodologies (observation, survey, experimental, and ex post facto). Each methodology is discussed and evaluated within the context of internal and external validity. This is followed by a discussion of a number of faulty and experimental designs. The final three sections consist of discussions related to variance control, basic statistical procedures, and notions of causal inference.

STATE OF THE FIELD

There has been a very noticeable shift away from a univariant approach toward a **multivariant approach**. The traditional way of doing research was to set up a horse race situation in which we tested for differences across groups on one or more dependent measures. For example, if we had a situation such as the one presented below with two groups (experimental and control) and a continuous dependent measure (achievement test scores) we would simply test for differences in achievement scores across groups.

> Experimental Control
> X1   X2
> _____
>
> Y1   Y2   -where a continuous variable (Y)
>   appears in the columns
>
> _____

Unfortunately, many experiments set up with this simple univariant design did not yield significant results because too much individual difference variability was not controlled for within groups. Today, most investigators attempt to control for more individual variability by building controls into their designs. A popular multivariant design is that of factorial ANOVA (Analysis of Variance). Take, for example, the same two groups situation we had before and control for individual differences among subjects using a 2 x 3 multivariant design.

		Experimental	Control
		Xa1	Xa2
	high Xb1	_____	
Intelligence	average Xb2	_____	
	low Xb3	_____	

> - where a continuous
> dependent measure (Y)
> appears in the cells

Instead of testing only one null hypothesis here, we are able to test three.

- There is no difference in achievement scores across methods of instruction (Xa1 & Xa2).
- There is no difference in achievement scores across aptitudes (Xb1 - Xb3).
- There is no interaction effect (A & B).

In this 2 x 3 multivariant instance, we are more likely to find significant results because we are controlling for more individual difference variability and are able to test more hypotheses.

    Another thing to consider when we discuss the present state of the field of research methodology is the relationship between the **tools of science** and the types of studies conducted. The point to be made here is that the tools of science (i.e., available instrumentation) determine what is studied. Twenty or so years ago, thinking, problem solving, and creativity were not the popular topics of study they are today. Why? Because twenty years ago we did not have the sophisticated computer simulation capabilities we now have. Advances in information-processing technology and instrumentation led to changes in what we were able to study. Likewise, development of psychometric instruments such as measures of social-adaptive behavior permitted the investigation of such behaviors. In sum, the available tools of science facilitate and/or constrain scientific developments.

A frequently asked question among researchers is whether we should engage in **basic or applied research**. Which approach is more likely to yield significant results? Perhaps the safest position to take in this instance is to straddle the fence. A noticeable trend among educational and psychological researchers today is to conduct field experiments. The desirability of a field experiment is that in field settings (intact classrooms, clinics, and/or workplace settings), strong treatment effects have a good chance to manifest themselves. Given the recent advances in more sensitive instrumentation related to the assessment of the complexities of variables within the context of a natural setting, more well-designed field experiments are now possible providing us with the opportunity to test hypotheses and articulate theory within natural contexts.

In addition to that which was stated above, it is important to note that special considerations are now being given to the **ethics** of conducting research. Today greater attention is being given to the importance of protection of both animal and human subjects. In addition, systematic attempts are being made to reduce the possibility of fraud within the research community.

Finally, it is important to keep in mind as we continue with our discussion of research methodology that the **short-term goal** of science is to **establish relationships**. The **long-term goal** is to **establish theory**. The point here is that our role as scientists is that of attempting to establish either correlational and/or cause and effect relationships. For some of us, we may be able to ultimately contribute to theory, but it is perfectly respectable for us to aim our sight at attempting to establish relationships.

AN OVERVIEW OF RESEARCH METHODOLOGY

One of the most basic approaches to science is that of **observation**. The investigator merely observes behavior without attempting to manipulate. A major advantage of this **field study approach** is that the observational data is being collected in a natural setting without the constraints imposed by a laboratory study. There are, however, a number of disadvantages associated with this approach. First of all, little control is possible. The only control is the observer's set to observe certain behaviors. That is to say that the checklist of behaviors to be observed provides some limited control. Furthermore, it is possible that some behaviors of interest (e.g., aggression) may not take place in the natural settings being observed. The observer's presence may also influence the behavior observed, but one could control for this problem by having the observer become a part of the natural environment before the study begins and/or by unobtrusively filming the natural situation. To ensure that you get an adequate sample of behavior, it is important to randomly select a number of times and events to be observed. It should be noted that the database in observational studies consist of frequency counts of the dependent measures of interest. If you merely observe one group, the data would be descriptively interpreted using graphs, figures, and tables to summarize what was observed. Should you have more than one group, let's say an experimental and control group, then it would be possible to statistically analyze the frequency data perhaps using a chi-square (X^2) procedure and testing for relationships between your independent and dependent measures.

A second approach to science is one of conducting **surveys**. This method consist of using questionnaires, rating scales, interviews, and psychological tests. If you use this approach to science, you are able to test for correlational relationships among variables. The advantage of the survey method is that you do present a standard stimulus to your respondents and you assume that differences in responses are attributed to something inside your respondents (e.g., intelligence, personality, attitudes, etc.). It should be noted that we are not manipulating anything here and are thus unable to nail down cause-effect relationships. In studies of this type, we are testing for correlational relationships using simple correlational procedures, multiple regression, factor analysis, and the related procedures of path analysis, canonical analysis, discriminant analysis, and LISREL (Linear Structural Relations). All independent and dependent variables are measured attribute variables, not active experimental variables. For example, if we wanted to determine the relationships of academic aptitude, grade point average, and need for achievement to college success, we would be conducting a psychometric survey study. In this instance we would have the following situation:

$$ACT + GPA + N\text{-}Ach \longrightarrow \quad \text{academic success}$$
$$X1 + X2 + X3 \longrightarrow \quad Y$$

The three variables on the left side of the equation would constitute the independent variables, and the academic success variable on the right would constitute the dependent variable. The analytic paradigm for the example would look like this:

		ACT (X1)		
		high	average	low
	nAch(X3)	high low	high low	high low
	high			
GPA(X2)	average			
	low			

-where a continuous measure of academic success (Y) appears in the cells

Since all independent variables are measured (nonexperimental variables in this instance), multiple regression would be an appropriate methodology to employ here. The null hypothesis to be tested would be that there is no relationship among the ACT scores, GPA, n-Ach scores, and academic success.

Of course, another basic research methodology is that of the **experiment**. Here we manipulate something and test for differences across groups, not relationships. If we had a two-group univariant situation, we would use a t-test to test our null hypothesis. If we had a three- or more groups univariant situation, we would use an F-test (ANOVA). Should the experiment be set up as a factorial design, then factorial analysis of variance (FANOVA) would be an appropriate analytic technique. For example, if the analytic paradigm looked like this,

		Method		
		Xa1	Xa2	Xa3
	Xb1			
Aptitude measure	Xb2			
	Xb3			

- where a continuous measure of achievement (Y) appears in the cells

we would be able to test three null hypotheses:
- There is no difference in achievement scores across methods (Xa1 - Xa3).
- There is no difference in achievement scores across aptitudes (Xb1 - Xb3).
- There is no interaction effect.

Note the difference between this example, where we have an experimental manipulation and test for differences, and the example used in the preceding paragraph, where we had measured independent variables (ACT, GPA n-Ach) and tested for relationships.

Finally, mention should be made of **ex post facto studies** where we examine relationships and/or differences after the fact. With ex post facto studies we can randomly select our subjects from existing data sets, but we cannot randomly assign our subjects to treatment groups since we are dealing with intact groups. Ex post facto studies are popular but permit only limited correlational and/or causal inference. For example, the early studies designed to examine the relationship of smoking to the incidence of cancer were essentially ex post facto studies. Since there was no random assignment of the treatments (smoking and nonsmoking conditions), it is possible that variables other than smoking could have produced the relationship. That is to say that the results could have been contaminated by self-selection differences not related to the smoking and nonsmoking condition. Through continuous systematic replications, these self-selection factors are controlled for to some degree, and we build up a case for the establishment of a strong relationship between (among) the variables of interest.

INTERNAL AND EXTERNAL VALIDITY

The frequently used concepts of internal and external validity were put forth by Donald Campbell and Julian Stanley in 1963 in a chapter in the *Handbook of Research in Teaching* (1963). Campbell and Stanley examined a number of basic faulty and experimental designs and evaluated each design with respect to its ability to control for components of internal and external validity. A design is internally valid to the extent that one is able to support the claim that the variable manipulated produced a change in behavior. On the other hand a design is externally valid to the extent that one is able to generalize the findings from the study to other situations. The general organizing basis of the Campbell and Stanley piece is that one should not make claims supporting external validity unless one can first of all support internal validity. The point being presented here is that you should not attempt to generalize your findings until you have something worth generalizing.

If we take each of the basic research methods discussed in the previous section and evaluate them with respect to their adequacy on the internal and external validity dimension, we would find the following relationships. Since nothing is manipulated in an **observational study**, internal validity is low, but external validity is high since the study took place in a natural setting. Likewise with **survey research**, since nothing is manipulated, internal validity is problematic. It should be noted here that one could apply the psychometric criteria of reliability, validity, and objectivity for evaluating psychological tests to partially support the internal validity of a survey research project. By using these psychometric indexes we are merely attempting to support the adequacy of the instrumentation being used to measure the variables of interest to the investigator. With respect to supporting the external validity of survey methods, we would provide evidence supporting the adequacy of the standardization and norming procedures used with the outcome dependent measures.

A **laboratory experiment** would have high internal validity since manipulation and control are present. However, given the artificial nature of most laboratory studies, external validity is low. On the other hand, **field experiments** have high internal and external validity since one manipulates variables, controls are present, and the field experiment is conducted in a natural setting. That said, it appears as though the field experiment fares best with respect to the adequacy of internal and external validity.

Finally, it should be noted that **ex post facto** studies may be observational, survey, and/or experimental. The internal and external validity of an ex post facto study would be dependent upon the type of study conducted. Once again, a field experiment would probably be given high marks for being the best combination of internal and external validity. The observational ex-post facto study would receive low marks for internal validity and high marks for external validity. Since manipulation was not involved in survey research, internal validity would be problematic.

FAULTY DESIGNS

In Table 8.1, a comparative summary of four faulty designs is presented. The first faulty design outlined in Table 8.1 is the **one-group (no control group) design**, which is frequently called a one-shot case study (XY). One subject and/or group is given a treatment, and then the subject and/or group is measured or evaluated. There is no comparison group, and no statistical analysis is appropriate to estimate or evaluate the treatment effect. Most would say that this design represents pre-science. The treatment effect may be biased because it is not clear if the effect is actually due to X (the treatment). Because there is no comparison or control group, it is not certain whether the treatment X is in fact what produces the Y dependent variable measure. Thus, numerous other independent variables, extraneous variables, history, experimental effects, and error may be operating and there is no way of determining whether this is the case.

Table 8.1
A Comparative Summary of Four Faulty Designs

1.   **Design 1:** A one group - one shot case study - **(XY)**
a) - This is a single group with no comparison group (it could be an individual subject).
- Given the one group design, no comparative statistical analyses is possible. The researcher would describe the data sets reported in the form of frequencies using a combination of narrative, figural, and graphic descriptions.
- The benefit of case studies is that they may be directed at interesting subjects (e.g., in Freud's case, ground breaking discoveries were made).
b) - Treatment effects may be biased because there is no comparison group. Hence, one is never sure if the treatment produced the effect in the individual(s) or if alternative sources of variance influenced the subject(s) as well.
- If this is a group of subjects, not randomizing may result in a non- representative sample.

2.   **Design 2**: A before-after, no control group, non-randomized design - **(Yb X Ya)**
a) - This is a single group design in which the subjects are given a pre-test and a posttest. There is no comparison group. The researcher is looking for differences in the post-test scores due to the treatment. The data can be analyzed using a simple t-test to test for differences between the pre- and post-test measures.
b) - Treatment effects may be biased because: there is no control group, there may be a sensitizing effect of the pretest measure in the posttest measure, and there may be reactive and/or regression effects (maturation, history, testing).

3.   **Design 3:** A simulated before-after, non-randomized

$$\text{design - } (\frac{XYa}{Yb})$$

a) - This is a design using 2 groups in which one group gets the pretest and a different group gets both the treatment and the posttest. The design is used in instances where giving the same groups a pretest and a posttest would be impossible and/or would make the results seriously suspect due to the pretest influencing the posttest. A t-test can be used to test for differences between the before-after measures.
b) - Treatment effects may be biased because the comparability of the groups is questionable. Since there is no randomization or matching, the researchers must have good evidence that the two groups represent the same population.

4.   **Design 4:** A two or more group(s), non-randomized

$$\text{design - } (\frac{XY}{XY})$$

a) - This design is the same as faulty design #1 with the addition of a control group. The first group of subjects is given the treatment and the second group is not. When only two groups are involved, a t-test is used for analysis. However, if the researcher desires multiple groups, an ANOVA design can be used to test for differences, either as a 1-way ANOVA or a factorial ANOVA.

b) - Treatment effects may be biased since the groups are not randomized or matched, they may not be truly comparable.

The second faulty design listed in Table 8.1 is the **one-group before-after (pre-test-post-test) design (YbXYa)**. In this design, the subject (or subjects) is (are) pretested before (Yb) the treatment (X) in order to determine its (their) effect as measured after the treatment (Ya). The appropriate statistic to use in most instances is a simple t-test applied to the before and after dependent measures. The possible treatment effect bias in this case is that since there is no control group (comparison group), it is not clear whether the change in Y is actually due to X. That is to say that there may be regression effects. History and perhaps maturation may have also operated between the Yb and the Ya measures in such a way so that other extraneous variables may have produced the observed effect. Also, because the subject is pretested, there may be reactive effects to the pretest measure in that the subjects may be changed more by the pretest than by the treatment.

The third faulty design outlined in Table 8.1 is the **simulated before-after design (XYa)**. In this design, the possible sensitizing or
                                              Yb
reactive effects of the pretest are guarded against by having two groups in which one group receives the treatment and the posttest and another group receives only the pretest. The assumption is that the groups are equivalent, and thus the Ya measures can be compared to the Yb measures of the second group by means of a t-test used to test for a possible treatment effect. The problem with bias here is that there was no attempt made to randomize or match the two groups. The groups may in fact be different and thus the dependent measure Y may be reflecting this more than X.

The fourth and final faulty design to be discussed here is **the two groups non-randomized design (XY)**. In this design, there is
                                                        XY
a comparison group. One group is exposed to the treatment and one group is not. In most instances, the appropriate statistic to be used here is a t-test with two groups, an F-test (ANOVA) with more than two groups, and a factorial analysis of variance (FANOVA) with multiple independent variables. The central problem with assessing the treatment effect estimate is

that the groups may not be equivalent at the outset. No randomization or matching is used to control for extraneous variance which could differentially effect Y since other independent variables and/or extraneous variables may in fact have been responsible for the changes in the dependent variable measured.

EXPERIMENTAL DESIGNS

In Table 8.2, a comparative summary of eight experimental designs is presented. The first basic experimental design outlined in the table is the simple randomized experimental-control group design ($\frac{XY}{XY}$ R).

Experimental	Control	
X1	X2	
Y1	Y2	- where continuous dependent measures (Y1 and Y2) appear in the columns

We would use a t-test to test for differences across groups should we have only two groups. If we had three or more groups, an F-test (ANOVA) would be the statistical analysis of choice.

$$\frac{XY}{XY} R$$

X1 X2 X3	
Y1 Y2 Y3	-where continuous dependent measures (Y1 - Y3) appear in the columns

It is also possible to have a situation where a factorial analysis of variance (FANOVA) procedure would be employed to test for differences across groups.

$$\underline{Xa1Y} \\ \underline{Xa2Y} \; R \\ \underline{Xb1Y} \\ \underline{Xb2Y}$$

	Xa1 Xa2	
Xb1		
Xb2		-where a continuous dependent measure (Y) appears in the cells

Table 8.2

A Comparative Summary of Eight Experimental Designs

1. **Design 1:**   A two (or more) group(s) randomized design -

$$(\frac{XY}{XY}R)$$

a) - This design is the same as faulty design 4 but randomization is present in this instance. As with faulty design 4, where only two groups are involved, a t-test is used for analysis. However, if the researcher has a multiple groups situation, an ANOVA design can be used to test for differences, either as a 1-way ANOVA or a factorial ANOVA.

b) - A frequently used design that is adaptable to many situations—bias is controlled for by the use of a comparison group and randomization.

2. **Design 2:**   A two (or more) group(s) matched group

$$design - (\frac{XY}{XY}MR)$$

a) - This design is the same as experimental design 1 with the addition of the matching condition. Remember that matching is not a substitute for randomization, since we can only match on a few variables at one time, after which we must randomize. Since matching is used in this instance, a correlated groups statistical analysis (simple correlated groups analysis, test of repeated measures, analysis of co-variance) of the data set would be used here.

b) - Bias is controlled through use of a comparison group, matching, and randomization.

3. **Design 3:**   A before-after randomized and/or matched

$$group\ design - (\frac{YXY}{YXY}R\ or\ \frac{YXY}{YXY}MR)$$

a) - The basic feature of this design is the pre- and post-test feature. For a two groups randomized design, one would use a t-test on the change scores to test for differences between pre- and post-test performance. For three or more randomized groups, a simple ANOVA performed on the change scores would be appropriate. Should the design be set up as a randomized factorial design, a factorial ANOVA procedure would be used to test for significance. If matching is used, then a correlated groups analysis could be employed.

b) - There are two special problems (the analysis of change scores and the possible sensitizing effects of the pre-test) related to experimental design 3. Alternatives to analyzing change scores include using multiple regression or using the pre-test as a covariant. In most situations, the sensitizing effects of the pre-test do not present a serious problem. However, should you wish to control for the possible sensitizing effects of the pre-test, you should use either experimental design number 5 or number 6.

4. **Design 4:**   A randomized simulated before-after design -

$$(\frac{XYa}{Yb}\ R)$$

a) - This design is the same as the faulty simulated before-after design, except that we use randomization with respect to selecting our subjects and assigning

treatment conditions to groups. The design is used in instances where giving
the same group a pre-test and a post-test would be impossible and/or would
make the results seriously suspect due to the pre-test influencing the post-test. A
t-test can be used to test for the differences in the before-after measures.

b) - Treatment effects may be biased because even though randomization is
present here, unless large numbers are used and special care is given to the
randomization procedures, the comparability of the groups is questionable.

5. **Design 5:**   A three group before-after randomized

$$\text{design} - \begin{array}{c} \text{YXY} \\ \text{(YXY R)} \\ \text{XY} \end{array}$$

a) - By adding the third group, we have set up a situation where we can control
for the possible sensitizing effects of the pre-test. To test for possible pre-test
sensitizing effects, one could apply a t-test to the change scores for the first two
groups to test for pre- and post-test differences across groups. One would then
compare t-test findings with the results of an overall F-test performed on the
post-test scores across all three groups. If the F-test were found to be significant
but the t-test were not, then there are possible sensitizing effects related to the
use of the pre-test.

6. **Design 6:**   A four group before-after Solomon design -

$$\begin{array}{c} \text{YXY} \\ \text{(YXY R)} \\ \text{XY} \\ \text{XY} \end{array}$$

a) - This design represents a combination of the best features of designs 1 and 3.
To test the hypotheses in this instance, Kerlinger (1986) suggested that a factorial
ANOVA be used where the pre-test condition becomes an independent variable
in addition to the treatment-control condition.

b) - Here we have an "ideal" design in which bias is controlled in numerous
ways (we avoid analysis of change scores, we control for the possible sensitizing
effects of the pre-test, and we randomize and have comparison groups). A
general rule of thumb is to save this sophisticated design for crucial experiments.

7. **Design 7:**   A compromise, non-randomized before-after

$$\text{design} - \left(\frac{\text{YXY}}{\text{YXY}}\right)$$

a) - This design is identical to design number 3. However, in this instance,
randomization procedures were not used, and this lack of randomization raises
questions with respect to the comparability of the groups. As with design
number 3, hypotheses could be tested by employing a t-test, an F-test, or
factorial ANOVA on the change scores. If one wished to avoid the use of change
scores, one could use multiple R or analysis of covariance as an alternative
procedure.

b) - Since we did not randomize here, it should be noted that we have in fact
violated the assumptions related to the recommended statistical tests cited in
part a above.

8. **Design 8:**   A longitudinal time design -
     (YYYXYYYXYYYXYYY)

   a) - An important consideration here is the necessity of establishing a stable
   baseline. Should you have only one group, a t-test could be used to selectively
   test for differences across pre- and post-test conditions. This situation is
   basically the same as that reported for faulty design number 2. Should you have
   more than one group, a test of repeated measures could be performed.

Given a situation where we have four groups with two of the groups (Xa1
and Xa2) representing an experimental-control group situation and two
groups (Xb1 and Xb2) representing an aptitude or attribute dimension, factorial ANOVA would be used to test for interaction effects and differences
across groups. From what is reported above, we can see that the first experimental design is easily adapted to many types of experimental situations.

The second experimental **matched subjects design** $(\frac{XY}{XY}$ **MR)**

listed in Table 8.2 is similar to design number one but the matching procedure has been added. It should be noted that matching (MR) is not to be
viewed as a substitute for randomization since it is difficult to match on
many variables simultaneously after which we must randomize. Should
we have a design where matching has been used to control for variability,
we would use a simple correlated groups analysis or perhaps a test of repeated measures, to test our hypotheses. Given the situation below, a simple
correlated groups analysis would be used to test the hypotheses of differences across groups and MR units.

		Experimental X1	Control X2	
MR	1			
units	2	Y1	Y2	-where a continuous dependent
	3			measure (Y) appears in the cells
	4			

Should we have three or more independent conditions such as that depicted
below, a test of repeated measures would appear to be the statistical method
of choice.

		X1	X2	X3	
MR	1				
units	2				-where a continuous
	3	Y1	Y2	Y3	dependent measure
	4				(Y) appears in the cells

Design number 3 consists of a **before-after control group design** which is either randomized and/or matched. Given the following randomized situation **YbX1Ya** R, we would use a t-test to test for the difference in the change
YbX2Ya

Experimental	Control
X1	X2
Yb Ya	Yb Ya
pre-post	pre-post

scores across groups. Should we have three or more groups, an F-test could be applied to test for differences in the change scores across groups.

Yb Xa1 Ya
Yb Xa2 Ya R
Xb Xa3 Ya

Xa1	Xa2	Xa3
YbYa	YbYa	YbYa

\- where a continuous before-after dependent measure (YbYa) appears in the columns

Finally, if we had a factorial design, we could use a factorial analysis of variance procedure to analyze the results. Note once again that the three

Yb Xa1 Ya
Yb Xa2 Ya R
Yb Xb1 Yb
Yb Xb2 Yb

	Xa1	Xa2
Xb1	YbYa	YbYa
Xb2		

\- where a continuous before-after dependent measure (YbYa) appears in the cells

examples cited above employ randomized designs and the change scores between the before-and-after measures would serve as dependent measures.

Should we have a matched group situation, a correlated groups analysis would be appropriate. For example, given the following, one would use a simple correlated groups analysis to test for differences across groups and

<u>Yb X1 Ya</u>
Yb X2 Ya MR

		Experimental X1	Control X2	
MR Units	1	YbYa	YbYa	- where a continuous
	2			before-after dependent
	3			measure (YbYa) appears
	4			in the cells

MR units. Analysis of covariance could also be employed here where the pre-test would serve as the covariant. If we had a three or more groups design, a test of repeated measures procedure could be applied to the change scores.

<u>YbX1Ya</u>
<u>YbX2Ya</u> MR
YbX3Ya

		X1	X2	X3	
MR Units	1	YbYa	YbYa	YbYa	- where a continuous
	2				before-after dependent
	3				measure (YbYa) appears
	4				in the cells

As can be seen from what is reported above, design number 3 is a very useful and flexible design. However, the design is not without a few difficulties. There are problems related to the possible sensitizing effects of the pre-test. Analysis of change scores are viewed by many as being problematic in that many times the instrumentation is not sensitive enough to detect change score differences. Furthermore, it is important to note that the change scores are reported to be less reliable than the scores from which they are derived. Should the investigator desire to employ an alternative methodology to avoid the use of the change scores, the pre-test could be used as a covariant permitting the analysis of covariance or the treatment groups could be coded as dummy variables and a multiple regression analysis could be performed on the data set.

The **three groups before-after randomized control group design** (design number 4) outlined in Table 8.2 is a design that permits control of the possible sensitizing effects of the pre-test. Essentially what we have here is design number 3 with the addition of a third group without a pre-test.

YbXYa
YbXYa R
XYa

To test for significant differences across groups, one could use a t-test on the change scores to test for differences across the first two groups in addition to performing an F-test on the post-test measures only across all three groups. If both analyses yielded significant findings, one could rule out the threat of the possible sensitization effects of the pre-test. If the overall F-test were found to be significant but the t-test was not found to be significant, then you have something to worry about with respect to the sensitizing effects of the pre-test scores. It is recommended that design number 4 be used with a pilot data set to rule out possible sensitizing effects of using a pre-test. However, in most situations where we are not too worried about the sensitizing effects of the pre-test, we would probably be better off taking the subjects who would have been in the third group without the pre-test and combining them with the subjects in the first two groups so as to increase our sample size and give variability a greater chance to manifest itself.

Design number 5 is a **randomized simulated before-after design** ($\frac{XY}{Yb}$ R). This design is better than the faulty simulated before-after design since randomization is involved. However, unless fairly large numbers of subjects are involved to give randomization a chance to manifest itself, it is a design of last resort used in those special instances where the investigator has only one opportunity to study an interesting situation where the pre-test and post-test groups must remain different. In sum, experimental design number 5 is a risky choice, but a possibility for really interesting methodologically constrained investigations. Since you have pre- and post-test means, you could use a t-test to test for significant differences in the change scores.

The sixth design appearing in Table 8.2, (**a Solomon four groups design**) permits one to control for the possibility of the sensitizing effects of the pre-test scores and at the same time utilize the strength of the pre-test-post-test comparison.

YbXa1Ya
YbXa2Ya R
Xa1Ya
Xa2Ya

This design is best reserved for crucial experiments when one desires maximum control of variability. One slight problem with the use of this design is the statistical imbalance among the groups since in two groups you have a pre-test-post-test condition and in two groups you have only a post-test condition without a pre-test. Given this rather cumbersome situation, Kerlinger (1986) recommended that the results be analyzed using factorial ANOVA. The analytic paradigm for such an analysis would be as follows:

	Xa1	Xa2	
	Experimental	Control	
	Group	Group	
Pre-test-post-test			- where continuous
Post-test only			post-test scores only
			appear in the cells (Y)

In this instance, the pre-test condition is used as an independent variable, and the post-test scores serve as the dependent measure. That is to say that you do not use the change scores here as your dependent measure; rather the post-test scores are tested for differences across experimental and pre- and post-test conditions.

The seventh experimental design is a **compromise before-after control group non-randomized design** ($\frac{YbXYa}{YbXYa}$). This design has the same basic characteristic as experimental design number three with the exception of the non-randomization condition. The investigator could analyze the data using the same statistical procedures as those recommended for use with design number 3. However, since randomization was not used in this instance, we are violating randomization assumptions here and we would be less certain as to the differences and/or relationships found.

The final design to be discussed here is the **longitudinal time design - (YbYbYb-X-YaYaYa)**. Of major importance with this design is that the investigator be able to establish a stable baseline measure against which to test for significant treatment effects. In a one group longitudinal time design, one could use a t-test to test for differences in the change scores across the averaged baseline and averaged post-testing conditions. Should you have two or more groups, the statistical procedures to be employed would be essentially the same as those used with experimental design number three.

VARIANCE CONTROL

There are several ways to control variance in a research design. **Randomization** is the hallmark variance control technique. It is thought of as the great equalizer. By randomizing (both subject assignments and treatment conditions) you equalize groups by equally distributing underlying factors or attributes (e.g., individual differences). That is to say that differences between groups tend to cancel each other out. **Matching** can serve a similar function, because when subjects are matched on some relevant variable (e.g., intelligence, personality, cognitive style), this tends to make groups more homogeneous with respect to that variable. It should be noted that matching should always be followed by randomization so that other extraneous variables will be equally distributed across groups and/or conditions.

In planning designs, it is critical that **treatment effects be maximized**, and in a sense, this is a deliberate attempt to control variance by making sure that the experimental variance (or the systematic variance when using a correlational design) is great.

Note that with a one-way ANOVA, when you randomly select subjects and randomize treatment conditions, what you are trying to do is keep within-groups variability fairly small so that between-groups variability has a chance to manifest itself. By doing this, you are, in a sense, attempting to minimize the size of the number in the denominator in the F ratio.

$$F= \frac{\text{between-groups variance (experimental variance) or systematic variance}}{\text{within-groups variance (error variance) or residual variance}}$$

Error variance and variance due to individual differences gets lumped into the within-groups variance number. An effective way of reducing within groups variance is to **partition out the variance due to individual differences**, thereby making the within-groups variance smaller. A factorial design is an excellent way to do this, since one of the independent variables in the design could be an attribute (i.e., individual difference) variable. Thus, when a factorial ANOVA is done, more individual difference variance is partitioned out of within groups variance which in turn enhances the **homogeneity** among the subjects. For example, if we wish to study the differential effectiveness of three psychotherapeutic methods, the design would look like this:

$$\underline{Xa1Y}$$
$$\underline{Xa2Y}\ R$$
$$Xa3Y$$

$$\begin{array}{ccc} \underline{Xa1} & \underline{Xa2} & \underline{Xa3} \end{array}$$

or

$$\begin{array}{ccc} Y1 & Y2 & Y3 \end{array}$$

Here we could use a one-way ANOVA (provided we had a continuous variable as our dependent variable). We may or may not find a significant difference across groups using this univariant approach. However, we could control for some individual differences (e.g., attributional styles) among our subjects and enhance the likelihood of finding significance, since the individual difference variance due to attributional style could be partitioned out and controlled. This factorial analysis of variance multivariant design would look like this:

		Xa1	Xa2	Xa3
Xb1	Internal			
Xb2	External Locus of Control			

Matching and **repeated measures procedures** yield, if properly done, similar effects. Using these procedures, homogeneity among subjects is increased so that the systematic variance due to the treatment has a chance to manifest itself. Analysis of **covariance** might also be used in this case to control for individual differences among the subjects before testing for differences in the post-test measures. In this case, the pre-test is used as a covariate which has the effect of accounting for differences between groups that are present at the time of the pre-test measure. Again, this is another way to partition and control individual difference variance.

Research designs control variance by accounting for and controlling for the variability within groups as much as possible and by maximizing the variance between groups as much as possible. Accounting for within groups variability, or partitioning out variance, involves techniques such as matching groups of subjects on a particular characteristic, using multivariate methods to assess the effects of several variables at once, statistically controlling for the shared variance (covariance) of subjects with regard to a measure, etc. Maximizing group differences means that the researcher tries to make the treatment effects as large as possible so a difference may be found.

A factorial design controls more variance than a one-way design, because subjects are grouped according to at least two variables in a factorial design, while they are grouped only by the single treatment variable in a one-way design. For example, when trying to assess the possible differential effects of three different teaching methods applied to third grade students, use of a one-way design would merely partition variability in the test scores across the three methods of instruction (e.g., lecture, computer-aided, group interaction). The design would look like this:

Xa1	Xa2	Xa3
Method 1	Method 2	Method 3

Y1	Y2	Y3

- where continuous achievement scores appear in the columns

Ho: The null hypothesis in this instance is:

There are no differences in test scores across teaching methods. Given the number of possible reasons for variations in the test scores across groups, a significant difference would be unlikely in this instance.

A factorial design applied to the same example could be used to separate the students and account for some of the within groups variability found among the subjects in the one-way design. For example, if the third graders were divided up by type of classroom (regular education classrooms Xb1 and special education classrooms Xb2) and gender (Xc1 and Xc2), much more individual difference variability could be partitioned out, and much more information could be gained.

The design would look like this:

		Xa1	Xa2	Xa3
		Method 1	Method 2	Method 3
Xb1	Xc1			
	Xc2			
Xb2	Xc1			
	Xc2			

- where continuous achievement scores appear the columns

The factorial ANOVA summary table would look like this:

Source of variance	F
Methods (Xa1 - Xa3)	*
Classrooms (Xb1 - Xb2)	*
Genders (Xc1 - Xc2)	*
A x B	*
B x C	*
A x C	*
A x B x C	*
Error	
Total	

The seven null hypotheses to be tested in this instance
would be as follows:

Ho1:   There are no differences in achievement scores across methods
       (Xa1-Xa3).
Ho2:   There are no differences in achievement scores across classrooms
       (Xb1-Xb2).
Ho3:   There are no differences in achievement scores across genders
       (Xc1-Xc2).
Ho4:   There is no A x B interaction effect.
Ho5:   There is no A x C interaction effect.
Ho6:   There is no B x C interaction effect.
Ho7:   There is no A x B x C interaction effect.

It should be noted that seven F values are obtained with this factorial design versus only one F value with a one-way design.

A design using **matched subjects, covariance,** or **repeated measures**
controls for variance by insuring the least amount of within groups variability possible, hence improving the possibility of finding significant F-
values. For example, if students are tested as to which of three teaching
methods is best, the results will have a better chance of being significant if
the students are grouped according to level of ability, (i.e., basic, standard,
honors). In the same way, the students could each be matched on their IQ
scores, with the IQ test being considered as a covariant. Likewise, if the
researcher were interested in assessing the effects of four different types of
music on memory task performance, a single subject could undergo each
treatment in a repeated measures design.

What was described and illustrated above may be summarized by using the **MAXMINCON principle** of variance control as an organizer. The
MAX component of the principle refers to attempting to maximize experi-

mental and/or systematic variance across groups. The **MIN** component refers to attempting to control for error variance among our subjects. This is done by making certain that the instruments we use are reliable and valid measures. Finally, the **CON** component refers to our ability to control extraneous variance. This control of extraneous variance is achieved by using randomization and matching procedures when selecting subjects and assigning treatments to groups. In addition, the design of the study (e.g., use of a factorial or correlated groups design as opposed to a simple one-way ANOVA design) may be used to control for extraneous variance. In sum, when attempting to determine the adequacy of any empirically based study, it is our recommendation that you carefully critique your study using each of the MAXMINCON evaluative components as an organizer.

A STATISTICAL ORGANIZER

In this section we present two summary tables in which the statistical procedures associated with each of the different research methodologies (field studies, surveys, laboratory experiments, field experiments, and ex post facto studies) are listed, described, and compared. **Table 8.3** consists of a listing and description of the statistical procedures (t-test, F-test, FANOVA, and correlated group analyses) to be used with data sets collected during the course of conducting laboratory experiments, field experiments, and some ex post facto studies. It should be noted that there are two commonalities among these **experimental** statistical procedures. In all cases we have some **experimental manipulation** and we design our hypotheses to **test for differences** between (among) groups. In addition, variance consist of experimental variance (between groups and/or columns) and error variance (within groups and/or rows). To test for statistical significance, the F-ratio is computed as follows:

$$F = \frac{\text{experimental variance (variance between groups and/or columns}}{\text{error variance (variance within groups and/or rows)}}$$

To obtain statistical significance using any of these procedures, the experimental variance must be larger than the error variance.

It should be noted that the **chi square (X^2)** procedure noted in Table 8.3 is a statistical procedure that is used to **test for relationships** among independent and dependent variables when the **dependent measure is reported as a frequency** count rather than a continuous measure. A X^2 procedure could be used to analyze data sets collected during the course of conducting laboratory experiments, field experiments, ex post facto studies, and surveys in which the dependent measure was reported as a frequency count. In addition, if you had a comparison group in an observational study (i.e., field study) where the dependent variable is reported as a frequency count, you could probably use a X^2 analysis to test for relationships between your X and Y variables.

Table 8.4 consist of a listing and description of the statistical procedures (multiple regression, canonical correlation, discriminate function, factor analysis, path analysis, and LISREL) to be used with data sets collected during the course of conducting **survey studies**. All of the correlational procedures listed in Table 8.4 were designed to **test for relationships**. They are applicable to data sets in which we have non-experimental (i.e., measured-attribute) independent and dependent variables. When using these statistical procedures, variance consist of systematic (regression) variance and residual (error) variance.

$$F = \frac{\text{systematic (regression variance)}}{\text{residual (error) variance}}$$

Three predictive situations (A-C) are depicted below:

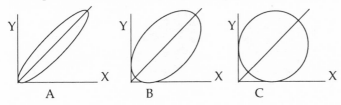

In situation A, we have a great deal of systematic (regression) variance (represented by a line of best fit among our data points) and very little residual variance (error variance represented by dispersion of data points from the line of best fit). In situation B, we do have considerable systematic variance (another straight line of best fit), but there is more residual (error) variance. In situation C, there is little if any systematic variance and far too much error variance to make any prediction with certainty. If F values were determined for each of these data sets, the F value for situation A would be high, B moderate, and C would be close to zero.

What we are trying to say here is that when using these multiple regression and structural modeling techniques associated with analyzing data sets collected during the course of conducting survey studies, the statistical procedure boils down to comparing the amount of systematic (regression) variance to residual (error) variance. Of course, you want the systematic variance to be larger than the uncontrolled residual variance.

Table 8.3

Statistical Procedures (t-test, F test, FANOVA, and Correlated Group Analyses) to Be Used with Data Sets Collected During the Course of Conducting Laboratory Experiments, Field Experiments, and Some Ex Post Facto Studies

Statistic	Design	Paradigm/Data Set	Hypothesis Tested	Sources of Variance	Comment
(chi-sq.X^2)	$\underline{XY}$ R XY	$\underline{\quad Y1 \quad Y2 \quad}$ Xa1 $\underline{\qquad\qquad}$ Xa2 - where frequencies appear in the cells	- There is no relationship between X and Y.	NA (not applicable in this instance)	- used when dependent measures are reported as frequencies
t-test	$\underline{XY}$ R XY	$\underline{\quad X1 \quad X2 \quad}$ $\underline{\quad Y1 \quad Y2 \quad}$ $\underline{\qquad\qquad}$ - where a continuous dependent measures (Y1 and Y2) appears in the columns	- There is no difference in the outcome measures (Y1 and Y2) across experimental conditions (X1 and X2).	- between-groups (experimental) variance and within-groups (error) variance $F = \dfrac{\text{experimental (between groups) variance}}{\text{error (within-groups) variance}}$	- used when you have only two experimental conditions and a continuous dependent measure

Statistic	Design	Paradigm/Data Set	Hypothesis Tested	Sources of Variance	Comment
ANOVA (F-test) (analysis of variance)	XX XX R XY	X1 X2 X3 Y1 Y2 Y3 - where a continuous dependent measure (Y1, Y2, and Y3) appears in the columns	- There is no difference in the outcome measures (Y1-Y3) across experimental conditions (X1-X3).	- between-groups (experimental) variance and within-groups (error) variance $F = \dfrac{\text{experimental (between groups) variance}}{\text{error (within groups) variance}}$	- used when you have more than two experimental conditions and a continuous dependent measure
FANOVA (factorial analysis of variance)	Xa1 Y Xa2 Y R Xb1 Y Xb2 Y	Xa1 Xa2 Xb1 Xb2 - where a continuous dependent measure (Y) appears in the cells	- There is no difference in the outcome measure (Y) across experimental conditions (Xa1 - Xa2). - There is no difference in the outcome measure (Y) across aptitudes (Xb1-Xb2). - There is no interaction effect.	- between-groups (experimental) variance and within-groups (error) variance $F = \dfrac{\text{between A}}{\text{error}}$ $F = \dfrac{\text{between B}}{\text{error}}$ $F = \dfrac{\text{A} \times \text{B (interaction)}}{\text{error}}$	- used when you have two or more independent variables arranged in an ATI (aptitude-treatment-interaction) design and a continuous dependent measure

261

Statistic	Design	Paradigm/Data Set	Hypothesis Tested	Sources of Variance	Comment
correlated groups analyses	(simple correlated groups design) Xa1 Y MR Xa2 Y	Xa1 Xa2 1 2 3 Y1 Y2 MR 4 Units 5 - where a continuous dependent measure (Y1 and Y2) appears in the columns	- There is no difference in the outcome measures (Y1 and Y2) across experimental conditions (Xa1 - Xa2). - There is no difference in the outcome measures (Y1 and Y2) across MR units.	- between columns, rows, and residual F = between columns / residual F = between rows / residual	- used when you have a matched group experimental designs
	(test of repeated measures) XY XY MR XY	X1 X2 X3 1 2 3 Y1 Y2 Y3 MR 4 Units 5 - where a continuous dependent measure (Y1 - Y3) appears in the columns	- There is no difference in the outcome measures (Y1 - Y3) across experimental conditions (X1 - X3). - There is no difference in the outcome measures (Y1 - Y3) across MR units.	- between columns, rows, and residual F = between columns / residual F = between rows / residual	- used when you have a matched group experimental design in which the matched units receive multiple exposure to the X1 - X3 conditions

Statistic	Design	Paradigm/Data Set	Hypothesis Tested	Sources of Variance	Comment
	(analysis of covariance- (ANCOVAR) $\underline{XY}$ MR XY	X1 X2 — Yc1 Y1 Yc2 Y2 — - where a continuous depedent measure (Y1 and Y2) and a covariant (Yc1 - Yc2) appear in the columns	- There is no difference in the outcome measures (Y1 - Y2) across X1 - X2 conditions with Yc1Yc2 serving as the covariant.	- between-groups (experimental) variance and within-groups (error variance) experimental (between groups F = variance) error (within groups) variance	- used in intact groups where differences in the covariant are statistically controlled before a test is made on the differences in the dependent variable of interest

263

Table 8.4
Statistical Procedures (Multiple Regression, Canonical Correlation, Discriminant Function, Factor Analysis, Path Analysis, and LISREL) to Be Used with Data Sets Collected During the Course of Conducting Survey Studies

Statistic	Design/Paradigm/Data Set	Hypothesis Tested	Sources of Variance	Comment
multiple regression (linear predictive regression)	$X1 + X2 + X3 = Y$ - where X1 - X3 are continuous independent measures (predictors) and Y is a continuous dependent measure (criterion)	- There is no relationship among X1, X2, X3, and Y.	- regression (systematic) and residual (error) variance $F = \dfrac{\text{regression (systematic) variance}}{\text{residual (error variance)}}$	- used when you have multiple independent predictors and one dependent measure
canonical correlation	$X1 + X2 + X3 = Y1 + Y2$ - where X1 - X3 are continuous independent measures (predictors) and Y1 and Y2 are continuous dependent measures (criterion)	- There is no relationship among X1, X2, X3, Y1, and Y2.	- regression (systematic) and residual (error) variance $F = \dfrac{\text{regression (systematic) variance}}{\text{residual (error variance)}}$	- used when you have multiple independent predictors and more than one dependent measure
discriminant function	$X1 + X2 + X3 = Y1$ $X1 + X2 + X3 = Y2$ - where X1 - X3 are continuous independent measures (predictors) and Y1 and Y2 are criterion groups	- There is no relationship among X1-X3 and Y1. - There is no relationship among X1-X3 and Y2.	- regression (systematic) and error (residual) variance $F = \dfrac{\text{regression (systematic) variance}}{\text{residual (error variance)}}$	- used in situations in which you desire to use a set of predictors to maximally differentiate between (among) two or more criterion groups

Statistic	Design/Paradigm/Data Set	Hypothesis Tested	Sources of Variance	Comment
factor analysis	- a systematic search for structural patterns (relationships) in a complex data set	- a systematic search for structural patterns (relationships) in a complex data set	- regression (systematic) and error (residual) variance regression $F = \dfrac{\text{(systematic) variance}}{\text{residual (error variance)}}$	- used in situations in which you desire to simplify a data set
path analysis (structural regression)	- where X1 - X3 are continuous independent measures (predictors) and Y is a continuous dependent measure (criterion).	- There is no relationship among X1, X2, X3, and Y.	- regression (systematic) and residual (error) variance regression $F = \dfrac{\text{(systematic) variance}}{\text{esidual (error variance)}}$	- used in situations in which you desire to determine the structural relationships among a set of predictors and a criterion measure
LISREL (linear structural relations)	- a systematic search for structural patterns (relationships) in a complex data set.	- a systematic search for structural patterns (relationships) in a complex data set.	- regression (systematic) and residual (error) variance regression $F = \dfrac{\text{(systematic) variance}}{\text{residual (error variance)}}$	- used in situations in which you desire to determine the structural relationships among a very complex set of predictors and multiple criterion measures.

PROBLEMS RELATED TO ACCEPTING
A TRUE NULL HYPOTHESIS

Accepting a "true null hypothesis" is a little bit like hunting for the Loch Ness monster. No matter how hard we look, if we do not find anything, you can always say we did not look hard enough.

If an experiment or correlational study yields no evidence to support the rejection of a null hypothesis, this does not really prove that there are no differences and/or relationships. Perhaps, the investigator did not have a strong treatment to begin with (quite possible in a contrived laboratory experiment). Perhaps the investigator was unable to effectively eliminate or control extraneous variables that influenced the dependent measures. Perhaps error variance—the "noise" of the experiment—was simply too great and overcame the experimental and/or systematic variance. If such factors were not adequately managed in the experiment, the investigator may have precluded finding a difference and/or relationship that is actually there. So how can an investigator ever say that the null hypothesis is true?

As was noted earlier in this chapter, in our attempt to apply the **MAXMINCON PRINCIPLE** to our research projects, we should attempt to:

1.   Maximize experimental variance by increasing differences between (among) treatment groups

2.   Minimize error variance by decreasing within groups differences (use of correlated groups, covariance, and factorial designs—use of reliable and valid instrumentation).

3.   Control for extraneous variance by:
    a.   randomizing subjects and treatments
    b.   matching whenever possible
    c.   have good evidence in support of a representative sample
    d.   using a comparison group and/or blocking variables in the design

When we apply the MAXMINCON evaluative criteria to a research project, we are essentially guarding against a **type II error** (accepting a false Ho) by maximizing treatment differences and enhancing homogeneity within groups via the careful selection of a large number of subjects, randomization, and matching. In addition, a researcher should attempt to guard against a **type I error** (rejecting a true Ho) by using a fairly conservative alpha-level (0.01-0.05) and thereby setting the stage for the achievement of high statistical power (i.e., making a correct decision). Of course internal and external validity and reliability must also be established for the results to have true meaning.

The point here is that none of these items on the researcher's MAXMINCON checklist is absolute: there are quantitative and qualitative decisions to be made at many levels of the design of the study and the interpretation of the results reflects these multitudinous decisions. Therefore, there are at least two reasons why we cannot accept the null hypothesis:

1.   We are not sure the statistical tests were sensitive enough to pick up differences or relationships that may have truly existed.
2.   We cannot say that all of the MAXMINCON principle components were adequately addressed by the researcher.

According to Thomas Cook and Donald Campbell (1979), there are several standards by which the researcher could estimate the confidence that can be placed in failing to reject the null hypothesis when results are not found to be significant. These standards are:

1.   When using a directional Ho, if there is a strong significant differ ence in the opposite direction of H1, or if there are no significant differences across several powerful subgroups, one may then accept Ho. (Make certain that you check to see if other relevant variables have hidden the treatment effect.)
2.   Prior to conducting a study, if a point-estimate of the size of the effect is not as large as desired. The researcher can use procedures to estimate the sample size and the variance required to obtain the desired effect with 95 percent confidence. If this is found to be

undesirable, accept the Ho.

3.   One can estimate retrospectively the sample size and variance esti-
        mates required to achieve significant results for the desired effects
        at the 95 percent level of confidence. If the results are still out of
        reach, then accept Ho.
4.   If results are not significant, but they are in the right direction, the
        researcher can then apply as much of the MAXMINCON principle
        as possible and match subjects, maximize treatment differences,
        increase N, etc., in an attempt to redesign the study and enhance
        the possibility of finding significant results in a future study.
5.   If results remain nonsignificant after redesigning the study, the re
        searcher can only say that this particular experiment provided no
        significant results. That is to say that given another systematic repli
        cation, a significant result may be found. **In sum, never completely
        accept a true Ho**.

CAUSAL INFERENCE

The notion of **causal inference** is understood differently, depending on
the philosophical position taken. The **positivist** position is that only that
which is observed is of relevance with respect to establishing causal inference. The strict positivist has no need to postulate causation because it is
not actually observed. Using David Hume (1711-1776) as an example, what
is observed is a contiguity between A and B, the temporal precedence of A
before B, and the constant conjunction of A and B. Another positivist,
Bertrand Russell (1913), advocated using only functional relationships to
describe the relation between A and B. In short, the emphasis in the positivist position is on what is actually observed. That is to say that if it can be
seen and controlled, study it. If it is not observable, it has no meaning and
cannot be studied.

From an **essentialist** perspective it is assumed that a cause may actually exist in reality. From this perspective, determination of a necessary
and sufficient cause is required for an effect to occur. The essentialists argue that there is a causal chain in which a certain cause (A) infallibly and
simultaneously results in an effect (B). Because of this emphasis on a causal
chain of events, this position tends to be rather mechanistic. Often, the
only way necessary and sufficient conditions which infallibly bring about
the effect are found is at the micromediational level. Thus, while the positivists have no need to point to "real causes," the essentialists do posit causes
which are actually believed to exist and serve as a focus of study.

The **falsificationist's position** is associated with the writings of K. R.
Popper (1972). Basically he argues that any theory of causation must have

the status of not yet being disconfirmed. The focus here is on the importance of using comparison groups. The positivists are confirmationists in that when a hypothesis is corroborated by observational procedures, this leads to confirmation of a theory. The theory is therefore considered to be useful and could be utilized again. In contrast, the falsificationists argue that no theory is ever truly confirmed. Even with a corroborated hypothesis, there may be an alternative explanation given to the interpretation of positive findings. One may find that a theory provides a verified hypotheses but that there is an even larger theory which generates these same hypotheses. For example, Isaac Newton's theory was later included in Albert Einstein's theory of relativity. Thus, a theory can never be proved and/or confirmed. Instead, it can only be said to be not yet disconfirmed until another alternative theory can be found which may account for the previous theories' successes and generate others not previously included in the first theory.

Those (Cook & Campbell, 1979) associated with the **evolutionary critical-realist** perspective, in contrast to the positivists, hold that causation actually exists in nature. But like the positivists and falsificationists, one must critically evaluate any causal inference. Like the falsificationists, those associated with this view hold that there may be alternative explanations. The evolutionary critical realists would agree with the essentialists that there is a chain of causation, but they would not emphasize the necessary and sufficient philosophical analysis; nor would they be greatly concerned with the micromediational level of the causal chain. Instead, they would discuss the evolutionary significance of causal inference. They would argue that such an ability to infer causation has survival value. The positivists would argue that this is not an ability and that causation does not actually, or necessarily, exist. The evolutionary critical realists argue that causes are real and humans have an ability to survive because of their causal inferential abilities. However, all inferences must be critically evaluated since the actual causal chain may not at first be clear and must be further studied.

What we are trying to say here is that causal inference is the conceptual umbrella under which all of the details of research methodology fall. The point of experimentation is to arrive at this conceptual mountaintop. The logical positivists were the first, and perhaps the most rigid team to attempt to scale the mountain. Cause, according to the positivists, could not be observed, so was not necessary. Hume's method of constant conjunction fits here. For *every* A (cause), there must be a B (effect). We may not infer from nonobservables that A causes B. Thus, the preference in language for advocates of this model was for quantitative intervening variables, not qualitative hypothetical constructs (i.e., because a billiard ball hits another does not necessarily mean that one caused the other to move— only a coincidence of time and space can be observed). Only from past correlations may we even begin to approach causation. This view, as well as the essentialist's perspective, are considered to be confirmationist's views.

The essentialists scaled the mountain (or attempted it) from the idea that a whole constellation of variables is necessarily, inevitably, and infallibly predictive of causality. Their task, working with observables, was to determine at what level of (micro) mediation one could observe the constellation of variables and thus arrive at cause. At the micromediational level, simultaneity of cause and effect could occur (A = 1000 degrees, B = iron glowing—both happen simultaneously). This view is associated with sophisticated logical analyses and considerable reductionism.

John Stuart Mill (1806-1873) was a kind of bridge between the confirmationists, who used theory as a convenient summary (and did not particularly care that others were equally plausible), and the falsificationists, who sought to disconfirm theories. Briefly, his method of concomitant variance (if A is present, B is too; if A is absent, B is too: if both of these conditions are met, causal inference strength exists) and use of a control group are important in the development/progression of philosophical causal-inference comparisons.

Popper's (1972) falsificationism view is closely aligned with Thomas Kuhn's (1970) paradigmatic shift notion. Popper sought to falsify theory and was not content to confirm it. Indeed, the alternative hypotheses were viewed as being critical. His point was to rule out all plausible alternative hypotheses but one. Even then, all that could modestly be said was that a theory is not yet disconfirmed. This leaves open the possibility (and acceptance) of anomalies of facts that do not fit the paradigm. This situation could become the genesis of a gateway to a new paradigm. Yet Popper put one theory into competition with others, and the problems related to theory-laden facts (Kuhn) and the Quine-Duhem thesis derail this view somewhat.

Theory-laden facts is a buzz term of sorts that is frequently used by the post-positivists (i.e., falsificationists). Coming out of Kuhn's (1970) framework, it refers to the ultimate impossibility of implying cause from a falsification approach even when we have been very careful to design a highly controlled experiment yielding significant results. Even using Popper's framework of falsifying a theory that is in competition with other theories, with the ultimate goal being elimination of rival plausible hypotheses, the objectivity of the facts which would or would not refute (confirm or disconfirm) a theory may be contaminated by the language in which the facts are clothed or couched. It is possible that in the very use of language there may be theoretical assumptions which have "impregnated" the description of facts and which may indeed be theory-bound.

A second problem related to the falsificationist perspective is perhaps best addressed by considering the **Quine-Duhem thesis**. The point here is that everything—all facts—may be disproved. The bottom line here is not to trust anything. Scientifically, this means that we may not give much credence even to evidence which may lead to disconfirming or confirming a theory, even when that theory is pitted against other plausible hypotheses. Quine-Duhem affiliates may need some psychodynamic therapy focused on the issue of building trust.

The evolutionary critical realist perspective yields a somewhat better climb up the mountain since cause is considered to exist outside the (contamination of) mind; critical because of our imperfect way of measuring cause; and evolutionary because of the survival value of inferring cause (i.e., to use a ladder in getting fruit off the tree) implies control and manipulation. It is a contemporary view (as is falsificationism) that backs off from the deeply ingrained philosophic debates related to supporting the notion of causal inference.

Cook and Campbell (1979) stated the following summary beliefs related to the evolutionary critical realist view of causal inference: (1) that molar laws are meaningful—though we may not know all micromediation stages; (2) that they (molar laws) are fallible; (3) that they (molar laws) stem from multiple causes; (4) that strong molar laws have reliable intermediate units; (5) that effect follows cause; (6) that cause and effect can be reversible; and (7) that finally, paradigmatic assertions state that if we manipulate cause (A), we will manipulate effect (B). Such is the primacy of experimentation in approximating causal inference.

TERMS TO KNOW

X^2
t-test
ANOVA (analysis of variance)
FANOVA (factorial analysis of variance)
correlated groups analyses
test of repeated measures
analysis of covariance (ANCOVAR)
analytic paradigm
interaction
type I error
type II error
power
MAXMINCON principle
causal inference
positivist views of causation
essentialist theories of causation
falsificationism
Quine Duhem thesis

theory-ladenness of facts
problem of "accepting" the "null hypothesis"
covariation
primacy of internal validity
internal validity
external validity
multiple regression (R)
canonical correlation analysis
discriminant analysis
factor analysis
path analysis
LISREL (Linear Structural Relations)

QUESTIONS AND PROBLEMS TO CONSIDER (SEE APPENDIX FOR A SAMPLE SET OF PROBLEM SOLUTIONS)

1. Compare and contrast the notion of causal inference from the positivist, essentialist, falsificationist, contextualist, and the evolutionary critical realist perspectives.

2. Discuss the following sets of issues related to faulty experimental and ex post facto designs. First, list four widely used faulty designs. Describe their general characteristics and the appropriate statistical treatment effect estimate each provides. Second, how and why might the treatment effect estimates be biased for each design?

3. How does research design control variance? Why would a factorial design control more variance than a one-way design? How does a design that uses matched subjects, covariance, or repeated measures of the same subjects control variance? How is variance controlled when a multiple regression procedure is used to analyze a data set? In responding to this question, you may find it helpful to provide a comparative figural representation of how each design controls variance. That is to say, make certain that you discuss how each design controls variance.

4. Sir Ronald Fisher, the inventor of analysis of variance, said, "it should be noted that the null hypothesis is never proved or established, but is possibly disproved in the course of experimentation. Every experiment may be said to exist only in order to give the facts a chance of disproving the null hypotheses." (Fisher, R. (1951).

The design of experiments. New York: Hafner, p. 16.) Present a detailed interpretation related to the meaning of this statement quoted from one of Fisher's books. In framing your response, consider the **MAXMINCON** principle and make certain that you give at least two reasons why the null hypotheses cannot logically be proven.

5. There is considerable controversy over the purpose of research. Two broad views are represented in the literature. One of these views takes the position that the purpose of scientific research is the development of theory and/or explanation. The other view, which seems particularly prevalent in psychology and education, is that the purpose of research is to help improve human and social conditions, to help find solutions to human and technical problems. In general, the scientist favors the former view, the person-in-the-street the latter view. Which position do you espouse? Why? Is there a rational middle position? If so, why? In answering this question, make certain that you discuss research methodological issues in need of resolution at the present time.

6. Four problems from the research literature are given below. Present analytic paradigms and construct hypotheses based on them.
   a. What is the influence of massive rewards on the reading achievement of potential school dropouts?
   b. Teachers who are perceived by students as dissimilar (to the students) in traits relevant to teaching are more attractive to students than teachers perceived as similar.
   c. How do sex-role stereotyping, sexual conservatism, adversial sexual beliefs, and acceptance of interpersonal violence affect attitudes toward rape and sexual violence?
   d. Does stimulus exposure have two effects, one cognitive and one affective, which in turn affect liking, familiarity, reognition, confidence, and accuracy?

7. Suppose a researcher has done an experiment in which he or she tested two methods of instruction (A1 and A2). A second independent variable was social class (middle class and working class, B1 and B2). The dependent variable was achievement. The results are summarized as follows (the tabled entries are means):

Methods

		A1	A2	
Social	B1	78	70	74
Class	B2	72	60	66
		75	65	(Mt = 70)

The A effect was reported to be significant at the 0.01 level. So was the B effect. The interaction was not found to be significant.

a.   Interpret the results by discussing the differences between the means and the relations they presumably reflect.

b.   Draw a graph describing the results, and interpret the graph.

Using the same problem presented above, assume that the table entries are a bit different:

		A1	A2	
Social	B1	70	78	74
Class	B2	72	60	66
		71	69	(Mt = 70)

The only change is that the A1B1 and A2B1 means have been inter changed. A factorial analysis of variance shows that the A means are not significantly different, but the B means are significantly different. The interaction is also significant.

a.   Interpret the results. Compare your interpretation to that of the first problem.

b.   Draw a graph describing the results and interpret it. Compare this graph to the one drawn for the first problem.

c.   What value does factorial analysis of variance have in research situations like this? Explain why you would not necessarily reach the same conclusions by conducting two separate experiments?

8.   Suppose that you are the principal of an elementary school. Some of the fourth- and fifth-grade teachers want to dispense with workbooks. The superintendent does not like the idea but allows you to test the notion that workbooks do not make much difference. (One of the teachers even suggests that workbooks may have bad effects on both teachers and pupils.) Set up two models (i.e., analytic paradigms) to test the efficacy of the workbooks (a one-way design and a factorial design). State a few possible null hypotheses related to your analytic paradigms and critically discuss the logic of each design from the standpoint of research design and statistics. Consider the variables of achievement, intelligence, and gender. Also consider the possibility of teacher attitude toward workbooks as an independent variable.

9.   Can memory be improved by training? William James performed a memory experiment on himself. He first learned 158 lines of a Victor Hugo poem, which took him 131 minutes; then he learned

the entire first book of John Milton's *Paradise Lost*. He returned to the Hugo poem and learned 158 additional lines in 151 minutes. Thus, he took longer after the training than before. Not satisfied, he had **others** do similar tasks—with similar results. Comment specifically on the adequacy of his two research studies. Which **two designs** among those discussed in this chapter do his designs approximate?

10. Suppose that you wish to study the relations among the following variables: intelligence, socioeconomic status, need for achievement, and school achievement. Set up **two alternative models** (analytic paradigms) that explain school achievement. Draw **path diagrams** of the two models.

11. In a study in which training on the complexities of art stimuli affected attitude toward music, the investigator used analysis of covariance, with the covariate being measures from a scale to mea sure attitudes toward music. This was a pre-test. There were three experimental groups. Sketch the design from this brief description. Why did the investigator use the music attitude scale as a pre-test? Why was analysis of **covariance** used?

12. Outline plans for the design of a laboratory experiment, a field experiment, and a field study of the same basic problem (the relation between the cohesiveness of a group and its productivity). Keep the designs simple. Do the three designs get at the same research problem? That is, is the problem altered by the differences in the three kinds of study? How? Which design is best? Why?

13. A college instructor was interested in testing the relationship between intrinsic and extrinsic motivation. The basic question of interest to the instructor was whether extrinsically manipulated grade contingencies negatively effected intrinsic interest in the course. Five hundred students (graduates and undergraduates, males and females) were randomly assigned to a **grade contingent condition** (groups in which the final examination grade was averaged with the cumulative course examination grades of the students prior to the taking of the final examination) and a **grade noncontingent condition** (groups in which the final examination grade could only improve but not lower a student's final course grade). After completing the final examination, all students returned a course evaluation rating (A, B, C, etc.) form to the instructor. Present the overall **analytic paradigm(s)** for this research project. Discuss the logic of your design(s) from the standpoint of research design and **statistics**. What statistical test(s) of significance would you use? State a few possible null **hypotheses** related to your analytic paradigm(s) and critically evaluate how the treatment effect estimates may be

biased. (Note: In addition to the course evaluation ratings, make certain that student performance on the final examination is included as one of the variables of interest in the study at hand.)

14.   Here are three sets of simple fictitious data, laid out for an analysis of variance procedure. Reconfigure the data set so that a multiple regression analysis could be performed. Use a dummy coding (1, 0) procedure.

X1	X2	X3
7	12	5
6	9	2
5	10	6
9	8	3
8	11	4

Imagine that X1, X2, and X3 are three methods of changing racial attitudes and that the dependent variable (Y) is a measure of change with higher scores indicating more change. Interpret the results ($R^2 = 0.75$; $F = 18$ is significant at the 0.01 level of significance with df = 2, 12).

15.   Cutright, in a study of the effect of communication, urbanization, education, and agriculture on the political development of 77 nations, found a **multiple correlation** of 0.82. The correlations between each of the independent variables and the dependent variable were also found to be high (0.81, 0.69, 0.74, and -0.72). The intercorrelations among the independent variables were also high (mostly in the 0.70s and 0.80s). What **conclusions** can you reach about the relations between the independent and dependent variables? The beta weights for the four independent variables were 0.65, 0.19, 0.02, and 0.00. How much dependence can be put on these weights? What could happen if we **reversed the order** of entry of the independent variables?

16.   An experiment was designed to compare the effects of prepassage questions quizzing information of different structural importance on college students' memory for expository prose passages. From the results reported in the following tables, it can be seen that in conditions in which information from a high-level passage unit was quizzed by the question, indirect recall (i.e., recall of nonquizzed information) was greater than recall in both the low-question condition and the no-question condition. The low-question condition exceeded the no-question condition only when the analysis was limited to recall of superordinate information from the subtopic

cluster containing the quizzed unit. These results indicate that questions which direct the subject's attention to material at the top of the organizational structure facilitate the effective encoding of the central organizational idea within the passage segment. A signifi cant interaction was also found between subjects' vocabulary abil ity and question condition. The facilitative effect of high questions declined with increasing vocabulary ability. This interaction is con sistent with the view that high-ability and low-ability people differ in their tendency to use the superordinate organizational structure of the passage and thus in their tendency to benefit from process ing aids such as adjunct questions. Present the overall analytic paradigm for this research project. Discuss the logic of your de sign from the standpoint of research design and statistics. State a few possible null hypotheses related to your analytic paradigm and present a graph and interpretation of the interaction effects.

Summary of Regression Analyses for Overall Indirect Recall

Factor	Specified Order of Entry	Percent Variance Explained	F	MS
Between-Subjects				
Vocabulary (A)	1	9.0	10.13**	.910
Extraversion (B)	2	2.5	2.84	.885
A X B	3	0.8	0.95	.876
Within-Subjects				
Recall level (C)	1	5.5	76.31**	.448
Question (D)	2	2.3	32.41**	.448
C X D	3	2.7	37.39**	.448
A X D	7	0.1	0.37	.448
B X C	8	0.1	0.28	.448
A X B X C	9	0.1	0.42	.448
A X D	10	1.3	6.19*	.448
B X D	11	0.4	1.94	.448
A X B X D	12	0.1	0.42	.448

Note. The degrees of freedom for all tests were 1,103.

$*p < .05$ $**p < .01$

Mean Number of Overall Indirect Recalls

Recall Level	High	Low	No	Combined
Superordinate				
M	2.38	1.76	1.65	1.93
SD	.86	1.05	.93	
Subordinate				
M	1.44	1.38	1.51	1.45
SD	.98	.97	1.07	
Combined	1.91	1.57	1.58	

*The maximum possible total score was 3.0.

SUGGESTED READINGS

Readers wanting to study more thoroughly the topics covered in this chapter will find the following references helpful.

Cook, D. T., & Campbell, D. T. (1979). *Quasi-experimental: Design and analysis issues in field settings.* Boston: Houghton-Mifflin.

Kerlinger, F. N. (1986). *Foundations of behavioral research (3rd edition).* New York: Holt, Rinehart, and Winston.

Kuhn, T. S. (1970). *The structure of scientific revolutions (2nd edition).* Chicago: The University of Chicago Press.

CHAPTER 9

METHODOLOGICAL ISSUES RELATED TO THE MULTICULTURAL REVOLUTION RESHAPING AMERICAN BUSINESS

INTRODUCTION

American management is running scared in the face of relentless global competition, multicultural issues, and the dizzying pace of technical and societal change. Diversity, multicultural sensitivity, equity, TQM, rightsizing, business process re-engineering, ISO-9000, and team building are among the current buzzwords and phrases being invoked in guiding corporate strategic planning. Many employers are asking in frustration, "How do I improve my employee's multicultural sensitivity, critical thinking, and problem-solving skills?" Many have claimed to have the answers. But few have delivered on the "how to." In this chapter we provide some answers by deconstructing and then reconstructing the complex topic of the multicultural revolution reshaping American business from a research methodological perspective.

The use of **narrative forms of inquiry** (ethnographic, participant observation, case study, phenomenological, constructionist, and interpretive) as an educational research method for describing teaching and learning processes has generated considerable controversy and excitement. The increasing attention given to postmodern and feminist views and the methodologies associated with these views has created chaos, confusion, and instability among many researchers. That is to say that the use of **qualitative narrative methodologies** have presented a number of challenges to many of the assumptions inherent to empirical forms of research inquiry. One of the contentions that empiricists typically confront narrative researchers with is the belief that every trainer has a story. Each told story that is documented by qualitative researchers purports to recount a **thick and rich description** of the experiences that trainers live in context-specific situations. Such descriptions are thought to play a powerful mediational role for trainers who engage in active reflection ranging from illuminating tacit wisdom that guides practice to assisting trainers in the generation of practice-based theory. Story represents an enormous database from which to develop a new understanding about the relationships among phenomena in workplace contexts. However, empiricists raise several questions about the utility, authenticity, and claims of veracity of story that beg the question of whether the research community will ultimately sanctify storytelling work as a viable methodological approach.

In this chapter, we will **analyze the utility of narrative as a legitimate workplace training research tool.** Tracing the historical development of research paradigmatic models, we will provide a comparative description of sociolinguistic (narrative) and empirical research methodologies, discuss the various definitions and conceptions of narrative/story, explore the sociopolitical conceptual and theoretical frameworks that guide both narrative and technical/empirical forms of research, highlight the disadvantages and advantages of using story as a methodological research tool in the workplace, examine future directions for the use of narrative inquiry, and conclude with a conceptual framework designed to grant story a practical and utilitarian role in the communication processes of trainers, researchers, and academicians. In sum, what we will attempt to do is present a case for balance and the complimentary use of narrative forms of inquiry within the workplace community.

CONCEPTUAL ROOTS AND MODELS OF RESEARCH

It is widely documented (Erickson, 1986; Shulman, 1986, 1987; Wittrock, 1986) that **three major educational research programs** have competed for attention during the past three decades (process-product research, process-mediator-product research, and process-psychological mediators-sociological mediators-product research).

During the 1960s and early 1970s, most educational researchers were engaged in **process-product research.** Efforts were made to establish relationships between what teachers do in the classroom and student outcomes. For the most part, these process-product studies were conducted as a **reaction to James Coleman** et al. (1966) who reported that individual differences among students were a result of differences in abilities (i.e., IQ) not school environments (i.e., public, private, rich, poor), **and Richard Rosenthal and Linda Jacobson** (1968), who claimed that a teacher's expectancy of whether or not a student would do well in school was related to school performance.

At this time, considerable attention was given to examining the **components of effective schools**. In addition, a number of field experiments were conducted. Many of these studies demonstrated that active teaching, direct instruction, time on task, emphasis on strong teacher control and behavior management were effective. In many ways, the timing of these studies was fortunate in that the empirically based process-product research programs served as a reaction against the laissez-faire culture of the late 1960s and early 1970s. There were some concerns related to the unnatural ecology of aggregating aptitude and treatment variability into manageable units of study. But the main reason for erosion of these efforts was probably the strong empirical, atheoretical approach given to addressing educational research problems. In sum, a focus was given to what worked, but not why. That is to say that there was an absence of explanation.

A program of research in which **time** was considered to be the primary mediator of student achievement was referred to as **process-mediator-product research**. Much of this research was anchored onto **John B. Carroll's (1963, 1989) mastery learning model**, in which attention was given to describing and manipulating a number of variables (e.g., learner attributes such as ability and aptitude, instructor attributes, and quality of instruction). However, it is important to note that the primary variable used to account for differences in student performance in Carroll's model was the time needed to learn. This **behaviorally anchored mastery learning approach** was somewhat more explanation oriented than the nonmediated process-product models. Overall, it could be described as a mediational variant of the atheoretical process-product research models of the 1960s. A behavioral bias persisted in the early 1970s and the focus remained on observations. As we moved into the **1980s and 1990s**, some attention was given to **adding cognitive science components** of instruction (e.g., the importance of active engagement, prior knowledge, cognitive conflict, etc.) **to Carroll's mastery learning model**.

A **sociological** (sociolinguistic) **component** was **added** to the paradigm in the 1990s. Today, the major paradigm is a process-psychological medicators-product research paradigm combined with a sociolinguistic perspective **(process-psychological mediators-sociolinguistic mediators-product research paradigm)**. Considerable attention is given to dynamic, interactive, context, and unobservable processes. Many questions are raised with respect to making contrasts between quantitative and qualitative science. Narrative inquiry and linguistic analysis are center stage. A radical, critical, political focus is taken. **Race, culture, and social class are used to explain differences among learners**. Advocates of this sociolinguistic position view social science as a **science of criticism** rather than a science striving for practical process-product answers. They view social science as a search for meaning rather than an experimental science in search of laws.

ADDRESSING DIVERSITY AND EQUITY IN THE
WORKPLACE: A SOCIOLINGUISTIC PERSPECTIVE

Sociolinguistic methods are **rooted** in **Western European intellectual history** (Erickson, 1986). Many of these qualitative methods (ethnographic, participant observation, case study, phenomenological, constructionist, and interpretive) developed out of interests in the lives and perspectives of people who had little or no voice in society. Focus was given to the dignity of manual labor. For the most part, these Western European views were compatible with those of Karl Marx, who viewed the self as shaped through concrete circumstances of daily living and Freud's subjective and unscientific notions. Of course, these views were **not compatible with the German natural science-Newtonian physics view that supported the process-product behaviorally anchored mastery learning and cognitive science research efforts of the 1960s, 1970s, and 1980s.** Sociolinguistic researchers focus on how social organizations and cultures relate to making choices. When looking for explanations related to individual differences, the search is not for abstract universals (e.g., intelligence and aptitude); rather a focus is given to finding concrete universals (e.g., race, culture, and class).

The **German natural science model** is frequently associated with **radical conservative views**. From this perspective, **schools and working environments have served a social sorting function.** Biased learning and workplace environments are believed to be established by teachers and employers who have set middle-class standards (the middle-class value laden normative gaze) of academic and workplace performance. **Individual differences** in school and job performance are attributed to genetic deficits (Herrnstein & Murray, 1994; Jensen, 1969), **socialization defects** (cultural deprivation, linguistic deprivation, family disorganization, negative attitudes, cultural deviance), and **cultural differences** (teacher-employer expectations, linguistic interference, second language-interactional interference, culturally incongruent instruction) which have been used to explain minorities lack of success.

In contrast, many advocates of the **sociolinguistic perspective** are aligned with the **radical left position.** Many of them believe that a social revolution is a necessary condition for school and workplace improvement. From a radical left sociolinguistic perspective, the **explanation for failure is rooted in politics** (i.e., in the inequitable distribution of power and privilege in society). It should be noted that these views are compatible with a Marxist dialectical view, a perspective usually found in those countries where institutions are controlled by the state (e.g., the former Soviet Union and Scandinavia). In sum, from a radical left, sociolinguistic perspective, **school and workplace failures are viewed as self-defeating resistance rather than inadequacy.**

Most sociolinguistic researchers use **qualitative methods** to collect their data sets. They conduct long-term, intensive participant observations in a field setting. They begin without prior conceptual explanations. In many respects, the process is believed to be unteachable. It is considered to be important to have a solid grounding in substantive courses in anthropology and sociology. By taking a **distanced observational stance** moving from the general to the specific (the final stages are more focused - zooming in/zooming out during the process), sociolinguistic researchers learn through **active participation, reframing as the analysis proceeds**. Focus is given to pattern discovery. The sociolinguistic researchers' aim is not proof in a casual sense, but the demonstration of plausibility. The analytic narrative and linguistic analysis are center stage. The focus is on a policy audience. It is considered to be important to teach the findings that emerge from sociolinguistic studies by teaching trainers and employers to be researchers and establishing a collaborative relationship among the trainers, employers, employees, and researchers.

From an empirical perspective, it could be argued that the yields of these sociolinguistic research programs are questionable. There are questions related to viewing social science as a source of criticism rather than obtaining practical, empirically based solutions to training problems. There are questions raised with respect to choosing political grandstanding and protest rather than confronting the job performance challenges that being in a highly competitive middle-class workplace environment present. From a sociolinguistic perspective, there is a **search for meaning and a demonstration of plausibility rather than an experimental science in search of laws**. The focus is on a policy audience (i.e., teaching the findings). However, empiricists would claim that conducting research and making social policy are rarely done by the same persons. That is to say that two cultures (researchers and policy makers) prevail.

In the sections that follow, we will attempt to **strike a balance among the various views**. What are the limitations of empirically anchored behavioral and cognitive science models of training? What are the virtues associated with postmodernism? Is social constructivism (narrative inquiry) research? Are the contemporary constructivists creationists? How can we relate narrative forms of inquiry to the workplace?

CONCEPTIONS OF STORY/NARRATIVE FORMS OF INQUIRY

Characteristically, story is a narrative with very specific syntactical shape (Scholes, 1981, 1982) and subject matter that allows for, or encourages, the projection of human values upon this material. Story places an emphasis on the connections between what humans think, know, and do as well as the reciprocal relationships between the way that human thinking shapes behavior and knowing shapes thinking. As an entity with its own parameters (beginning, middle, and end), story has a dynamic that is created and interpreted through the lived experiences of a person or a participant observer who offers a vicarious interpretation of an individual's personal story. A synthesis of the lived experiences results in a narration that occurs through a **process of active construction**. Two factors are involved in this reconstruction process (temporality and causality). These factors related to the time, place, specific situation, and cultural context provide a framework for systematically interpreting the events and outcomes within a story.

Consider the similarities between story and other forms of representation. For example, the structure of a story parallels that of a musical exposition. Musical works have an introduction, a development, recapitulation or variation on a theme, and denouement. As the theme is developed, the listener may become acutely engaged in attending to the melody, often referred to as the thematic content, or the listener may focus on the harmony, the dynamics, the tonality, the metric movement, the intervalic patterns, or the tempo. As with the situation of hearing or reading a story, the listener constructs his/her own personal experience and meaning while listening. It is recognized that there is no assurance that the listener's experience is synonymous with that of the composer's intentions. The representation of the listener's **experience is contextualized** and embedded in their previous experiences, tacit knowledge, and their connectedness to the exposition. Similar to the way listeners **construct meaning** when they hear a musical composition, narrative researchers employ codes and conventions so as to construct stories, relay their interpretations (as exemplified by the musical elements of melody, dynamics, or harmony), convey the sequence of incidents (demonstrated by musical conventions such as meter, intervalic patterns, or tempo), and describe a synthesis of events that occurs by way of a story (also illustrated by the musical structures of development, recapitulation, variation on a theme, or denouement). By its very nature, a story involves an agent who acts to achieve goals that can be interpreted in understandable ways. Story establishes the "ordinary" and the demonstration of the truth as it is experienced.

Story or narrative belongs to the **classroom-workplace ecology paradigm** that includes sociolinguistic mediation research on teaching, as well as more methodologically qualitative, interpretive, and critical forms of inquiry (Martin & Sugarman, 1993). Story telling is an **ethnographic form of qualitative research** that involves telling or recounting. Research involving narrative forms of inquiry have included microanalyses of teacher-student interactions taking place in classrooms and workplace settings in which the focus is given to specific curriculum and content areas (Clandinin & Connelly, 1988; Connelly & Clandinin, 1986, 1988), documentations of teachers' and workplace trainers' reflections (Cochran-Smyth & Lytle, 1990, 1993; Elbaz, 1991; Kagan, 1988; Leinhardt, 1990; Schon, 1987; Shulman, 1987; Yinger, 1987), and longitudinal microanalyses of social and community factors that influence schooling, teaching, and learning activities over extended periods of time (Peshkin, 1978).

Story research, which falls within the category of components that emphasize **learning how to teach and consult in the workplace**, has focused on **elucidating trainers' ways of knowing**. Use of narrative as a form of inquiry suggests that it is **trainers' thought processes**, not solely their behavior, that is essential to the knowledge base on research on trainer thinking. Knowledge that results from narratives is qualitatively different from formal theoretical knowledge, which represents the synthesis of interactions taking place within a particular context and the classroom and workplace situations in which knowledge is transformed into action. Story knowledge attempts to relate predefined observables to theoretical contexts. In story research, the **trainer is the unit of analysis**.

By highlighting the workplace trainer, the research suggests that a basic assumption is sustained which holds that the trainer is an individual who brings a specialized set of social relationships and experiences to the workplace learning situation. These particular social relationships and experiences are considered to be the important components in the development of knowledge. Although the practical knowledge that coalesces as trainers interact in the workplace results in knowledge in action, the quality and type of knowledge is integrally interwoven with the trainers' level of expertise. Additionally, workplace training experience may not be the best teacher since teachers and workplace trainers are generally very isolated while experiencing and perceiving events (Feiman-Nemser & Buchmann, 1986). That is to say that the perceptions formed may be limited by the depth and breadth of their own experience or the trainers' own bias. Others argue that the workplace training experience integrated with **active reflection** acts as a powerful instructor that facilitates a trainers' development of beliefs and perceptions of themselves as learners and teachers, while helping them to acquire practical knowledge (Connelly & Clandinin, 1986). Narrative inquiry acknowledges the importance of the workplace trainer's role by placing a value on trainer autonomy and reflection.

The overall purpose of story is to fill a gap in the knowledge base of training by crafting a mode for trainer voice and to provide a means to understand the interpretive frames that trainers use to improve their workplace training practices (Cochran-Smith & Lytle, 1990). Narratives emphasize trainers' own **interpretations of context-specific workplace training situations**. Focus is given to the context in which decisions are made. An attempt is made to bring to a conscious awareness the nature of a trainer's professional reasoning. The common thread in studies involving narrative is the overacting emphasis on the validity of workplace trainers' judgments that are drawn from their own experiences.

G. M. Sparks-Langer and A. Bernstein-Colton (1991) claim that several major benefits are derived from research that utilizes narrative forms of inquiry. First, these studies heighten an awareness regarding what motivates a trainer's action and provide a detailed description of a trainer's everyday life. Second, trainers' narratives provide material for instructional case study material. Third, narratives can provide workplace trainers with insight gained as a result of self-reflection. Sparks-Langer and Bernstein-Colton (1991) contend that narrative research represents a bridge to a new way of thinking about thinking.

Characteristic of the narrative inquiry paradigm is that meaning sought from workplace training experiences relies upon **interpretive and analytical frameworks**. Narrative inquiry attempts to explicate an understanding of the events that occur in specific educational and workplace contexts under investigation. This method relies heavily upon creating **rich and thick descriptions** without reliance on causal, associative data treatments and analyses. One of the fundamental assumptions underlying narrative is that teachers' and workplace trainers' personal biographies interact with particular situations that help them understand their use and application of practical knowledge. Narrative also seeks to explicate trainers' ways of knowing and their origins by analyzing the reflective thought processes and related behaviors of particular trainers.

Other environmental factors that may also influence teacher and workplace trainer thinking behaviors and reflection in action include the contextual, organizational, or bureaucratic structures indigenous to specific school and workplace environments. In spite of the fact that narrative is a special type of sociolinguistic mediational research, it is somewhat remarkable that there has been little attention given to understanding the relationship between the ways that environmental structures such as the contextual, organizational, or bureaucratic elements might influence a teacher and/or workplace trainers' behavior or how these elements possibly mediate a display of practical knowledge. In laboratory or role play situations, responses can be predicted; however in real world or actual classroom and workplace contexts, responses we planned to elicit may be sacrificed for behaviors that are perceived as normative within the context of the culture in which they are expressed. Teachers and workplace trainers may also experience **pressure to conform to the contextual (systemic) influences of the power structures within which they have to coexist**. Having provided a framework for what constitutes story and narrative forms of research, we now turn our attention to the conceptual frameworks that amplify the utility of story in context-specific situations.

CONCEPTUAL FRAMEWORKS AND
ADVANTAGES OF STORY

In this section, we outline the advantages of story, the criticisms re-garding the use of story as an educational research tool, the limitations that remain unaddressed by researchers who advocate story, and discuss what we consider to be relevant epistemological issues.

Advocates of the use of story as a form of inquiry assert that story has benefits that cannot be realized solely by empirical methodologies. A list of several advantages which have been reported to be transacted from the use of story as a methodological approach to conducting research on teacher and workplace trainer thinking is presented below:

1.   Stories are believed to be **constructions that give meaning** and con-vey a sense of experience.
2.   Story has been used as a **frame to counter the technical/empirical modes of inquiry** that have dominated research on teacher and workplace trainer thinking.
3.   Narrative has been **used by women as a means to portray their specialized ways of knowing** (Belensky, Clinchy, Goldberger, & Tarule, 1986; Helle, 1991) and to provide them with a representa-tive voice in the research literature.
4.   Storied knowledge can be **organized into explanatory frameworks**. The cultural and contextual variables that serve as interpretive lenses for comprehending one's experiences can be analyzed.
5.   Experienced teachers and workplace trainers use narrative struc-tures (story) as a **frame for organizing and interpreting knowl-edge structures** (Gudmundsdottir, 1991).
6.   Knowledge derived from teachers' and workplace trainers' stories results in the acquisition of event-structured knowledge (Carter, 1993; Carter & Doyle, 1987; Carter & Gonzalez, 1990) and **promotes expertise**. This process is driven by the complexity of social events taking place within the context of the educational and/or work-place training environment.

CRITICISMS OF STORY

Critics of story claim that story telling suffers from an **absence of an "authenticity judge"** (Kleine & Greene, 1993) **and an inability to "distin-guish a scholarly interpretation of a learning event from that of a deliri-ous observer"** (Salomon, 1991, p. 10). Others suggest that the use of story research results from a researcher's inability to utilize experimental design methods and statistical techniques for data analysis. Summarily, according to the aforementioned views, story is portrayed as an indefensible form of inquiry owing to the fluidity that characterizes the context in which data is collected. Even Connelly and Clandinin (1986, 1988), who rely heavily on narrative inquiry in their own research, seem to suggest that perhaps narrative inquiry provides a research agenda that gives professors something to do (Schwab, 1983).

Other criticisms of story include the view that it places **extreme emphasis on personal meaning** and exaggerates the significance of the person recording the story. Such an emphasis tends to confer an unwarranted level of authenticity upon the storyteller's experience and to reward narcissism. Basic problems of knowledge claims that are associated with elevating a teachers' and/or workplace trainers' stories to a "privileged status" have yet to be systematically addressed.

In an overall sense, **storytelling is a variation on reflection**. Reflection may be the type of experience in which individuals analyze, question or privately rethink their own behaviors and perceptions. During this kind of experience, individuals are offered an opportunity to incorporate the wisdom and perceptions of others. While reflection is essential to the processes involved in analysis, clearly this technique is not emergent. Reflection has been around for a long time. Reflection seems to be a quality of good practitioners, who are generally thought to be intuitive individuals. As such, some researchers assert that the current use of the term **reflection is equivalent to fadism**.

LIMITATIONS OF STORY/NARRATIVE

Several limitations regarding the disadvantages of story have been cited in the research literature. If this method is likely to be accepted by the research community at large, it seems that the aforementioned concerns obligate disputation or at the very least a consideration of whether or not to modify the techniques involved with gathering story telling data. A few related limitations are enumerated below:

1. The **relationship between story and reality** as defined by the experiences of an outside observer **does not necessarily portray a one-to-one correspondence**.
2. The study of a story as case descriptive material usually involves the view of only one individual. Of course, these descriptions are open to **multiple meanings**. The complexities portrayed in narrative descriptions, along with the possible inaccuracies, sometimes leads to confusion in teaching because there are many interpreta-

tions inherent in a complex story. The possibilities for different interpretations are also a function of the perspectives and experiences that students engaged in the study of story bring to the task.

3. Story does not represent a consensually agreed upon and/or scholarly knowledge base. Therefore the use of story as a knowledge base for training others raises questions regarding what knowledge is worth most. Similarly, if **told stories represent solely those of the dominant culture**, how does this promote pedagogical practice for people of color, women, underrepresented populations, and/or the underprivileged classes? How do the findings that are associated with ethnography inform the field or advance our knowledge theoretically? How does contextualized ethnographic research that generally is reported in a case study format help us in terms of recommending what teachers and workplace trainers should consider doing in classrooms and workplace settings?

4. Analyzing an individual narrative does not lend itself to empirical investigation. Furthermore, interpretations that emerge in narrative are **not open to verification** since they emanate from beliefs that are the collaborative construction of a teacher and/or workplace trainer (interviewee) and/or researcher (interviewer).

5. **Interpretations** of narratives are influenced by belief systems that **are a product of one's own cultural framework**. Are neutrality or unbiased perceptions possible? Can we claim that the evidence derived from interpretations truly corresponds to an objective reality or renders any universally valid principles or laws (Greene, 1994)? The generalizability and utility of interpretations is also open to considerable argumentation.

6. Paradigmatic assumptions about the value of various research methodologies also play a role in interpretations that emerge from narrative research. **Story has been criticized for amplifying moralistic, narcissistic, and omnipotent representations**. Illuminating related concerns, Andy Hargeaves (1994) claims that the voice given to a storyteller through the use of narrative has come to represent the storyteller as an entity, but that this notion is a highly morally laden and perspective voice, not an empirical or actual representation of all storytellers. It is interesting to note that research on teachers' and workplace trainers' thought and voice is characteristically replete with teachers and workplace trainers who are humanistic and caring, but not about teachers and workplace trainers who are cynical, lack knowledge, and/or demonstrate a lack of pedagogy. That is to say that the positive, moral characteristics are not grounded in representation of all teachers and workplace trainers.

According to Hargeaves (1994), this **moral singularity of teachers' voice needs to be deconstructed**. It is interesting to note that research on teaching and workplace training shows that teachers' and trainers' didactic moralistic instruction seems to dominate classrooms and workplace training situations even today. Many instructors tend to see classrooms and other types of workplace training situations from the position of power, authority, privileged status, and role instead of from the viewpoint of their students. One can build a strong case for the notion that understanding teachers' voice should be a priority, but we must be **careful not to romanticize these voices** according unwarranted authenticity to them. One of the most poignant criticisms leveled against stories is that they amplify a sense of narcissism, by exemplifying delusions of omnipotence and highlighting the sense of a boundless self (Hargeaves, 1994).

EPISTEMOLOGICAL ISSUES

Assumptions Underlying Interpretation

Connelly and Clandinin (1986, 1988) claim that the primary value of narrative inquiry is its quality as subject matter and its capacity to render life experiences. However, certain **inherent difficulties** exist since **falsehood may be substituted for meaning** and narrative truth by using criteria that give rise to significance, value, and intention. Meanings told are not necessarily representative and secondary or tertiary levels of interpretation may be falsely created. Methodological errors in interpretation of narrative can occur from attempts to generalize the events of story. One **may misrepresent the truth** and alter actualities by fabricating a recounting of the events. Narrative smoothing (Spence, 1986) may result from an obscurity of facts, leaving open the question of what is not being told. H. G. Gadamer (1960) concurs and reminds us that "the interpreter experiences two claims: one from the object of the interpretation . . . and one from the interpreters' own lived circumstances" (pp. 124-125). Prejudgments and prejudices cannot be set aside, since they have so much to do with shaping those interpretations" (Greene, 1994, p. 438; our emphasis).

Sanctifying storytelling work and formulating an epistemology to support this methodology is insufficient for creating a new paradigm for research on teacher and workplace trainer thinking without addressing the assumptions that underlie this method or without considering those posited by empirical researchers. In the same connection, story has been criticized on epistemological grounds because the **criteria of acceptance are rooted in contextualism**. Furthermore, the interpretations gathered from story data don't necessarily yield practical information, and the meanings embedded in story are not always accessible to the reader. Nespor and Barlyske (1991) contend that when researchers use narrative as a tool for constructing knowledge they are describing, discovering, or identifying objects that really exist. However, they use instructors' constructions of the object which has been fashioned according to the needs of the researcher. In this sense, narratives are **frequently used to express relations of power and political agendas of researchers,** not as a tool to discover truth and expand the pluralistic knowledge base of research on teacher and workplace trainer thinking.

J. Nespor and J. Barlyske (1991) point out the fallacy associated with the premise that narratives index fundamental structures of thought or experience as D. Polkinghorne (1988), J. Bruner (1986), M. Gergen and K. Gergen (1986), F. M. Connelly and D. J. Clandinin (1986, 1988), and others suggest. The **representational fallacy** is that entities that emerge within story actually preexist and contribute to the creation of that discourse. Researchers reify narrative discourse, make inferences from nonobservable mental processes, and then use discourse as evidence for the existence of the inferred processes. Thus the **creation of a** sophisticated and esoteric, but **circular and indefensible system of reasoning** has been created to forge the acceptance of a nontraditional method of research. However, one must also ask whether narrative research is actually more prevalent than the empirical/ technical (traditional) forms of inquiry than previously acknowledged. How much of current research, case studies, and the like are grounded in empirical interpretations that represent forms of story?

Connelly and Clandinin (1986 and 1988) have defined criteria for narrative as grounded in white, educated, and Anglo-American society. This perspective contradicts their assumption that narrative reflects basic human cognitive structures that mirror normative methodological inquiry. The historical specificity that defines criteria for narrative is **class biased, gender biased, and culturally biased** if the criteria of acceptance is based solely on the dominant Eurocentric and middle-class cultural values system. Using these criteria as the standard ignores the diversity, richness, and thickness of experience that narrative portends to exemplify.

Narrative is a culturally specific communication that imposes certain societal structural characteristics. There is inherent difficulty in determining whose narrative is being told, that of the respondent (the storyteller) or the researcher (interviewer). According to J. Willinsky (1989), representation is always a matter of power that should be treated with some skepticism. Recounting one's history and related social events does not always portray the lived experience of the teacher's or workplace trainers' discourse. An account may be told through the lived experiences or interpretation of the researcher not the actual lived experience and interpretation of the story teller (Crapanzano, 1980, pp. 9-10).

CONCEPTUAL ROOTS OF STORY

On an epistemological level, story is **conceptually rooted in mentalis-tic psychology** as opposed to empirically based behavioral psychology. Howard Kendler (1993) stated that the differences between the two are methodological, not theoretical. He asserted that selecting behavior as the dependent variable does not negate the use of hypotheses about mentalis-tic processes as long as theoretical mentalistic assumptions have testable behavioral implications. In contrast, the behaviorists would argue that by promoting techniques of self-observation, "the unbiased scrutiny of expe-rience" (MacLeod, 1986), is unachievable because conscious experience is a private and only available to the self-observer. Most people are incapable of self-awareness. Behaviorists also claim that it is only when an event can be observed by more than one person that socially agreed-upon criteria can be adopted that might lead to observational agreement. The overarching dilemma is that researchers engaged in narrative inquiry cannot provide veracity or socially agreed-upon criteria by which to judge the content and/ or value of story. Pondering the notion of either/or perspectives, E. F. Keller (1985) contends that this dichotomy is akin to the male/female opposition. She links the abstract and objectivist to masculine modes of thinking and self-interpretation but challenges male claims to universalism and neutral-ity. M. Greene (1994) concurs with Keller (1985) and states that "For main-stream and technical thinkers (often including some doctrinal Marxists), so-called subjective views are suspect in part because they are associated with embeddedness or situatedness and, by extension, with the female" (p. 433).

Psychology cannot resolve the conflict that ensues during a debate re-lated to **which is better, qualitative or quantitative methodology.** How-ever, psychology can shed some light on the consequences of adopting com-peting principles. **The dilemma facing the empiricists is that they cannot provide value-free information that is not an expression of the researcher's political or value commitments. Some will insist that behavioral empiri-cally based methodologists seek to attain political power (control), not truth (explanation). On the other hand, the subjective conceptions asso-ciated with qualitative research can be criticized for failure to distinguish between those value judgments intrinsically associated with empiricism (e.g., emphasis on controlled observations, use of comparison groups, statistical significance) from those that can be detached from empirical evidence.**

One of the major issues that empiricists have yet to grapple with lies in **the limitations associated with the knowledge claims that empirical re-searchers offer.** Greene (1994) asserts that "Too many researchers still find it difficult to confront the effects of technicism on their thinking or to face the problem of objectivity. The desire for precision and disinterestedness continues, sometimes as a corrective against what is viewed as uncontained relativism and reliance to mere opinion" (p. 432). One of the limitations associated with empiricism lies in its inability to discern whether the quality of research illuminates the social consequences associated with competing methodologies. Technocratic research varies in its ability to empirically predict consequences associated with assumptions underlying qualitative and quantitative methods of research. Second, knowledge claims that emanate from the notional quality of behavioral concepts may or may not be socially defensible. In contrast, the difficulty associated with narrative inquiry as a phenomenological and mentalistic conception of psychology resides in the observation that it suffers from an inability to offer persuasive knowledge claims that society can trust. Kendler's (1993) claim that empirical researchers need to abandon their assumptions that quantifiable research can identify definitive principles which describe predictable human behavior should be instructive to those who believe that a strict use of empirical methodology can guide teaching and workplace training programs. Kendler (1993) also suggests that empiricists must give up the notion that a gap between what is and what ought to be can be bridged only by the application of empirical evidence.

Kendler (1993) receives support from assertions by Jack Martin and Jeff Sugarman (1993) who contend that research on teaching and workplace training that relies primarily on an empirical enterprise is ill-fated because of an overemphasis on methodology. Furthermore they assert that empirical researchers have failed to adequately address the epistemological problems that confront assumptions underlying their work. Much of the empirical research on teaching and workplace training: (1) lacks an underlying theory that identifies specific variables; (2) provides an insufficient description of the characteristics of focal variables that are particularly worthy of empirical scrutiny; or (3) fails to explain why empirically based evidence is pragmatically unmanageable (Martin & Sugarman, 1993). On the other hand, one might ask how research based on **narrative inquiry** can be advocated when it seems to be **based purely on rationally biased assumptions.**

Many of the current debates on teaching and workplace training have been focused on concerns related to methodological and epistemological paradigms to the exclusion of providing a theoretically defensible argument for the empirical preoccupation. However, it is notable that during the proliferation of empirical studies, as observed by Martin and Sugarman (1993), that no new scientific understandings or heuristics have been made available for practitioners.

FUTURE DIRECTIONS

The use of story has become an emergent power in educational and psychological research, but in their current framework, teachers' and workplace trainers' stories do not provide us with a political or paradigmatic base from which to create new understandings. We need to establish the contextual parameters in order to illuminate the potential contributions of research that relies on story. One avenue to capitalizing on the unrealized benefits of story research may involve macrolizing the location of story. Macrolizing means to take a macro or more global perspective, moving beyond the analysis of individual stories as they exist in micro or singular educational contexts. Macrolizing refers to the process of creating a quantifiable database from story research by analyzing all of the stories that emerge in a particular location (educational context) or assessing common themes, patterns, or traits that emerge across locations (educational contexts). Since the ultimate aim of story as an educational research tool is to mediate pedagogically, politically, and educationally what we want to share, categorizing and organizing information gleaned from story research seems to be a logical progression from accumulating individual stories.

What does continued research on classroom and workplace ecology with narrative as the methodological vehicle portend for training teachers and/or workplace trainers? Perhaps the time is ripe to create teacher and workplace training programs that are designed to focus on using individualistic, sociolinguistic, and psychoanalytic anchored approaches (Combs, 1965). A recapitulation of the predominant purpose of story reveals that story ostensibly tries to create an awareness about what teachers and workplace trainers do and how they teach. Each story seeks to impart something of a practical nature regarding how that particular storyteller copes with instructional and curricular matters in the context of his/her environment. However, the emergent insights desired from one's own story or a study of stories has implications only in the context in which the story was located. Perhaps we need to reassess the potential utility of story and advance narrative methodology to the next level, that is, beyond the often asked question So what? For example, if the descriptive findings that emerged from studies which used narrative inquiry were organized into analytical or classificatory systems, then tangible connections between practice and theory might be synthesized. Suppose we obtained narratives from many teachers and/or workplace trainers in several contexts and created a database of multiple stories. Perhaps patterns or classificatory systems of action would coalesce that are suggestive of how teachers and workplace trainers use story, their professional reasoning, or the reciprocal relationships between their thinking styles and behaviors.

Story is purposeful in that it attempts to create self-awareness for the storyteller. **Organizing the data into logical categories by quantifying multiple stories,** as well as the contextual and demographic variables related to the occurrences of and characterizations of self-awareness, and then collapsing this information into a **graphic display,** might reveal the utility of this method of inquiry.

Within medicine, particularly psychiatry, documentations of patients' case histories have been systematically chronicled. They became codified sources for illustrating classificatory systems of mental disorders. This information has become a database for the creation of the diagnostic statistical manuals in which characterizations of symptomatology have been organized. **Volumes of case studies** have been written into books that are used as primary sources for training psychologists, psychoanalysts, and psychiatrists to guide them to the effective treatment of their patients. Using these same sociolinguistic approaches, stories could be used to clarify effective teaching and workplace training practices in context-specific environments and highlight effective instructional strategies for learners in characteristic or chronicled situations.

COMPARATIVE EXAMPLES

In this section, we provide a few brief comments related to a sample of articles that we believe reflect contrasting prevailing views of educational research. As noted earlier, we are attempting to strike a balance among the various views. What are the limitations of behavioristic psychology? What are the virtues associated with postmodernism? Is social constructivism (narrative inquiry) research? Are the contemporary constructivists creationists?

B. F. Skinner and Control

Many view behaviorism as both a science and/or a framework for explaining and/or understanding certain behaviors, as well as a technique that has behavioral management applications under certain circumstances. Most of us probably give little thought to the political and social contexts in which behavioral theories were developed. Laurence Smith (1992) wrote an article entitled "On Prediction and Control: B. F. Skinner and the Technological Ideal of Science" in which he related Skinner's views to those of Francis Bacon (1561-1626). Tracing behaviorism's philosophical roots back to Sir Francis Bacon and drawing parallels between behaviorism as a technique of behavioral control with Bacon's view of epistemology gives a reader a great deal to think about.

Smith (1992) presented Skinner's views and arguments so as to support the notion that behavioral control, or control in general, is the basic aim of science. The primary flaw with control being the chief aim of science is the unexpected side effects and societal impacts which may result from manipulating environmental events. Smith pointed out, citing Rachel Carson's (1962) book Silent Spring, the impact of technology and/or control and the possible undesirable side effects associated with use of environmental manipulations. He also cited M. R. Lepper and D. Greene (1978) and B. Schwartz (1982), who raised the issue of potential risks associated with the use of behavioral interventions. Although these down sides have been receiving increasing attention, behaviorism remains a relatively active area of study. Smith (1992) cited several factors for this, the most potent being the empirically validated use of behavioral techniques designed to manage behaviors and control specific behavior problems.

For many, Skinner's view of science as one of establishing control does not adequately define the overall purpose of science. For Aristotle, understanding has a practical and productive component. But should understanding be viewed as inferior to practical control? We do not exult the artisan (productive knowledge) as Sir Francis Bacon did, nor do we place more value upon the practical as Aristotle did. In our view, the production of knowledge to further our understanding of particular phenomena in order to build a foundation upon which to then further increase knowledge is as important as effecting change through a series of pragmatic behavior control techniques. The value of knowledge, whether it be to establish control or to lay a theoretical foundation, should be measured against various goals (prediction, explanation, and/or control) established for the pursuit of that knowledge. If the intent of a particular pursuit of science is to establish a theoretical framework, the value of that effort should be measured by how strong (or flexible) the framework is. Similarly, if the purpose of a particular pursuit is to effect a change or result in control, goals to reflect that purpose should be used to define success.

Virtues of Postmodernism

J. L. Kincheloe and S. R. Steinberg (1993) presented a discussion of the virtues of postmodernism in an article entitled "A Tentative Description of Post-Formal Thinking: The Critical Confrontation with Cognitive Theory." In trying to determine why this article and other similar articles have affected us in such a negative way, we offer the following four possibilities.

First, and potentially foremost, our negative reaction could be due to our Eurocentric normative gaze. The ideas put forth by the authors continually challenged our current Eurocentric views, past training, and knowledge of learning. This was a difficult article for us to read without reacting either defensively or in response to key components presented by the authors. Second, the writing style of the authors is one that frequently makes use of derogatory terms or words with negative connotations to refer to ideas other than their own, while framing their own views in more politically acceptable and humanistic ways. Describing formal operational thinkers à la Piaget as believers of a "Cartesian-Newtonian mechanistic worldview" locked in "monolithic essentialism of the past" illustrates our point. The authors conceptualize their way of thinking as "post-formal" and describe moving beyond the formality of Piaget, thus implying that they are functioning at a qualitatively higher level of formal thought than any of us. Our understanding of formal operations in Piaget's theory was a level of thought characterized by a theoretical or conceptual understanding of the assumptions underlying thought. Formal operations, therefore, are not necessarily bound to one set of assumptions. Thus, post-formal thought, as described by these authors, is not quantitatively or qualitatively higher or at a different level than formal thought, but rather formal thought which uses a different set of assumptions. This view of Piaget's contributions stated by the authors in the first two pages of the article, seemed to reflect such a biased view that it was difficult for us to read the rest of the article without continually questioning and critiquing the authors' bias within every paragraph. That is not to say that the authors presented no thoughts of value, but rather that they created a negative mind-set that took on the tone of dogma in their zealousness of critiquing cognitive theory.

The authors also made reference to feminist theory, citing the inseparability of rationality and emotion, the point being that intelligence may take many forms and should not be dominated by the masculine view of the proper path for human cognitive development. The only thing the authors seem to be stating is that any assumption cannot be separated from the social-political ideas of the individuals from whom the assumptions are born. We don't think that this idea by itself represents an earth-shaking revelation, but it does bring to the foreground the idea that we must not be complacent in our blind acceptance of assumptions which undergird any philosophy and/or theory. In this way, the authors serve the reader well by encouraging the reader to question the various assumptions the reader may hold dear.

In the authors' presentation of the features of what they classify as post-formal thinking, they fall into the same errors, pitfalls, and problems that they themselves have raised as areas of concern with respect to formal operational thought. In their quest of etymology, they state that post-formal thinking involves the ability to remove ourselves from socio-interpersonal norms and expectations, thus disembedding ourselves from the context in which we think and live. To us, this appears to be as realistic as a three-dimensional creature attempting to conceptualize fourth-dimensional space. Isn't this objective approach advocated by the authors precisely what empirical researchers attempt to do? It is difficult to imagine how anyone could totally remove him- or herself from any set of assumptions that lacks a political and/or ideological bias. The most one can hope for is to be cognizant of the possible presence of bias and its potential impact. In their presentation of pattern discovery (a second feature of post-formal thinking), Kincheloe and Steinberg state that the patterns are sometimes impenetrable to empirical methods of inquiry. We don't disagree with this assumption. However, we are reluctant to fully embrace this ideal for fear that any thought could be set forth and then challenges to the thought refuted with the idea that it cannot be subject to measurement and empirical verification. To us, this view is similar to many religious doctrines presented 500 years or so ago, in which all answers to questions were met with a statement that God's will or design was responsible for the shape and form of the universe as it exists. Similarly, though we do not disagree with the author's contention that the dominant cultures influence results with respect to creating biased assumptions and/or expectations, we are uncomfortable with a massive reinterpretation of knowledge structures based solely upon a feminist and/or postmodernist perspective. In fact, it could be argued that this revisionistic approach would be a trade-off of one set of assumptions for another.

A third characteristic of post-formal thinking places considerable value on deconstruction in a sense that the world in totality should be interpreted as opposed to specific events in the world. Would not this type of holistic deconstruction be subject to the same flaws as the empirical methods that the post-modern authors criticize with such zeal?

Finally, contextualization as the fourth characteristic of post-formal thought is presented in such a way so as to be beyond the realm or capacity of the Cartesian-Newtonian researchers. Empirical researchers certainly have a great deal of difficulty generalizing to real-life situations. We agree with this point. The desirable alternative, as put forth by Kincheloe and Steinberg, is the narrative holistic description of the world. This is presented by postmodernist thinkers as desirable and sufficient to be an alternative to the more commonly accepted empirical views. We remain more than skeptical and more than a little concerned with the thought that empirical research, with all its limitations of generalization and reliance upon assumptions that may in fact reflect a Eurocentric normative gaze, would or could be replaced by interpretations, descriptions, and thoughts that would defy any systematic inquiry, empirical test, or criticism from an individual or group of individuals whose views do not reflect what is contained in the socially and politically charged narrative, sociolinguistic analysis approach.

Social Constructivism

In an article entitled "The Value of Ideas: Problems Versus Possibilities in Learning", Richard Prawat (1993) puts forth the idea of restructuring education toward the goal of understanding the world in the holistic sense, as opposed to viewing the understanding of the world as a series of problems to be solved. His term for this educational direction, "idea-based social constructivism," has an Eastern philosophical flavor and is Zen-like in its approach. The major idea seems to be that individual facts or bits of knowledge "blind" one to a more thorough understanding of relationships and the world. He concedes that the specific problem-solving approach lends itself more or better to measurement because of the overt results of such study and, further, that the information-processing model tends to decrease the emphasis on more mechanical, technical, or rote skills with a positive emphasis given to teaching problem-solving strategies. Despite the benefits of the information-processing model over more simplistic behavioral ways of knowing, Prawat claims that the model cannot account for how new thoughts or organizations of concepts are acquired. This shortcoming forms the core of his argument: How can educators "cling to performance models" yet "incorporate insights from more recent cognitive constructivism and cultural anthropological theory?" (1993, p. 10).

Prawat (1993) explains that the information-processing model is fashioned as a parallel between the way a computer functions and the way the human mind interprets information. The main distinction, however, is that humans can "create representations, but they are not limited to them" (p. 7). Computers, on the other hand, may operate only with that information which has already been clearly defined. According to informational-processing theory, change (learning) occurs when currently held schema or cognitive structures cannot easily assimilate new data or information. This perturbation of organization is reconciled through a process of accommodation in which new schematic organizations are then formed. Piaget explains this accommodation-assimilation process as one of "perturbating the equilibrium" and defines it as being necessary in the learning process. Many cultural anthropologists have been greatly influenced by the work and theorizing of Vygotsky (1986), who embodies some of the information-processing approaches, though in a more global, less specific sense. The focus that is given to the importance of shared learning through apprenticeships is a good example of Vygotsky's approach to learning. Though some differences apparently exist in the interpretation of Vygotsky's work, he does appear to go beyond Piaget's work with respect to trying to encompass additional learning concepts that are social in nature.

Prawat (1993) presents the notion that idea-based social constructivism, not the information-processing model, should guide the direction of education. Following the idea-based social constructionism as a guide would result in curricula that are organized around big ideas and not merely tied to teaching specific competencies. This is referred to as a learner-centered as opposed to a subject-centered approach. Although Prawat (1993) stated that current research and theory on learning does not yet clearly justify an approach that combines elements of both learner-centered and subject-centered instruction, he does concede that it may represent the most realistic option for changing the nature of teaching at this time.

We see much of what Prawat (1993) sets forth as being the direction of much of our current teaching. For example, the emphasis of interdisciplinary lessons and global approaches in place of more specific content-based instruction seems to reflect contemporary views of teaching and learning. Where there is a great departure, however, is in his minimizing the importance of various aspects of content contained within a given subject matter. However, as long as there is public education, by which the education itself is funded by the people through the government, there would seem to be a need for some mechanism of accountability. And where there is accountability, there will need to be mechanisms in place to measure progress. The mechanisms will have to be objective, and this implies that educational outcomes can be measured. This takes us back to an approach that is at least partially subject centered and which is closely aligned with an empirically focused specific content laden information-processing approach to learning and instruction.

Constructionists and Creationists

In an article entitled "Constructionists and Creationists" F. E. McManus (1993) described his major concerns with postmodernist or constructivist views as opposed to empirical study and methodologies. He claimed that there is an analogy between constructivism and creationism. Constructionists have impact on the domains of humanities and politics, while creationists affect areas of religion and politics. He made reference to the fight biologists engage in to keep the views of creationists out of textbooks and science classes because creationism is not a science in the true sense of the word. McManus claimed that elevating the views of constructivists to the level of empirical science is not in the best interest of psychology or the acquisition of knowledge in general. According to McManus, what is lost in the constructivist's views is objectivity and objectivity is a major distinguishing characteristic between scientists and witch doctors. He argues that knowledge passed along from witch doctor to witch doctor is similar to the way knowledge would be passed along from constructivists to constructivists. McManus views the primacy constructivists give to personal experience and meanings as a reflection of a current humanistic fad of "conspicuous compassion" (p. 57). He summarizes his view of constructivists and post-modernists, with the idea that postmodernism is merely a term that means "after the era of science" (p. 58).

All things considered, we do share many of the concerns of the postmodernist and constructivist thought set forth by McManus. However, we are not comfortable with the notion of completely discounting the possible value that these creationists (constructionist) philosophies may offer us with respect to the acquisition of knowledge. On the one hand, it is difficult for us as individuals trained to respect and see value in empirical and objective research, to discount empirical methodologies in favor of a more subjective, less scientific method. However, it is recognized that the art of teaching is not one which always lends itself well to a systematic analysis and subsequent determination of effectiveness. Thus, these two opposing thoughts probably represent the shortcomings of both empirical inquiry and the appeal of the postmodernist views. We are willing to concede to the shortcomings of the empirical method, but not to the extent of completely discounting it. Further, the narrative or constructive approach may allow us to add to our knowledge base. However, unless there is some mechanism to ensure its validity or "objectivity," it needs to be approached with the same hesitancy or skepticism that an empiricist must apply to research assumptions and data. In sum, intellectual honesty is considered to be necessary but not sufficient to ensure the quality of narrative inquiry required for the acquisition of knowledge (see Training Application 9.1).

THE ROLE OF NARRATIVE INQUIRY

How can narrative inquiry be incorporated into the process-psychological mediators-sociolinguistic mediators-product research agenda outlined in the first section of this chapter? It is recognized that stories are important in that they constitute a legitimate arena of formal knowledge about teaching. Teacher research makes knowledge about teachers' expertise accessible and provides different perspectives on teaching and learning that cannot be known by other forms of inquiry. All forms of research rely on assumptions and while it is crucial to question assumptions that underlie different conceptions of research inquiry, most of us would probably support the notion that absolute truths will never be known about the truths of assumptions.

As Linda Behar-Horrenstein and Ronald R. Morgan (1995) noted, concerns about the limitations of the technique of narrative research have focused upon the descriptive nature of narrative and have highlighted the lack of objective standards to guide improvement or gauge effectiveness. To be truly effective, **narrative research should be evaluated within the**

context of standards that would be used to ensure appropriate classroom and workplace practice. The responsibility of the teacher and/or workplace trainer must progress beyond the development of his/her own idiosyncratic theory and/or practice in the development and incorporation of these standards into his or her teaching and/or training practices (Buchmann, 1986). Incomplete considerations about story involve examining the possibilities for the use of story that have not been previously suggested. Using narrative as the sole form of methodological inquiry will require agreed upon and rigorous methodological procedures, clear conceptualizations, the formulation of key assumptions, and common referents that have precise meanings that are consistently used across varied situations.

Given the importance of stories, the next step should focus on **making the information** that is likely to emerge from story **accessible by looking at recurring patterns across different contexts and variables**. A conceptual framework (Hargeaves, 1994) that could be used to guide such research includes four process-oriented principles: (1) situating teachers' stories in relationship to other stories; (2) contextualizing stories in relationship to other considerations; (3) raising questions about story in relationship to social and political considerations; and (4) regrounding stories.

The implementation of the first principle is predicated on increasing the use of story and **building large databases of multiple stories**. For example, suppose that workplace trainers' stories were compiled for many trainers in many workplace training situations. Each trainer would be asked to maintain a daily journal. **Content analysis procedures** would be employed to systematically examine individual journals. The occurrence of recurrent themes would be identified, categorized, and quantified within each journal and across all journals. These activities would address the first principle.

Related to the second principle, the occurrence of various themes would be categorized in relationship to a trainers' gender, age, level of education, area of specialization, socioeconomic status, country of origin, ethnic orientation (European, Asian, Native American Indian, Caucasian, Hispanic, or African-American), demographic context of training location (urban, suburban, or rural sectors), and type of work setting (public, private, factory, service, etc.). If a series of patterns began to emerge, or similarities across variables and contexts within thematic categories were illustrated, then correlation techniques might be employed to test for significant relationships among various subgroups. Statistical techniques such as the Kolomogorov-Smirnov test of agreement (to assess the homogeneity of the subgroups within the sample), **path analysis**, or **cluster analysis** might be used to establish patterns of interrelations among many cognitively and/or socially situated variables. Path analysis techniques permit testing the validity of causal inferences for pairs of variables while controlling for the effects of other variables. Models can be specified and the influence of exogenous variables that correspond to independent constructs (themes that occur within multiple stories) on endogenous trainer variables (trainers' gender, age, level of education, area of specialization, socioeconomic status, country of origin, ethnic orientation) and other variables (e.g., demographic context of business and/or type of business) present in educational and/or workplace contexts (locations) can be formulated and empirically tested. Limitations on the meaningfulness of parameters are predicated on the researcher's ability to demonstrate the extent to which models can be shown to fit the ongoing data sets. If the pattern of variances and covariances derived from the models do not differ significantly from the pattern of variances and covariances related to the observed variables, then a given model is said to fit the data sets (Behar, 1994; Leithwood, Jantzi & Fernandez, 1993). This evidence might serve to identify strengths and weaknesses of storytelling as a research tool. In a similar connection, these pattern matching activities would amplify the third principle, by encouraging researchers to raise questions about story themes that emerged in relationship to social and/or political considerations. A total analysis of the findings would then lead to regrounding stories as suggested by the fourth principle.

A second approach to expanding the use of story involves **examining the outcomes of certain emergent themes** among trainers, such as trainer isolation, working with a learner with disabilities, and the professional disequilibrium (Cochran-Smith & Lytle, 1993) that occurs during the transition from a novice to advanced beginner teacher and/or trainer. This approach would focus on the nature of outcomes. If the teachers' and/or trainers' actions were the same for each situation reported, we might ask whether these outcomes were coincidental, or influenced by one variable or a combination of many variables. While it might be tempting to assume that a pattern exist while conducting this type of research, the only way to know for sure if sysmtematic and reproducable patterns exist is to perform a series of studies.

A third approach would be to have several researchers analyze the respondents' stories. There can be little doubt that the interviewer interjects his/her interpretive reality while recounting a respondent's story. For example, if one teacher's and/or trainer's story were distributed among a group of researchers rather than just to one or two, what is the likelihood that the analysis or identification of thematic content would be the same? How do we separate the framework of one's own culture, experiences, or tacit knowledge from their interpretation of the stories? If we gathered seven to ten stories and engaged five to seven researchers to systematically analyze the content, what degree of agreement or inter-rater reliability might be achieved?

Voracious debates about the limitations of story and empiricism are difficult to evaluate. Surely there are other productive approaches to take in addressing this matter, rather than engaging in seemingly unresolvable debates. **A marriage of empiricism and mentalistic psychology** is not unreasonable given that the underlying assumptions from both camps cannot be clearly verified. Research in the field may be strengthened by a combination of these methods. The power of story to make new things possible and important in educational research becomes a reality when researchers' aims are focused on expanding our understanding rather than providing the one right methodology. If we begin to quantify the contexts in which the storyteller's themes occur, then the potential value of story as an educational research tool may be known. The substantial and quantified framework offered by these approaches may eventually affirm Noddings' (1991) belief that it is by engaging educators regardless of gender, class, and culture and giving them a voice through story that we may realize the use of story as a vehicle to direct and change lives.

Within the educational and research community, we appear to be coming full circle in our exploration of what constitutes truth, knowledge, and viable educational research constructs worthy of study. Ultimately, we must disengage ourselves from the notion of renegotiating which research method is worth most and examine the essential means by which research methodology can inform workplace training practices. If we do not challenge the value or utility of story as a viable methodology, we will remain mired in the usual undisciplined circular discourse that characterizes much of what educators and workplace trainers do. To challenge these assumptions might give rise to an emergent linkage that we believe exists in macrolizing the location of multiple stories. Also, creating a classificatory system supported by an empirically derived system will serve to illustrate the relationship between the storyteller's reflection, thought, philosophy, and their subsequent actions. Attempts to systematically codify thematic material could serve as the basis to exemplify the notional value of story and illustrate the importance of using this methodology in workplace training situations.

SYNTHESIS AND CRITIQUE

The decade of the 1960s was a time of great enthusiasm for educational and societal reforms (Biddle & Anderson, 1986). It was assumed that we could eliminate the effects of race, sex, culture, and socioeconomic status on the quality of education. During the 1970s and 1980s, social deficit models (cultural deprivation, linguistic deprivation, family disorganization) and culturally different models (linguistic interference, second-language instruction, teacher expectancies, culturally incongruent instruction) were used to explain individual differences among students. Today deconstructed models in which school failure is viewed as self-defeating resistance rather than inadequacy prevail.

It is recognized that many contemporary researchers who have philosophical differences to or a predisposition against the use of empirical forms of methodological inquiry have chosen to superimpose the sociolinguistic techniques of the humanities onto the overall context of educational research. If we consider all research methodologies from a macro perspective and graphically represent them on a continuum, it becomes apparent that **the sociolinguistic techniques complement empirical methods of inquiry** (see Figure 9.1). That is to say that educational research paradigms have evolved from the strict behaviorally anchored empirically validated models of the 60's and 70's to models that are mediated by behavioral and cognitive science models and sociolinguistic models of inquiry.

Figure 9.1
Chronological Representation of Major Educational Research Paradigms

1960s 1970s	1970s 1980s	1990s
Process-product paradigms	Process-psychological mediators-product paradigms (Carroll's mastery learning model, cognitive science, and components of effective schools)	Process-psychological mediators-sociolinguistic mediators-product paradigms (sociolinguistic models, narrative inquiry, and linguistic analysis)

Overall, it could be argued that educational/psychological research has made little contribution to educational and/or workplace practices. It is recognized that social science research cannot provide the kind of hard information about human behavior that physics provides about atoms. Perhaps there is no such thing as a science of teaching and/or education. But the synthesis of research on teaching (Walberg, 1984, 1986; Wang, Haeartel & Walberg, 1993) has yielded some agreement on the ingredients of effective teaching. However, the procedures remain inexplicit. Most would probably agree that the documented consistency of educational effects has put teaching on a sound scientific foundation. That said, perhaps it is a good tactical position for us to hold on to all of these models at this time in the evolution of our thinking. Since we simply don't know what the best course of action is at this time, perhaps it is best to keep all the models in mind when attempting to solve educational and/or workplace problems. Some **promising areas of research** suggested by Glaser (1978, 1982, 1984, 1986, 1990) are:

1. Expert-novice comparisons/behavioral-cognitive task analyses/ computer simulations of thinking and problem solving
2. Early interventions
3. Prose learning/schema activators
4. Tutoring/mastery learning/PSI
5. Intelligence and personality
6. Behavior management

It is recommended that we try to strike a balance between empirical views and sociolinguistic views. Consider the utility of taking a middle position. Assume that there are individual differences in academic aptitude and motivation. Accept the reality of cultural differences. Consider the utility of taking an at-risk view and that schools and working environments serve a sorting function. Finally, consider the utility of taking a **cognitive science view** in which it is assumed that:

1. Individual differences can be modified.
2. The differences between typical and atypical learners consist of:
    a. attention
    b. memory organization (the literate bias in schooling)
    c. expectancies (cognitive styles)
3. Biological constraints consist of maturation, temperament, and attention.
4. Psychological constraints consist of knowledge, memory organization, emotion-state dependent memory, mood, language, personality, cognitive style, and motivation.
5. Expert-novice differences reflect differences in:
    a. content
    b. procedural content
    c. procedural knowledge (general problem solving skills)

QUESTION TO CONSIDER

Is the postmodern beast eroding psychologies' scientific foundation? Although empiricism may be dead as a theory of truth, it is very much alive as a method of discovery and finding evidence. Discuss your views related to the complimentary use of empirical and narrative forms of inquiry within the educational research community. Can we strike a methodological balance between the continuities and discontinuities inherent in the modern and postmodern eras? Can we use the traditions of our past as building blocks to catalyze the development of new solutions to many old problems related to learning theory and teaching that continue to confront us? Explain your position.

Training Application 9.1
States of Growth

"Growth states" refer to differences in levels of activity that indicate an individual's disposition to interact productively in the training environment (Joyce, Weil, & Showers, 1992). Trainers can use knowledge of growth states to inform instruction2al design decisions. Rich content, well organized training experiences, and positive training environments encourage productivity and changes in growth states. Data about growth states can be gathered by observation and reflective journal writing during training.

The Gourmet Omnivore. Mature, highly active people who pursue resources in the training environment and exploit them successfully. They volunteer, initiate ideas, influence events. They learn a lot from information interaction with peers. They are highly persistent even in difficult tasks.

The Active Consumer. Happy participators who easily engage in training activities but who look for confirmation that what they are doing is a good thing. They tend to look a lot toward the omnivores. They will try anything but need support and encouragement.

The Passive Consumer. They are relatively amiable and conform to the training environment but are highly influenced by the social context (i.e., their degree of activity depends on whom they are with). They also tend to be adamant about sitting with someone they know.

The Reticent Consumer. They are reluctant learners; generally they are participating because they have been told that they must. They are often angry about being there, try to negate the content, and avoid participating in activities. They tend to look with suspicion on participants who seem to enjoy being involved in training activities. They see more defects than possibilities.

Joyce, B., Weil, M., & Showers, B. (1992). *Models of teaching* (pp. 280-289). Boston: Allyn and Bacon.

APPENDIX

PROBLEM SOLUTIONS

1. Define the following terms or concepts:

   a. **Theory-ladenness of facts.** Theory-ladenness of facts is considered to be one of the underlying problems with the falsificationist's position of causal inference. It is a conviction that the objectivity of the facts that would be used to confirm or disconfirm a theory may be contaminated by the language we use. Therefore, we will never be able to infer cause no matter how hard we try, because in our use of language there are likely to be many hidden theoretical assumptions.

   b. **Quine-Duhem thesis.** Quine-Duhem thesis, another problem associated with the falsificationist's position of causal inference. Any theory of causation must have the status of not yet being disconfirmed and no theory is every truly confirmed. We as scientists cannot trust anything because all facts may be disproved, even evidence that may lead to disconfirming or confirming a theory.

   c. **Meta-analysis.** Meta-analysis is a way of approaching a particular research problem by pulling out the relevant studies that have been previously carried out and reanalyzing the findings. For a meta-analysis of teenagers' self-esteem, for instance, a psychologist would pull together all of the studies conducted in the past ten years on this subject and systematically reanalyze the entire data set across all studies.

   Distinguish between/among the following terms or concepts:

   a. **Factorial ANOVA and ANOVA correlated groups.** Because they are both capable of reducing the error variance by partitioning out the variance due to individual differences, the systematic variance due to the treatment has a chance to manifest itself. Factorial ANOVA and ANOVA correlated groups are both more effective and desirable than ANOVA since not much can be done to control for individual difference variability when we use a simple one-way ANOVA procedure.

Factorial ANOVA and ANOVA correlated groups differ from each other. For Factorial ANOVA no attempts are made to match the subjects, and both main effects and interactions are analyzed (for instance, for a 2 x 2 factorial design, there will be three HO hypotheses: two for main effects and one for interaction). An ANOVA of correlated groups, on the other hand, is based on the matching of subjects on variables significantly related to the dependent variable, and instead of main effects and interactions we analyze the variance between columns and between rows.

b. **Type I error, Type II error, and power.** A type I error is rejecting the null hypothesis when indeed we should not reject it. We often increase the alpha value in order to reduce the possibility of making a type I error. A type II error is the opposite (i.e., retaining the null hypothesis when indeed it should be rejected). The possibility of making a type II error can be reduced by increasing homogeneity, increasing n, and maximizing treatment differences. Power means the probability of rejecting the null hypothesis when, in reality, it should be rejected (i.e., making a correct decision).

c. **ANOVA and multiple regression.** ANOVA is used to test for differences across different treatment conditions, while multiple regression is used to examine the association between several independent variables and one dependent variable. Another difference between the two is that ANOVA is most often used in experimental research, while multiple regression is most often used for survey research and ex post facto studies because it is most suitable for analyzing attribute (measured) variables rather than active (experimental) variables. It should be noted that multiple regression is often employed in cases where the Ns are not equal or as an alternative to an analysis of change scores.

2. Compare and contrast the notion of causal inference from the positivist, essentialist, falsificationist, contextualist, and the evolutionary critical-realist perspectives.

a. **The positivist position.** This position is atheoretical and lays emphasis on actual observation, saying that if something is not observable, then it cannot be studied. Therefore, in research, the positivists regard quantitative intervening variables as the only way to study the phenomenon under investigation rather than qualitative hypothetical constructs.

b. **Essentialist position.** The essentialists emphasize looking for necessary and sufficient conditions in examining cause. They also think that there is a causal chain in which a certain cause infallibly and simultaneously results in an effect. Critics claim that this emphasis on a causal chain of events leads people to be rather mechanistic in their investigations.

c. **Falsificationist position.** According to this position, any theory of causation must have the status of not yet being disconfirmed, and a theory can never be proved and/or confirmed. Instead, it can only be said to be not yet disconfirmed until another alternative theory can be found that accounts for the previous theories successes and generate others not previously included in the original theory. Practically, advocates of this position use comparisons to rule out all plausible alternative hypotheses but one. Even then, all that could modestly be said was that the theory is not yet disconfirmed. This leaves open the possibility of anomalies of facts that do not fit the paradigm.

d. **Evolutionary critical realist position.** These people accept the notion that causation does exist, but they have to be very careful in accepting cause because there might be alternative explanations. Instead of emphasizing the necessary and sufficient philosophical analysis and the micromediational level of the causal chain, people holding this position discuss the evolutionary significance of causal inference and use observations and comparison groups to support their argument.

3. Discuss the following sets of issues related to faulty experimental and ex post facto designs. First list four widely used faulty designs. Describe their general characteristics and the appropriate statistical treatment effect estimate each provides. Second how and why might the treatment effect estimates be biased for each faulty design?

a. **The four faulty designs and appropriate statistical treatment effect estimates.**

1. One group - one shot case study: X Y
    Use: a narrative and figural description of the data set.

2. Before-after, no control group, nonrandomized design:
    Yb-X-Ya
    Use: a t-test

3. Simulated before-after, non-randomized design: X Ya
    Use: a t-test   Yb

4. Two or more group(s), non-randomized design: X Y
    Use: a t-test for two groups; F-test for more   X Y
    than two groups; or FANOVA

b. **Their general characteristics.** One thing characteristic of all four designs is that no randomization or matching is used to control for extraneous individual difference variance that could differentially affect Y since other independent variables or extraneous variables may in fact have been responsible for the differences in the dependent variable measured.

Another characteristic that is true of the first three designs is the lack of a comparison group. Hence we have no way of knowing if the changes in Y are indeed the result of X, because other factors, such as reaction (maturation and history) and regression effects, may also play a significant part in the change process.

c. **How and why might the treatment effect estimates be biased for each design.**

Design a: Since there is no comparison group, we are not sure whether it is the treatment that produces the effect in the subjects or other possible sources of variance. Also, since no randomization is involved here, the representativeness of the sample remains questionable.

Design b: There is no comparison group. In addition, there can be a sensitizing effect of the pre-test measure in the post-test measure, and there may be reactive and/or regression effects.

Design c: Same as design b.

Design d: We are not sure if the two groups are comparable since there is no randomization or matching. Therefore, there is a possibility that the treatment effects may be biased.

4. How does research design control variance? Why would a factorial design control more variance than a one-way design? How does a design that uses matched subjects, covariance, or repeated measures of the same subjects control variance? How is variance controlled when a multiple regression procedure is used to analyze a data set? In responding to this question, you may find it helpful to provide a comparative figural representation of how each design controls variance. That is to say, make certain that you discuss how each design controls variance.

a. Research design controls variance by maximizing experimental variance (increasing differences between/among treatment groups), minimizing error variance (decreasing within groups difference), and controlling extraneous variance (through randomization, matching, subject selection procedures designed to ensure a representative sample, and using a design that has a comparison group).

b. If, for example, a researcher wants to investigate the effects of two teaching methods, he or she has the following design:

Treatment Conditions

X1	X2
Y1	Y2

- where a continuous dependent measure (achievement) appears in the columns

However, with this simple one-way ANOVA design, the investigator may not be able to find a significant difference between the two methods because he or she has very little control over the individual differences among the subjects. But if a factorial design is used, the individual differences among the subjects could be better controlled. In this FANOVA arrangement the systematic variance due to the treatment has a chance to manifest itself as shown in the following analytic paradigm (here, the researcher adds another independent variable such as intelligence):

Treatment Conditions

	X1	X2
High		
IQ Middle		
Low		

- where a continuous dependent measure of
achievement appears in the cells

c. Similarly, a matched subjects design also helps control individual difference variance among subjects. The above study could also be done using a matched subjects design (i.e., the subjects would be matched on intelligence):

Treatment Conditions

MR Unit	X1	X2
1		
2		
3		
4	Y1	Y2
:		
:		
30		

- where a continous dependent measure of
achievement appears in each column

Thus, the variance due to individual differences in intelligence is partitioned out (i.e., controlled) and the detection of systematic-experimental variance is more likely to surface. The rationale for using a repeated measures design of the same subjects is the same.

d. Analysis of covariance is another way to partition (control) variance. Here, the investigator controls for individual differences among the subjects before testing for differences in the post-test measure(s). In analysis of covariance, the pre-test is used as a covariate that has the effect of accounting for differences between (among) groups that are present at the time of the pre-test measure:

Treatment Conditions

X1		X2	
Yb	Ya	Yb	Ya

- where a continuous before-after dependent
measure of achievement appears in columns

Another possibility here is to use intelligence as a covariant. In this type of situation, you would statistically control for individual difference in intelligence among your respondents before you would test for differences in achievement across treatment groups.

Treatment Conditions

X1		X2	
YCovar	Y1	YCovar	Y2

- where YCovar = intelligence and Y1 and Y2 = a
continuous measure of achievement

5. Four problems from the research literature are given below. Present analytic paradigms and construct hypotheses based on them.

a. What is the influence of massive rewards on the reading achievements of potential school dropouts?

b. Teachers who are perceived by students as dissimilar (to the students) in traits relevant to teaching are more attractive to students than teachers perceived as similar.

c. How do sex-role stereotyping, sexual conservatism, adversial sexual beliefs, and acceptance of interpersonal violence affect attitudes to ward rape and sexual violence?

d. Does stimulus exposure have two effects, one cognitive and one affective, which in turn affect liking, familiarity, recognition confidence, and accuracy?

a)   Experimental Conditions

     Massive Rewards (X1) Non-Massive Rewards (X2)

     _____

                  (Y1)   (Y2)

     _____

          - where a continuous measure of reading achievement appears in the columns

HO: There is no difference in reading achievement scores between massive reward and nonmassive reward conditions (Use a t-test.)

b)   Attractive   Non-Attractive

     _____

     Similar

     _____

     Dissimilar

     _____

          - where frequencies appear in the cells

HO: There is no relationship between student-teacher similarity and teacher attractiveness.
       (Use a X^2-test.)

6. Suppose a researcher has done an experiment in which he or she tested two methods of instruction (A1 and A2). A second independent variable was social class (middle class and working class, B1

and B2). The dependent variable was achievement. The results are summarized as follows (the tabled entries are means):

Methods

		A1	A2	
Social	B1	78	70	74
Class	B2	72	60	66
		75	65	(Mt = 70)

The A effect was reported to be significant at the 0.01 level. So was the B effect. The interaction was not found to be significant.

   a. Interpret the results by discussing the differences between the means and the relations they presumably reflect.
   b. Draw a graph describing the results, and interpret the graph.

Using the same problem presented above, assume that the table entries are a bit different:

		A1	A2	
Social	B1	70	78	74
Class	B2	72	60	66
		71	69	(Mt = 70)

The only change is that the A1B1 and A2B2 means have been inter changed. A factorial analysis of variance shows that the A means are not significantly different, but the B means are significantly different. The interaction is also significant.

   a. Interpret the results. Compare your interpretation to that of the first problem.
   b. Draw a graph describing the results and interpret it. Compare this graph to the one drawn for the first problem.
   c. What value does factorial analysis of variance have in research situations like this? Explain why you would not necessarily reach the same conclusions by conducting two separate experiments.

a)

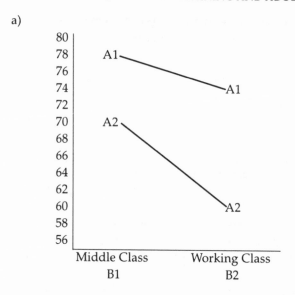

Since the mean of A1 is significantly higher than the mean of A2, it can be said that method A1 is the method of choice for students of both classes. The diagram indicates that there are differences between the two methods. There is no significant interaction effect.

b)

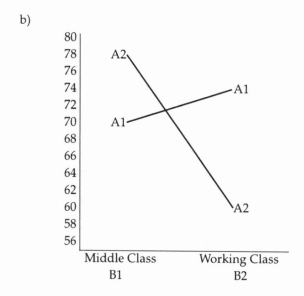

In contrast to the first problem, there is no significant difference between the two teaching methods, but the social classes differ from each other (i.e., students from middle-class families learn better than those from working-class families regardless of teaching methods). There is a significant interaction effect between the two variables that can be interpreted as follows: Methods are related to achievement, but the kind of relation depends on social class (i.e., method A2 is the method of choice for middle-class students while method A1 is the method of choice for working-class students).

This example also clearly shows the advantages of a factorial design, which allows us to study interactions among different independent variables, increase precision, and decrease type II error. This cannot be done with the univariant approach. For instance, two one-way analyses in this case will show only that there is no significant difference between two methods and that there is a significant difference between the two social classes. But we would not know anything about the interaction effect of the two variables. The specific information regarding each method and its relation to achievement for each social class would not be discerned from a simple one-way analysis.

7. Suppose that you are the principal of an elementary school. Some of the fourth- and fifth-grade teachers want to dispense with workbooks. The superintendent does not like the idea but allows you to test the notion that workbooks do not make much difference. (One of the teachers even suggests that workbooks may have bad effects on both teachers and pupils.) Set up two models (i.e., analytic paradigms) to test the efficacy of the workbooks (a one-way design and a factorial design). State a few possible null hypotheses related to your analytic paradigms and critically discuss the logic of each design from the standpoint of research design and statistics. Consider the variables achievement, intelligence, and sex. Also consider the possibility of teacher attitude toward workbooks as an independent variable.

a

| | | Experimental Conditions | |
| | | (X1) | (X2) |
MR	Unit	With Workbooks	Without Workbooks
1			
2			
3			
4			
5			
6			
7			
:			
:			
30			

- where a continuous measure of achievement
appears in each column

HO1:   There is no difference in the achievement scores between
the experimental conditions

HO2:   There is no difference in achievement scores across the units

This is a matched subjects design ($\frac{XY}{XY}$ MR) in which the subjects
are matched according to intelligence and sex and then a randomization procedure was used. A simple correlated group analysis would be
used to test for differences between the two experimental conditions.
In this design, variance due to individual differences of the subjects is
partitioned out by the matching procedure. Thus the researcher has a
better control of the individual difference variance which, as a result,
will enable the experimental variance to manifest itself. It is important
to note that for this kind of design that after matching on a few variables, that a randomization procedures be used. One limitation with
this design is that it cannot provide the detailed information of a factorial design related to the interaction effects.

b)

	Experimental Conditions			
	With Workbooks (X1a)		Without Workbooks (X1b)	
	(X3a)	(X3b)	(X3a)	(X3b)
	High Att.	Low Att.	High Att.	Low Att.
	F(X4a) M(X4b)	F(X4a) M(X4b)	F(X4a) M(X4b)	F(X4a) M(X4b)
High (X2a)_____				
Middle (X2b)_____				
Low (X2c)_____				

- where a continuous dependent measure of
achievement appears in each cell.

HO1:   There is no difference in the achievement scores between
the experimental conditions (X1a, X1b).

HO2:   There is no difference in the achievement scores across different levels of intelligence (X2a - X2c).

HO3:   There is no difference in the achievement scores between
the genders (X4a, X4b).

HO4:   There is no difference in the achievement scores across the
levels of teacher attitude (X3a, X3b).

HO5:   There is no interaction effect between the experimental conditions and the levels of intelligence.

HO6:   There is no interaction effect between the experimental conditions and the genders.

HO7:   There is no interaction effect between the experimental condition and the levels of teacher attitude.

HO8:   There is no interaction effect between the levels of intelligence and the genders.

HO9:   There is no interaction effect between the levels of intelligence and the levels of teacher attitude.

HO10: There is no interaction effect between the genders and the levels of teacher attitude.

This is 2 x 2 x 2 x 3 factorial design where four independent variables are simultaneously put together. Variance due to individual differences is highly controlled in this situation. The analysis also reveals the characteristics of each variable and its relation with the dependent variable in the presence of other independent variables.

8.   In a study in which training on the complexities of art stimuli affected attitude toward music, the investigator used analysis of covariance, with the covariate being measures from a scale to measure attitudes toward music. This was a pre-test. There were three experimental groups. Sketch the design from this brief description. Why did the investigator use the music attitude scale as a pretest? Why was analysis of covariance used?

Experimental Conditions

        X1   X2   X3
    _____

    1 Yb Ya Yb Ya   Yb Ya
    2
    3
    4
    :

                - where a continuous before-after dependent
                measure appears in each column

An analysis of covariance (ANCOVAR) would be performed where attitude towards music (the pretest) is the covariant. Music attitude is chosen as a covariant because it has the effect of controlling for individual differences between groups that are present prior to obtaining a measure on the dependent variable of interest (the post-test measure of attitudes toward music in this instance). An analysis of covariance enables the researcher to control for variance by ensuring the least amount of within groups variability possible, hence improving the possibility of finding a significant difference across the treatment groups.

9. Outline plans for the design of a laboratory experiment, a field experiment, and a field study of the same basic problem (the relation between the cohesiveness of a group and its productivity). Keep the designs simple. Do the three designs get at the same research problem? That is, is the problem altered by the differences in the three kinds of study? How? Which design is best? Why?

a. Laboratory experiment. Randomly select 200 subjects from a very large population and put them in a special location where extraneous influences are kept at a minimum. The subjects are randomly assigned into two equally large randomly assigned groups (the experimental group and the control group). It is so designed that the experimental group spend some time together in an effort to develop high group cohesiveness. The control group subjects are kept separated from one another (therefore developing no cohesiveness). Then two groups are then   placed in similar conditions to work on some task that requires some degree of cohesiveness. The productivity scores or the number of products produced by the two groups would be compared using a t-test.

While a relevant study and being able to provide some control for experimental variance, this design has limitations. Since it is not done in a natural setting, the treatment effect is probably not strong, and the findings are not very generalizable. Thus, the research problem can not be fully addressed by this experimental design.

b. Field experiment. Randomly select 30 students who have been in a homogeneous setting and have become familiar and friendly with one another to form the experimental group. Then randomly select another 30 subjects who do not know one an other. Ask the two groups to perform some problem-solving task that requires some degree of cohe-siveness. One half of the subjects in each group would be rewarded for their efforts, and the other half would not. Then the problem-solving scores and or products of the two groups would be compared using a factorial analysis of variance procedure.

In this design, since we are able to investigate the cohesiveness phenomenon in a natural setting, and more experimental and error variance can also be controlled, the research problem can be better addressed.

c. Field study. Since no treatment manipulation is possible for field studies, we simply select a group of 30 students who we find to be cooperative with each other and another group of 30 students who are not cooperative, observe them and count how many times they successfully complete some particular problem solving task. After that we will test for differences between the two groups using a t-test.

All in all, because the field experiment is done in a natural setting and we are able to exercise considerable control over two independent measures, we can address the research problem. This is probably the best method for a research problem of this nature. Given the difficulties associated with manipulation of cohesiveness in a laboratory setting, the field study is probably the second best method.

10. A college instructor was interested in testing the relationship between intrinsic and extrinsic motivation. The basic question of interest to the instructor was whether extrinsically manipulated grade contingencies negatively affected intrinsic interest in the course. Five hundred students (graduates and undergraduates, males and females) were randomly assigned to a grade contingent condition (groups in which the final examination grade was averaged with the cumulative course examination grades of the students prior to the taking of the final examination) and a grade noncontingent condition (groups in which the final examination grade could only improve, but not lower, a student's final course grade). After completing the final examination, all students returned a course evaluation rating (A, B, C, etc.) form to the instructor. Present the overall analytic paradigm(s) for this research project. Discuss the logic of your design(s) from the standpoint of research design and statistics. What statistical test(s) of significance would you use? State a few possible null hypotheses related to your analytic paradigm(s) and critically evaluate how the treatment effect estimates may be biased. (Note: In addition to the course evaluation ratings, make certain that student performance on the final examination is included as one of the variables of interest in the study at hand.)

Design #1

Final Examination Grades

Higher Maintenance Lower

Grade contingent   graduate

condition
_____

undergraduate

Non-grade   graduate

contingent
_____

condition
undergraduate

- where frequencies appear in the cells (Use a X^2 test)

HO1:   There is no relationship between grade contingent condition and performance on the final examination.

HO2:   There is no relationship between graduate and undergraduate student status condition and performance on the final examination for the grade contingent condition subjects.

HO3:   There is no relationship between graduate and undergraduate student status condition and performance on the final examination for the non-grade contingent condition subjects.

X1	X2
Grade Contingent	Non-Grade Contingent
Condition	Condition

Y1	Y2

- where a continuous course evaluation measure appears in each
     column (Use a t-test)
  HO: There is no difference in the course evaluation measures
        across treatment conditions.

Design #2

	Grade Contingent Condition	Non-grade Contingent Condition
Graduate		
Undergraduate		

- where a continuous final examination measure and a continuous
   course evaluation measure appear in the cells (Use two FANOVA
   analyses-one analysis for each dependent measure.)
  HO1: There is no difference in the final examination scores across
         grade contingency conditions.
  HO2: There is no difference in the final examination scores across
         the graduate-undergraduate student status conditions.
  HO3: There are no interaction effects.

HO1: There is no difference in the course evaluation scores across grade contingency conditions.

HO2: There is no difference in the course evaluation scores across the graduate-undergraduate student status conditions.

HO3: There are no interaction effects.

Both the combined X^2/t-test statistical design and the 2 FANOVA statistical designs address the research question. Does the use of extrinsic rewards (the two grade contingency conditions) undermine intrinsic interests (assessed by the course evaluation measure)? On the positive side, we have many subjects and some control over experimental variance and the individual differences among our subjects. However, the weakness of the course evaluation scores as a measure of intrinsic interest is a serious one requiring further refinement.

REFERENCES

Ames, C., & Ames, R. E. (Eds.). (1985). *Research on motivation in education: Vol. 2. The classroom milieu*. Orlando, FL: Academic Press.

Ames, C., & Ames, R. E. (1989). *Research on motivation in education: Vol. 3. Goals and cognitions*. Orlando, FL: Academic Press.

Ames, R. E., & Ames, C. (Eds.). (1984). *Research on motivation in education: Vol. 1. Student motivation*. Orlando, FL: Academic Press.

Amsel, A. (1962). Frustrative nonreward in partial reinforcement and discrimination learning. *Psychological Review, 69*, 306-328.

Anastasi, A. (1982). *Psychological testing* (5th ed.). New York: Macmillan.

Anderson, J. R. (1982). Acquisition of cognitive skill. *Psychological Review, 89*, 369-406.

Anderson, L. W., & Burns, R. B. (1987). Values, evidence, and mastery learning. *Review of Educational Research, 57* (2), 215-224.

Anderson, R. R., & Spiro, R. J. (1977). *Schooling and the acquisition of knowledge*. New York: John Wiley and Sons.

Annis, L. F. (1983). The processes and effects of peer tutoring. *Human Learning, 2*, 39-47.

Archer, R. P. (1992). *MMPI-A: Assessing adolescent psychopathology*. Hillsdale, NJ: Lawrence Erlbaum.

Ausubel, D. (1968). *Educational psychology: A cognitive view*. New York: Holt, Rinehart and Winston.

Ausubel, D. P. (1978). In defense of advance organizers: A reply to the critics. *Review of Educational Research, 48*, 251-257.

Bandura, A. (1978). The self system in reciprocal determinism. *American Psychologist, 33* (4), 344-358.

Bandura, A. (1989). Human agency in social cognitive theory. *American Psychologist, 44* (9), 1175-1184.

Bar-Tal, D. (1979). Interactions of teachers and pupils. In I. H. Frieze, D. Bar-Tal, & J. S. Carroll (Eds.), *New approaches to social problems: Applications of attribution theory*. San Francisco, CA: Jossey-Bass.

Bar-Tal, D., & Daron, E. (1979). Pupil's attributions of success and failure. *Child Development, 50*, 264-267.

Bartlett, F. C. (1932). *Remembering: A study in experimental and social psychology*. London: Cambridge University Press.

Bass, B. M. (1990). *Bass and Stogdill's handbook of leadership* (3rd ed.). New York: Free Press.

Bates, J. A. (1979). Extrinsic reward and intrinsic motivation: A review with implications for the classroom. *Review of Educational Research, 49* (4), 557-576.

Beck, A. T. (1976). *Cognitive therapy and the emotional disorders.* New York: International Universities Press.

Beck, A. T. (1991). Cognitive therapy: A 30-year retrospective. *American Psychologist, 46,* 4, 368-375.

Behar, L. S. (1994 October). *Student selected curriculum tracks as a mediating influence on academic achievement.* Paper presented at the Annual Meeting of the Midwestern Educational Association, Chicago, IL.

Behar-Horrenstein, L. S., & Morgan, R. R. (1995). Narrative research, teaching, and teacher thinking: Perspectives and possibilities. *Peabody Journal of Education, 70* (2), 139-161.

Belensky, M., Clinchy, B., Goldberger, N., & Tarule, J. (1986). *Women's ways of knowing.* New York: Basic Books.

Bellak, L. (1993). *The Thematic Apperception Test, the Children's Apperception Test, and the Senior Apperception Technique in clinical use* (5th edition). Boston, MA: Allyn and Bacon.

Bender, L. (1946). *Instructions for the use of the Visual Motor Gestalt Test.* New York: American Orthopsychiatric Association.

Benjamin, L. T. (1988). A history of teaching machines. *American Psychologist, 43* (9), 703-712.

Bentz, V. J. (1985 August). *A view from the top: A thirty year perspective of research devoted to discovery, description, and prediction of executive behavior.* Paper presented at the 95th Annual Convention of the American Psychological Association, Los Angeles, CA.

Biaggio, M. K., & Mauro, R. D. (1985). Recent advances in anger assessment. In C. D. Speilberger, & J. N. Butcher (Eds.), *Advances in personality assessment* (Vol. 5, pp. 71-112). Hillsdale, NJ: Lawrence Erlbaum.

Biddle, B. J., & Andersen, D. S. (1986). Theory, methods, knowledge, and research on teaching. In M. C. Wittrock (Eds.), *Handbook of research on teaching* (3rd. ed. pp. 230-254). New York: Macmillan.

Bindra, D. (1974). A motivational view of learning, performance, and behavior modification. *Psychological Review, 81,* 199-213.

Block, J. H. (Ed.) (1971). *Mastery learning: Theory and practice.* New York: Holt, Rinehart and Winston.

Block, J. H. (1974). Mastery learning in the classroom: An overview of recent research. In J.H. Block (Ed.), *Schools, society, and mastery learning.* New York: Holt, Rinehart and Winston.

Block, J. H., & Burns, R.B. (1976). Mastery learning. In L. S. Shulman (Ed.), *Review of research in education* (Vol. 4). Itasca, IL: Peacock Publishers.

Bloom, B. S. (1968). Learning for mastery. *Evaluation Comment, 1* (2). (University of California Center for the Study of Evaluation, Los Angeles)-460,463-465.

Bloom, B. S. (1971). Mastery learning. In J. H. Block (Ed.), *Mastery learning: Theory and practice* (pp. 47-63). New York: Holt, Rinehart and Winston.

Bloom, B. S. (1974). Time and learning. *American Psychologist, 29,* 682-688.

Bloom, B. S. (1976). *Human characteristics and school learning.* New York: McGraw-Hill.

Bolles, R. C. (1972). Reinforcement, expectancy, and learning. *Psychological Review, 79,* 394-409.

Boring, E. G. (1923). Intelligence as the tests see it. *New Republic*, 35, 35-36.

Bower, G. H. (1981). Mood and memory. *American Psychologist*, 36 (2), 129-148.

Bower, G. H., & Hilgard, E. R. (1981). *Theories of learning* (5th ed.). Englewood Cliffs, NJ: Prentice-Hall.

Bowers, K. S. (1973). Situationism in psychology: An analysis and a critique. *Psychological Review*, 80, 307-336.

Brainin, S. S. (1985). Mediating learning: Pedagogic issues in the improvement of cognitive functioning. In E. W. Gordon (Ed.), *Review of Research in Education* (Vol. 12). Washington, DC: American Educational Research Association.

Bransford, J., Sherwood, R., Vye, N., & Rieser, J. (1986). Teaching, thinking and problem solving. *American Psychologist*, 41 (10), 1078-1089.

Breland, K., & Breland, M. (1960). The misbehavior of organisms. *American Psychologist*, 16, 661-664.

Brody, N. (1992). *Intelligence*. New York: Academic Press.

Brophy, J. (1981). Teacher praise: A functional analysis. *Review of Educational Research*, 51, 5-32.

Brophy, J. (1988). Research linking teacher behavior to student achievement: Potential implications for instruction of chapter 1 students. *Educational Psychologist*, 23 (3), 235-286.

Brophy, J. E. (1983). If only it were true: A response to Greer. *Educational Researcher*, 12 (10), 10-12.

Brown, A. L. (1978). Knowing when, where, and how to remember: A problem of metacognition. In R. Glaser (Ed.), *Advances in instructional psychology*. Hillsdale, NJ: Erlbaum.

Brown, A. L., & Campione, J. C. (1986). Psychological theory and the study of learning disabilities. American Psychologist, 41 (10), 1059-1068.

Bruer, J. T. (1993). *Schools for thought: A science of learning in the classroom*. Cambridge, MA: MIT Press.

Bruner, J. (1986). *Actual minds, possible worlds*. Cambridge, MA: Harvard University Press.

Bruner, J. S. (1966). *Toward a theory of instruction*. Cambridge, MA: Harvard University Press.

Buchmann, M. (1986). Role over person: Morality and authencity in teaching. *Teachers' College Record*, 87, 529-544.

Buchwald, A. M. (1967). Effects of immediate vs. delayed outcomes in associative learning. *Journal of Verbal Learning and Verbal Behavior*, 6, 317-320.

Burghardt, G. (1985). Animal awareness: Current perceptions and historical perspectives. *American Psychologist*, 40 (8), 905-919.

Buss, A. H. (1989). Personality as traits. *American Psychologist*, 44 (11), 1378-1388.

Buss, A. R. (1976). The myth of vanishing individual differences in Bloom's mastery learning. *Instructional Psychology*, 3, 4-14.

Butcher, J. N. (1992). Providing psychological test feedback to clients: A special section. *Psychological Assessment*, 4 (3), 267-287.

Butcher, W.G., Dahlstrom, W. G., Graham, J.R., & Tellegen, A. (1990). *Minnesota Multiphasic Personality Inventory-2*. Minneapolis, MN: NCS Assessments.

Calhoun, J. F. (1973August). *Elemental analysis of the Keller method of instruction.* Paper presented at the annual meeting of the American Psychological Association, Montreal, Canada.

Campbell, D., & Stanley, J. C. (1963). *Experimental and quasi-experimental design for research.* Boston, MA: Houghton-Mifflin.

Capaldi, E. J. (1966). Partial reinforcement: An hypothesis of sequential effects. *Psychological Review*, 73, 459-477.

Caplan, G. (1970). *The theory and practice of mental health consultation.* New York: Basic Books.

Carroll, J. B. (1963). A model of school learning. *Teachers College Record*, 64, 723-733.

Carroll, J. B. (1989). The Carroll model: A 25-year retrospective and prospective view. *Educational Researcher*, 18 (1), 26-31.

Carson, R. (1962). *Silent spring.* Boston, MA: Houghton Mifflin.

Carter, K. (1993). The place of story in the study of teaching and teacher education. *Educational Researcher*, 22 (1), 5-12, 18.

Carter, K., & Doyle, W. (1987). Teachers' knowledge structures and comprehension processes. In J. Calderhead (Ed.), *Exploring teachers' thinking* (pp. 79-98). Hillsdale, NJ: Erlbaum.

Carter, K., & Gonzalez, L. (1990, April). *Beginning teachers' knowledge of classroom events.* Paper presented at the Annual Meeting of the American Educational Research Association, Boston, MA.

Case, R. (1978). Piaget and beyond: Toward a developmentally based theory and technology of instruction. In R. Glaser (Ed.), *Advances in instructional psychology* (Vol. 1). Hillsdale, NJ: Erlbaum.

Case, R. (1985). A developmentally based approach to the problem of instructional design. In S. F. Chipman, J. W. Segal, & R. Glaser (Eds.), *Thinking and learning skills* (Vol. 2). Hillsdale, NJ: Erlbaum.

Cattell, R. B. (1965). *The scientific analysis of personality.* New York: Penguin.

Ceci, S. J. (1990). *On intelligence ... more or less. A bio-ecological treatise on intellectual development.* Englewood Cliffs, NJ: Prentice-Hall.

Cherry, E. C. (1953). Some experiments on the recognition of speech, with one and with two ears. *Journal of the Acoustical Society of America*, 25, 975-979.

Chi, M. T. H. (1985). Interactive roles of knowledge and strategies in the development of organized sorting and recall. In S. F. Chipman, J. W. Segal, & R. Glaser (Eds.), *Thinking and learning skills* (Vol. 2). Hillsdale, NJ: Erlbaum.

Chomsky, N. (1968). *Language and mind.* New York: Harcourt, Brace, and Jovanovich.

Clandinin, D. J., & Connelly, F. M. (1988). Studying teachers' knowledge of classrooms: Collaborative research, ethics, and the negotiation of narrative. *The Journal of Educational Thought*, 22 (2A), 269-282.

Cochran-Smith, M., & Lytle, S. (1990). Research on teaching and teacher research: The issues that divide. *Educational Researcher*, 19 (2), 2-11.

Cochran-Smith, M., & Lytle, S. (1993). *Insight/outside: Teacher research and knowledge.* New York: Teachers' College Press.

Cohen, P. A., Kulik, J. A., & Kulik, C. C. (1982). Educational outcomes of tutoring: A meta-analysis of findings. *American Educational Research Journal*, 19 (2), 237-248.

Coleman, J. S., Campbell, E. Q., Hobson, C. J., McPartland, J., Mood, A. M., Weinfield, F. D., & York, R. L. (1966). *Equality of educational opportunity.* Washington, DC: Government Printing Office.

Combs, A. W. (1965). *The professional education of teachers: A perceptual view of teacher preparation.* Boston, MA: Allyn & Bacon.

Connelly, F. M., & Clandinin, D. J. (1986). On narrative method, biography, and narrative unities in the study of teaching. *Journal of Research in Science on Teaching, 24* (4), 293-320.

Connelly, F. M., & Clandinin, D. J. (1988). *Teachers as curriculum planners: Narratives of experience.* New York: Teachers' College Press.

Cook, D. T., & Campbell, D. T. (1979). *Quasi-experimental: Design and analysis issues in field settings.* Boston, MA: Houghton-Mifflin.

Costa, P. T., & McCrae, R. R. (1988). *NEO Five-Factor Inventory.* Odessa, FL: Psychological Assessment Resources.

Costa, P. T., & McCrae, R. R. (1992). *NEO Personality Inventory-Revised.* Odessa, FL: Psychological Assessment Resources.

Craik, F. I. M., & Lockhart, R. S. (1972). Levels of processing: A framework for memory research. *Journal of Verbal Learning and Verbal Behavior, 11,* 671-684.

Crapanzano, V. (1980). *Tuhami.* Chicago, IL: University of Chicago Press.

Cronbach, L. J. (1975). Beyond two disciplines of scientific psychology. *American Psychologist, 30* (2), 116-127.

DeCharms, R. (1976). *Enhancing motivation.* New York: Irving Press/Wiley.

Deci, E. L. (1975). *Intrinsic motivation.* New York: Plenum.

Deitz, S. M. (1978). Current status of applied behavior analysis: Science vs. technology. *American Psychologist, 33* (9), 805-814.

Diagnostic and statistical manual of mental disorder: DSM IV. (1994). 4th ed.). Washington, DC: American Psychiatric Association.

Digman, J. M. (1990). Personality structure: Emergence of the five-factor model. *Annual Review of Psychology, 41,* 417-440. Palo Alto, CA: Annual Reviews.

Domjan, M. (1987). Animal learning comes of age. *American Psychologist, 42* (6), 556-564.

Edwards, A. L. (1954). *Manual - Edwards Personal Preference Schedule.* New York: The Psychological Corporation.

Edwards, A. L. (1992). *Revised Manual - Edwards Personal Preference Schedule.* New York: The Psychological Corporation.

Elbaz, F. (1991). Research on teachers' knowledge: The evolution of a discourse. *Journal of Curriculum Studies, 23,* 1-19.

Erickson, F. (1986). Qualitative methods in research on teaching. In M. C. Wittrock (Ed.), *Handbook of research on teaching* (3rd ed.) (pp. 119-161). New York: Macmillan.

Estes, W. K. (1969). Reinforcement in human learning. In J. Tapp (Ed.), *Reinforcement and behavior.* New York: Academic Press.

Exner, J. E. (1974). *The Rorschach: A comprehensive system* (Vol. 1). New York: Wiley.

Exner, J. E. (1978). *The Rorschach: A comprehensive system* (Vol. 2). New York: Wiley.

Exner, J. E. (1993). *A Rorschach workbook for the comprehensive system.* Bayville, NY: Rorschach Workshops.

Exner, J. E., & Andronikof-Sanglade, A. (1992). Rorschach changes following brief and short term psychotherapy. *Journal of Personality Assessment*, 59, 59-71.

Exner, J. E., & Weiner, F. (1982). *The Rorschach: A comprehensive system: Assessment of children and adolescents* (Vol. 3). New York: Wiley.

Eyman, J. R., & Eyman, J. R. (1991). Personality assessment of suicide. *Suicide and Life-Threatening Behavior*, 21 (1), 37-55.

Eysenck, H. J. (1982). The psychophysiology of intelligence. In C. D. Speilberger, & J. N. Butcher (Eds.), *Advances in personality assessment* (Vol. 1) (pp. 1-33). Hillsdale, NJ: Lawrence Erlbaum.

Feiman-Nemser, S., & Buchmann, M. (1986). Pitfalls of experience in teacher preparation. In J. Rathes, & L. Katz (Eds.), *Advances in teacher education*, 1, 61-73. Norwood, NJ: Ablex.

Feuerstein, R., Jensen, N., Hoffman, N. B., & Rand, W. (1985). Instrumental enrichment, an intervention program for structural cognitive modifibility: Theory and practice. In J. W. Segal, S. F. Chipman, & R. Glaser (Eds.), *Thinking and learning skills* (Vol. 1). Hillsdale, NJ: Erlbaum.

Fisher, C., Filby, N., Marliave, R., Cahen, L., Dishaw, M., Moore, J., & Berliner, D. (1978). *Teaching behaviors, academic learning time, and student achievement*. Final report of Phase III-B Beginning Teacher Evaluation Study. San Francisco, CA: Far West Laboratory for Educational Research and Development.

Flynn, J. R. (1991). *Asian Americans: Achievement beyond I.Q.* Hillsdale, NJ: Lawrence Erlbaum.

Foster, S. F. (1986). Ten principles of learning revised in accordance with cognitive psychology: With implications for teaching. *Educational Psychologist*, 21 (3), 235-243.

Fosterling, F. (1985). Attributional retraining: A review. *Psychological Bulletin*, 48, 495-512.

Gadamer, H. G. (1960). *Truth and method*. New York: Seabury Press.

Gage, N. L., & Berliner, D. C. (1992). *Educational psychology*. Boston, MA: Houghton Mifflin.

Gagne, R. M. (1985). *The conditions of learning* (4th ed.). New York: Holt, Rinehart, and Winston.

Gagne, R. M., & Briggs, L. J. (1979). *Principles of instructional design*. New York: Holt, Rinehart, and Winston.

Gallagan, I. E. (1985). Psychoeducational testing: Turn out the lights, the party's over. *Exceptional Children*, 52, 288-299.

Gardner, B. T., & Gardner, R. A. (1980). Two comparative psychologists look at language acquisition. In K. E. Nelson (Ed.), *In childrens' language* (Vol. 2). New York: Halsted.

Gardner, H. (1983). *Frames of mind*. New York: Basic Books.

Gardner, H., & Hatch, T. (1989). Multiple intelligences go to school: Educational implications of the theory of multiple intelligences. *Educational Researcher*, 18 (8), 4-10.

Gardner, R. A., & Gardner, B. T. (1969). Teaching sign language to a chimpanzee. *Science*, 165, 664-672.

Garner, R., & Alexander, P. A. (1989). Metacognition: Answered and unanswered questions. *Educational Psychologist*, 24 (2), 143-158.

Gazzaniga, M. S. (1983). Right hemisphere language following brain bisection: A 20-year perspective. *American Psychologist, 38* (3), 525-549.

Geen, R. G. (1984). Human motivation: New perspectives on old problems. In The G. Stanley Hall Lecture Series (pp. 5-58). Washington, DC: American Psychological Association.

Gelman, R. (1969). Conservation acquisition: A problem of learning to attend to the relevant attributes. *Journal of Experimental Child Psychology, 7* (1), 67-87.

Gelman, R. (1983). Recent trends in cognitive development. In The G. Stanley Hall Lecture Series (pp. 145-176). Washington, DC: American Psychological Association.

Gergen, M., & Gergen, K. (1986). The social construction of narrative accounts. In K. Gergen & M. Gergen (Eds.), *Historical social psychology* (pp. 173-189). Hillsdale, NJ: Lawrence Erlbaum.

Glaser, R. (1978). *Advances in instructional psychology* (Vol. 1). Hillsdale, NJ: Erlbaum.

Glaser, R. (1982). *Advances in instructional psychology* (Vol. 2). Hillsdale, NJ: Erlbaum.

Glaser, R. (1984). Education and thinking: The role of knowledge. *American Psychologist, 39,* 93-104.

Glaser, R. (1986). *Advances in instructional psychology* (Vol. 3). Hillsdale NJ: Erlbaum.

Glaser, R. (1990). The reemergence of learning theory within instructional research. *American Psychologist, 45* (1), 29-39.

Glaser, R. (1993). *Advances in instructional psychology* (Vol. 4). Hillsdale, NJ: Erlbaum.

Glaser, R., & Resnick, L. B. (1972). Instructional psychology. *Annual Review of Psychology, 23.*

Glaser, R., & Takanishi, R. (1986). Special issue: Psychological science and education. *American Psychologist, 41* (10), 1025-1168.

Goldberg, L. R. (1993). The structure of phenotypic personality traits. *American Psychologist, 48,* 26-34.

Good, T. L., & Brophy, J. E. (1987). *Looking in classrooms.* New York: Harper & Row.

Gordon, E. E., & Gordon, E. H. (1990). *Centuries of tutoring: A history of alternative education in America and Western Europe.* Latham, MD: University Press.

Gordon, E. E., Morgan, R. R., & Ponticell, J. A. (1994). *FutureWork: The revolution reshaping American business.* Westport, CT: Praeger Books.

Gordon, E. E., Ponticell, J. A., & Morgan, R. R. (1989). Back to basics. *Training and Development Journal,* (August), 73-76.

Gordon, E. E., Ponticell, J. A., & Morgan, R. R. (1991). *Closing the literacy gap in American business: A guide for trainers and human resource specialists.* Westport, CT: Quorum Books.

Gough, H. G. (1987). *California Psychological Inventory administrator's guide.* Palo Alto, CA: Consulting Psychologists Press.

Greene, M. (1994). Epistemology and educational research: The influence of recent approaches to knowledge. *Review of Research in Education, 20,* 207-218.

Greene, R. L. (1991). *The MMPI-2: An interpretive manual.* New York: Allyn &Bacon.

Greeno, J. G. (1978). Review of Bloom's human characteristics and school learning. *Journal of Educational Measurement,* 67-76.

Greeno, J. G. (1980). Psychology of learning, 1960-1980: One participant's observations. *American Psychologist, 35* (8), 713-728.

Greeno, J. G. (1989). A perspective on thinking. *American Psychologist, 44* (2), 134-141.

Greer, R. D. (1983). Contingencies of the science and technology of teaching and prebehavioristic research practices in education. *Educational Researcher, 12,* 3-9.

Gudmundsdottir, S. (1991). Story-maker, story-teller: Narrative structures in curriculum. *Journal of Curriculum Studies, 23,* 207-218.

Guskey, T. R. (1987). Rethinking mastery learning reconsidered. *Review of Educational Research, 57* (2), 225-230.

Guskey, T. R., & Gates, S. L. (1986). Synthesis of research on the effects of mastery learning in elementary and secondary classrooms. *Educational Leadership, 43* (8), 73-80.

Guthrie, E. R. (1959). Association by contiguity. In S. Koch (Ed.), *Psychology: A study of a science* (pp. 158-195) (Vol. 2). New York: McGraw-Hill.

Halpern, D. E. (1989). *Thought and knowledge: An introduction to critical thinking.* Hillsdale, NJ: Lawrence Erlbaum Associates.

Halpern, D. E. (1991). *Sex differences in cognitive abilities* (2nd ed.). Hillsdale, NJ: Lawrence Erlbaum.

Hargeaves, A. (1994 April). *Dissonant voices: Teachers and the multiple realities of restructuring.* Paper presented at the Annual Meeting of the American Educational Research Association, New Orleans, LA

Hayes, S. L., Nelson, R. O., & Jarret, R. B. (1987). The treatment utility of assessment: A functional approach to evaluate assessment quality. *American Psychologist, 42,* 963-974.

Heckhausen, H., Schmalt, H. D., & Schneider, K. (1985). *Achievement motivation in perspective.* Orlando, FL: Academic Press.

Heinrichs, R. W. (1993). Schizophrenia and the brain: Conditions for a neuropsychology of madness. *American Psychologist, 48* (3), 221-233.

Helle, A. P. (1991). Reading women's autobiographies: A map of reconstructed knowing. In C. Witherell & N. Noddings (Eds.), *Stories lives tell: Narrative and dialogue in education* (pp. 233-249). Chicago, IL: University of Chicago Press.

Heppner, P., & Krauskoff, C. (1987). An information processing approach to personal problem solving. *Counseling Psychologist, 15* (3), 371-447.

Hermstein, R. J. (1977a). Doing what comes naturally: A reply to Professor Skinner. *American Psychologist, 32* (12), 1013-1016.

Hermstein, R. J. (1977b). The evolution of behaviorism. *American Psychologist, 32* (8), 593-603.

Hermstein, R. J., & Murray, C. (1994). *The bell curve: Intelligence and class structure in American life.* New York: Free Press.

Hilgard, E. R., & Bower, G. H. (1975). *Theories of learning.* Englewood Cliffs, NJ: Prentice-Hall.

Hogan, R., Curpky, G. J., & Hogan, J. (1994). What we know about leadership: Effectiveness and personality. *American Psychologist, 49* (6), 493-504.

Hogan, R., & Hogan, J. (1992). Hogan Personality Inventory manual. Tulsa, OK: Hogan Assessment Systems.

Hogan, R., & Nicholson, R. A. (1988). The meaning of personality test scores. *American Psychologist*, 43 (8), 621-626.

Howard, A., & Bray, D. W. (1990). Predictions of managerial success over long periods of time: Lessons for the management progress study. In K. E. Clark & M. B. Clark (Eds.), *Measures of leadership* (pp. 113-130). West Orange, NJ: Leadership Library of America.

Hughes, R. L., Ginnett, R. A., & Curpky, G. J. (1993). *Leadership: Enhancing the lessons of experience.* Homewood, IL: Irwin.

Hull, C. L. (1943). *Principles of behavior.* New York: Appleton-Century- Crofts.

Hunt, M.McV. (1961). *Intelligence and experience.* New York: Ronald Press Co.

Huttenlocher, J. (1976). Language and intelligence. In L. B. Resnick (Ed.), *The nature of intelligence.* Hillsdale, NJ: Erlbaum.

Jensen, A. R. (1969). How much can we boost IQ and scholastic achievement? *Harvard Educational Review*, 39 (1), 1-123.

Jensen, A. R. (1980). *Bias in mental testing.* New York: Free Press.

Kagan, D. M. (1988). Teaching as critical problem solving: A critical examination of the analogy and its implications. *Review of Educational Research*, 58 (4), 482-505.

Kagan, J. (1966). Reflection-impulsivity: The generality and dynamics of conceptual tempo. *Journal of Abnormal and Social Psychology*, 71, 17-24.

Kamin, L. J. (1974). *The science and politics of IQ.* Potomac, MD: Erlbaum.

Kaufman, A. S. (1979). *Intelligent testing with the WISC-R.* New York: Wiley.

Keller, E. F. (1985). *Reflections on gender and science.* New Haven, CT: Yale University Press.

Keller, F. S. (1968). Good-bye teacher! *Journal of Applied Behavioral Analysis*, 1, 79-84.

Kendler, H. H. (1993). Psychology and the ethics of social psychology. *American Psychologist*, 48 (10), 1046-1053.

Kendler, H. H., & Kendler, T. S. (1962). Vertical and horizontal processes in problem solving. *Psychological Review*, 69, 1-16.

Kendler, T. S. (1964). Verbalization and optional reversal shifts among kindergarten children. *Journal of Verbal Learning and Verbal Behavior*, 3, 248-436.

Kenny, D. A., & Zaccaro, S. J. (1983). An estimate of variance due to traits in leadership. *Journal of Applied Psychology*, 68, 678-685.

Kerlinger, F. N. (1986). *Foundations of behavioral research* (3rd Ed.). New York: Holt, Rinehart, and Winston.

Killeen, P. R. (1992). Mechanics of the animate. *Journal of the Experimental Analysis of Behavior*, 57, 429-463.

Kimble, G. A. (1989). Psychology from the standpoint of a generalist. *American Psychologist*, 44 (3), 491-499.

Kincheloe, J. L., & Steinberg, S. R. (1993). A tentative description of post- formal thinking: The critical confrontation with cognitive theory. *Harvard Educational Review*, 63 (3), 296-320.

Kipnis, D. (1987). Psychology and behavioral technology. *American Psychologist*, 42 (1), 30-36.

Kirby, J. R., & Biggs, J. B. (1980). *Cognition, development, and instruction.* New York: Academic Press.

Kleine, P. F., & Greene, B. A. (1993). Story telling: A rich history and a sordid past—a response to Berliner (1992). *Educational Psychologist*, 28 (2), 185-190.

Koffka, K. (1935). *Principles of Gestalt psychology*. New York: Harcourt, Brace and World.

Kohler, W. (1925). *The mentality of apes*. Translated by E. Winter. New York: Harcourt, Brace and World.

Kohler, W. (1929). *Gestalt psychology*. New York: Liveright.

Koppitz, E. M. (1975). *The Bender-Gestalt test for young children: Research and application, 1963-1973*. New York: Grune & Stratton.

Korchin, S., & Schuldberg, D. (1981). The future of clinical assessment. *American Psychologist*, 36 (10), 1147-1158.

Kosulin, A. (1986). The concept of activity in Soviet psychology: Vygotsky, his disciples and critics. *American Psychologist*, 41 (3), 264-274.

Kuhn, T. S. (1970). *The structure of scientific revolutions* (2nd Ed.). Chicago, IL: University of Chicago Press.

Kulik, J. A., Kulik, L. C., & Cohen, P. A. (1979). A meta-analysis of outcome studies of Keller's personalized system of instruction. *American Psychologist*, 34, 307-318.

Lachar, D. (1982). *Personality Inventory for Children: Revised format manual supplement*. Los Angeles, CA: Western Psychological Services.

Lanyon, R. I., & Goodstein, L. D. (1992). *Personality assessment*. New York: University Press of America.

Lazarus, R. S. (1991). Cognition and motivation in emotion. *American Psychologist*, 46 (4), 352-367.

Leinhardt, G. (1990). Capturing craft knowledge in teaching. *Educational Researcher*, 19 (2), 18-25.

Leithwood, K., Jantzi, D., & Fernandez, A. (1993 April). *Secondary school teachers' commitment to change: The contributions of transformational leadership*. Paper presented at the Annual Meeting of the American Educational Research Association, Atlanta, GA.

Lepper, M. R., & Greene, D. (Eds.) (1978). *The hidden costs of reward*. Hillsdale, NJ: Erlbaum.

Levin, J., & Pressley, N. (1983). *Cognitive strategy research: Educational applications*. New York: Springer-Verlag.

Levinson, H. (1994). Why the behemoths fell: Psychological roots of corporate failure. *American Psychologist*, 49 (5), 428-436.

Levy, R. (1985). *The new language of psychiatry: Learning to use D.S.M. III*. Boston, MA: Little, Brown.

Limber, J. (1977). Language in child and chimp. *American Psychologist*, 32 (4), 280-295.

Lippitt, P. (1969). Children can teach other children. *The Instructor*, 789, 41, 99.

Lippitt, P., & Lippitt, R. (1970). The peer culture as a learning environment. *Childhood Education*, 47, 135-138.

Lippitt, R., & Lippitt, M. (1968). Cross-age helpers. *National Education Association Journal*, 57, 24-26.

Logan, F. A. (1968). Incentive theory and changes in reward. In K. W. Spence & J. T. Spence (Eds.), *The psychology of learning and motivation* (Vol. 2). New York: Academic Press.

Luria, A. R. (1966). *Higher cortical functions in man*. New York: Plenum.

Lykken, D. T., McGue, M., Tellegen, A., & Bouchard, T. J. (1992). Emergenesis: Genetic traits that may not run in families. *American Psychologist, 47* (12), 1565-1577.

MacLeod, R. B. (1986). Phenomenology. In D. L. Stills (Ed.), *International encyclopedia of the social sciences* (pp. 68-72). New York: Macmillan & Free Press.

Mahoney, M. J. (1989). Scientific psychology and radical behaviorism: Important distinctions based in scientism and objectivism. *American Psychologist, 44* (11), 1372-1377.

Martin, J., & Sugarman, J. (1993). Beyond methodolatry: Two conceptions of relations between theory and research in research on teaching. *Educational Researcher, 22* (8), 17-24.

Maslow, A. H. (1954). *Motivation and personality.* New York: Harper and Row.

Matarazzo, J. D. (1978). The interview: Its reliability and validity in psychiatric diagnosis. *Clinical Diagnosis of Mental Disorders.* New York: Plenum Press.

Matarazzo, J. D. (1986). Computerized clinical psychological test interpretations. *American Psychologist, 41* (1), 14-25.

Matarazzo, J. D. (1990). Psychological assessment versus psychological testing: Validation from Binet to the school, clinic, and courtroom. *American Psychologist, 45* (9), 999-1017.

Matarazzo, J. D. (1992). Psychological testing and assessment in the 21st century. *American Psychologist, 47* (8), 1007-1018.

McCombs, B. L. (1984). Processes and skills underlying continuing intrinsic motivation to learn: Toward a definition of motivational skills training interventions. *Educational Psychologist, 19* (4), 199-218.

McCrae, R. R., & Costa, P. T., Jr. (1987). Validation of the five-factor model of personality across instruments and observers. *Journal of Personality and Social Psychology, 52,* 81-90.

McKeachie, W. J. (1974). The decline and fall of the laws of learning. *Educational Researcher, 3,* 7-11.

McKeachie, W. J. (1976). Psychology in America's bicentennial year. *American Psychologist, 31* (12), 819-833.

McKeachie, W. J. (1986). Teaching psychology: Research and experience. In V. P. Makosky (Ed.), *The G. Stanley Hall Lecture Series* (Vol. 6). Washington, DC: American Psychological Association.

McKeachie, W. J., Pintrich, P. R., & Lin, Y. G. (1985). Teaching learning strategies. *Educational Psychologist, 20* (3), 153-160.

McLane, J. B. (1987). Interaction, context, and the zone of proximal development. In M. Hickmann (Ed.), *Social and functional approaches to language and thought.* San Diego, CA: Academic Press.

McManus, F. E. (1993). Constructionists and creationists. *American Psychologist, 48* (1), 57-58.

McReynolds, P. (1968). *Advances in psychological assessment.* Palo Alto, CA: Science and Behavior Books.

McReynolds, P. (1982). The future of psychological assessment. *International Review of Applied Psychology, 31,* 117-139.

McReynolds, P. (1989). Diagnosis and clinical assessment: Current status and major issues. *Annual Review of Psychology*, 40, 83-108.

Meehl, P. E. (1954). *Clinical vs. statistical prediction*. Minneapolis, MN: University of Minnesota Press.

Meehl, P. E. (1959). Some ruminations on the validation of clinical procedures. *Canadian Journal of Psychology*, 13, 102-128.

Megargee, E. I. (1985). Assessing alcoholism and drug abuse with the MMPI: Implication for employment screening. In C. D. Speilberger & J. N. Butcher (Eds.), *Advances in Personality Assessment* (Vol. 5, pp. 1-40). Hillsdale, NJ: Lawrence Erlbaum.

Miller, G. A. (1956). The magical number seven plus or minus two: Some limits on our capacity for processing information. *Psychological Review*, 63, 81-97.

Miller, N. E. (1969). Learning of visceral and glandular responses. *Science*, 163, 434-445.

Millon, T. (1981). *Disorders of personality DSM-III: Axis II*. New York: Wiley.

Millon, T. (1984). On the renaissance of personality assessment and personality theory. *Journal of Personality Assessment*, 48 (5), 450-465.

Mischel, W. (1968). *Personality assessment*. New York: Wiley.

Mischel, W. (1973). Toward a cognitive social learning reconceptualization of personality. *Psychological Review*, 80, 252-283.

Mischel, W. (1977). On the future of personality measurement. *American Psychologist*, 32 (4), 246-254.

Mischel, W. (1979). On the interface of cognition and personality: Beyond the person-situation debate. *American Psychologist*, 34 (9), 740-754.

Mischel, W. (1981). Current issues and changes in personality. The G. Stanley Hall Lecture Series (pp. 81-100). Washington, DC: American Psychological Association.

Mischel, W. (1984). Convergence and challenges in the search for consistency. *American Psychologist*, 39 (4), 351-364.

Monahan, J. (1992). Mental disorder and violent behavior: Perceptions and evidence. *American Psychologist*, 47 (4), 511-521.

Morgan, M. (1984). Reward-induced decrements and increments in intrinsic motivation. *Review of Educational Research*, 54 (1), 5-30.

Morgan, R. R. (1975). An exploratory study of three procedures to encourage school attendance. *Psychology in the Schools*, 12 (2), 209-215.

Mowrer, O. H. (1956). Two-factor learning theory reconsidered, with special reference to secondary reinforcement and the concept of habit. *Psychological Review*, 63, 114-128.

Mueller, D. J. (1976). Mastery learning: Partly boon, partly boondoggle. *Teachers College Record*, 78, 41-52.

Murray, H. A. (1938). *Explorations in personality*. New York: Oxford University Press.

Murray, H. A. (1943). *Thematic Apperception Test manual*. Cambridge, MA: Harvard University Press.

Myers, G. L., & Fisk, A. D. (1987). Training consistent task components: Applications of automatic and controlled processing theory to industrial task training. *Human Factors*, 29 (3), 355-368.

Neimark, E. D. (1975). Current status of formal operational thought. *Genetic Psychology Monographs*, 91 (2), 171-225.

Nelson, K. (1977). Cognitive development and the acquisition of concepts. In R. Anderson, R. Spiro, & W. Montague (Eds.), *Schooling and the acquisition of knowledge.* Hillsdale, NJ: Erlbaum.

Nespor, J., & Barylske, J. (1991). Narrative discourse and teacher knowledge. *American Educational Research Journal*, 28 (4), 805–823.

Noddings, N. (1991). Stories in dialogue: Caring and interpersonal reasoning. In C. Witherell & N. Noddings (Eds.), *Stories lives tell: Narrative and dialogue in education* (pp. 155-170). New York: Teachers' College Press.

Norman, D. A., & Rumelhart, D.E. (1981). The LNR approach to human information processing. *Cognition*, 10 (1-3), 235-240.

Olson, D. (1977). The languages of instruction: On the literate bias of schooling. In R. C. Anderson & R. J. Spiro (Ed.), *Schooling and the acquisition of knowledge.* Hillsdale, NJ: Erlbaum.

Paivio, A. (1971). *Imagery and verbal processes.* New York: Holt, Rinehart, and Winston.

Palinscar, A. S., & Brown, A. L. (1984). Reciprocal teaching of comprehension fostering and comprehension-monitoring activities. *Cognition and Instruction*, 1 (2), 117-175.

Passini, F. T., & Norman, W. T. (1966). A universal conception of personality structure? *Journal of Personality and Social Psychology*, 1, 44-49.

Pavlov, I. P. (1960). *Conditioned reflexes.* Translated and edited by G. V. Anrep. New York: Dover. (Original translation, Oxford University Press, 1927).

Perry, J. C. (1992). Problems and consideration in the valid assessment of personality disorders. *American Journal of Psychiatry*, 149 (2), 1645-1653.

Peshkin, A. (1978). *Growing up in America: Schooling and the survival of community.* Chicago, IL: University of Chicago Press.

Piotrowski, Z. A. (1983). The perceptanalytic dream system (PDS) as a tool in personality assessment. In J. N. Butcher & C. D. Spielberger (Eds.), *Advances in personality assessment* (Vol. 2) (pp. 1-12). Hillsdale, NJ: Lawrence Erlbaum.

Polkinghorne, D. (1988). *Narrative knowing and the human sciences.* Albany, NY: State University of New York.

Polyson, J., Peterson, R., & Marshall, C. (1986). MMPI and Rorschach: Three decades of research. *Professional Psychology: Research and Practice*, 17 (5), 476-478.

Popper, K. R. (1972). *Objective knowledge: An evolutionary approach.* Oxford, England: Clarendon Press.

Prawat, R. S. (1993). The value of ideas: Problems versus possibilities in learning. *Educational Researcher*, 22 (6), 5-16.

Premack, D. (1965). Reinforcement theory. In D. Levine (Ed.), *Nebraska Symposium on motivation* (Vol. 13, pp. 123-180). Lincoln, NB: University of Nebraska Press, 243-244.

Premack, D. (1983). The codes of man and beast. *Behavioral and Brain Sciences*, 6, 125-167.

Pressley, N., & Levin, J. (1983). *Cognitive strategy research: Psychological foundations.* New York: Springer-Verlag.

Reese, E. P. (1986). Learning about teaching from teaching about learning: Presenting behavioral analysis in an introductory survey course. In V. P. Makosky (Ed.), The G. Stanley Hall Lecture Series (Vol. 6). Washington, DC: American Psychological Association.

Rescorla, R. A. (1987). A Pavlovian analysis of goal-directed behavior. *American Psychologist*, 42 (2), 119-129.

Resnick, L. (1981). Social assumptions as a context for science: Some reflections on psychology and education. *Educational Psychologist*, 16, 1-10.

Resnick, L. T. (1976). Task analysis in instructional design: Some cases from mathematics. In D. Klahr (Ed.), *Cognition and instruction*. Hillsdale, NJ: Erlbaum.

Resnick, L. T. (1977). Assuming that everyone can learn everything, will some learn less? *School Review*, 85, 445-452.

Restak, R. M. (1984). *The brain*. New York: Bantam Books.

Restak, R. M. (1988). *The mind*. New York: Bantam Books.

Restak, R. M. (1994). *Receptors*. New York: Bantam Books.

Reznikoff, M., Aronow, E., & Rauchway, A. (1982). The reliability of inkblot content scales. In C. D. Spielberger & J. N. Butcher (Eds.), *Advances in Personality Assessment* (Vol. 1) (pp. 83-114). Hillsdale, NJ: Lawrence Erlbaum.

Rorschach, H. (1921). *Psychodiagnostik*. Bern: Bircher.

Rosenthal, R., & Jacobson, L. (1968). *Pygmalion in the classroom*. New York: Holt, Rinehart, & Winston.

Rothkopf, E. Z. (1977). The concept of mathemagenic activities. In M. C. Wittrock (Ed.), *Learning and instruction*. Berkeley, CA: McCutchan Publishing Corporation.

Rotter, J. B. (1954). *Social learning and clinical psychology*. Englewood Cliffs, NJ: Prentice-Hall.

Rotter, J. B. (1966). Generalized expectancies for internal versus external control of reinforcement. *Psychological Monographs*, 80 (1, Whole No. 609).

Rumelhart, D. E., & Ortony, A. (1977). The representation of knowledge in memory. In R.C. Anderson & R.J. Spiro (Eds.), *Schooling and the acquisition of knowledge*. Hillsdale, NJ: Erlbaum.

Russell, B. (1913). On the notion of cause. *Proceedings of the Aristotelian Society* (New Series), 13, 1-26.

Salomon, G. (1991). Transcending the qualitative-quantitative debate: The analytic and systematic approaches to educational research. *Educational Researcher*, 20, 10-18.

Samelson, F. (1980). J. B. Watson's Little Albert, Cyril Burt's twins, and the need for a critical science. *American Psychologist*, 35 (7), 619-625.

Sattler, J. M. (1982). *Assessment of children's intelligence and special abilities*. Boston, MA: Allyn and Bacon.

Savell, J. M., Twokig, P. T., & Rachford, D. L. (1986). Empirical status of Feuerstein's "instrumental enrichment" (FIE) technique as a method of teaching thinking skills. *Review of Educational Research*, 56 (4), 381-410.

Scardamalia, M., & Bereiter, C. (1983). Child as co-investigator: Helping children gain insight into their own mental processes. In S. Paris, G. Olson, & H. Stevenson (Eds.), *Learning and motivation in the classroom*. Hillsdale, NJ: Erlbaum.

Schaie, K. W. (1980). Age changes in intelligence. In R. L. Sprott (Ed.), *Age learning, ability, and intelligence*. New York: Van Nostrand Reinhold.

Scholes, R. (1981). Language, narrative, and anti-narrative. In W. J. T. Michell (Ed.), *On narrative* (pp. 200-208). Chicago, IL: University of Chicago Press.

Scholes, R. (1982). *Semiotic and interpretation.* New Haven, CT: Yale University Press.

Schon, D. A. (1987). *Educating the reflective practitioner.* San Francisco, CA: Jossey-Bass.

Schraa, J. C., Jones, N. F., & Dirks, J. F. (1983). Bender-Gestalt recall: A review of the normative data. In J. N. Butcher & C. D. Spielberger (Eds.), *Advances in personality assessment* (Vol. 2) (pp. 133-160). Hillsdale, NJ: Lawrence Erlbaum.

Schwab, J. J. (1983). The practical four: Something for curriculum professors to do. *Curriculum Inquiry, 13* (3), 239-265.

Schwartz, B. (1982). Reinforcement induced behavioral stereotypic: How not to teach people to discover rules. *Journal of Experimental Psychology: General,* 111, 23-59.

Sheffield, F. D. (1965). Relation between classical conditioning and instrumental learning. In W. F. Prokasy (Ed.), *Classical conditioning: A symposium.* New York: Appleton-Century-Crofts.

Shuell, T. J. (1986). Cognitive conceptions of learning. *Review of Educational Research,* 56 (4), 411-437.

Shulman, L. S. (1986). Paradigms and research programs in the study of teaching: A contemporary perspective. In M. C. Wittrock (Ed.), *Handbook of research on teaching* (3rd Ed.) (pp. 3-36). New York: Macmillan.

Shulman, L. S. (1987). Knowledge and teaching: Foundations of the new reform. Harvard Educational Review, 57 (1), 1-22.

Sivan, E. (1986). Motivation in social constructivist theory. *Educational Psychologist,* 21 (3), 209-233.

Skinner, B. F. (1938). *The behavior of organisms: An experimental analysis.* Englewood Cliffs, NJ: Prentice-Hall.

Skinner, B. F. (1977). Herrnstein and the evolution of behaviorism. *American Psychologist,* 32 (12), 1006-1012.

Skinner, B. F. (1989). The origins of cognitive thought. *American Psychologist,* 44 (1), 13-18.

Slavin, R. E. (1987a). Mastery learning reconsidered. *Review of Educational Research,* 57 (2), 175-214.

Slavin, R. E. (1987b). Taking the mystery out of mastery: A response to Guskey, Anderson, and Burns. *Review of Educational Research,* 57 (2), 231-235.

Snow, R. E. (1992). Aptitude theory: Yesterday, today, and tomorrow. *Educational Psychologist,* 27 (1), 5-32.

Smith, L. D. (1992). On prediction and control: B. F. Skinner and the technological ideal of science. *American Psychologist,* 47 (2), 216-223.

Sorcher, M. (1985). *Predicting executive success: What it takes to make it in senior management.* New York: Wiley.

Spady, W. G., & Marshall, K. J. (1991). Beyond traditional outcome-based education. *Educational Leadership,* 49, 67-72.

Sparks-Langer, G. M., & Bernstein-Colton, A. (1991). Synthesis of research on teachers' reflective thinking. *Educational Leadership,* 48 (6), 37-44.

Spence, D. P. (1986). *Narrative truth and historical method.* New York: Norton & Company.

Spence, K. W. (1960). *Behavior theory and learning: Selected papers.* Englewood Cliffs, NJ: Prentice-Hall.

Spielberger, C. D., & Butcher, J. N. (1982). *Advances in personality assessment* (Vol. 1). Hillsdale, NJ: Lawrence Erlbaum.

Spielberger, C. D., & Butcher, J. N. (1983). *Advances in personality assessment* (Vol. 2). Hillsdale, NJ: Lawrence Erlbaum.

Spielberger, C. D., & Butcher, J. N. (1983). *Advances in personality assessment* (Vol. 3). Hillsdale, NJ: Lawrence Erlbaum.

Spielberger, C. D., & Butcher, J. N. (1984). *Advances in personality assessment* (Vol. 4). Hillsdale, NJ: Lawrence Erlbaum.

Spielberger, C. D., & Butcher, J. N. (1985). *Advances in personality assessment* (Vol. 5). Hillsdale, NJ: Lawrence Erlbaum.

Spielberger, C. D., & Butcher, J. N. (1986). *Advances in personality assessment* (Vol. 6). Hillsdale, NJ: Lawrence Erlbaum.

Spielberger, C. D., & Butcher, J. N. (1988). *Advances in personality assessment* (Vol. 7). Hillsdale, NJ: Lawrence Erlbaum.

Spielberger, C. D., & Butcher, J. N. (1990). *Advances in personality assessment* (Vol. 8). Hillsdale, NJ: Lawrence Erlbaum.

Spielberger, C. D., & Butcher, J. N. (1992). *Advances in personality assessment* (Vol. 9). Hillsdale, NJ: Lawrence Erlbaum.

Stallings, J. (1980). Allocated academic learning time revisited or beyond time on task. *Educational Researcher, 9*, 11-16.

Stein, D. J., & Young, J. E. (1992). Cognitive science and clinical disorders. New York: Academic Press.

Sternberg, R. J. (1985). *Beyond IQ: A triarchic theory of human intelligence.* Cambridge, MA: Cambridge University Press.

Sternberg, R. J. (1986). *The triarchic mind: A new theory of human intelligence.* New York: Cambridge University Press.

Sternberg, R. J. (1986). *Intelligence applied: Understanding and increasing your intellectual skills.* New York: Harcourt, Brace, Jovanovich.

Stogdill, R. M. (1948). Personal factors associated with leadership: A survey of the literature. *Journal of Personality, 25*, 35-71.

Stogdill, R. M. (1974). *Handbook of leadership.* New York: Free Press.

Stricker, G. (1992). The relationship of research to clinical practice. *American Psychologist, 47* (4), 543-549.

Swartz, J. D., Reinehr, B. P., & Holtzman, W. H. (1983). Personality development throughout the lifespan: Assessment by means of the Holtzman Inkblot Technique. In C. D. Speilberger & J. N. Butcher (Eds.), *Advances in personality assessment* (Vol. 3) (pp. 35-52). Hillsdale, NJ: Lawrence Erlbaum.

Thorndike, E. L. (1949). *Selected writings from a connectionist's psychology.* New York: Appleton-Century-Crofts.

Tolman, E. C. (1932). *Purposive behavior in animals and men.* New York: Appleton-Century-Crofts. Reprinted, University of California Press, 1949.

Travers, R. M. (1982). *Essentials of learning: The new cognitive learning for students of education.* New York: Macmillan.

Tulving, E. (1972). *Episodic and semantic memory.* In E. Tulving & W. Donaldson (Eds.), Organization of memory. New York: Academic Press.

Tulving, E. (1985). How many memory systems are there? American Psychologist, 40 (4), 385-398.

Turkington, C. (1986a). Aversives: Report faulting institute refuels debate on its use. *APA Monitor,* 17 (6), 24.

Turkington, C. (1986b). Dolphins: Responses to signs, sounds suggest they understand our orders. *APA Monitor,* 16 (4), 32-33.

Vane, J. R., & Guarnaccia, V. J. (1989). Personality theory and personality assessment measures: How helpful to the clinician? *Journal of Clinical Psychology,* 45 (1), 5-19.

Viney, W. (1989). The cyclops and the twelve-eyed toad: William James and the unity-disunity problem in psychology. *American Psychologist,* 44 (10), 1261-1265.

Voeks, V. W. (1950). Formalization and clasification of a theory of learning. *Journal of Psychology,* 30, 341-363.

Vosniadow, S., & Brewer, W. F. (1987). Theories of knowledge restructuring in development. *Review of Educational Research,* 57 (1), 51-68.

Vygotsky, L. S. (1978). *Mind in society: The development of higher psychological processes.* Cambridge, MA: Harvard University Press.

Vygotsky, L. S. (1986). *Thought and language.* Cambridge, MA: MIT Press.

Walberg, H. (1984). Improving the productivity of America's schools. *Educational Leadership,* 41 (8), 19-30.

Walberg, H. (1986). Synthesis of research on teaching. In M. C. Wittrock (Ed.), *Handbook of research on teaching* (3rd. ed.) (pp. 214-229). New York: Macmillan.

Walberg, H. J. (1984). Improving the productivity of America's schools. *Educational Leadership,* 41 (8), 19-27.

Wang, M. C., Haertel, G. D., & Walberg, H. J. (1990). What influences learning? A content analysis of review literature. *Journal of Educational Research,* 84 (1), 30-43.

Wang, M. C., Haertel, G. D., & Walberg, H. J. (1993). Toward a knowledge base for school learning. *Review of Educational Research,* 63 (3), 249-294.

Watson, J. B., & Raynor, R. (1920). Conditioned emotional reactions. *Journal of Experimental Psychology,* 3, 1-14.

Wegner, K. W. (1988). Review of the California Psychological Inventory, 1987 rev. ed. In D. J. Keyser & R.C. Sweetland (Eds.), *Test critiques Volume VII* (pp. 66-75). Kansas City, MO: Test Corporation of America.

Weiner, B. (1986). *An attributional theory of motivation and emotion.* New York: Springer-Verlag.

Weiner, B. (Ed.) (1974). *Achievement motivation and attribution theory.* Morristown, NJ: General Learning Press.

Weiner, B., & Exner, J. E. (1991). Rorschach changes in long term and short term psychotherapy. *Journal of Personality Assessment,* 56, 453-465.

Weiner, I. B. (1994). Rorschach assessment. In M. E. Maruish (Ed.), *The use of psychological testing for treatment planning and outcome assessment* (Ch. 11). New York: Erlbaum.

Weinstein, C. E., & Marges, R. E. (1986). The teaching of learning strategies. In M. C. Wittrock (Ed.), *Handbook of Research on Teaching.* New York: Macmillan.

Wertheimer, M. (1923). Laws of organization in perceptual forms. In W. D. Ellis (Ed.), *A source book of gestalt psychology* (pp. 71-88). New York: Harcourt, Brace and World.

Wertheimer, M. (1923). Untersuchung zur Lehre von der Gestalb, II. Psychol. Forsch, 4:301-50. Translated and condensed as Laws of organization in perceptual forms. In W. D. Ellis (Eds.), *A source book of gestalt psychology* (pp. 71-88). New York: Harcourt, Brace and World, 1938.

Westermeyer, J. (1987). Cultural factors in clinical assessment. *Journal of Consulting and Clinical Psychology*, 55, 471-478.

Willinsky, J. (1989). Getting personal and practical with personal practical knowledge. *Curriculum Inquiry*, 19 (3), 247-264.

Winne, P. H. (1985). Steps toward promoting cognitive achievement. *Elementary School Journal*, 83, 673-693.

Winne, P. H. (1991). *Motivation and teaching*. In H. C. Waxman & H. J. Walberg (Eds.), *Effective teaching: Current research*. Berkeley, CA: McCutchan.

Wirt, R. D., & Lachar, D. (1981). The Personality Inventory for Children: Development and clinical applications. In P. McReynolds (Ed.), *Advances in psychological assessment* (Vol. 5). San Francisco, CA: Jossey-Bass.

Wirt, R. D., Lachar, D., Klinedinst, J. K., & Seat, P. D. (1984). *Multidimensional description of child personality: A manual for the Personality Inventory for Children*, Revised 1984. Los Angeles, CA: Western Psychological Services.

Witkin, H. A., Moore, C. A., Goodenough, D. R., & Cox, P. W. (1977). Field- dependent and field-independent cognition styles and their educational implications. *Review of Educational Research*, 47, 1-64.

Wittrock, M.C. (1978). The cognitive movement in instruction. *Educational Psychologist*, 13 (2), 15-30.

Wittrock, M.C. (1979). The cognitive movement in instruction. *Educational Researcher*, 8 (2), 5-11.

Wittrock, M.C. (Ed.) (1986). *Handbook of research on teaching* (3rd ed.). New York: Macmillan.

Wolpe, J. (1981). Behavior therapy versus psychoanalysis: Therapeutic and social implications. *American Psychologist*, 36, 159-164.

Woolfolk, R., & Richardson, F. (1984). Behavior therapy and the ideology of modernity. *American Psychologist*, 39 (7), 777-786.

Yesselydke, J., Thrulow, M., Graden, J., Wesson, C., Deno, S., & Algozzine, B. (1982). Generalizations from five years of research on assessment and decision making. *Exceptional Education Quarterly*, 4, 75-93.

Yinger, R. (1987). Learning the language of practice. *Curriculum Inquiry*, 17 (3), 293-318.

Yuki, G. A. (1989). *Leadership in organizations* (2nd ed.). Englewood Cliffs, NJ: Prentice-Hall.

Zajonc, R. B. (1984). On the primary of affect. *American Psychologist*, 39 (2), 117-123.

Zilbergeld, B. (1984). *The shrinking of America*. New York: Little, Brown and Co.

Zuriff, G. E. (1980). Radical behaviorist epistemology. *Psychological Bulletin*, 87 (2), 337-350.

Authors Index

Adams, H., 199
Alexander, P.A., 104
Algozzine, B., 134
Ames, C., 25
Ames, R.E., 25
Amsel, A., 38, 54, 58, 61, 62, 212, 213
Anastasi, A., 164
Andersen, D.S., 304
Anderson, L.W., 17, 103
Anderson, R.R., 80
Andronikof-Sanglade, A., 176
Annis, L.F., 20
Archer, R.P., 167, 199
Aristotle, 296
Armstrong, T., 116, 117
Aronow, E., 178, 192
Ausubel, D., 78, 83, 86, 97

Bacon, F., 295, 296
Bandura, A., 45, 109, 138
Barlyske, J., 291
Bar-Tal, D., 107, 140
Bartlett, F.C., 76, 83, 86
Bass, B.M., 194
Bates, J.A., 43, 75, 215
Beck, A.T., 157, 176, 181, 215
Behar, L., 303
Behar-Horrenstein, L., 301
Belensky, M., 287
Bellak, L., 172, 174, 175, 189, 199
Bender, L., 170
Benjamin, L.T., 65
Bentz, V.J., 195
Bereiter, C., 25
Berliner, D.C., 20
Berman, 181
Bernstein-Colton, A., 286
Biaggio, M.K., 193
Biddle, B.J., 304
Biggs, J.B., 81
Bindra, D., 58
Block, J.H., 17, 18, 19, 29
Bloom, B.S., 17, 29

Bolles, R.C., 58
Boring, E.G., 121
Bouchard, T.J., 185, 197
Bower, G.H., 21, 38, 69, 77, 78, 79, 84, 99, 137
Bowers, K.S., 158, 193
Brainin, S.S., 25
Bransford, J., 24, 28, 104
Bray, D.W., 194
Breland, K., 134
Breland, M., 63, 134
Brewer, W.F., 92
Briggs, L., 93
Brody, N., 123, 128, 146, 147, 148, 152
Brophy, J., 18, 24, 25, 66
Brown, A.L., 9, 16, 20, 21, 81, 84, 87, 92, 94, 96, 103, 104, 106, 130, 131, 139, 226, 230
Bruer, J.T., 16, 20, 22, 24, 28, 30, 78, 113, 224, 232
Bruner, J., 86, 87, 126, 291
Buchmann, M., 285, 302
Buchwald, A.M., 38, 61
Burghardt, G., 58
Burns, R.B., 17, 18, 19, 29
Buss, A.R., 17, 158, 193
Butcher, J.N., 190, 192, 199
Butcher, W.G., 164

Calhoun, J.F., 19
Calhoun, K., 199
Campbell, D., 242, 267, 269, 271, 278
Campione, J.C., 104, 130, 131
Capaldi, E., 61
Caplan, G., 207
Carroll, J.B., 6, 16, 18, 22, 30, 281
Carson, R., 296
Carter, K., 287
Case, R., 16, 20, 21, 81, 87, 92, 136
Cattell, R.B., 160
Ceci, S.J., 113, 152
Cherry, E.C., 87, 106, 139
Chi, M.T.H., 103

Subject Index

About the Authors

RONALD R. MORGAN is an expert in the psychology of learning and instruction. He serves as the director of the educational and school psychology programs of study at Loyola University of Chicago.

JUDITH A. PONTICELL is an Assistant Professor of Curriculum and Instruction at Texas Tech University. Her research focuses on adult learning, school effectiveness, and establishing educational partnerships in the workplace.

EDWARD E. GORDON is President of Imperial Corporate Training and Development and teaches at Loyola University in Chicago.

Together they have co-authored *FutureWork: The Revolution Reshaping American Business* (Praeger, 1994) and *Closing the Literacy Gap in American Business* (Quorum Books, 1991).

ISBN 0-275-95016-6